COMING TO OUR SENSES

Coming to Our Senses

AFFECT AND AN ORDER OF THINGS
FOR GLOBAL CULTURE

DIERDRA REBER

COLUMBIA UNIVERSITY PRESS   NEW YORK

COLUMBIA UNIVERSITY PRESS
Publishers Since 1893
NEW YORK   CHICHESTER, WEST SUSSEX
cup.columbia.edu

Library of Congress Cataloging-in-Publication Data
Reber, Dierdra
    Coming to our senses : affect and an order of things for global culture / Dierdra Reber.
        pages   cm.
    Includes bibliographical references and index.
    ISBN 978-0-231-17052-9 (cloth : alk. paper) — ISBN 978-0-231-54090-2 (e-book)
    1. Aesthetics—Psychological aspects 2. Affect (Psychology) 3. Capitalism.
4. Globalization—Religious aspects—Christianity. I. Title.

BH301.P78R43 2015
306—dc23
                                    2015017754

Columbia University Press books are printed on permanent and durable acid-free paper.
This book is printed on paper with recycled content.
Printed in the United States of America

c 10 9 8 7 6 5 4 3 2 1

COVER DESIGN: Christopher King

References to websites (URLs) were accurate at the time of writing. Neither the author
nor Columbia University Press is responsible for URLs that may have expired or changed
since the manuscript was prepared.

For my grandmother
 who gave me a room of my own
and my daughters
 who fill it with light

Contents

Preface

Tracking the Feeling Soma

In my childhood, I had the persistent impression of having been born into a cultural aftermath. Everything had already happened, and I had missed it all: wars of indiscernible quantity, presidents and cultural heroes assassinated, the civil rights movement, Woodstock, Vietnam. I intuited that the "events" that marked my childhood were of an entirely different nature: the opening of the Golden Triangle Mall in Denton, Texas, where I spent my earliest years, and its eventual upstaging by Walmart, the Pepsi Challenge, the John Williams Star Wars theme virtually looped on the radio, and, more important for me, Star Wars action figures, Cookie Crisp cereal (which my grandmother unfeelingly obliged me to mix with All-Bran), the Hispanic Hispanica Barbie doll (whose redundancy is still baffling), the Sony Walkman, the Commodore 64, Atari, Apple computers, Rubik's Cubes, Pac-Man, Ms. Pac-Man, Super Mario Brothers, Michael Jackson, Michael Jordon, Air Jordans, Cabbage Patch Kids, jelly beans (because Ronald Reagan loved them), Jordache jeans, neon T-shirts and socks, crocodiles and polo players, asymmetrical haircuts, Madonna, the Beastie Boys, and the division of the school cafeteria into first, second, and third world dining levels in support of Oxfam. Even the fall of the Berlin Wall is archived thus in this history of life as a history of consumption: what I most clearly recall about that monumental event is the news that pieces of the wall were being sold as souvenirs.

In my mind's eye, a persistent juxtaposition serves as a conceptual distillation of the cultural juncture into which I perceived myself to have been born: on the one hand, grainy and chaotic images on the evening news of men running with guns in a faraway arid-looking place; on the other, people from around the world singing in candlelit unity about such delightful and friendly things as apple trees, honey bees, buying the world a Coke, and keeping it company. The men with guns, I thought, should really learn this song.

As an adult, I am still trying to make sense of the enduring power of this television commercial, which I know now must have been the 1977 Coca-Cola "Candles" ad, a Christmas-themed remake of the original 1971 "Hilltop" ad whose jingle was so instantly and intensely popular that Co-ca-Cola's advertising team at McCann Erickson had it recorded by not one but two pop groups, the Hillside Singers and the New Seekers, whose versions of the same song moved to the top of the U.S. pop charts with the title "I'd Like to Teach the World to Sing (In Perfect Harmony)." McCann Erickson "Hilltop" art director Harvey Gabor recalls that the release of the commercial drew over one hundred thousand fan letters for Coca-Cola (Google *Project Re: Brief*); one *Huffington Post* blogger calls "Hilltop" "the most popular and iconic . . . television ad ever created" (Amato).

The key content common to both the original 1971 and Christmas 1977 commercials is the extended camera pan, first in close-up, then from an aerial view, of an eclectic grouping of people of diverse ethnicity and fashion of dress, in an apparent microcosm of humanity the world over. Indeed, Gabor is credited with the guiding foundational vision for the ad of wanting to create what he called the "First United Chorus of the World" (Ryan). In both commercials, these singers embody harmony by standing at elbow's distance of one another, with relaxed, peaceful, and smiling expressions as they "sing" (in truth, lip-sync) lyrics about harmony, love, and company. In the "Hilltop" ad the singers all raise an iconic glass Coca-Cola bottle in one hand, in the "Candles" ad, a lit white candle. In the "Hilltop" ad, the closing aerial shot reveals this group on a bucolic Italian hillside in a triangular shape that connotes progressive growth from the singular point person at its head to the increasingly broad rows that fan out expansively behind. In the "Candles" ad, the closing aerial shot reveals the group on an equally pastoral hillside seated together, again in a triangle, this time forming the classic shape of a Christmas tree, their swaying candles making it seem like a single living being.

Coca-Cola and McCann Erickson were intentionally trying to pioneer a new message—the lyrics in the "Hilltop" ad suggest that the commercial is seeking to embody what the world wants "now," though it leaves the contrapuntal "then" unspoken; what it is that the commercial sees itself as breaking with is not spelled out for the viewer. For me as a child, it seemed that this ad broke with segregation, violence, hierarchy, and vertical authority. Of course, I couldn't articulate all this at the time, but I could sense that "Candles" represented the antithesis of the televised warfare I was also seeing. It wasn't therefore as much a break from history per se that "Candles" was staging—for I was seeing the men with guns at the same point in time that I was seeing these people singing together—as it was staging a break in cultural modality of thought. In other words, an epistemological break, which this book proposes to trace.

"Candles," and "Hilltop" before it, proposed absolute heterogeneity and absolute unity in simultaneity. Each singer was clearly meant to represent a discrete ethnic profile, yet the togetherness of the group was as important as its members' individuality—these became perfectly interchangeable in the sense that any given individual could represent the whole. In this sense, the representation was perfectly democratic, for each face was understood to be equally important and valuable as any other; in this vision the intention was to signal an emphasis on the absolute equality of the members of this group. (Certainly, a face-by-face analysis of each ad might reveal imbalances favoring Caucasian faces or other asymmetries of ethnic or regional representation, but in general terms the overarching denotative function of the ad seems clearly to have been to represent the purest possible multiculturalism.)

It is significant that the singers in both ads form a large enough group of people that they become too many to count easily with the eye; they are so many that the only distinguishing characteristic of them all, from the distance of the final take, is their common humanity. In the "Candles" ad, even this much is not visible in the closing image, where the members of the group become, simply, moving points of light. In each case, the togetherness and unity of the group is represented as a single unified body; the concluding "Candles" shot of the living Christmas tree takes the representation of this organicity one conceptual step further than "Hilltop"—if in "Hilltop" the growth of the group is suggested by its positioning into the frame of an ever expanding shape, in "Candles" the group is organized into a shape that represents organic life itself in the form of an arborescent body.

The logic of this body is one of perfect harmony of its internal parts, a harmony predicated on equality of diversity and mutual love, respect, and honor for fellow beings. This oneness is symbolically situated in the heart of nature, as a metaphor for both the lush greenery that surrounds each group and the love that that setting is meant to connote and to afford—and even, perhaps, to foster. The constantly roving pan of the camera in both commercials insists on the visual leveling of the singers; the angle of the camera is not adjusted for height, but rather moves along the continuum of a horizontal average, safeguarding the integrity of the singers' faces, but not necessarily of the tops of their heads or the apparel on their torsos. In this sense, the viewer intuits a valorization of democracy through the lens that is afforded for spectatorship; what is privileged, above all, is eye-level status as a kind of visual connective tissue between singers themselves as well as with respect to the viewer. The viewer is enveloped into this relationship of horizontal equality without the "old" distinctions of ethnicity, race, nationality, class, or gender—though this is a markedly youthful group, signaling a "new" aesthetic and conceptual modality. And, clearly, if I am to judge by the desire that persists all these decades later to have the men with guns from the evening news lay down arms and join in song, the commercial is meant to inspire a sentiment of universal application to all humanity.

There is no leader in either of these commercials; even in "Hilltop," where there is a clearly introductory face—"that 'right' face, which was filled by a young lady on vacation in Rome from Mauritius" (Ryan)—that face, for all its "rightness" (not to mention any persistent racialized preference it might imply), immediately fades from view as the camera moves on to other faces and, moreover, is shown to be one of many in a back row of the group. The single person at the tip of the final "Hilltop" triangle also receives no emphasis as such; the shape of propagation is what is visually patent. In "Candles" there is even less emphasis through either camerawork or positioning of singers' bodies on the primacy of any given members of the group. Their togetherness is what is most clearly of interest and at conceptual stake; that is what Roland Barthes (1980) might have called the "punctum" of this moving image, to borrow from *Camera Lucida*'s photographic terminology for the penetrating effect of emotional recognition, bonding, and understanding that happens between viewer and image, yielding the deepest meaning of the photograph.

We might pause here to absorb the significance of Barthes's very approach to the formulation of meaning in decidedly emotional terms, as a kind of felt communion between viewer and image. By way of citing a related iconic cultural landmark, it also bears mention that, when Barthes's contemporary Susan Sontag rejects the classic terms of interpretation in her famous 1966 essay "Against Interpretation," she nevertheless embraces a new framework of interpretation when she calls for an affective "eros" to replace a rational "hermeneutics" of interpretation. I offer this brief tangential discussion of the role of emotion in the interpretive frameworks theorized by Barthes and Sontag as a quick cross-sectional consideration of their perhaps unexpected but surprisingly similar conceptual resonance with the "Buy the World a Coke" ad series, in which emotion becomes the new measure of meaning, ethics, and morality. It is the common disposition of emotional positivity of the singers, reinforced by the song lyrics that foreground love, sharing, and harmonious companionship, that defines this new horizontal formation of humanity as an implicit rejection of geopolitical asymmetries of power and their characteristic patterns of conflict and separation.

This is what the world wants now, the commercial claims by performing its own declaration: humanity gathered in the unity of common positive feeling and communion, joining together in fully self-reflexive action that narrates what that unified body is doing as it is doing it—singing about gathering in harmony while gathering in harmony. The "Candles" ad is my earliest memory of the cultural instantiation of what I propose to call a *feeling soma*: a model of human knowledge and action based on the conceptual framework of a body governed by moral standards, a morality defined on an emotional spectrum (positive is good, negative is bad). The feeling soma is heterogeneous and unified, bound together in the same principles of autonomic internal functioning that guide any living organism, with a premium on homeostasis and happiness as intrinsically and indissolubly unified conditions. No leader or authority need—or, indeed, ought—intervene within this model. The feeling soma self-regulates intuitively and nonrationally, at the level of "wanting" a supremely ethical and egalitarian human experience. The feeling soma is self-forming, self-determining, self-governing, and self-loving. As a child, I perceived something about the "Candles" commercial to be "new" in a profound way; as an adult, I offer the model of the feeling soma as a means of explaining that profound newness as a shifting of epistemological terrain in which the casting of knowledge of self and world becomes a process of "coming to our senses"—that is, a coming into "reason" by way of the nonrational, in which feelings and togetherness become the new basis of forming knowledge and political action aligned with fundamentally horizontal—democratic—moral principles of equality and well-being.

I began this meditation with the characterization of my childhood—of my generation—as being primordially defined by product consumption. Indeed, it is not casual that the feeling soma carries bottles of Coca-Cola in its many hands. In order to understand this relationship qualitatively, I would like to point to the New York-based advertising agency Saatchi and Saatchi's coining of the notion of brands as "lovemarks," a concept that builds product consumption *as* loving community, thus not only viewing human affect as the principal determinant of consumer behavior but also, therefore, erasing any difference between consumer behavior and what it means to be human in the most foundational of terms.[1] This study of the feeling soma and its relationship to free-market capitalism more broadly is, quite simply, an attempt to trace how and why we might possibly have come to think—rather, feel—this way.

*   *   *

Coming to Our Senses argues that even the most cursory inventory of the cultural present turns up instance after instance of a logic more affective than rational in nature. This logic may be defined as a knowledge generated by the ascendant homeostatic sequence of sensory perception, emotion, and feeling; thoughts produced by the feeling body; a comprehension of the self and of that self in the world occasioned by a new cogito: "I feel, therefore I am." This feeling cogito functions through analysis, judgment, and interpretation realized through affective processes and produces a social—and political—life protagonized by a sentient subject. If we take analytic stock of the diverse roles and representations of affect visible in the current cultural mainstream, we will appreciate how in the aggregate these cultural appearances evince the contours and function of an episteme—a vehicle for the approximation, organization, and production of knowledge.

To explain the emergence of epistemic affect, I posit the following historical periodization in the hypothetical mode: that epistemic affect has been developing for two and a half centuries since the birth of free-market capitalism, but that it has only now, in the past two decades, become eminently visible during the contemporary era of globalization underwritten by the universal triumph of capitalist liberal economics and democracy. The late eighteenth-century age of revolution displaces the mercantilist colonial monarchy to make way for a capitalist democratic bourgeoisie. Free-market capitalism and liberal democracy—two facets of the same prism of bourgeois power—relocate the control of economic resources and political governance from the monarchy to the body politic ("of the people, by the people"). If vertical monarchical fiat had found epistemic support in the Cartesian notion of a reasoning mind subjugating an "irrational" body driven by the affects, now horizontal capital flow vindicates precisely those affects as the basis of a nonrational homeostatic self-regulation that neutralizes the hierarchy between bourgeoisie and monarchy by requiring no intervention from on high (e.g., Adam Smith's "invisible hand"). Affect thus emerges as a new discourse for an entirely new model of power, redefining the category of social order and the limits of knowledge.

Epistemic affect may have been born in the age of revolution, but for the next two centuries it would have a hybrid coexistence with reason—the episteme of colonial imperialism—in the context of (neo)imperialist state apparatuses engaged in both free-trade and colonialist practice and discourse. It is only with the end of the cold war and, with it, formal colonialism, that free-market capitalism has enjoyed total epistemic dominance in the form of global neoliberalism—a radical realization of free-market principles and politics. Although in practice neoliberalism may be said to be a rationalizing neocolonial force seeking total global conquest—in the spirit of Max Weber's classic analysis of capitalism—its self-justifying discourse affirms just the opposite: that it is an engine of perfect democracy and social harmony whose epistemic vehicle is that of a body self-regulated by homeostatic principle. Post-Soviet capitalism has assumed the shape and "spirit," as Boltanski and Chiapello (2005) prefer to call its ideology, of a network—homologously referenced in theoretical currents as an "assemblage" (Deleuze and Guattari, Latour)—that is, a single and all-encompassing model of immanent and continuously interconnected participation in social life, a life now defined predominantly by its economic character. We inhabit, in Manuel Castells's formulation, a "network society" (2010) in which the network—uneven in its practical application over variegated contexts, though constitutive of a "global system" (xviii) in its structural self-conception and capacity—predominates as the conceptual and organizational model equally operative in the spheres of technology, society, and the economy. Alongside the notion of a "network," we might equally consider the notions of "community" (e.g., Jean-Luc Nancy's "being-with" in *Être singulier pluriel* [*Being Singular Plural*, 2000]) or the "common" (e.g., Michael Hardt and Antonio Negri's meditations on the shared cultural space of the global "multitude" in *Commonwealth* [2009]), which have become central conceptual topoi in the theorization of current culture. Whether we speak of a network society, a global community (whether understood ontologically or abstractly), or a multitudinous common, a "one-world" ethos emerges as a recurrent and vertebral characteristic of social life.

The iconic Irish-gone-global rock group U2's signature song "One"— consistently hailed as one of the greatest songs of all time—appeared in 1991 as a commitment to HIV research and AIDS awareness, but we might equally consider it an anthem of the post-Soviet years in which a heterogeneous multitude is rhetorically interpellated as constitutive of a cultural "we" in which this subject at once singular and plural—the world in all its diversity—is markedly focused on horizontal action that is perhaps best conceived as an endlessly expansive community (or network, or multitude) born of loving interaction.

This same conceptualization of a singular yet diverse "we" whose public action derives from what we might consider a kind of emotionally derived sense of social justice is to be found in the Occupy movements that have sprung up across the globe since the original phenomenon of coordinated mass public protests in Spain by the so-called *indignados* ("the outraged"), whose emotionally plaintive rubric—which denotes a decidedly political stance—signals a rejection of the asymmetrical political economics of neoliberalism. This posture is echoed by the some thousand protests that have since taken place worldwide in inspired emulation of the *indignados*, which consistently interweave the idea of love and positive emotion with the political platform of a perfectly democratic horizontality in which there is a full rejection of hierarchy in either the political or economic sphere. Occupy Wall Street's Facebook "cause" page (as distinct from its "political party" or "community" pages), for example, featured a wall photo, at the time of this writing, of a block-lettered graffiti-style caption, Separation of Corporation and State, thus recommending the purging of economic verticality and phenomenon of "super" wealth that it has spawned from the structure of political governance. To this image, the group moderator added the following comment: "'and us' would be an appropriate addition to the banner," thus underscoring a first-person plural understanding of the collective "99 percent" motif of the Occupy Wall Street group as a multitude differentiable only with respect to the 1 percent economic elite. The same Occupy Wall Street group, which is "liked" by almost two-hundred thousand Facebook users (the "political party" group by almost five-hundred thousand), has also given rise to the interrelated "community page" subgroups, among myriad others: "Occupy Together" and "Occupy Your Heart." The idea of a loving togetherness—a heartfelt "being-with," to borrow Nancy's term anew—is underscored in the titles of two documentaries, one a 2011 short, the other a 2012 feature film, "Love Is the Revolution" and *Occupy Love*, respectively, that chronicle the Occupy movements from the inaugural Spanish manifestation forward. The films' titles propose love as the mechanism for social change and, implicitly, for an alternative and "revolutionary" social order, with the collective living in love as a kind of communal and emotional habitus. Living-together-in-love is thus foregrounded as the conceptual synthesis of the Occupy movements the world over.

This real-life global multitude, the sentient—outraged and loving—"we," constitutes a thoroughly hegemonic commitment to the principle of organization by self-governance and through the affective transfer of communication and knowledge.[2] We may trace this affective self-governance further back in time—here signaling just one example among many, as I will consider in greater depth in the introduction—to the watershed acceptance of the emergent concept of emotional intelligence (Goleman) in a relationship of primacy vis-à-vis its rational counterpart, a notion that emerged to optimize the organizational functionality of the network as a single collective social actor. What is knowable is defined by the extremes of homeostatic success and failure: well-being and ill-being (my neologism to mimic the opposition between the Spanish *bienestar* and *malestar*), expressions of a somatic condition heavily inflected by emotion. In the age of all-out free-market capitalism, this vertebral dichotomy becomes—significantly—the new language of both social knowledge and its critique.

Comprehension of our dominant cultural episteme matters because without it we will understand neither mechanisms of cultural control nor the possibilities of their contestation. The battle to define who we are takes place as a function of what we may know—indeed, what we *can* know, because the cultural imaginary of epistemic dimension determines the shape and terms of our collective knowledge. If we fail to understand this battle of knowledge, then we will fail to perceive how it is dictating the terms of our cultural intervention. I argue that we need to understand our profile as contemporary cultural subjects in order to conceive of the limits and possibilities of that cultural subjectivity.

It is to this end that I propose an inquiry into the epistemic state of contemporary cultural affairs. My conceptual anchor and point of departure for this exercise is the identification of what we might call "free-market democracy" as the single most important characteristic of contemporary culture, a term that denotes the comprehension of liberal democracy and free-market capitalism as the political and economic—and never mutually exclusive—faces of a single social system that manages power and resources.

I interpret the political-economic cultural system of democratic capitalism as a text: one that most insistently proposes a relationship of radical horizontality among its integrants, radical horizontality being terminologically and conceptually interchangeable with perfect democracy. This perfectly horizontal—perfectly democratic—relationship between constituents is one in which there is a perfectly equitable flow of power (politics) and resources (economics). This perfectly equitable flow is represented as one guided without intervention—without regulation, without dictates. Rather, the equitable flow of power and resources within the constituency of this perfectly horizontal field is accomplished as though by force of nature. As though the integrants of this new perfect democracy were constitutive of the body politic, that body is organized along the laws of organic order. Having lost its head—its monarch, its rule by fiat—that headless but perfectly harmonious soma now self-regulates (instead of having regulation imposed from on high) and self-sustains (dictating the terms of its own existence) through the laws of internal equilibrium in which the notion of well-being—represented through the concept of health and, more specifically, through the flow of emotions—becomes a metaphorical analogue for the distribution of resources (capital) and power.

The role that this logic of affectively driven homeostasis plays as the epistemic instrument of social organization and action is evident in cultural texts past and present. Indeed, we should be able to locate this figure in some modality at any point in the cultural life of the capitalist West. This book offers a synecdoche of that extended set of proofs in the form of a doubly comparative analysis meant to gesture toward a more fully diachronic and panoramic circumstance. First, I draw an arc between contemporary global (post-Soviet) culture and the age of revolution, connecting these periods on the strength of the argument that they bookend capitalist life as we know it. This arc serves largely as a conceptual support for thinking through the cultural content of the second arc, which I draw between the United States and Latin America in the global present, and which constitutes this study's principal material for analysis.[3]

The age of revolution gives birth to free-market democracy; the current era of post–cold war capitalism has witnessed its global hegemony. (If the systemic oppositionality of the Soviet Union were ever considered to have been succeeded by that of the culturally Islamist Middle East, then the popular and new media-propelled Occupy "revolutions" toward free-market democracy in that region only affirm Francis Fukuyama's perestroika-era hypothesis of the universal triumph of liberalism.) If I create an interepochal bridge between the age of revolution and globalization for the sake of fleshing out the epistemic similarities between the two periods—that is, their shared assumptions about cultural subjectivity and the possibilities of knowledge—then, after an initial broad-based theoretical consideration of the epistemological status of affect, I turn my most intense focus in the extended analysis that follows on the global moment. I approach the global moment with a comparative methodology, bringing the United States and Latin America together as an intercontinental microcosm of the broader global West in which there is a shared cultural experience in spite of a relationship of continental asymmetry with respect to power and resources. In representative comparatist modules across time and space, I discover the same textual patterns of epistemic representation.

In this sense, mine is a study of aesthetics—not in the sense of beauty as either ineffability or cultural privilege, but in the sense of the capacity of cultural production to represent social meaning through internal constructs of signification. Cultural studies–dominated discourse has rejected aesthetics as a category of analysis because of its association with a class-based system of valorization. I would like to move beyond this political overdetermination in order to recuperate the value of aesthetic analysis. Does not narrative fundamentally encode meaning in its aesthetic? In its textual patterns, images, metaphor, dialogue, description, (self-)analysis, structure? Where else are we to look for stronger and more compelling evidence of meaning and message?

In 2007 Hispanist literary critic Josefina Ludmer—of hemispheric intellectual presence, with one foot in Yale University and the other in her native Argentina—argued that all culture is economic, and all economics cultural. Yet—in keeping with the cultural-studies ethos, whether intentionally or not—Ludmer does not make any attempt to define how such

XX PREFACE: TRACKING THE FEELING SOMA

an epistemological fusion would be discernible in contemporary cultural narrative produced under these new circumstances. This study seeks to answer that question by showing how the economic may be found in the cultural not in the guise of exchange value or so many ciphered transactions, but rather as a recurrent set of tropes: networked multitudinous subjects understood as a heterogeneous singularity, affective flow within that body as an organizational dynamics, representations of well-being and its lack as critical poles of judgment within that affective systematicity. Indeed, my contention, in its simplest terms, is quite spare: I argue that affect, in its epistemic dimension, is persistently figured as what I have earlier defined as a "feeling soma"—that is, a headless body that "thinks" by feeling—whose operational dynamics are best summarized as an affectively oriented homeostasis—that is, an internal order that is based on the logic of an affective balance sheet, inherently and autonomically striving toward a positive yield of well-being. Together—the feeling soma and its self-organization through affective homeostasis—constitute what I seek to lay bare as the central dynamic concept undergirding epistemic affect. The feeling soma is not by any means a static model, but one whose shifting contours reveal the political exigencies of the forces behind these representations. The central conceit of the present exercise is the distillation of a Western ideal of capitalist homeostasis from the particularities of its recurrent representation. In other words, the goal is to discern a repeating pattern—a stable echo—across a broad and diverse range of cultural texts. To some extent every act of representation is idiosyncratic and irreducible. Yet when a cultural pattern repeats itself with a strong enough frequency, it is possible to draw parallels across representations allowing for broader generalizations that do not violate those idiosyncrasies—do not collapse the specificities of and differences between discrete instances of cultural production. The patterns I foreground in this study are thus necessarily general in scope. I have attempted to trace affective epistemicity to its lowest common denominator of cultural representation and I believe I have found it in the figure of the feeling soma. To push further would be to distort the objects of study; to push less would be to compromise the meaning, and therefore the value and utility, of a broad analysis of the global cultural moment.

I argue that, once we have become sufficiently familiar with the contours of epistemic affect, we should be able to identify its trace not only in the global cultural present, where it has become eminently visible, but also—in varying degrees of visibility—in Western cultural production since the advent of free-market capitalism. Though this last idea that the reach of epistemic affect is commensurate with the lifespan of free-market capitalism is certainly one that I would venture to posit as a corollary to my main hypothesis regarding the genesis of affect as episteme, the present study makes its ultimate objectives the location and intelligible rendition of the feeling soma—the epistemic figure of affective homeostasis—in contemporary culture.

My study takes as its inspirational model and guiding example Michel Foucault's 1966 *Les Mots et les choses: Une archéologie des sciences humaines* (*The Order of Things: An Archaeology of the Human Sciences*), in which he masterfully lays out, in a sweeping panoramic and diachronic analysis, what he views as the vertebral conceptual modalities within the modern Western discourse of knowledge. Foucault seminally defines therein an "episteme" as a conceptual paradigm that delimits what it is possible to know and how we may know it. He speaks of the episteme as if it might be multiple—as though it could take on more than one guise—yet, in the end, reason is the only episteme that is operative within his analysis. Foucault explores what he considers shifting modalities of epistemic reason, and, though he never views them as more than variations upon a singular rational theme, it is here that he leaves the door open for further thoughtwork.

In his study of the sixteenth to the nineteenth centuries, Foucault identifies many subpatterns of the way in which reason manifests itself discursively in epistemological terms, but he underscores only one major shift: a significant break, he declares, between the taxonomical external locus of rational order predominant in the sixteenth to the eighteenth centuries and the "organic" internal locus of rational order that suddenly comes into being toward the end of the eighteenth century and holds sway through to the end—and indefinitely beyond, it is to be presumed—of Foucault's study that concludes in the nineteenth century. This latter internalization along a logic of organicity of the formerly outward conceptually gridlike taxonomies of order is what Foucault calls the "invention of man"—that is, the "invention" of the human body as a paradigmatic model of order. It is precisely this time period and rubric that I wish to plumb for its possibilities of being reconceived as an era when *affect* emerges as an episteme vying to displace reason.

Whereas Foucault's is a chronological analysis distributed among epochs, mine trains its gaze on the current cultural moment, which was both where my interest in affective discourse began and what I most wanted the project of its analysis to explicate in theoretical terms. My analysis of contemporary culture was, from its first moments, cross-cultural in the sense that I had one eye on the United States and the other on Latin America, constantly comparing what I was seeing in both regions and probing for a common bottom line of discursive logic in regard to the representation of affect.[4] When I began to see a consistent pattern across continents and media, I began to frame what I was seeing as a phenomenon most properly addressed at the level of the conceptualization and production of knowledge itself—that is, in the epistemological dimension. But to speak of epistemology begs the question of periodization—a question I faced repeatedly from interlocutors and readers across disciplines as I developed this project—and so I sought to strengthen my analysis of contemporary culture with a long meditation on what might be the possible sources of its markedly affective discourse. That meditation—on the politics of affect; on consumer culture and capitalism; on globalization; but particularly on the relationships between reason and colonial imperialism, on the one hand, and affect and capitalist democracy, on the other—slowly brought a genealogy of affective discourse into view that stretched back in time to the inception, on a global scale, of free-market capitalism and democratic politics in the age of revolution at the end of the eighteenth century, the moment that Foucault heralds, in his rubric, as the "invention of man."

My analysis thus has two axes of focus: first and foremost, the analysis of U.S. and Latin American cultural production of the post-Soviet period, especially the first years of the twenty-first century; second, a theoretical hypothesis about how the current moment relates to capitalist democracy in its origins and how we may map the twists and turns of that relationship over the intervening centuries. I think of the overarching conceptual structure of my study as a double set of arcs: one spanning the Americas in contemporaneously in the global present, the other spanning the epochs from the rise of capitalism to that global present. This latter arc bookends my analysis in the introduction and conclusion, both of which consider the broader theoretical ramifications of affective cultural discourse. But the arc that joins Latin America and the United States constitutes the bulk of my analysis, for, though what I seek to evidence may be simple—namely, the recurrence of the feeling soma and its homeostatic dynamics—its proof can only be approximated through the extensive examination of cultural evidence.

Exploiting the tension between the cultural homogeneity produced by globalization and the persistence of cultural difference, I seek to show, on the one hand, how the fundamental epistemic model of capitalist homeostasis (and its neocolonial counterpart of growth) are at play in both hemispheres and, on the other, how the particularities of its representation reflect hemispheric difference. To speak of either the United States or the twenty-one countries of Latin America as a monolith may inevitably aggrieve some sensibilities, particularly those scholars who champion cultural difference as a morally weighted category in which the question of continental sovereignty is vested. It is not my intention to impose an exogenous theoretical model upon Latin America, or upon the United States, for that matter—though there are far fewer concerns in the latter regard given the generally undisputed nature of U.S. sovereignty. I emphasize that my model of capitalist homeostasis derives from a long apprenticeship in the study of both Latin American and U.S. cultural production—the former as a trained scholar, the latter as a studious citizen—and that my overarching analyses are built from the ground up, not imposed downward from some a priori top-heavy and ideologically charged theoretical structure. I should also emphasize that it is none other than the very question of sovereignty, or the perceived threat thereto, that I find salient in the hemispheric analysis of representations of the epistemic figure of homeostasis. In U.S. cultural production the representation of capitalist homeostasis tends to revolve around a narcissistic contemplation of self that may decry sickness and ill-being instead of well-being and health, but does not always move beyond a symptomatology toward a structural cultural diagnosis, much less formulate a proposal for cultural change. In Latin American cultural production, on the other hand, the representation of capitalist homeostasis tends to revolve around a contemplation of self in relation to the other—chiefly, the United States, though also its own history of internal colonization by a cosmopolitan elite—as a source of external cultural pressure and economic dictates. Together, in the aggregate, the two sets of cultural analyses form what we might call an inverted specular whole in which the two sides evince a differential sense of cultural sovereignty, but express those differences in the same language of cultural discourse at the epistemic level.[5]

And yet I would take issue with those who insist upon an a priori ontology of regional difference—which, to my mind, only belies an ideologically motivated need for the same. Even as I am willing to stand by the broad assessment of continental difference that I have just outlined, I am also acutely aware that I harbor a certain misgiving about capitulating to the political dictates of my field, which demand the categorical preservation of regional difference as a proof of cultural sovereignty. Under postcolonially inflected politics, which places a premium on difference, comparative cultural analysis has accordingly focused on what differentiates cultural representations; in contrast, I use comparative hemispheric analysis to show the similarities of two regions that we have, by force of scholarly cultural politics, come to expect to be different. In this sense, I have endeavored to answer Erin Graff Zivin's call in *The Ethics of Latin American Literary Criticism* to "read otherwise" (7), propelled by a sense of ethical responsibility to set forth and interpret the patterns I see, to the best of my abilities, to their furthest consequences. The principal objective of this book—to reiterate it anew—is, therefore, to render visible and intelligible a composite epistemic portrait of affectivity built from analyses of cultural production in both hemispheres.

The prelude to this study offers an anecdotal account of the genesis of my understanding of affective discourse, which originated with the realization that a pair of U.S. and Latin American films that I happened to see in close range of one another, Mel Gibson's *The Passion of the Christ* (2004) and Rodrigo Bellott's *Dependencia sexual* (*Sexual Dependency*, 2003), made similar use of affective narrative strategies in a way that I began to understand as epistemological. I use the remainder of the prelude to define for academic readers what I mean by this epistemological dimension of affective discourse by entering into three texts that have had a particularly significant role in shaping it within interdisciplinary scholarly discourse: Raymond Williams's "Structures of Feeling" (literary analysis, 1977), Antonio Damasio's *Looking for Spinoza* (neurology, 2003; the last in a trilogy of trade books initiated in 1994), and Kathleen Stewart's *Ordinary Affects* (anthropology, 2007). This preliminary inventory of a progressive evolution of epistemic affect in the language of scholarly analysis is meant to serve as a preparatory exercise in defining my own terms as well as beginning to signal the stakes of the study in showing that critical—as well as cultural—production is equally implicated in participation within affective discourse.

The introduction that follows seeks to give an even broader and more detailed account of the representational girth and epistemological significance of affect in the contemporary moment. It also spells out in greater depth the hypothesis laid out in shorthand at the outset of this preface in regard to the cultural origins of the feeling soma—what I understand as the figure that foundationally structures epistemic affect—linking the emergence of that figure to the cultural logic of free-market capitalist democracy. The introduction lays out the diachronic arc that spans the age of revolution and the contemporary moment of globalization.

The body chapters of the book establish the interregional arc between Latin America and the United States within the global present and concern themselves with a singular task: mapping the epistemic figure of affective homeostasis within that comparative contemporary cultural landscape. These four chapters and the diverse sampling of contemporary cultural texts that comprises them are intended as extensive evidence, simply, of the frequency with which the feeling body and its homeostatic dynamics inform contemporary cultural discourse by shaping its epistemological framework. They are meant in the aggregate as a set of cultural proofs demonstrative of the central hypothesis that affective discourse has become so pervasive as to warrant our understanding of it on the scale of the epistemological.

The four chapters are divided into two parts. Part 1 treats the feeling soma, tracing how the sentient "we" is represented as a cultural subject. Part 2 treats the homeostatic dynamics of the feeling soma, tracing how the nonrational balance between well-being and ill-being constitutes the basis of social interaction by—or among or even within, to signal the ambivalence between its singularity and multiplicty—that cultural subject. Each part reiterates in its two chapters, the first of which lays out the general pattern at hand (i.e., the feeling soma or its homeostatic dynamics) in order to revisit that pattern in a successive chapter that considers it more properly in the context of a specific cultural politics: sustainability discourse, which I posit as the crowning political-economic-cultural narrative of our present moment and the most significant contemporary arena—now global in scope—for the negotiation of capitalist practice and ethics in broad terms. If epistemic affect was once used to legitimize the birth of capitalism, then its role in sustainability discourse shows that it is now at play in the global debate over its future. Rather than view sustainability discourse as a choice among many as a possible lens through which to conduct an interrogation of cultural epistemology, I argue that we instead view sustainability discourse as an outgrowth of affective epistemicity in which the feeling soma and its homeostatic dynamics underwrite from the foundation up the debate about the future of humanity, economic and political affairs, and the planet itself. In this regard my location of the feeling soma and its operational dynamics in the geographical arc between U.S and Latin American sustainability discourse of the global present also explores the contemporary end of the diachronic arc that I draw temporally between the discursive expressions of global neoliberalism of the present moment and originary free-market capitalism of the late eighteenth century.

Chapter 1 thus examines the construction of a collective but organically singular subject across all of humanity: the feeling soma, the immanent "we." Chapter 2 revisits the feeling soma in its avatar as a compound social actor of people and planet in sustainability discourse. Chapter 3 analyzes the expression of that subject in the homeostatic terms of well-being or ill-being, in which health and disease become categories of political affirmation or critique; I examine how homeostasis constitutes the organizational dynamics of the feeling soma and defines its possibilities of action. Chapter 4 analyzes the homeostatic logic of the affective subject's possible avenues of social action. These chapters thus make two passes, respectively, at the identification of the feeling soma and its homeostatic dynamics, in order to consider them first in general terms and second as foundational to the framework of contemporary cultural politics. As a whole, they are intended as a single compound portrait of affective epistemicity in global cultural discourse.

I conclude my study with a meditation on affective epistemicity as a form of biopower and make a case for the importance of its comprehension as such, without which, I argue, we will not fully understand our contemporary global cultural politics. In an advance discussion of that conclusion, I will say that my hypothesis will certainly raise objections on the basis of its supposition that affective epistemicity stakes its claim as a visceral form of cultural command that exercises a potent influence over its subject, interpellating that subject, as it does—to recast Althusser in affective terms—at the nonrational level of sensory perception, emotion, and feeling, all of which culminate in a conscious, but *involuntary*, response. To suggest, moreover, that such a powerful cultural model of the limits of knowledge originates with capitalism may strike many readers as a gesture of complicit fatalism. In anticipatory response, I ask why we would avoid—and even eschew—a serious analysis of the terms of affective discourse that motivate such critical interventions as the body without organs. Why do we accept a critique of capitalism, but not an analysis that departs from an acknowledgment of its power? Why do we regard such an analysis, which explains affective contestation as epistemically derivative instead of autonomous, as an insult to that contestation instead of an explanation—likewise—of its power? I hold dear Foucault's maxim that knowledge is power—of contestation as much as of hegemony—and it is in that spirit that I set forth, for contemplation, critique, and improvement, a hypothesis of the epistemic mechanisms of cultural knowledge and power in this era of unchallenged free-market capitalism.

Acknowledgments

The debts of intellectual generosity, collegiality, companionship, encouragement, and criticism that I have incurred in the course of this project are too numerous to count. So many iterations of this thought puzzle that has finally come together in these pages have passed through so many kind and capable hands that it is a vertiginous proposition to name them all. I am unendingly grateful to one and all and will endeavor to the best of my abilities, to the end of my academic days, to pay those debts forward whenever and wherever possible.

The small kernel of an idea about the epistemological dimension of affect that was born by listening to NPR and going to the movies found many generous sources of interlocution, support, and encouragement through the years from gestation to realization. There is no one I should thank before Carlos J. Alonso, mentor extraordinaire. I am grateful to Carlos for awakening my love of criticism to the fullest, for embodying intellectual gravitas, and for encouraging me to be both disciplined and courageous in my scholarly life, all of which inspired me to undertake the project of writing this book and, more important, to stay the course.

I am also grateful for invaluable early feedback from Michael Solomon, Reinaldo Laddaga, Yolanda Martínez-San Miguel, and Heather Love, Heather's own work reassuring me, several years before the affect boom had consecrated a disciplinary niche, that there was indeed a "there there" to my budding project. Erica Miller Yozell, Elisabeth Austin, Meghan McInnis Domínguez, Emilio Irigoyen, Rachel Burke, Tania Gentic, Elena Lahr-Vivaz, and eagle-eye Jennifer van Frank were go-to readers during first drafts when I was still piecing the project together. Phill Penix-Tadsen, Sam Steinberg, and Craig Epplin have given me earnest critiques at various points along the way, with no punches held.

At Emory I have been lucky to have capable and adventurous Spanish majors willing to try out my thought experiments on affect in the classroom. My intrepid undergraduates in "Social Currency of Love in Twenty-First-Century Media" tickled my funny bone with a speed-dating game in Spanish; in "Coming to Our Senses in the Global Americas" they formulated comparatist analyses of hemispheric pairings of smiles, frowns, and tears; in "Green with Love: Sustainability Discourse in Latin American-U.S. Media," they considered the relationship between love and ecostories in film and advertising, such as the polar bear's embrace of a startledNissan LEAF owner that I discuss in chapter 4. My graduate students, for their part, thoughtfully engaged with "Dollars and Sense: Neoliberal Capitalism and Emotional Social Meaning" and "Love in the Media: Toward a Social Meaning of Affect in the Twenty-First-Century Global Americas." I cotaught the latter seminar in a magical semester alongside Michele Schreiber of Emory's Film and Media Studies, with whom I once chatted the entire day away about films and the representation of emotion.

In writing the manuscript, I leaned heavily on the faculty writing group to which Michele and I belonged together with the indomitable Monique Allewaert and the wise Andrea White. Their friendship was every bit as important as their interdisciplinary critical insight for bringing my chapters into being. This group was convened by Amy Benson Brown, at that time the founding director of Emory's Author Development Program, whose superlative crash course in academic publishing gave me the tools to search for a press and the faith that my project might find one when the time came. During a visit to Duke, Michael Hardt read my draft introduction at this stage and offered generous and insightful feedback. Brian Massumi also gave me a detailed and helpful critique.

I thank Laurie Patton and Allison Adams, for their vote of confidence in awarding me the pilot grant from the Center for Faculty Development and Excellence for a pre-editorial manuscript review conference, and Donna Troka, for her stewardship in seeing it through to fruition. For my conference, Priscilla Wald agreed to make the trip from Durham sight unseen, which presaged her boundless energy, generosity, and acumen; Carlos J. Alonso found time during his busy graduate deanship to attend; and, from Emory, Lynne Huffer, Matthew Bernstein, Jeff Lesser, Larry Barsalou, and my stalwart colleague and chair Karen Stolley offered their time and countless pearls of inveterate wisdom. I recall that some thirty students and faculty attended the public portion of the review conference, including Peggy Barlett, Bob McCauley, and Laura Otis, colleagues who have all been kind and venerable sources of guidance and know-how, both interdisciplinary and institutional. My graduate advisee Anne Garland Mahler, who broke the mold of stellar on every front, graciously took notes for me at the conference; I believe she has inquired more often about my book than I ever had to about her spectacular thesis.

Within my department, I must offer special thanks to Hernán Feldman, who was always a meticulous and skeptical reader, giving especially sage advice on how to strengthen my historical hypothesis about the relationship between religion, free-market capitalism, and affect, my characterization of the place of affect in the Enlightenment, and my references to Argentine culture, politics, and history. Robert Goddard has engaged me in many a hallway volley of ideas about the *Economist*, Adam Smith, and neocolonialism. Don Tuten and Hazel Gold also have my thanks for their support.

Yanna Yannakakis gave me brilliant guidance in streamlining the articulation of my project as a grant proposal; I am thankful for a semester's leave to work on the book granted by Emory's University Research Committee and for gratifying recognition by the American Council of Learned Societies as an alternate. David Nugent and Chris Krupa joined me in a collegial interdisciplinary reading group that grew out of discussions at Latin American and Caribbean Studies Program faculty meetings.

Thanks to Bob McCauley and Laura Namy for inviting me to dialogue with Jocelyne Bachevalier in a humanities-sciences conversation on emotion hosted by Emory's Center for Mind, Brain, and Culture; thanks, more broadly, to the CMBC for serving as my lunchtime haunt for cutting-edge thought on affect across the disciplines throughout my writing process. I thank Karla Oeler of Emory's Film and Media Studies for taking interest in my work on affect and for subsequently inviting me to present what eventually became my book chapter 4 in her departmental graduate seminar series.

Within the profession more broadly, I am grateful to Jill Kuhnheim, Jonathan Culler, Bruno Bosteels, Doris Sommer, Hilda Chacón, Susan Martin-Márquez, and Ignacio Sánchez Prado for affording me the opportunity to present some aspect of the book on conference panels of the divisions on Twentieth-Century Latin American Literature and Literary Criticism at the Modern Language Association Convention. Additional thanks to Nacho, and to Mabel Moraña, for inviting me to the Washington University in St. Louis conference on "Reading Emotions in Latin America" and for including me in their published volume of conference proceedings, *El lenguaje de las emociones: Afecto y cultura en América Latina*. Their conference and anthology put affect on the Hispanist map. Josh Lund recommended me for the Wash U conference; he has my thanks for this and also for inviting me to coauthor "False Parity and the Politics of Amnesia," a memory studies response piece that begins the work of considering the relationship between affect and "democratic" free-market violence. I also thank Eugenio Di Stefano, Emilio Sauri, and Todd Cronan for inviting me to contribute a Hispanist take on epistemological affect to the "Latin American Issue" of *nonsite*.

If this book has an intellectual patron saint, it is Nancy Armstrong. Nancy is a force of nature within the scholarly world, with the gravitational pull of a planet and a fearsome talent for discernment. Had she not seen a glimmer in the last few paragraphs of a talk I gave, I would likely have tarried in conceptual gestation far longer than I did. Nancy published the talk in the *Novel* anniversary conference proceedings and then encouraged me to submit my book introduction to *differences*, where it became "Headless Capitalism: Affect as Free-Market Episteme." I must offer thanks to Ellen Rooney, and especially to managing editor Denise Davis, who indulged my final rounds of revisions with generous and unflappable equanimity. I will never know just what compelled Nancy to cross multiple disciplinary lines of field, time period, region, language, and medium to take me under her wing, but her mentoring has made all the difference. She has my endless admiration and humble gratitude.

Lynne Huffer changed my life by making the introduction to her editor at Columbia University Press. Wendy Lochner is the stuff of academic lore: enthusiastic, engaged, lightning-quick, razor sharp, knowledgeable, savvy, sage. She sized up the project instantly, sifted through my pre-editorial conference advice with ease and authority, and guided me toward a sound plan of action while I was still pinching myself. Wendy, her assistant Christine Dunbar, and manuscript editor Susan Pensak (who is also, amazingly, a translator of Latin American literature) have been a first author's dream come true. I also thank the two anonymous Columbia UP readers who generously provided detailed and astute critiques of the manuscript that I strove to honor in final revisions. I am grateful to Cynthia and Robert Swanson for a meticulous and conceptually complete index, and to Emory College and the Emory Laney Graduate School for a book subvention to fund it. And I am honored by the spare elegance Julia Kushnirsky's cover design, which feels like just the right way to enclose this long labor of love.

In all truth, this project began with the development of a certain way of looking at the world that long preceded my professional scholarly life. I have lived my days as the fatherless child of lesbian parents during the conservative 1980s, granddaughter to the first college graduates in families of rural Kentucky farmers and Dutch Pennsylvania factory workers, one of few white faces in a predominantly African American and Latino inner-city neighborhood, a scholarship student at elite New England private schools, and an Anglo scholar in the Hispanic field. The sustained education of being an outsider on the inside has given me a kaleidoscopic view of class, gender, sexuality, race, and language from my earliest years. I understood normativity as an arbitrary and contingent construct decades before I knew how to articulate it as such; I understood that humans mount narratives of self-legitimation as a mechanism of self-empowerment and that the axes of those stories trace lines of inclusion and exclusion on a spectrum from the sympathetic to the violent.

If, in this book, I have taken my gaze on that strange patchwork quilt of stories and stretched it to the scale of epochs and world systems, it is because the fiercely independent minds of my grandparents, my mother, and my aunts allowed me to grow up thinking that it was only natural to aim so high; this book is foundationally underwritten by their imprint on my character. But mine would be a starless sky without the love and support of Chris Blais and our combined firmament: Lucia, Stella, Ziya, Celeste, and Autumn Moon. They are my heart and soul, my light in the dark, my reason for being, my inspiration for writing.

COMING TO OUR SENSES

Prelude

Affective Contours of Knowledge

The first and most foundational seed of *Coming to Our Senses* dates to an afternoon in 2004 when I saw the Bolivian director Rodrigo Bellott's *Dependencia sexual* (*Sexual Dependency*, 2003) in the annual Philadelphia International Film Festival, only to realize that it was most unexpectedly related to both the McDonald's on the street corner opposite the theater and *The Passion of the Christ*, another film that I had been discussing with friends in view of the golden arches as we waited for the festival screening to begin. What intrigued me about Mel Gibson's film was not its sudden authoring of a global Christ franchise or the scandal swirling through the media ether on the strength of reports of anti-Semitism in the director's family, but rather the narrative strategy that Gibson had adopted of having Christ's bleeding body do the bulk of the storytelling. Having this narrative blood on my mind as I watched *Dependencia sexual*, I was struck by its somatic parallel with the strange denouement of this latter film in which five central protagonists vomit one by one as a culminating critique of the violent sexual addiction produced by global consumer culture. Nor was this blood and vomit far removed from McDonald's first global advertising campaign, which it had recently launched, "i'm lovin' it," which sought to market hamburgers through smiles, laughter, and the exuberance of general well-being represented in a commercial campaign based on visual images of people having fun together against the background of audio tracks by pop stars like Justin Timberlake and Tony Santos in the English- and Spanish-speaking worlds, respectively. The rational metalanguage of old—the language of Christ's teachings, of politically inflected cultural critique, of product promotion—had all ceded, it suddenly seemed to me, to what we might, for the sake of contrast, call an affective intralanguage: a language (or, simply, semiotics) figured in the logic of the feeling soma, understanding that logic to be immanent to the feeling soma—a knowledge produced by and for the soma, without rational intervention or transcendence.

Once I had begun to appreciate the degree to which cultural production was operating on an affective paradigm of knowledge, my interpretive lens retrained its focus accordingly, seeking out instances of emotionally coded narrative meaning in any medium—a search that became a nearly ten-year project. Over the course of a decade of gathering evidence, I also began to see how the same paradigm of affective signification was at work in critical production—that is, the emotional knowledge implicitly figured in cultural production was explicitly theorized in critical discourse.

As a prelude to the more panoramic and theoretical consideration I will give to the role of affect in cultural discourse in the introduction, I would like to pause in order to show how we might appreciate an intensification of affective discourse in critical scholarly writing over the past several decades. I will suggest a more precise periodization for this intensification in the introduction; here I would like to focus on the qualitative shift in the conceptual place afforded to affect in a close reading of a series of groundbreaking interventions in affective discourse across scholarly disciplines.

The key concepts I will present for comparative analysis are Raymond Williams's structures of feeling (1977), Antonio Damasio's brain science of emotion (2003, the culminating text in a trilogy begun in 1994), Kathleen Stewart's ordinary affects (2007), and, by way of Stewart, Gilles Deleuze and Félix Guattari's bodies without organs (1972). I have selected these interventions for analysis on the strength of how authoritative and even canonical they have come to be regarded in their respective fields, but my intent is not to present them as authorities upon which my analysis seeks to rest. Rather, I seek to historicize these incursions into affective discourse—

monumental incursions, with respect to their investigative fields—as illumi-
nating a continuum along which scholarly affective discourse has developed
a progressively epistemological face. In other words, I seek to give skeletal
evidence of an intensification of the scholarly tendency—across disciplines—
to locate innovation in the domain of the affective.

In his essay "Structures of Feeling"—arguably the section of *Marxism
and Literature* (1977) of the most significant posterity, having become a
cultural studies commonplace—British literary critic Raymond Williams
theorizes the process by means of which social institutions come into being, as though to investigate the prelife of Louis Althusser's Ideological
State Apparatuses (ISAs, 1970). Althusser and Williams write only a few
years apart during the decade of the 1970s, but this is a time of intense and
swift change in the aftermath of the repression by the recently colonyless
French bourgeois state of the May 1968 student-worker strikes, on the one
hand, which would seem to be Althusser's point of reference, and, on the
other, the emergent culture of neoliberalism that would seem to be that of
Williams. Althusser writes of social structure as a rigid and ever present force
constituted by the ISAs as "toujours déjà donnée" ("always already given"),
whereas Williams, who periodizes his book simply by saying it is "written in
a time of radical change" (1), conceives of these structures as much more in
flux, with a life cycle of their own. As a point of departure, Williams avers
that "in most description and analysis, culture and society are expressed in
an habitual past tense" (128). What follows makes clear that this observation is not free of judgment: "The strongest barrier to the recognition of
human cultural activity," Williams continues, "is this immediate and regular
conversion of experience into finished products" (128). Against this conversion of the social into a preterit mode, Williams posits the alternative of "a
kind of feeling and thinking which is indeed social and material, but each
in an embryonic phase before it can become fully articulate and defined
exchange" (131).

This dichotomy between the "habitual past tense" and an "embryonic
phase" of cultural expression calls to mind the contemporaneous characterization of Hollywood cinema by Cuban filmmaker and New Latin American
Cinema ideologue Julio García Espinosa as being defined by the preterit
mode; against this, he calls for "un cine imperfecto" (1967)—a cinema "imperfect" in the grammatical sense of a present tense coming into being that
resists the reification of finality. For García Espinosa, the preterit is the epistemic modality of imperialist culture, the imperfect that of its revolutionary

counterpart. Williams does not overtly politicize the preterit-imperfect dichotomy in the same manner; rather than casting it as a question of poles, either of which might trump the other, and each of which is associated with an opposing political system, Williams instead presents it as a Hegelian dialectic in which the process of social becoming eventually gives rise to its own perfection in the grammatical sense of having been fully realized, a completion that, the reader is left to infer, will usher in a new phase of becoming followed by its full realization, and so on.

It is significant that Williams leaves the reader to infer the cyclical nature of his model, instead lingering in the consideration of the structures of feeling. Even though Williams is presenting a dialectical model within which the so-called structures of feeling are integrated as one phase in a two-part process, his real interest, as the title of his essay conveys, lies in this phase of becoming, the inchoate stage of cultural forms "*in solution*" (133) as opposed to their eventual "*precipitated*" (134) structure. It is this structural stage of being "still in process" and, "methodologically . . . a cultural hypothesis" (132) that constitutes the novel aspect of Williams's proposed dialectic, as his labor of terminological definition makes clear:

> The term [*structures of feeling*] is difficult. . . . An alternative definition would be structures of *experience*: in one sense the better and wider word, but with the difficulty that one of its senses has that past tense which is the most important obstacle to recognition of the area of social experience which is being defined. We are talking about characteristic elements of impulse, restraint, and tone; specifically affective elements of consciousness and relationships: not feeling against thought, but thought as felt and feeling as thought: practical consciousness of a present kind, in a living and interrelating continuity.
>
> (132)

Despite the fact that Williams is sketching out an ontology of the life cycle of social structures, there is a certain value judgment discernible in the relationship he attributes to each phase of that dialectic in which the structures of feeling occupy a position of privilege with respect to fixed forms insofar as these latter finished past-tense structures of social institutionalization are, in one instance, "barriers," and, in another, "obstacles" to the recognition of "meanings and values as they are actually lived and felt" (132). Williams argues that structures of feeling "do not have to await definition, classification, or rationalization before they exert palpable pressures and set effective limits on experience and on action"; "it is the reduction of the social to fixed forms that remains the basic error" impeding the productive analysis of these pressures and limits. Williams also rescues all of Marxist doctrine from this pitfall with the retrospective claim that an appreciation of structures of feeling is evident within Marx's writing—"Marx often said this," Williams tersely avers—the fault instead lying with "some Marxists [who] quote him, in fixed ways, before returning to fixed forms" (129). The structures of feeling are what Williams is "discovering"—in an act of "recognition" (128, 132), to use his own terminology of epistemological encounter—and validating in theoretical and ideological terms.

Structurally speaking, Williams's self-styled groundbreaking intervention in the field of cultural analysis finds an analogue two decades later in the groundbreaking intervention made by Antonio Damasio in the field of neuroscience. In *Descartes' Error* (1994)—and later in the *Feeling of What Happens* (1999) and *Looking for Spinoza* (2003)—Damasio elaborates a model of the "relation between emotion and reason" (x). "The new proposal in *Descartes' Error*," Damasio writes, "is that the reasoning system evolved as an extension of the automatic emotional system, with emotion playing diverse roles in the reasoning process" (xi–xii). Emotion, in other words, is not only connected to reason but is foundational to reason in an ascending relationship in which reason operates as a secondary process on the primary process of emotion. Emotion can stand alone, Damasio argues, giving us the ability "to *act* smartly"; reason, he clarifies, gives us the ability "to *think* smartly" (xi).

But, again, in a strong echo of Williams, it is not really this "smart reasoning system" (xi) per se—that is, as an *integrated* system of smart action and thought—that interests Damasio as much as it is the "brain science of emotion" (x) *alone*. In a ten-year retrospective preface to *Descartes' Error* published in 2005, Damasio describes the disciplinary terrain within which he sought to introduce his study of the brain science of emotion as one that had, throughout the twentieth century, given "the cold shoulder to emotion research" (ix). Likewise, in *Looking for Spinoza*, where Damasio turns his attention to feelings as the conscious—but prerational—mapping of emotions within the brain, he explains he had had to counter the "established advice that feelings were out of the scientific picture," "beyond the bounds of science" (4) in order to "map the geography of the feeling brain" (6). Like Williams, Damasio builds a two-part model in which feeling occupies the ground floor of human experience, with reason (the structural analogue of Williams's rationalized social forms) occupying the higher and secondary floor of analysis carried out on the basis of that ground floor of feeling. Also like Williams, Damasio argues that the novelty of his contribution lies in its treatment of feeling, not of reason. And, again, like Williams, Damasio perceives himself to be thinking against the grain of disciplinary—indeed, epistemological—convention.1

To this pattern that I have identified in Williams and Damasio, I would like to add anthropologist Kathleen Stewart, whose book *Ordinary Affects* (2007) seeks to develop a new scholarly language for the analysis of contemporary culture.2 Stewart's opening paragraphs establish a parallel with the feeling-reason divide centrally asserted by Williams and Damasio and the self-positioning as a groundbreaking voice for feeling in a discipline rooted in the terrain of the rational. Yet, where Damasio and Williams stop short of abandoning reason and its analogous social structures, Stewart brings to mind García Espinosa's privileging of the imperfect over the preterit in her will to allow what she calls "ordinary affects" to take center stage over their cultural opposite, "dead effects" (1). Stewart's evocation of Williams himself evidences this determination in the sense that she cites only his structures of feeling and their independence ("they [ordinary affects, now followed by Williams's definition of structures of feeling] 'do not have to await definition, classification, or rationalization before they exert palpable pressures,'" she sparely cites, obviating any contextualization of this assertion within the dialectic that he proposes). This dispensing with reason in the characterization of affect as fully autonomous marks a break with Williams and Damasio, who, in spite of patently foregrounding feeling in structures of culture and of the brain, both nevertheless maintain one foot in the territory of the rational: Williams presents his structures of feeling as inextricable from structures of definition, classification, rationalization; Damasio defends against the erroneous interpretation of his work as dispensing with reason ("I never suggested that emotion was a substitute for reason," xi). Stewart, on the other hand, moves decidedly into the territory of affect over reason. She is "trying to create a contact zone for analysis" (5) now exclusively of the affective variety.

Stewart's procedure is diarylike, "an experiment, not a judgment" (1), she declares—again recalling García Espinosa's ideologically charged distinction between imperfect and preterit modes—in which she links anecdotes about contemporary cultural experience and glosses them with intermittent and minimalistic references to theorizations about neoliberal global capitalism (Gilles Deleuze—theorist of capitalist immanence—being the most insistent such reference). In contrast to Williams and Damasio, whose subjects resist historiography (Williams's has pretensions of ahistoricity; Damasio's is physiological), Stewart begins her book by locating her diary-study in the present moment of neoliberalism, following that periodization with the claim that this new experimental language of ordinary affects is an attempt to develop a discourse more adequate to that cultural reality than the customary language of rational analysis:

> This book is set in a United States caught in a present that began some time ago. But it suggests that the terms neoliberalism, advanced capitalism, and globalization that index this emergent present, and the five or seven or ten characteristics used to summarize and define it in shorthand, do not in themselves begin to describe the situation we find ourselves in. The notion of a totalized system, of which everything is always already somehow a part, is not helpful (to say the least) in the effort to approach a weighted and reeling present. This is not to say that the forces these systems try to name are not real and literally pressing. On the contrary, I am trying to bring them into view as a scene of immanent force, rather than leave them looking like dead effects imposed on an innocent world.
>
> (1)

Further on in her introduction, Stewart returns to the matter of fleshing out her definition of the language of ordinary affects and why "bottom-line arguments about 'bigger' structures and underlying causes"—coding the discursive procedure of rational synthesis in economic terms—miss the mark of the affective knowledge that her new experimental mode seeks to communicate. In the following two paragraphs, which are worth quoting at length, Stewart gives a definition that borders on the poetic of the model of thinking that she is rejecting and the model of thinking that she is embracing.3 Note the use of metaphor that anthropomorphizes the affective model of thinking she champions, making the components of this model "habitable and animate," in opposition to what she posits as the shortsighted and implicitly cold, and even less than humane, ambition of synthetic rational analysis:

Models of thinking that slide over the live surface of difference at work in the ordinary to bottom-line arguments about "bigger" structures and underlying causes obscure the ways in which a reeling present is composed out of heterogeneous and noncoherent singularities. They miss how someone's ordinary can endure or can sag defeated; how it can shift in the face of events like a shift in the kid's school schedule or the police at the door. How it can be carefully maintained as a prized possession, or left to rot. How it can morph into a cold, dark edge, or give way to something unexpectedly hopeful.

This book tries to slow the quick jump to representational think-ing and evaluative critique long enough to find ways of approaching the complex and uncertain objects that fascinate because they literally hit us or exert a pull on us. My effort here is not to finally "know" them—to collect them into a good enough story of what's going on—but to fashion some form of address that is adequate to their form; to find something to say about ordinary affects by performing some of the intensity and texture that makes them habitable and animate. This means building an idiosyncratic map of connections between a se-ries of singularities. It means pointing always outward to an ordinary world whose forms of living are now being composed and suffered, rather than seeking the closure or clarity of a book's interiority or riding a great rush of signs to a satisfying end.

(4–5)

First and foremost, what I would like to emphasize about Stewart's new model of thinking is that it asserts a fully independent status for affective discourse. Unlike Williams, who reserves a difference between "terms of analysis" and "terms of substance" (129), Stewart expressly seeks to "fash-ion some form of address that is adequate to [ordinary affects'] form." This mimetic form of address is intentionally fenced off from the traditional reg-ister of scholarly analysis—"my effort here is not to finally 'know' [ordinary affects]," Stewart declares, effectively eschewing the operation and language of rational synthesis. Only a handful of chapter headings—which have to be teased from the text since Stewart rejects a traditional chapter index, presumably as part of the undesired scholarly format "seeking the closure or clarity of a book's interiority or riding a great rush of signs to a satisfy-ing end"—serve as vestigial markers of that traditional scholarly language: "The Politics of the Ordinary" (15–16), "Learning Affect" (40), "Games of

Sense" (41–42), "The Self" (58), "The Affective Subject" (59), "Power Is a Thing of the Senses" (84), "Agencies" (86), "Beginnings" (128). These tropes of social science analysis—politics, subjectivity, agency—are in no way defined in the classical sense; the chapter content that they announce presents anecdotes, metaphors, stream-of-consciousness narration of emotional landscapes of self and others. Indeed, on the back jacket, fellow anthropologist Michael Taussig elegizes Stewart's rendering of scholarly language in a strictly affective register: "Anything but ordinary, this book rewrites the social sciences from top to bottom through its bleak and beautiful honesty as to the human condition and the conditional nature of our language and concepts." Taussig's evaluation of Stewart's work locates her attempt to create an affective language of scholarly inquiry on the same cutting-edge horizon as Williams, whose theorization of "structures of feeling" has become a touchstone for the consideration of affect, and Damasio, whose work has pioneered a now significant subfield in neuroscience dedicated to the exploration of emotion. We might understand the thirty-year passage from Williams to Damasio to Stewart as a progressive—and progressively radical—epistemological affirmation of affect as a vehicle for knowledge.

It is important to note that Stewart's assertion of independence for affective scholarly discourse is not politically neutral. Her naturalization of Deleuze and Guattari's terminology (e.g., her definition of the ordinary as a "shifting assemblage of practices and practical knowledges, a scene of both liveness and exhaustion, a dream of escape or of the simple life" [1] and of ordinary affects as the "varied, surging capacities to affect and to be affected that give everyday life the quality of a continual motion of relations, scenes, contingencies, and emergences" [1–2]) and her steady citation of their scholars (Alphonso Lingis, Brian Massumi, John Rajchman) codes her intervention as contestatory with respect to the cultural fact of capitalism that motivates this collective theoretical corpus. (Stewart in fact recognizes Deleuze and Guattari's influence on her central conceptual definitions in a general footnote acknowledging her intellectual debt to their *Anti-Oedipus* [1972] and *A Thousand Plateaus* [1980].) In the face of capitalist immanence, which this de facto Deleuzean school most centrally posits, it is as though affect were to have emerged as the substance of its nonconformist— dissident—cultural expression.

The "bodies without organs" elaborated in *Anti-Oedipus* is an abstract model of rebellion anthropomorphized as a body whose parts have seceded from the homeostatic union, the latter posited as a metaphor for—or,

better yet, an epistemological figuring of—the teleology of capitalist production. Deleuze and Guattari's "hero" of anticapitalist nonproductivity is
the schizophrenic, whom they theorize as the maximum embodiment of the
pleasure principle, understanding pleasure as a drive that seeks only its own
fulfillment, in obeisance to no other dictates. Whereas capitalism demands
the capitulation of every bodily organ, yoking each and all to the project of
streamlined output in satisfaction of capitalist production plans, the schizophrenic liberates its body by taking pleasure, rather than work, as its telos.
Its organs are freed from the harness of productivity; they are not forced to
serve as cogs in the capitalist wheel. Using the body's autonomic system as
the conceptual raw material to represent models of political captivity and
resistance, Deleuze and Guattari effectively create two different types of
homeostasis: one in which all organs are working in synchronicity toward a
prescribed capitalist end and another in which the body ("without" organs
because they are freed from duties as such) chases its own bliss in perfect
disregard for teleology of any kind except the program of self-pleasuring.4

What is privileged is this alternative homeostasis driven by pleasure and
represented by the schizophrenic that declines on the organic level of physiology to participate in the discipline imposed on the body by the dictates
of capitalist productivity. Although the entire conceptual system of negative critique and positive affirmation is somatic—that is, both constitute a
homeostasis, whether in service of production or pleasure—Deleuze and
Guattari nevertheless inscribe within that conceptual field of the somatic an
antagonism between productivity and pleasure. Productivity is associated
with a body held captive to a mechanistic rationalizing force and therefore
conceptually estranged from that body and realigned with the reasoning
mind, whereas pleasure is associated with the liberated body—within the
plane of immanence, unbridled affect rules supreme. In the same way that
Stewart's new model of affective thinking is charged with emotion, and
the rejected model of rational thinking incapable of such sentience, there
is a strange way in which, in Deleuze and Guattari, the body obedient to
capitalist logic is rendered devoid of affect, whereas the rebellious body that
flouts capitalist logic is affectively charged with pleasure and desire. Pleasure
and desire—the feeling body and affect per se—become connotative of dissident autonomy.

In this Deleuzean model that Stewart inherits and reproduces, although
the negative side of capitalist hegemony is anthropomorphized and cast in
the somatic-affective terms of a harnessing of homeostasis for the telos of

productivity, it is nevertheless not critiqued as such—that is, not critiqued as a force of affect but rather of its absence. The cold, distant, transcendent, and rationalizing mind of epistemic neocolonialism is what is imputed to the negative model of the body colonized toward productivity, whereas its contestatory counterpart appropriates for itself the discourse of affect. If we think of capitalism and bourgeois revolution as having come about on the strength of the expropriation of affect as an epistemic category from its position of abjection in the schema of colonial reason, then what Deleuze and Guattari and company are staging is, in effect, the reenactment of this very act of epistemic rebellion. That is, casting capitalism as a neocolonial force and enacting a democratizing revolution—each organ perfectly horizontal with its peers, none in the service of a higher command, in which epistemic affect is expropriated from capitalism qua new colonial power. On the politically liberal side of affective revolution, there is no longer any need to "know"—terminologically casting knowledge as part of the repudiated schema of rational and vertical power—as Stewart asserts in regard to the avowed purpose of her book.5

How do we make sense of the epistemic representation of capitalism? Is it a democratic feeling soma or a colonial rationalizing mind? I argue that cultural and critical representations have long presented us with a case of epistemic fusion within which, if we are to parse them, the democratic feeling soma—born when capitalism *was* revolutionary, quite literally in the era of bourgeois revolution—is the originary model, and the colonial rationalizing mind constitutes a subsequent development corresponding to capitalism's gradual ascendance as a de facto colonizer. Yet it is also true, as "degrowth" theorist Serge Latouche asserts, that capitalism-as-colonizer's guiding practical concept of infinite growth may be fruitfully interpreted as an intrinsically biological model. But even if we argue that colonial epistemicity is thus retrofitted in affective terms—Manifest Destiny as the somatic rendering of the Crusades, if you will—I would argue that, biological though the model may be, the notion of an organism in endless expansion was not the originary model justifying the political economics of capitalism. In a watershed study of this very relationship between emotion and bourgeois capitalist revolution, Nicole Eustace (2008) claims that the American Revolution was underwritten by a gradual but decisive shift in the discursive status of emotion: from being socially abject—associated with the uncouth masses—emotion was vindicated as a universal aspect of the human condition, a shift that allowed "passion [to become] the gale" of this inaugural liberal-democratic revolution. In this same spirit, I posit the hypothesis that homeostasis, and not growth, was the original epistemic justification of the replacement of the colonial monarchy with the democratic free-market bourgeoisie: a perfectly self-directed—and therefore democratic and horizontal—harmony of the internal parts that needed no interference from a master mind. This figure of bourgeois independence is, in other words, the soma orchestrated headlessly by its own internal invisible hand.

As I began to argue in the preface—an argument I will further develop in the introduction and that is foundational for the logic of *Coming to Our Senses*—I propose that we read Foucault's "invention of man" in analogy to this figure of somatically rendered bourgeois autonomy. Foucault defines "man" in epistemic dimensions as the organic internalization of an erstwhile externally directed taxonomizing order. Whereas, however, Foucault posits that this epistemological figure of the "invention of man"—which he dates, precisely, to the Age of Revolution—constitutes yet another avatar of reason, I argue that we instead revisit the "invention of man" as the birth—in Western modernity, at least—of an epistemicity that is affective rather than rational.

The conceptual mechanics of capitalism are complex because they are both neocolonizing (growth) and democratizing (homeostasis). What happens in Deleuze and Guattari—to take their writing as representative of the discourse of capitalist contestation—is that there is an accusation of the neocolonizing aspect of capitalism (growth in the form of endless productivity) packaged as homeostatic colonization. In other words, the image of somatic homeostasis is portrayed with characteristics of vertical neocolonial growth. Homeostasis is thus emptied from the outset of its positive connotations; these positive connotations are, in turn, reattributed to its subversion in the form of bodies without organs. Bodies without organs—a schizoid homeostasis—becomes the democratizing principle. What is elided is the direct consideration of how capitalism, in its epistemic genesis, casts itself effectively as what Foucault calls the epistemic modality of "man"—as a self-contained, self-regulating, happy, and harmonious interconnectivity between all internal parts connected by the vital flow of capital as the infrastructural network that would also support, in a relationship of perfect analogy, its politics and culture.

It is thus not pleasure and desire or affect as a category that counters capitalism, but rather their specifically schizoid or "ordinary" aspect entering into battle with an antagonist—the affective subject in pursuit of happiness, we might say—that has only been partially fleshed out. Likewise, if we are to accept feelings of structure and the brain science of emotion as revolutionary by virtue of positing a "living" and affectively oriented model of the cultural and the physiological in opposition to the alleged petrification of rationally oriented intellectual and scientific discourse, then I argue we must consider the epistemic role of the capitalist-democratic complex that might inform such triumphalism. If the epistemic underpinnings of capitalist democracy validate a social protagonism structured on an ordering principle of nonrational feeling in opposition to rational thought—affective homeostasis versus rational cogitation—then it behooves us to contemplate the extent to which the epistemology of the feeling soma underwrites the very conceptualization of those cultural and scientific models by shaping our understanding—our *imagination*—of what it is possible to know. It is to this exploration of the relationship between the feeling soma and cultural knowledge that I will turn in the introduction that follows.

Introduction

Headless Capitalism

The New Cogito: "I Feel, Therefore I Am"

In 1999 Slavoj Žižek warned that the liberal academy should grant the Cartesian subject a stay of execution. Charged with colonial Europe's rationalized crimes against humanity, the Cartesian subject had come to shoulder the burden of racism, heterocentrism, sexism, elitism, imperialism, teleology, master narratives, and phallogocentrism, the linguistic vehicle of this totalizing oppression. In the cultural studies–dominated intellectual aftermath of global decolonization, reason became the worst discursive criminal of the modern West. The rational political subject born of the mid-seventeenth-century cogito of transcendent mind had fallen into seemingly irreparable disgrace. Yet, when a prescient Žižek saw in neoliberal culture a rising leviathan that would bring the already debilitated left to its knees, he was clinging to the Cartesian subject as though it were the last hope: if the left were to stand a chance in this epic battle, it had better not turn its back on reason. In 2007 Al Gore, too, publicly lamented the loss of reason within the political sphere, decrying its "assault" by neoconservative politics of fear and greed. How curious that, although both Gore and Žižek sought the rehabilitation of a common fallen hero, each blamed the diametrically opposed end of the political spectrum for its demise.

These defenses of reason from attacks issuing from both extremes of the political spectrum suggest that the rejection of rationality is not the exclusive work of any given political camp but rather a phenomenon far more culturally hegemonic. If reason has been demonized and abandoned by both the political left and right, it is because a new avatar of social agency has begun to emerge: affect. My proposition is simple: that we may currently be witnessing the radical apogee of an epistemic shift from reason to affect, a shift that may have only become fully visible in the present era of "one-world" capitalist globalization, but that we can trace to the birth of free-market capitalism in the age of revolution.

We tend to think of capitalist practice and discourse as one of expansionist and neocolonizing growth. Yet I argue that in its revolutionary genesis capitalism—together with liberal democracy—validates the bourgeois body politic as the new site and source of economic and political power that is always already self-contained and autonomically self-governing within its own limits and constructs itself epistemologically on the model of immanent and foundationally affective homeostasis. When liberal democracy and free-market capitalism move beyond their revolutionary inception to become players in a world theater dominated by imperialism, the rational and expansionist epistemological discourse of outward growth overshadows the discourse of harmonious equilibrium—though it could also be argued that the two discourses of growth and homeostasis are complementary in that episodic expansionist growth is balanced by a continual return to a necessarily contingent state of homeostatic equilibrium. Whether we view growth and homeostasis as competing or complementary epistemological discourses, what I wish to argue most centrally is that once the imperialist world system comes to an end along with the cold war, the discourse of capitalist-democratic homeostasis markedly eclipses that of growth, and with this shift affective logic begins to supersede its rational counterpart.

Indeed, in the years immediately following the fall of the Soviet Union, an event that Francis Fukuyama heralded—albeit infamously—as proof of the universal triumph of liberal democracy, affect began to come into view as the driver and protagonist of cutting-edge research and innovation in academic and public cultural discourse alike, freely traversing this terrain.

If we take stock of the diversity of these interventions by affect as a vehicle for the construction of knowledge—the exercise of thinking of and through affect—then we begin to appreciate the extent to which affect has had the effect of creating a field of inquiry unified in this respect across disciplines and ideologies. With particular intensity over the past two decades, affect (understood as both topic and optic) has been forging an epistemological immanence of inquiry—not at the micro level of specific content, but at the macro level of the constitution of a transformative discourse that is pushing toward the radical redefinition of fields and their foundational theoretical assumptions and tools.

In 1995, for example, Eve Kosofsky Sedgwick championed the insertion of affective discourse within theoretical currents as a nonlinguistic alternative mode of signification that quietly and defiantly bypassed the Cartesian subject's prison house of rational discourse. In *Shame and Its Sisters: A Silvan Tomkins Reader*, Sedgwick and her coeditor Adam Frank imported the groundbreaking mid-century work of the eponymous psychologist in affect and cognition for use in queer studies, introducing to the humanities the unorthodox idea of feeling as the basis of subjectivity. This markedly liberal and contestatory use of affect notwithstanding, it is essential to note again that, like the demise of reason, the rise of affect on the cultural horizon has not been the monopoly of any one political perspective. To wit, whereas Sedgwick borrowed one psychologist's theorization of affect to reconceive marginalized social identity, another psychologist's theorization of affect propelled the reconceptualization of identity within the decidedly conservative economic mainstream: with *Emotional Intelligence: Why It Can Matter More Than IQ*—also published in 1995—Daniel Goleman caused a minor revolution in the business world, where suddenly affective skills were heralded as more accurate markers of professional success than raw brain power. *Time* magazine featured the story and baptized this form of intelligence "EQ" (Gibbs).

Yet a third title from 1995, neurologist Antonio Damasio's *Descartes' Error: Emotion, Reason, and the Human Brain*, pioneered the concept and study of what would come to be known as "grounded cognition," a model of affective or "hot" cognition that stands in opposition to the "cold" cognition of reason (see, e.g., Barsalou). Against the grain of Cartesian dualism—and against disciplinary convention that rejected emotion as a nonsubject of scientific investigation—Damasio argued that affect (defined as a sequence proceeding in complexity from sensory perception to emotion to feeling) underlies and ensures competent reasoning. Healthy reason is dependent upon healthy affect; where sensory-emotional-feeling capacities are irrevocably compromised, rational capacities, in turn, suffer an equally irrevocable debilitation, particularly in the areas of decision making and planning for the future.

In *Looking for Spinoza: Joy, Sorrow, and the Feeling Brain*, Damasio maps a model of the feeling brain in which he locates affective process within homeostasis, the mechanism of self-regulation that drives toward well-being—i.e., health, whose emotional face is happiness—as the natural point of equilibrium.[1] In this theory of affective process, the senses, emotions, and feeling are ascending rungs on the ladder of homeostasis. The human autonomic system, Damasio argues, is crowned by feeling, which he defines as a mental map of the body's emotional state—a form of consciousness that is nevertheless nonrational.

By way of caveat, I would like to emphasize that I am not debating the empirical merits of Damasio's characterization of affective process as homeostatic, but rather reading his intervention in the brain science of emotion as a cultural text that participates in and further confirms a pattern of the generalized privileging of affect whose major coordinates I am here trying to map out in a culturally diagnostic mode. In this light, although it is true that Damasio seeks to elaborate a mind-body continuum inspired by the philosophical thought of Descartes's contemporary Baruch Spinoza in which affective and rational systems are mutually interdependent, it is nevertheless fair to say that affect is really the star of Damasio's work (just as Spinoza has displaced Descartes as the star of an established strain of contemporary politico-cultural theory).[2] Affect, Damasio asserts, is the foundation of the human condition. The furthest reaching implication of this radical shift in neurological perspective is to usher in a new "cogito." Indeed, a *New York Times* review of *Looking for Spinoza* is titled, simply, "I Feel, Therefore I Am" (Eakin).

This new cogito seems to issue forth from every area of social life. Artificial intelligence has moved away from binary computation and toward the analog programming of human emotion. Psychologist and Silvan Tomkins disciple Paul Ekman has published a new critical edition of Charles Darwin's virtually forgotten *The Expression of the Emotions in Man and Animals* (1872) in which Ekman vindicates Darwin's characterization of affective communication through facial expressions as a hard-wired and universal "language of the emotions." Ekman went on to achieve media representation by actor

Tim Roth as Dr. Cal Lightman on the Fox television series *Lie to Me*, an exploration of the truth as ciphered in emotional microexpressions, which ran for three seasons. Advertising has begun to plumb recent work in psychology and neuroscience on this alleged universality of the emotions for its relevance to marketing; a simple online search will turn up both a lengthy list of titles in business studies literature purporting to exploit emotion for commercial advantage and an array of conferences convened in recent years for the purpose of disseminating and refining those strategies of emotional exploitation.

The biggest food and drink companies in the world have adopted the mantra of affect: McDonald's launched its first worldwide campaign in 2003 under the slogan "i'm lovin' it" ("McDonald's"); Coca-Cola followed suit with "happiness in a bottle" in 2006 ("Welcome"). Subaru of America, Inc. was named "Automotive Marketer of the Year" for 2008 by Mediapost.com in part for its "Love. It's What Makes a Subaru, a Subaru" and "Share the Love" campaigns ("Mediapost.com"). Politics have adopted analogous emotional brandings. In 2004 George W. Bush won his second term in office on the strength of a so-called—albeit tacit—politics of fear; Barack Obama triumphed in 2008 with a campaign explicitly defined by "hope" (Organizing).[3] Political scientist Drew Westen argues in *The Political Brain* that the electoral process is, in fact, motivated by affective rather than dispassionate choice. Strategies of political lobbying also reflect this affective shift, for example in regard to the movement to overturn California's illegalization of same-sex marriage in Proposition 8, which has adopted the slogan "love conquers H8." In an edited volume of cultural criticism, Patricia Ticineto Clough and Jean Halley have diagnosed the contemporary circumstance as one that has taken an "affective turn" in which the social is only intelligible when viewed through the lens of affect.[4]

Likewise, theories of the affective are springing up with particular intensity in media studies. These theories examine the media's appeal to the senses, a perspective neatly summarized in Vivian Sobchack's postulate that "our aesthetic and ethical senses merge and emerge 'in the flesh'" (1) and further exemplified in Laura U. Marks's characterization of global media and consumer culture as a "portable sensorium" (243), Brian Massumi's reading of mediated affect in the form of "parables for the virtual," and Linda Williams's definition of hard-core pornography as a "frenzy of the visible" (36). These theorists push toward an ontological understanding of affect as foundational to the experience of media culture, making an interpretive tradition—or even school within media studies—of Gilles Deleuze's late-blooming writings on cinema from the perspective of an affective temporality, that is, a narrative experience apprehended as such by the sensory perception of a passage of time.[5]

Whereas this strain of media studies theory focuses largely on the relationship of affect to form and reception (Marks proposes the metaphor of the "skin" of the film; Massumi insists on the "intensity" of representation), we would also do well to interrogate the ways in which affect shapes narrative itself—that is, the way we approach storytelling. Two recent films are of special interest in this regard, for they revisit canonical cultural figures—both notorious "men of words"—and cast them as men of feeling. In Mel Gibson's *The Passion of the Christ* (2004), Jesus's extended and notoriously graphic pain encapsulates his scriptural teachings. In Walter Salles's *Diarios de motocicleta* (*The Motorcycle Diaries*, 2004), the young Ernesto Guevara metamorphoses into the revolutionary "Che" not by evincing a capacity to give reasoned attacks on the asymmetries of neoimperialist capitalism, but rather by giving himself over in a profoundly somatic love to the oppressed of Latin America, which he accomplishes by conquering the debilitating pain of what the film's narrative codes as a fundamentally bourgeois asthmatic condition. No longer do teachings and long speeches characterize these enduring cultural icons. Their significance is reaffirmed in the stoic endurance of agony; their relationship to pain for the sake of love tells the story that used to be reasoned in words.

This cinematic rendering of cultural narrative—and politics—as affective finds a striking echo in the words of the insurrectionary Subcomandante Galeano, formerly Marcos, who makes a pithy formulation of political agency as the rights "to opine, and *to feel*, and to dissent" ("a opinar y a *sentir* y a disentir"; Galindo and Muñoz, emphasis added). Where we might expect—in the rationalist tradition of social agency that Gore and Žižek struggle to uphold—to find reasoning as the bridge transforming opinion into political self-expression, we instead find feeling as the motor driving activist political intervention.

Furthermore, the ways in which we have begun to narrate and represent our social selves and how we know those selves and the world around them now hinge on our capacity to feel. As a model of meaning, affect-as-episteme rests on the notion of homeostasis; hence, well-being and its opposite—"ill-being"—become its poles of evaluative judgment. In an economy of meaning epistemically centered on affect, the force of social denunciation is carried by sadness, pain, and disease; social affirmation by joy, pleasure, and good health.

I have proposed that the phenomenon I am examining represents an epistemic shift. We may remember that in "The Confession of the Flesh" ("Le jeu de Michel Foucault"), Foucault defines the episteme as a function of a second term, the *apparatus*. This latter term denotes "a thoroughly heterogeneous ensemble consisting of discourses, institutions, architectural forms, regulatory decisions, laws, administrative measures, scientific statements, philosophical, moral and philanthropic propositions" (194) that we should understand as a "formation which has as its major function at any given historical moment that of responding to an *urgent need*" (195). If the apparatus, then, embraces "the said as much as the unsaid" (194) in pressing all its heterogeneous elements into the service of "a dominant strategic function[ality]" (195), then the episteme is the "specifically *discursive*" (197) avatar of this apparatus. "I would define the episteme retrospectively [for its first use comes in the 1966 *Order of Things*] as the strategic apparatus which permits of separating out from among all the statements which are possible those that will be acceptable within, I won't say a scientific theory, but a field of scientificity, and which it is possible to say are true or false. The episteme is the 'apparatus' which makes possible the separation, not of the true from the false, but of what may from what may not be characterised as scientific" (197).[6]

Yet, for Foucault, the organizing principles of the episteme are inherently bounded by reason. I propose here that we break with that assumption in order to contemplate the possibility that we are witnessing on a broad cultural scale—from the representational to the empirical—the full-blown emergence of an episteme inherently bounded by affect. If we take inventory of our epistemological tools for conceiving of and delimiting the possible coordinates of human knowledge, we will find them critically amassed around an affective center that throws over the transcendent mind and thought for the immanent soma and feeling. In the affective epistemological landscape, feeling *becomes* "thought" in a knowledge of self and world produced through nonrational means.

We lack as yet an adequate vocabulary to express the idea of embodied knowledge, one that does not conjure up at every turn the specter of Cartesian rationality. For, within the cultural straits of the Enlightenment, affect has been the long-standing and abject obverse of reason. The very notion of an affective cogitation, judgment, or analysis seems most immediately oxymoronic because these faculties are so firmly associated with reason as to repudiate the possibility of affect-as-episteme in and of themselves. Yet contemporary cultural discourse presents us at every turn with bodies that cogitate, judge, analyze through sensory perception, emotion, feeling. Felt realities, sensed truths, guts that advise and hearts that remember, tears and smiles are what have begun to reconstitute social discourse along the semantic axis of affect. From this wide-ranging cultural discourse and the necessarily partial representation that I have given to it herein as a kind of epistemological symptomatology (of both the representational and the empirical, the tropological and the ontological), I have extrapolated a composite definition of affect as the prerational set of dispositions toward the self in the world given by sensory perception, emotion, and feeling, a set of dispositions that constructs a somatic knowledge organized on the autonomic principle of homeostasis. Organicity as a logic of organization, emotional disposition as a form of moral judgment, internal equilibrium as a means of analysis (through the constant tally of positive and negative affects and somatic states of being as ease or dis-ease): these are what Foucault would call the "rationalities"—again, the problem of vocabulary—of an epistemically affective approximation of being in the world.

There are many different affects—these understood, moreover, on an imprecise continuum from the empirical to the tropological. The discussion of affect in the singular is not meant to reduce this diversity to a monism except to signal the possibility that we might speak of an all-encompassing epistemic mode in which meaning is produced in a way that sharply contrasts with its production by reason. To take a concrete example of the potential utility of thinking through the implications of this shift, we might consider the twentieth-century treatment of culture, for example, in which we make a decisive switch of paradigm from one of hierarchy to one of relativism. If we analyze the epistemological currency of each position, we see that the former hierarchical model corresponds to a taxonomizing tendency that is racialized, as Mary Louise Pratt discusses (31–33), and guided by a vertical and transcendent power dynamic informed by epistemic reason. The latter relativist model, on the other hand, emerges in the aftermath of decolonization as a remediation of colonialism's cultural hierarchies and corresponds to an egalitarian tendency guided by a horizontal and immanent power dynamic and informed by epistemic affect. In the remainder of this introduction, I will flesh out these two terminological constellations—reason, verticality, and transcendence, on the one hand, and affect, horizontality, and immanence, on the other—in conjunction with colonialism and free-market capitalism, respectively. This analysis builds upon other considerations of the relationship between emotion and capitalism, arguably foremost among them *Cold Intimacies: The Making of Emotional Capitalism*, in which Eva Illouz posits the preeminence of emotional logic as a function of capitalism. I seek here to consider the epistemological reach of that logic and to theorize its genesis.

Headless Free-Market Capitalism

If we seek out modern origins of affect-as-episteme, we might, as a starting point, first consider how the Reformation challenged the vertical hierarchy of the Catholic Church, a hierarchy that we could productively view as analogous to the verticality of Cartesian dualism, in which a transcendent and exalted mind governs an immanent—and abjectly residual—body. Let us take the Religious Society of Friends, the Quakers, originating in the mid seventeenth century, as an apt example of how we might understand the Reformation to have metaphorically taken the governing "head" off of the religious body. If, a century earlier, Martin Luther had rejected the authority of the Pope, dispensed with confession, and lobbied for the free interpretation of the Bible, then Quakerism took this initial dismantling of Catholic hierarchy to a plane of full horizontality. Most significantly, the fundamental tenets of Quakerism hold that there is no mediation necessary between individuals and God—no priest, no minister, no preacher—and, moreover, that divinity is manifest in the form of an "inner light" within every living being. Quakerism does away with institutional hierarchy and establishes a perfectly horizontal relationship between the faithful. In fact, declared faith is not even requisite for the natural enjoyment of equal access to God: the inner light is universal and germane to life itself. The Quakers thus give the transcendent godhead a thoroughly somatic rendering in a somaticization that represents the social conviction of absolute equality between all people and constitutes a conceptual act of democratization ahead of its time. In a 1661 treatise on proper business conduct, Society of Friends founder George Fox emphasizes love as the ultimate guiding principle for transactions of exchange, signaling emotional harmony as the rule and measure of social harmony.[7] The very terminology of the sect itself indicates a horizontal rather than vertical disposition of relationships defined by affective bonds among members. Conceptually, the belief in an inner light joins humans together from within, creating an organic, immanent, and perfectly democratized totality. The result is a feeling soma that has dispensed altogether with the need for a thinking head.

In the *Protestant Ethic and the Spirit of Capitalism* (1905), Max Weber defined the "spirit of capitalism" as the wholesale cultural application of Protestant vocation—the concept of a "calling"—to the pursuit of profit. But where Weber interprets this pursuit of profit as "continuous, rational, capitalistic enterprise" (5), famously insisting on the rationalizing character of capitalism, I wish to reiterate the proposal that we entertain a productive discrepancy between capitalist discourses of colonizing expansion and democratizing immanence. If, indeed, capitalist expansionism is rationalizing and produces what contemporary sustainability critics have called an ideology of "growth"—expansive in an infinite linearity—then I would like, for a moment, to hold the consideration of this rationalizing ideology in abeyance, as a posterior and diachronic development to which we will later return, and in the meantime to examine capitalism's originary discursive definitions and justifications, which posit a different model of capitalist intercourse as a kind of organic homeostasis—an immanent harmony of the sum total of interconnected and integrated parts produced through nonrational self-regulation to maintain the healthy order and functionality of the whole as a kind of eternal (atemporal, ahistorical) circumstance equivalent to the circumstance of life itself.

Where Weber dedicates himself to the analysis of what I would consider the rational imperialist discourse of capitalism, I propose to analyze its revolutionary discourse of affective immanence. From this perspective, in full consonance with Weber's central claim, I posit that the Quaker soma finds its economic analogue a century later in Adam Smith's invisible hand (*Theory, Wealth*). In departure from Weber, however, I would like to turn my attention to the ways in which this consonance is constructed of an affective—rather than rational or rationalizing—conceptual fabric. Just as the Quakers envision an inner light connecting the religious body politic, Smith's writings evince a conceptualization of capital as the substance that flows organically through the social body politic. Just as the Quakers reject the institutional hierarchy of church and exogenous God, Smith likewise rejects the institutional trappings of military colonialism as a top-heavy redundancy in favor of a strictly economic relationship with Britain's American subjects. The Quakers locate authority and divinity within the illuminated body; Smith locates power within the flow of capital itself. Although the concept of laissez-faire had already been a hundred years in the making—coinciding with the robust expression of the Reformation and the robust development of commerce with the New World—it is Smith's writings that seminally theorize free-market capitalism.

If Smith theorizes free-market capitalism in 1776, then it is the revolutionary American bourgeoisie that brings it into being that same year under the political mantle of liberal democracy. In the logic of monarchy the bourgeoisie had been economically endowed through commerce but politically subaltern; in undertaking the self-ordained passage to sovereignty, the subaltern needed a conceptual logic to accompany and legitimize that change of social station. Here Nicole Eustace's *Passion Is the Gale: Emotion, Power, and the Coming of the American Revolution* explains the role of affect in accomplishing that legitimization. Eustace argues that it was a tectonic shift in the cultural status of emotion that underwrote the bourgeois revolutionary cause: whereas in the early modern culture of monarchical Europe, emotion had been rendered conceptually abject through association with the vulgar body politic, in the years preceding the American Revolution emotion was redeemed as a universal aspect of the human condition and exploited discursively as a means of defining that same formerly subject body politic—within whose ranks, after all, the bourgeois elite nevertheless found itself with respect to the monarchy—as a new and legitimate sovereign political force.[8]

Contemporaneously, Smith proposes a model for an economic sovereignty that, likewise, has a systemic—and not hierarchical—derivation. In other words, the economic sovereignty Smith proposes is one that does not need a crown or an empire; in fact, this kind of hierarchical apparatus is precisely what threatens to impede the optimization of capital flow. In tracing out what *will* optimize capital flow, Smith creates a narrative of organizational dynamics that echoes the trope of affective universality Eustace argues is all-important to the success of the American Revolution.

I approach Smith's construction of this universality in two passages that I will consider in the composite: one on morality and the other on the distribution of wealth, both of which, in consonance with Eustace's analysis, evince a vision of the human condition as one of universal organicity in which there is a perfectly democratic distribution of morality and wealth, as though these two were not only homologous resources but innately—and definitionally—human characteristics. Universal morality (the conceptual platform for a democratic model of governance, following Eustace) and universal access to resources along a homeostatic model of democratizing organic flow—from all parts through all parts of the universal soma—obey the same epistemological dynamics in Smith's thought. (If we read Smith with one eye to the present—considering Smith a starting point for an uneven but continuous trajectory of affective discourse through to the current global moment—we will also readily appreciate how his notion of a universal soma traversed by a flow equally moral and economic resonates strongly with Damasio's model of homeostasis as an affective form of nonrational somatic self-regulation. Reading the two authors side by side shows how Damasio's model of affective homeostasis appears in effect as the biological counterpart, two centuries later, of Smith's model of the moral-economic homeostasis of the capitalist body politic.)

In the *Theory of Moral Sentiments* (1759)—the foundation for his capitalist treatise *The Wealth of Nations*—Smith claims that morality is an intrinsic part of the self-interest that famously drives human nature and capitalism alike (this last pair posited, as always within capitalist discourse, as a homology). It is with this fundamental assertion that Smith opens his disquisition on the moral sentiments:

> How selfish soever man may be supposed, there are evidently some principles in his nature, which interest him in the fortunes of others, and render their happiness necessary to him, though he derives nothing from it, except the pleasure of seeing it. Of this kind is pity or compassion, the emotion we feel for the misery of others, when we either see it, or are made to conceive it in a very lively manner. That we often derive sorrow from the sorrow of others, is a matter of fact too obvious to require any instances to prove it; for this sentiment, like all the other passions of human nature, is by no means confined to the virtuous and humane, though they perhaps may feel it with the most exquisite sensibility. The greatest ruffian, the most hardened violator of the laws of society, is not altogether without it.
>
> (13)

The self-interest, then, that moves the capitalist machine, is not at odds with the moral sentiments—empathy, sympathy, feeling for others—but inextricably bound together with them. This morality—this capacity for a social life of emotions—is portrayed emphatically by Smith as a universal attribute, a characteristic proper to the human condition.

For Smith, nature mirrors this equitable distribution of morality in the equitable distribution of resources, which, in spite of an asymmetrical distribution of wealth, nevertheless achieves a perfect symmetry in its support of humans irrespective of class difference:

> The produce of the soil maintains at all times nearly that number of inhabitants which it is capable of maintaining. The rich only select from the heap what is most precious and agreeable. They consume little more than the poor, and in spite of their natural selfishness and rapacity, though they mean only their own conveniency, though the sole end which they propose from the labours of all the thousands whom they employ, be the gratification of their own vain and insatiable desires, they divide with the poor the produce of all their improvements. They are led *by an invisible hand* to make nearly the same distribution of the necessaries of life, which would have been made, had the earth been divided into equal portions among all its inhabitants, and thus without intending it, without knowing it, advance the interest of the society, and afford means to the multiplication of the species. When Providence divided the earth among a few lordly masters, it neither forgot nor abandoned those who seemed to have been left out in the partition. These last too enjoy their share of all that it produces. In what constitutes the real happiness of human life, they are in no respect inferior to those who would seem so much above them. In ease of body and peace of mind, all the different ranks of life are nearly upon a level, and the beggar, who suns himself by the side of the highway, possesses that security which kings are fighting for.
>
> (215, emphasis added)

Making our way back to the analysis of the invisible hand as the key figure of the homeostatic principle foundational to epistemic affect, here it guides the wealthy to play the part of nature by "mak[ing] nearly the same distribution of the necessaries of life, which would have been made, had the earth been divided into equal portions among all its inhabitants." The invisible hand is the force of democratization that counters vertical hierarchy and the disproportionate hoarding of resources, goods—and, later, capital—by setting them into a circulation salutary to the entire body politic, favoring equally beggars and kings. Just as in *The Wealth of Nations*, where the invisible hand will make another cameo appearance in which the integrant of capitalist society is described as being "led by an invisible hand to promote an end which was no part of his intention" (4.2.9) and yet which accomplishes the greatest social good, in *Theory of Moral Sentiments* this process of the democratic satisfaction of needs happens "without intending it, without knowing it," as though by force of an unthinking autonomic process. And it is this process that "advance[s] the interest of the society, and afford[s] means to the multiplication of the species." Within Smith's discourse, asymmetries of wealth are local and incidental; the most important figure, ultimately, is that of the human collective—the single soma of boundless parts—in which such asymmetries disappear, drowned out by the wash of democratizing uniformity that humanity, on a scale so large as to be one with nature, imposes organically upon itself through the visceral logic of the invisible hand, which mindlessly, through somatic wisdom, achieves a perfect distribution of resources throughout the greater human body.

Rather than being governed—impeded, restricted, constrained, regulated—by a thinking head, the free market is intrinsically governed, in Smith's now canonical metaphor, by an invisible hand. The invisible hand assumes the responsibilities of a higher transcendent power of organization, but puts an end to the discrete and external verticality of that power by internalizing it. The rational head is entirely excised through its functional cannibalization by Smith's epistemically affective invisible hand. Reason and rational order are submitted to affective expression. If the invisible hand represents a manifestation of divinity, it is a divinity that is relocated downward into the soma, a force of methodical organization and balance that is thoroughly *disintellected,* a self-rule of the soma by the soma.

The Quakers had developed just such a model of spiritual religiosity, yet persisted in the belief in an exogenous godhead as the source of the inner light. Smith's invisible hand does away with all exogeny, granting the soma a status of pure immanence. When liberated from all regulatory and executive administrative obstacles, capital will naturally flow, as though guided by this disintellected invisible hand freed from the constraints of an authoritative thinking head, in a pattern that will maximize its potential for accumulation and profit. Unfettered capital will circulate like blood through the body politic—now conceptually homologous with the market—carrying economic oxygen to and fro according to organic demands for its movement. The disintellected hand represents an autonomic, rather than rational, orchestration of this movement, a movement that will always tend toward the

well-being of the market-public as a whole. The somatic regulation of the
invisible hand represents a homeostatic model in which unrestricted capital
flow maximizes good social health.

Shortly after the birth of liberal democracy and the invisible hand, France
followed suit with a bourgeois revolution of radically egalitarian ideology
that literally severed the heads of its monarchy. If we view this will to de-
capitate as a rejection of transcendent vertical dualism in favor of immanent
somatic monism, then we will find in contemporary philosophical discourse
the European analog of the American universalization of emotion that Eustace lays out as the foundation of bourgeois revolution. In 1739 David
Hume claimed in *A Treatise of Human Nature*, "Reason is and ought only
to be the slave of the passions, and can never pretend to any office other
than to serve and obey them" (2.3.3.4, 266). Half a century later—in synchronicity with the French Revolution—we find this inversion of Cartesian dualism to be even more emphatically articulated in Jeremy Bentham's
Principles of Morals and Legislation, which, from its opening lines, locates
sovereignty in affect, dressing the feeling soma triumphantly in the language
of the repudiated thinking head:

> Nature has placed mankind under the governance of two sovereign
> masters, pain and pleasure. It is for them alone to point out what we
> ought to do, as well as to determine what we shall do. On the one
> hand the standard of right and wrong, on the other the chain of caus-
> es and effects, are fastened to their throne. They govern us in all we
> do, in all we say, in all we think: every effort we can make to throw
> off their subjection, will serve but to demonstrate and confirm it. In
> words a man may pretend to abjure their empire: but in reality he will
> remain subject to it all the while. The principle of utility recognises
> this subjection, and assumes it for the foundation of that system, the
> object of which is to rear the fabric of felicity by the hands of reason
> and of law.
>
> (1)

The ratio of pleasure to pain is what indicates the political action optimal to the maintenance of homeostasis in the body politic, a homeostatic
equilibrium defined in affective terms as "felicity" (in a note to the second
edition of 1823, Bentham observes that the term "principle of utility" has
come to be known equally as the "principle of happiness" [1*n*1]). Indeed, it

is the capacity of the body to move autonomically toward maximal well-being that becomes the guiding conceptual principle for political life. The body's affects have become the new social monarch, ruling headlessly from within. Reason is here no longer glorified as an epistemic ontology—that is, as a viable terrain for the acquisition of knowledge and order—but rather as a secondary posture of recognition of the a priori dominion of the affects over all aspects of human affairs. The strategic management of this primordially affective condition is the purview of reason, but the human condition itself—and its social and civic life—is affirmed as being foundationally affective. Once more, the ruling head is relocated downward to the soma, where it is recast as internal affective process: a contest between pain and pleasure in which a pleasurable equilibrium is the model for the optimal social ideal.

Capitalism—as Weber argues—may well be said to have harbored reason as a dominant organizational paradigm for the following two centuries; for evidence of this rationalization, one need only think of the Fordist assembly line and its Taylorist refinement in the optimization of physical movement or the contemporary calculation of industrial productivity to the ten thousandths of a second.[9] Yet we should remember that its originary—revolutionary—self-legitimizing discourse was one rooted in the primacy of the passions and the resultant vision of a social compact based on the moral balance of homeostatic health and well-being. Since its inception, capitalism has been culturally naturalized as a system whose benefits may be quantified in a calculus of the social good. Its proponents argue that capitalism brings about a prosperity that is tantamount to robust health; its detractors, making the opposite claim from within the same symbolic terrain, assess its faults in terms of social malaise or ill-being: disease, desperation, dehumanization. In the late nineteenth century Charles Dickens decries these latter ills as the product of capitalist industrialization. If we accept that Dickens, like other authors of his day, may—approaching Herbert Marcuse through Nancy Armstrong's reading—participate in an "inward turn" that places onto "each individual [the responsibility] for finding within him- or herself emotional, spiritual, or aesthetic compensation for whatever forms of compensation he or she may lack in material terms" (Armstrong 143), then we could consider a work like Diamela Eltit's *Mano de obra* (*Work Hand*, 2002) as a modern-day Dickensian dystopia without the compensatory inward turn. Here the concepts of "love" and "respect," indeed, the entire interior moral landscape, have been colonized by the culture of the megasupermarket in a patently perverse utilitarian discourse of "good" that is profoundly bad. On the opposite end of the discursive spectrum, Lloyd Blankfein, current CEO of the powerful global investment bank Goldman Sachs, defends the "good" of capitalism by asserting a "social purpose" for the banking industry: the "virtuous cycle" of the creation of companies, wealth, and jobs from capital. That Goldman Sachs has maintained vertiginous holdings in spite of the current economic recession and crisis of capitalist faith should, in Blankfein's view, make "everybody . . . frankly, happy" at this success story of bankers "doing God's work" (Arlidge). (Never mind that months after Blankfein's claim to godliness, Goldman Sachs was accused by the U.S. Securities and Exchange Commission of defrauding investors in the recession-provoking housing market collapse [Goldstein].)

There is a recent convergence of interest among cultural theorists around the end of the eighteenth century, precisely the moment in which Smith and Bentham are writing, in which the birth of free-market capitalism, liberal democracy, and the Industrial Revolution all come into being (in turn recasting formal empire, from this point forward, as an "imperialism of free trade," to borrow John Gallagher and Ronald Robinson's landmark 1953 term for neocolonialism). Michael Hardt and Antonio Negri look back to the American Constitution as the genesic model of twenty-first-century empire (in which there is neither formal empire nor formal colony, but rather all-encompassing systemic immanence—echoing the furthest-reaching implications of Gallagher and Robinson's model of neocolonial imperialism—and also of Smith's theoretical dispensation with crown and empire). Giorgio Agamben finds in the French revolutionary Declaration of the Rights of Man and Citizen (1789) a decisive biopolitical shift in which "bare life," heretofore "clearly distinguished as *zoē* from political life (*bios*), now fully enters into the structure of the state and even becomes the earthly foundation of the state's legitimacy and sovereignty" (127). Michel Foucault argues in *The Order of Things* that the end of the eighteenth century witnessed a profound epistemic shift, which he characterizes as the "transformation of structure into character . . . based upon a principle alien to the domain of the visible—an internal principle [that] is *organic structure*" (227). The end of the eighteenth century, in synthesis, witnessed the birth of a neoempire of bare organic life. A critical mass of scholarship is also growing around the eighteenth century that redefines it as a function not of its rationality, but of its *sentimentality* (e.g., Brooks, Dupré, Festa, Frazer, among myriad others).

Let us review in brief the multiple threads of the conceptual investiture of the late eighteenth century that we have traced herein: the invisible hand

and autonomic self-regulation of the economy as the specular homologue of the entire social order (Smith); pain and pleasure as the absolute sovereigns of human, and therefore political, life (Bentham); the positioning of bare life as the foundation of political life (Agamben); the democratic constitution as the foundational principle of immanent empire (Hardt and Negri); and the notion of organicity as the operative epistemic modality (Foucault). The homeostatic principle embraces all of these ideas: a self-contained, self-regulating, organic model of immanent organization and control in which the feeling soma rules itself on moral grounds without the intellectual interference of transcendent rational authority. This is the constellation of *affective positivities*, to employ Foucault's term for the key topoi of epistemic thought and discourse.

Foucault implicitly assumes that epistemes were inherently rational, yet he also muses on the difficulties of explaining what he characterizes as the "enigmatic event" of the emergence of "organic structure" within "some progress made by rationality" (*The Order of Things* 238). Might we not consider that what Foucault has trouble characterizing within a trajectory of rational epistemicity signals, precisely, its rupture? The point in time Foucault links to this irrevocable tear in the epistemic fabric is the same point in time that we have characterized as the age of bourgeois independence and the birth of the democratic principle, in parallel with the emergence of free-market capitalism and a new form of colonial imperialism that prefers economic neocolonialism to the formal imperial fact. Could we identify this tear in the epistemic fabric of the West as one that ushers in affect as a new epistemic principle? In other words, that affect becomes, henceforth, a competing cultural logic?

Persistence of the Rational Colonizing Head

If this epistemic rupture ushers in affect as the new vehicle for modeling knowledge and framing discourse in the era of free-market capitalism, then it is important to note that what affect-as-episteme bursts forth to interrupt and challenge is the era of first-wave colonial imperialism and its epistemic handmaid, the rational discourse of the modern West. We might view reason as the episteme of Western colonial imperialism—which would begin with late fifteenth-century Spain—with the cogito as the conceptual expression of an imperial practice that Ángel Rama describes, in an analysis of

Spanish imperialism, as "a whole series of transmitted directives . . . from the governing head [of empire] to the physical body [of the colony]" (7). The bipartite affirmation "I think, therefore I am" creates a dichotomy between authoritative reason and subject body, with rational thought taking on a sovereign role of effectively authoring the body into being. The rational mind observes the subject body from on high, codifying, regulating, taxonomizing. The intellectual head remains the supreme locus of organizational power, ruling over the subject body that is at once exalted, as the living proof of the head's creational genius, and abject, as necessarily inferior to its creator. Instead of characterizing the head's activity in terms of creation, perhaps we ought to substitute the term *discovery*—as intentionally suggestive of the relationship between the Old and New Worlds. The thinking head—with its transcendent mind—discovers, through its thought, the fact of physical being, just as the Old World "discovered" the New and sought to organize this new terrain in its likeness, but without allowing it to progress from abject savagery to rational civilization. The New World is the future of Europe, its paradise and promised land, but, paradoxically, it must nonetheless be eternally inferior to the original model. We may conceive of Old World colonialism as formal (during the period of Spanish dominion), epistemological (following Pratt's view of Europe's early modern global intellectual hegemony), or informal (as per Gallagher and Robinson's argument regarding the free-market imperialism of Britain over Latin America—along with the school of economic dependency theory). Regardless of how we characterize Old World colonialism, its living New World subjects constitute the body "discovered"—now glorified, now reviled—by this distant governing head.

And so we come full circle to our initial observation in regard to the thorough repudiation of the Cartesian subject as the administrator of Western colonialism (arguably nowhere more explicit than in Frantz Fanon's *The Wretched of the Earth*). But reason does not die away completely with the final twentieth-century "decapitation" of the colonial head. The colonial head, we must remember, has already long since given itself over to the management of free-market capitalism, whose practice—and companion discourse—of growth has been engaged in a lengthy process of rationalization—and, many argue, neocolonial exploitation: perfectly abstracted imperial structure, now absent of both formal empire and colony. The ideology of growth associated with rationalizing imperialist capitalism could be considered an epistemically hybrid discourse in the sense that it takes on the biological contours of affective epistemicity but adapts them to the neocolonial project of vertical rationalization.

The collapse of the Soviet Union represents the bitter end of formal, albeit quasi, colonization. The first and second worlds had openly vied to control the globe. With this collapse, as Fukuyama gave us to understand in his essay "The End of History?" and later in his book *The End of History and the Last Man*, free-market capitalism—alternately known as "liberal democracy"—assumed universal proportions as the "last man" standing. Affect-as-episteme has no further challenge, no further obstacle to its cultural hegemony. On balance, growth is rendered epistemologically obsolete; full expansionism has been conceptually guaranteed, and now the discourse of perfect immanence may come to the epistemological fore.

It is not only the eradication of obstacles to its diffusion that marks the global capitalism of the post-Soviet period but also the simultaneous development of a technology in the form of the World Wide Web that accomplished the realization—and reactivation—of its inherent originary potentialities.[9] Regarding the historical convergence between the emergence of the Web and the triumph of neoliberalism, new media studies critic Lev Manovich has the following meditation:

> Although causally unrelated, conceptually it makes sense that the end of [the] Cold War and the design of the Web took place at exactly the same time. The first development ended the separation of the world into parts closed off from each other, making it a single global system; the second development connected [the] world's computers into a single network. The early Web (i.e., before it came to be dominated by big commercial portals toward the end of the 1990s) also practically implemented a radically horizontal, non-hierarchical model of human existence in which no idea, no ideology, and no value system can dominate the rest—thus providing a perfect metaphor for a new post–Cold-War sensibility.
>
> (25)

There may be no causal relation between the end of the cold war and the launching of the World Wide Web—or at least no single cause—but we might ask ourselves whether new media technology (the Web and its mechanisms of massive intercommunicativity) emerge in satisfaction of the dictates of capitalist needs. Manovich's characterization of the Web as "implement[ing] a radically horizontal, non-hierarchical model of human existence in which no idea, no ideology, and no value system can dominate the rest" is a concise paraphrasis of the epistemic fundaments of capitalist homeostasis. In this sense Manovich's identification of the Web as a "perfect metaphor for a new post–Cold War sensibility" invites the interpretation of new media technology as a vehicle to realize on a virtual plane the structure and operation of the affective monosubject—the homeostatic feeling soma. In media and cultural studies discourse, the network has emerged as a signal trope of global capital (Castells, Dyer-Witheford, Fisher, Latour) and, from the perspective of affective epistemicity, the material realization of its discursive body.

In practice, networks may assume a heterogeneity of aspects and functions—including the production of systems of control, as Alexander R. Galloway and Eugene Thacker argue in *The Exploit: A Theory of Networks* (2007), systems of control that facilitate what I would call colonialist expansionism in the service of capitalist elitism. Yet, as a general descriptor for the wired interconnectivity that defines our social state of affairs on an increasingly global level, the "network society," as Manuel Castells calls it, "made of networks in all the key dimensions of social organization and social practice" (xviii), is neither more nor less than the manifest architectonic rendering of the infinitely capacious soma guided by Smith's invisible hand—with the fact that this architecture is now virtual as well as physical only increasing the girth and expanse of the collective capitalist subject.

It is in this context that we have witnessed the explosion of affect in every field of knowledge, most strikingly within the natural sciences, which had for two centuries endured and thwarted, as the last bastion of epistemic reason, the incursions of affect. Suddenly, in the post-Soviet era, the flirtations with the scientific study of affect that had begun in the post–World War II era of U.S. economic, military, and cultural preeminence exploded in scale. Now, well into the second decade of the twenty-first century, the cutting edge of research in each of the three major disciplines is, in some way, an inquiry into affect, whether physiological or discursive, empirical or representational, material or symbolic. Contemporary culture and politics likewise reflect this discursive shift in the same measure that free-market capitalism—neoliberalism in its most contemporary iteration—has achieved unprecedented heights of both hegemony and contestation.

It may be that the development of new media network culture affords capitalism with the technological realization of its epistemologically idealized homeostatic structure, causing its discourse of growth comparatively to wane, but its practice does not cease to be what Weber called "identical with the pursuit of profit" (5). The global neoliberal variant of capitalism presents a paradox. On the one hand, the ideological and technological circumstances are such that capitalism's epistemologically affective discourse can come to the fore virtually unchallenged, confronting the problem of conversion—from markets to epistemologies—rather than any problem of competition. On the other hand, this very condition of global hegemony allows neoliberal capitalism to take its practice of profit making to new extremes of neocolonialism, yielding a vertiginous divide between a tiny global elite and the heterogeneous masses.[10] Where capitalist apologies maintain that such radical asymmetry—and the poverty and social injustice that accompany it—are accidental, David Harvey argues that they are structural—the "raison d'être" of the system as opposed to a mere "side-product" (98).

Hence neoliberal capitalism's greatest and most persistent difficulty: the reconciliation of its practical telos of profit (growth) with its epistemic self-portrait of harmony (homeostasis). For, in theory, the sprouting of a monarchical—colonialist—"head" constitutes the most powerful allegation of immoral hypocrisy that could be leveled against capitalism in its revolutionary iteration, because it strikes at the core of the capitalist discourse of epistemic affect itself, which staunchly maintains an ethic of anti-intellectual and anti-vertical headlessness—the sovereign self-regulation of the body by the body.[11]

Affective Terms of Social Critique: The Contest to Define Homeostatic Well-Being

The allegation that neoliberalism has sprouted a colonizing "head" where it claims there ought to be none frames the current struggle between hegemon and dissident as a contest for the definition of affective homeostasis. If free-market capitalism has laid claim to the homeostatic principle, maintaining a monopoly on the notion of somatic well-being, then its global-era critics have begun to take it to task on its own epistemic terms, decrying this well-being as an illusion, a mere question of smoke and mirrors behind which lies a reality of profound ill-being. In other words, the critics of capitalism traffic in the same conceptual terrain epistemically dictated by capitalism itself. That is, critics take aim at capitalism precisely at the disjuncture between its rationalizing (neocolonialist) practice and its affective (anticolonialist revolutionary) discourse, charging—in the language of affect-as-episteme itself—that its practice is one that produces an ill-being entirely at odds with its discourse of well-being. (Nike, for example, staged a so-called Human Race event in 2008 meant to epitomize global harmony and health even as it faced renewed accusations of maintaining sweatshop labor conditions across the world.) In this sense, I submit that we can comprehend neither our current discourse of political contestation nor the insistence with which mainstream capitalist discourse clings to its hegemonic position without comprehending their shared epistemically affective motor.

Ulrich Beck's concept of "risk society" (*Risk Society*)—which he has since rendered in a global framework as "world risk society" (*World Risk Society*) and as a menace to the planet itself in "world at risk" (*World at Risk*)—holds that the growth of capitalist modernity is predicated on dangerous risk at the individual, social, and planetary levels. (Addiction and obesity induced by the fat-sugar-salt fast food triumvirate, manufacturing waste and run-off into local water supplies, carbon emissions, and fracking are several high-profile examples from current public discussion and debate.) In other words, the unseen axis of the pursuit of prosperity is the constant risk of adverse consequences, consequences of ill-being. These risks have come to be called *externalities* of production and development— that is, ill-effects that are socialized outside the formal ledger of industrial and business accountability. Annie Leonard's online animated historiography and analysis of consumer culture, "The Story of Stuff," denounces this unseen part of consumer culture as that which pillages and pollutes people and the environment on a linear model, as though the resources at the disposition of this capitalist machine were infinite and infinitely disposable. A published version of Leonard's video content succinctly makes its case in the book's subtitle: *How Our Obsession with Stuff Is Trashing the Planet, Our Communities, and Our Health*. A documentary film titled, simply, *The Corporation* diagnoses the eponymous entity as a psychopath using a checklist of symptoms defined by the World Health Organization. The film posits as an amalgamation of these symptoms the disregard for both social and planetary well-being that is exhibited in the linear capitalist exploitation of resources and flagrant indifference toward the noxious effects of this exploitation on the health of individuals, communities, and nature. The central accusation: capitalism produces deadly imbalance. Yet if neoliberal practice produces deadly imbalance, then it is an imbalance discursively cloaked in equilibrium.

Addiction is the key concept that increasingly surfaces to explain the cultural permissiveness toward this capitalist devastation and acceptance of the mitigating illusion of homeostatic well-being. Exposés of the food and drug industry, of shopping, and of gambling (whether at casinos or on the stock market) make this charge. Americans are addicted to fast food, mall culture, big cars, credit cards, and pharmaceuticals. They are obese, diabetic, diseased, indebted beyond repair, virtually buried in material goods. They are almost completely alienated from their own humanity and starved for real love, as the Pixar film *WALL·E* asserts in its apocalyptic vision of how consumer culture destroys planetary life and leads humans to a mechanized existence of consumption in which they are so obese they cannot walk and so enslaved to onscreen virtuality that they no longer see or touch one another. Their cerebral reward center gives the positive somatic interpretation of pleasurable gratification to the effects of even the most lethal of addictive substances, thereby disabling the homeostatic principle of balanced self-regulation that tends toward truly healthy well-being like a pendular return to center.

Mad Men, a period AMC cable television series that explores the powerful culture of Madison Avenue advertising, has turned its gaze on the unbridled and unscrupulous marketing of the 1960s as a critical originary moment in the U.S. ascent to current global hegemony. (It is important to note that within the United States and elsewhere—in Latin America, for example—the leftist revolutionary discourse of the 1960s is also turning up anew, precisely as a discursive antidote for this exploitation by capitalist consumer culture.) The pilot episode of *Mad Men*, "Smoke Gets in Your Eyes," introduces our protagonist, creative genius Don Draper (Jon Hamm), in the midst of an uncharacteristic crisis about to how to pitch the product of his mainstay client, Lucky Strike. The adverse circumstance is a recent publication by the surgeon general conclusively linking smoking to cancer. Draper ultimately resolves this quandary by tossing the report in the trash. Advertising is about producing comfort, security, and happiness, he concludes, not about morbidly peddling in death. Accordingly, Draper arrives at the simple slogan, "It's toasted," succinctly reassuring in its connotations of nature, health, and home. This portrait of homeostatic equilibrium thus perversely obscures the calculated misrepresentation of profound ill-being. Lucky Strike becomes the synecdoche for the turning of profits on certain death through the promotion of toxic addiction to a product that activates the reward center of gratification—all to the fatal detriment of the consumer. Happiness becomes purely discursive, covering up a diametrically opposed reality of ever increasing ill-being as both source and effect of capitalist success.

In an affective register, neoliberal critique decries a discrepancy between neoliberal practice and discourse in which neoliberal discourse promises a perfect equity of happiness and harmony for all, yet its neocolonial practice produces wealth—happiness and harmony—for an elite at the expense of the many that it submerges into poverty, pain, and discord. Lauren Berlant, for example, takes this disjuncture as the focal point of her analysis in *Cruel Optimism*, in which she argues that the cultural promise of happiness for all is belied by a contrary reality. Neoliberalism contests this critique by reasserting its claim to well-being, which has become the key trope—underwritten by epistemic affect—of social legitimacy.

Empathic Imaginaries of the Social: Altruism, Posthumanism, Sustainability, Revolution

If the act of distinguishing between ill-being and well-being has become the basis of imagining alternative social realities, then it is no wonder that empathy has surfaced as a key concept in cultural discourse, for empathy is, simply, the ability to comprehend the feelings of another. Empathy might be defined as the art of affective diagnosis—with the implication that the agent of empathic diagnosis will be led by the affective information derived from this diagnosis to adopt a behavior that will tend toward the well-being of the Other. Empathy, then, is a behavioral method of achieving social homeostasis, with a constellation of positive affects—care, compassion, love—motivating the empathic act. We might understand empathy, in other words, as a social practice of the construction of collective well-being based on love (to take love as a metonym for the positive affects motivating empathy).

In biology Frans de Waal's ideas about morality in the primate world serve as the main text for an edited theoretical inquiry into the evolution of morality in *Primates and Philosophers* that de Waal expands into a social model in *The Age of Empathy: Nature's Lessons for a Kinder Society* (2009) on the strength of the central idea that altruism—and not selfishness, as was accepted for decades following Richard Dawkins's *The Selfish Gene*—is the basis of adaptive behavior. In *The Bonobo and the Atheist: In Search of Humanism among Primates* (2013) de Waal argues that morality—in humans considered the purview of religion—should more accurately be understood as biologically innate and the result of evolutionary adaptation. Economist Jeremy Rifkin, likewise, postulates the concept of "empathic civilization" as the only viable remedy for the apocalyptic course set by our synthetic human-made environment. The business world, as the originary producer of this discourse, is also repositioning itself to learn from those who would hold it to the letter of its own epistemic law, as is evidenced, as just one example among many, by Dev Patnaik's *Wired to Care: How Companies Prosper When They Create Widespread Empathy.*

In the same vein as de Waal, poststructuralist theory—most notably, Jacques Derrida with his "The Animal That Therefore I Am (More to Follow)"—has been evolving into a so-called posthuman modality for well over a decade. Cary Wolfe gathers these interventions together in his edited volume *Zoontologies,* which, in combination with his own analysis of "posthumanist theory" in *Animal Rites,* and his more sustained development of a theoretical model in *What Is Posthumanism?,* elucidates the phenomenon of theoretical interest in the animal as fundamentally rooted in the expulsion of humanity from its self-arrogated throne of ecological dominance. This kind of "decapitation" of cultural anthropocentrism mimics the logic of affect-as-episteme in that it effectively dethrones "man" from the rule of the animal kingdom—from the rule of the universe. For *man* as a discursive invention comes into being, according to Foucault (*The Order of Things*), precisely with the birth of the logic of "organic structure," which we might consider under the alternative terminology of affect-as-episteme. And so the notion of a self-governing, homeostatic, headless—organic—structure of order replaces a vertical one in which the rational and externally imposed monarchical head governs from above. What posthuman theory decries is the way in which "man"—though apparently involved in a thoroughly democratic and horizontal relationship with "him"self—nevertheless lords over the rest of the animal world in a kind of reemergence of the monarchical head that had to be repudiated as a founding condition of "his" conceptual emergence. The posthuman position is one of affective—organic—purism in that it rejects this de facto head. In other words, what this posthuman theory proposes is, first, that the model of epistemic affect—of organicity—not be designated in homology with the human body, but rather with the entire animal kingdom, a diversity of life united, in the most basic regard as explored by posthuman theory, by emotion, and, second, that an ethics of well-being—practices of empathy—be negotiated within that entire corpus of living beings, not just

among humans. This democratized vision of a horizontal web of life is epistemologically analogous to the decentralized network structure of the feeling
soma—now conceptually expanded to embrace all humanity and, in even
more radical conceptualizations of life, the planet itself.

Indeed, the emergent discourse of sustainability takes both altruism and
posthumanism to their ultimate consequences by proposing that the homeostatic model ought to expand to include the whole of life itself at the
intersection of the environmental, the social, and the economic, and that
a concern for all-inclusive planetary well-being replace a concern for profit as the central motor of social life. Far beyond simply turning off lights
or recycling paper, the concept of sustainability poses the most significant
challenge to capitalist powers since the revolutionary discourse of the 1960s.
In a 2006 speech before the United Nations General Assembly, Bolivian
president Evo Morales developed a conceptual dichotomy between "living
well" (*vivir bien*) and "living better" (*vivir mejor*) that sets in clear relief
how sustainability may be understood in the dimension of comprehensive
social contestation. In Morales's incendiary definition, the capitalist way of
life—living *better*—is "to pillage, to rob, to exploit"; the alternative way
of life—living *well*—is to live in respectful harmony with Mother Earth, in
peaceful community, and with collective property. For Morales, the linear
excess of "living better" is as environmentally untenable as it is socially
cruel and economically self-interested. The interconnectivity of nature and
people in a system of balanced exchange of "living well," on the other hand,
is sustainable because it is environmentally conscientious, socially kind (empathic), and free from the imbalances of economic asymmetry.[12]

Whether in its most modest or radical variant—and understanding it as
a simultaneously three-way intervention into the domains of people, planet,
and profit—sustainability may well be said to constitute the new discourse
of social change, on a spectrum from reform to revolution. Yet sustainability
discourse maintains a relationship with capitalism that is one of epistemic solidarity rather than epistemic aggression. That is, sustainability may
seek to change capitalism—from meekly "greenwashing" it to aggressively
countering its neocolonial practice, but, regardless of its position along this
continuum, sustainability only works to reaffirm capitalism's affective epistemological supports insofar as it constructs itself out of the same model of
universal homeostatic organicity.

The lesson here is that for the immanent "we" that has no outside,
revolution may only assume the form of therapy, a movement away from

ill-being and toward well-being; violence has no place in revolution by the feeling soma. Under the sway of epistemic affect, revolution becomes a practice of empathy in which the battle is over the right of the immanent "we" to well-being. This understanding of revolution as being founded on and driven by an exercise in empathy (a diagnosis of self and of the countless others in the immanent "we" as so many proximate selves) helps to explain what goes emphatically expressed but completely unglossed in Hardt and Negri's estimation, namely, that the militant of immanent empire wages a battle that becomes a "project of love" (*Empire* 413). The concept of affect-as-episteme allows us to understand that this project may contest capitalist empire, but it in no way moves outside its epistemological logic.

Toward the Epistemic Recognition of Soma-as-Knower

The very visceral immediacy of affective signification that makes it so powerful is also what blinds us to its legitimacy as a vehicle for social representation. Like Žižek and Gore, on a cultural level, we still fail to recognize—and valorize as significant—the phenomenon of affectively figured social meaning that surrounds us, instead training our expectations on a rational model that has come to prove elusive time and again. If we look closely, we will see that theoreticians across the disciplines are providing us with the material to revisit and revise our consciously held conceptions regarding the epistemic foundations of self and knowledge. Rei Terada has revisited poststructuralist theory to foreground an emotional content—a "feeling in theory"—that no one had ever supposed was there; Daniel Heller-Roazen performs a sweeping survey of the philosophical canon to elucidate the heretofore unstudied references to the senses—the "inner touch," as he calls it. Jon Protevi gives an exposition of the conceptual importance of the body in modern political philosophy. In Peninsular Hispanism, the collaborative project "Emotional Cultures in Spain from the Enlightenment to the Present" directed by Jo Labanyi (New York University), Elena Delgado (University of Illinois at Urbana Champaign), and Pura Fernández (Consejo Superior de Investigaciones Científicas, Madrid), seeks to reread Spanish literary and cultural history as a function of affect. Emotion has been there all along; its status has simply experienced an epistemic shift, and scholars are, in effect, returning to the Western canon to give the presence of emotion a new epistemic interpretation. The interest in affect that is bubbling up in every discipline is a sign of the times, an indicator that a common model of knowledge—a common epistemic cultural fabric—is guiding thought on the cutting edge of every major field of investigation in a like-minded direction. We all know that we are conceptually captivated by affect; my intervention seeks to address—and take first steps to remedy—the fact that we don't yet know why.

Until we know the whys and wherefores of this captivation, we will continue to willfully misunderstand—to second-guess and devalorize—our own interpretations of affective discourse. In spite of the ready intelligibility of affective narrative on its own terms, as cultural subjects steeped in its logic we will nevertheless continually seek to reinscribe affect within reason.[13] We will continue to profess scandal at Mel Gibson's overwhelmingly graphic representation of Jesus's torture (*The Passion of the Christ*) instead of analyzing the dialogue of suffering and empathic facial expressions as the film's most powerful narrative motor. We will, along with A. O. Scott, conclude that Alejandro González Iñárritu's *Babel* is, "like that tower in the book of Genesis . . . a grand wreck," because it "does not seem to be tethered to any coherent idea or narrative logic," even though we have titled our very review "Emotion Needs No Translation" and have astutely observed that the director's "own visual grammar tries to go deeper [than a banal lingua franca] to suggest a common idiom of emotion."[14] We will assert, like Anthony Lane, that Fernando Meirelles's *Blindness* "forgets to tell a story—to keep faith with the directives of common sense" even though we give a full account and profound analysis of the film's figuring of blindness as a social parable and moral challenge: "That is why [Meirelles] opens with traffic, choked not merely with pollutants but with the emissions of our haste and rage, and why he closes, two hours later, with the prospect of paradise regained, around a dinner table, and with a hint of sight restored. It was all our fault, and the healing is up to us."

Taking these three films as a microcosmic yet representative sample of the kind of discourse that contemporary global cultural production is yielding, what an awareness of affect-as-episteme allows us to see about them is what they unexpectedly share, in spite of the ideological differences of their directors: namely, a strategy of politicized storytelling in which sensory experience culminates in emotional landscapes that represent moral and ethical positions.[15] All three films, moreover, present corrective social models based on the transit from hurtful indifference—strongly associated in each with the capitalist status quo—to loving empathy, a condition that reconfigures the terms of social bonds along new lines no longer defined by money, status, possessions, and hierarchical power. What is essential to note is that this critical position derives foundationally from the very fabric of the discourse it seeks to contest.

In late 2010, popular political uprisings around the globe became the real-life counterparts of these cinematic texts whose analysis I suggest is unproductive if not versed in affective epistemology. The Spanish *indignados* and the successive so-called Arab Spring of collective protest throughout the Middle East initiated this chain reaction of imitation worldwide, challenging and even toppling governments on the strength of new-media driven resistance to regimes diverse in character but sharing the common objectionable characteristic—as articulated by the narratives of protest—of an elitism that has disenfranchised the general populace.

In September 2011 the United States bore witness to its own self-proclaimed counterpart to the Arab Spring in the form of a popular New York City–based resistance movement called "Occupy Wall Street" that has since been interchangeably represented with its Twitter tag as "#OccupyWallStreet." The new-media propelled movement defines itself as "leaderless" and undefined by social markers ("people of many colors, genders, and political persuasions") with the exception of the sheer force of numbers: "We Are the 99% that will no longer tolerate the greed and corruption of the 1%," the movement's emphatically "unofficial" Web page reads (*Occupy Wall Street*). Against the "heads" of capitalist excesses, this movement posits itself as a headless soma, an immanent "we" that reasserts—in symbolically lowercase presentation—the principles of democracy as a discourse of self-legitimation: "we the people, of the united states, in order to form a more perfect union, establish justice, insure domestic tranquility, provide for the common defense, promote the general welfare, and secure the blessings of liberty to ourselves and our posterity, do ordain and establish this social movement" (*We Are the 99%*). Protest discourse features empathy as a guiding logic of the action and objectives of this collective: "Compassion is the gold of the new paradigm," one protest sign reads, an image captured in a photo that is posted in an online album with the caption "Occupy Wall Street with Love" (Perez).

Cultural and political analysts have been torn between interpreting Occupy Wall Street and the Arab Spring as an interruption or a perfection of global capitalism (see, e.g., Thomas L. Friedman's characterization of these positions as "The Great Disruption" versus "The Big Shift"). They have also been uncertain as to how to interpret these movements' goals or political potential; a chorus of incomprehension—"What do they want?"—swept across the U.S. media in the immediate wake of Occupy Wall Street's inception. Speaking in particular of the Spanish "15-M" movement that has broadly come to be known as one of "indignation," Zygmunt Bauman accuses it of being "emotional" and lacking "thought" (Verdú).[16] A minority voice, however, warns against an overly dismissive attitude, suggesting—in conceptual affinity with this essay—that we must learn to read the political landscape in a new light rather than discount it as incongruent with our traditional lens and expectations. Douglass Rushkoff, for example, calls Occupy Wall Street "America's first true Internet-era movement" and notes that it does not have a "traditional narrative arc," but is rather a "product of the decentralized networked-era culture" that is "about inclusion and groping toward consensus." "It is not like a book," Rushkoff concludes; "it is like the Internet." If this is so, then the collective protests of the immanent "we" against capitalist neocolonialism are, ironically, a rekindling of capitalism's originary epistemology of revolution.

It may—or may not—be true that the master's tools will never dismantle the master's house. But, even before advancing to the debate of this question in the context of global capitalism, there is an antecedent consideration that this essay seeks to address—all the more urgently given this current turn in global politics—which is that we will never fully comprehend our own attempts at either construction or deconstruction without fully comprehending the nature of our instruments. I submit that, as yet, we only partially understand capitalism's tools and house.

We have long been familiar with the concept of capitalist growth because it is epistemically consonant with the dominant rationalist paradigm of the modern colonialism—including its neocolonial avatar—operative from the Conquest to the fall of the Soviet Union. What we do not yet know how to consciously read and critique—because it is so thoroughly naturalized within our cultural discourse and simultaneously dismissed as an inferior source of knowledge (in keeping with the self-styled superiority of epistemic reason that is only just now beginning to cede ground to affect in the intellectual sphere)—is the concept of capitalist homeostasis, that is, a model of systematicity rooted in the principle of the rule of the body by the body, in which that body has absorbed the head. This soma thus establishes a paradigm of immanence and self-governs through harmonious and automatic (nonrational) organic flow. The social actor that results from this epistemicity is a singular collective—a unified body, an organic network—of diverse and even infinite composition nevertheless constitutive of a single "we" of immanent agency (an agency that works toward the absorption of any exogenous Other or "they" because such external agency is epistemologically anathema). The dynamics of action of this immanent "we" are those of homeostatic flow that governs over the soma's moral state by tending toward an equilibrium whose status quo is not neutrality but rather well-being. The homology to moral flow is the organically equitable networked distribution of resources and wealth. Where the latter flow of wealth and resources is in balance, there is well-being (health and happiness); where it is imbalanced, there is ill-being (disease and unhappiness).

When we comprehend homeostatic affect as an independent epistemic modality—a full-fledged mechanism for the representation of knowledge of self and world—then we will begin to understand the discursive forces already at work around us: those that seek to hold us captive with the promise of well-being and those that denounce ill-being and propose a new model of organic health. We may revisit our notions of power—particularly Foucault's concept of biopower (*The History of Sexuality, The Birth of Biopolitics*)—to ask not only how the body is controlled by the modern sovereign but also how those narratives of control are written in the language of the feeling soma itself. We will be able to conceive of an affective political actor with an agenda epistemologically driven by affect, with principal concerns over collective health and well-being. We will also be able to periodize our currently fervent epistemic interest in affect within a historical continuum that runs parallel to the evolution of headless free-market capitalism. Sense, emotion, feeling: these will be recognized as ways of knowing. Organicity and flow will be denaturalized as epistemological constructs manipulated discursively to produce social meaning. Affect-as-episteme will be intelligible as a tool of social domination as well as a tool of liberational contestation. We will, at last, render cognitively visible the discursive movements of the invisible hand.

I *The Feeling Soma*

1 The Feeling Soma

Humanity as a Singular "We"

The status of the group within cultural logic has fluctuated over time, always in tension with the status of the individual. More often than not, the group appears in cultural discourse as an unstable entity requiring the control—whether positive or negative—of an elite command. The masses need taming by a firm fascist or dictatorial hand; the people need guidance by an enlightened revolutionary vanguard. Historically the collective has rarely been figured as capable of self-control, self-guidance, or self-enlightenment. The singular and unique individual must always rise up and out of the group in order to serve as a driver of human progress. Conversely, where the group oppresses the individual or constrains this potential, the right to freedom becomes the basis for a call to arms.

Although this hierarchy of individual over group may persist as received knowledge, current cultural discourse suggests that both the terms of the relationship between individual and group and the terms of their relative valorization are shifting. Whether the figure of the collective makes its appearance as a direct referent of humanity or as an abstract conceptual category, it tends increasingly to subsume the individual—even to occupy the very position of the individual by being cast as one large body—and to carry a positive epistemological charge. In other words, the group is becoming a vehicle for the conceptualization and articulation of knowledge and the social.

It may be that this shift toward the valorization of the collective has a discrete genealogy—that is, a set of intellectual or public interventions that may be said to have decisively influenced this change. Richard Dawkins's *The Selfish Gene* (1976), for example, could be located within such a genealogy for proposing a "gene's eye view of nature" (xv) that revolutionized biology as a discipline and captured the attention of the mainstream reading public by arguing that organisms be regarded as vehicles for the reproduction of genes and not the other way around. The image of a vast gene pool controlling living beings like a puppet master from behind the scenes—as the unseen collective mastermind of life—begins to approximate the conceptual protagonism that the collective has begun to take on in recent years. In this emerging vision, the collective tends to be cast as a single body with an internal composition on the order of the infinite that propels itself toward self-evolution on the strength of a kind of unthinking—or at least not rational, but rather visceral—intelligence.

Here I will not attempt to establish a definitive genealogical archaeology of the evolving representation of the collective in cultural discourse, but rather to extrapolate a composite working model of how the collective is figured from a diverse sampling of cultural materials culled from major news journals, popular U.S. nonfiction, Latin American film, and U.S. television and advertising. My sources reflect daily life in the U.S. and Latin American cultural mainstream—that is, cultural production that has widespread dissemination and reception, and is in the aggregate representative of big-picture cultural patterns. To be sure, I am not actively seeking out exceptional or minoritarian voices, but, on the contrary, generally privileging the analysis of voices that enjoy, in varying degrees, a broader scale of influence. I am conscious of the persistence of academic canons and their importance for establishing nodes of scholarly knowledge, but I am equally cognizant that the plumbing of a canon will not, on its own, yield the kind of evidentiary data that I am seeking in this study, which is instead conceived as an analysis of lived culture in all its textual heterogeneity across diverse fora and media. Throughout, as the epistemological figure of the collective comes into view, I will argue that its conceptual representation as a feeling soma—as an organism regulated by homeostatic principle—strongly echoes the notion of a society given over—as though it were a soma—to the organic movements of free-market capital and the democratic principle that is their political analogue.

In the classic capitalist imaginary, the accumulation of capital is not fixed and static, but rather contingent and constantly shifting according to the balance of needs that naturally maximizes the welfare of the social order bound by this economy. Society does not create the economy; the economy creates the society. Further, to recall Margaret Thatcher's words during her guidance of Britain into the throes of neoliberalism, "there is no such thing as society but only individuals" (Harvey 82). One might be inclined to interpret this statement as the ultimate affirmation of individualism—of uniqueness, of idiosyncrasy, of standing out from the crowd. But Thatcher meant for the dissolution of "society" in favor of a mass of "individuals" to underwrite the shift she was engineering toward extreme free-market principles. As such, Thatcher's was not a liberation of individuals, but only an uprooting from traditional social moorings to facilitate their reimbrication within the economy as a social structure so naturalized as to be equated with the human condition itself (as is evident, for example, in the argument about implicitly neoliberal trade as an adaptive characteristic that I analyze further on in this chapter).

The imaginary of the collective economic soma is one in which two discursive narratives are at odds. In the colonialist-empire-inflected vertical narrative of infinite growth, capitalism legitimates its creation of a rigid social hierarchy and class power differential; in the originary revolutionary narrative of universal harmony, capitalism claims to afford every social element—every individual within its collective corpus—a purely democratic opportunity for prosperity and economic well-being. In this latter narrative, which the present study argues is increasingly the more pervasive of these two threads of self-definition, capitalism thus arranges its constituents in a relationship of perfect horizontality, connecting them as though by force of perfectly distributed resources. This body politic shares the same lifeblood of capital flow. "A rising tide lifts all boats" and the "trickle-down" effect—the latter principally translated for Latin American rhetoric as *goteo* (Argentina) or *chorreo* (Chile), both meaning a "dripping," though *chorreo* can also imply a flow of greater force—are turns of phrase associated with capitalist philosophy that demonstrate the operative conceptual equivalency between water and capital, in which water acts as a unifying agent, bathing all individuals democratically in the same wealth. Thus conceptualized, the movement of capital as autonomically regulated—and therefore deregulated from rational intervention—is best interpreted on the epistemological level as an affective process. Involuntary processes involved in homeostasis—the body's unthinking mechanism for achieving a steady-state maximization of well-being—are what metaphorically guide the somatic dynamics of capital: breathing, circulation, sensory perception, emotion, feeling.

The Collective in the News:
Crowd Sourcing, Glial Cells, and Ideas That Have Sex

A set of three contemporaneous stories in prominent news sources illustrates the apparent cultural hegemony—or, more precisely, the epistemological ascendance—of this notion of the collective. These three journalistic pieces appeared independently within days of one another, treating diverse subject matter but coinciding in evincing a common conceptual privileging of the group. I selected these stories for analysis as an exemplary cross-section of daily media reports—in this grouping, from the U.S.—that demonstrate the quantitative frequency with which epistemic affect undergirds a diversity of cultural media communication. But this grouping also serves as a qualitative point of entry for the consideration of the politics—or, we might say, economics—of the collective as a discursive trope because it demonstrates the following: a privileging of groups over individuals as sources of information collection and knowledge production, a privileging of interstitial connectivity as the source of communicativity, and the currency of affective metaphor for the description of human affairs understood as such—on the scale of humanity, and, moreover, humanity analyzed in adaptive evolutionary terms, whose diachrony extends the notion of the human collective to its greatest possible dimensions.

In the first instance, the *Chronicle of Higher Education*—the premiere academic news journal in the United States, boasting a monthly online readership of almost two million users—announced a shift in scientific research paradigm as a move away from individual inquiry and toward "large-scale collaborations" (Young, May 28, 2010). This new "crowd science," as the author dubs it, engages a broad base of data collectors ("crowd sourcing") and makes the focus of the principal investigator's work the interpretation of the large body of data that results from its collaborative capture. Although academia continues to assign merit and promotion based on the model of individual achievement, one of the furthest-reaching implications of the article is that crowd science will force a change of paradigm in institutional assessment toward the recognition of shared knowledge as more and more disciplines embrace this model—astronomy, genetics, and oceanography are cited, along with interest from pharmaceutical companies, thus indirectly acknowledging capitalist business as a nonacademic driver of this new trend in information sharing as the basis of scientific inquiry. "If only Newton, Planck, and Einstein had had any idea of the possibilities inhering in not going it alone," one reader comments, evincing the belief that group investigation may be capable of bringing human genius to untold heights.

A story on glial cells that aired on NPR—the U.S.'s most prestigious nonprofit news source with over twenty million listeners weekly—less than a week after the crowd science report suggests that it is not only the method of conducting scientific inquiry that has assumed collective proportions but also the manner of conceiving the inquiry itself (June 2, 2010). Whereas the crowd science article commentator wondered how Einstein's discoveries would have been shaped had he conducted his research through "crowdsourcing," here—in a poetic coincidence—it is Einstein's brain that is cited at the root of a new way of formulating central questions in neurobiology. The story discusses the findings of a twenty-year sequence of research that originates with the claim that Einstein's brain had more glial—connective—cells than average, giving rise to the possibility that his genius was not, contrary to all expectation, a result of exceptional neuronal capacity, but rather of an abundance of cells that R. Douglas Fields, the most recent in the line of these researchers, describes as having been heretofore considered inconsequential. Fields's findings, published in *The Other Brain* (2009), successfully reproduce a landmark 1990 experiment that showed that glial cells were "eavesdropping on the chemical conversations between neurons, and rebroadcasting them to distant areas of the brain. . . . [Says Fields,] 'I just wish I could get across the amazement of that finding—that these cells that were thought to be stuffing between neurons were communicating'" (Hamilton). That the neuron, the longtime protagonist of neurobiological study, should be displaced by newfound interest in its supporting cells—cells that serve to shoulder and maintain neurons, as well as to communicate neuronal activity through their own chemical signals—would seem to indicate a new open-mindedness in setting the parameters of scientific inquiry. Indeed, as Fields remarks with respect to the evidence of glial cell

communicativity, their chemical signals are "easy to miss if you're not looking for them" (Hamilton). In order to look for them, one has to start out
with the notion of communication as a full-brained phenomenon in which
every kind of tissue is engaged.

Within this model of participatory communication, the verticality of the
old premise of neuronal superiority with respect to other cerebral matter
becomes outmoded; epistemological hierarchy gives way to horizontality
in which a democratic conceptualization of the brain has allowed the glial "plebians" to claim a functional and investigative significance equal or
greater to that of the cells they support. The final step in this epistemological movement from verticality to horizontality, from the privileging of
powerful "kings" of the brain to a holistic valuing of the scientific and physiological worthiness of the entire "body politic," would be to progress on a
mainstream disciplinary level from the democratization of the brain to the
democratization of the entire body. That is, to cease to privilege the brain
above the rest of the body, instead beginning to formulate investigative
questions that seek to prove how, as neuroimmunologist Candace Pert argues from an iconoclastic position in *Molecules of Emotion* (1997), the entire
body—and not just the brain—constitutes an interconnected "information
highway." Pert, accordingly, vociferously challenges Cartesian brain-body
dualism—which has found institutional hypostasization, she argues, in a
jealously guarded divide of purview in the United States between the National Institutes of Health and the National Institutes of Mental Health.
In Pert's view, Cartesian dualism continues to thwart the necessarily interdisciplinary research that could yield a unified theory of the body as an
integrated set of systems. Pert's position may as yet occupy outlier status
with respect to the scientific establishment, but it nevertheless serves as an
indicator of the cutting edge of future inquiry that resonates with the conceptual comeuppance of the collective.

Just prior to these two reports, the *Wall Street Journal*—among the top
daily business journals in the world with a daily circulation to over two million paid subscribers—featured a story likewise privileging the group over
the individual, this time claiming collective intelligence as the explanation
for the triumph of humans over other species (Ridley, May 22, 2010). Just
as crowd science effectively expands the individual investigator to group
proportions, and glial cell research turns its focus away from the neuron
and toward its mass of connective tissue, here the theory of human triumph
abandons the biology of the brain and embraces species behavior. Matt

Ridley, prominent British science writer, former banker, and author of the human triumph story—which he subsequently gave as a TED talk on the same subject that has been seen over two million times—writes, "Scientists have so far been looking for an answer to this riddle [of why humans prevailed over other species] in the wrong place: inside human heads. . . . But the sophistication of the modern world lies not in individual intelligence or imagination. . . . The answer lies in a new idea, borrowed from economics, known as collective intelligence: the notion that what determines the inventiveness and rate of cultural change of a population is the amount of interaction between individuals."

Here the collective is defined as an unquantifiable set—on the order of the species in absolute diachrony—of "interaction between individuals." How are we to understand this "interaction between individuals"? Is the quality, intensity, or specificity of this interaction significant in giving rise to the adaptive benefits of collective intelligence? Does or must the interaction have a particular telos? Ridley does not explicitly define the group interaction in these terms, but rather shifts metonymically among implicit equivalencies in a way that allows his reader to appreciate his underlying assumptions. Thus we may piece together the tacit assertion that the "sophistication of the modern world" results from an "interaction between individuals" that constitutes a "collective enterprise." Even without knowing how Ridley defines "sophistication," we already surmise that it is the end result—and possibly the teleological objective—of a collective human project across time and space. That Ridley should use the word *enterprise* to characterize human interaction suggests that if there is indeed a teleology of the collective to be discovered, it is one associated with business and economic activity. The further characterization of this "interaction" in terms of its effects, "innovation," "invention," and "discovery"—a set of contemporary business catchwords—only strengthens the implication that business, and perhaps science in its service, is the organically arising product of human interaction and synonymous with "collective enterprise."

Indeed, as Ridley develops his argument, he posits that "exchange" and "trade" are at the root of human success, even pointedly arguing that, contrary to the sequence of social evolution that has become common wisdom, commerce precedes—and even foundationally paves the way for—agriculture. Of interest here is not the veracity of Ridley's anthropological assumptions, but what their assertion reveals about the contemporary cultural narrative in which they participate. The reader of Ridley's intervention will come away with the unspoken thesis that capitalism has been the social telos of humanity and its adaptive strength. The species evolved to do business; business is at once its vehicle and reason for being. Humans, in other words, were born to trade—a term that becomes loosely and implicitly synonymous with free-market capitalism in the course of Ridley's intervention. Ridley makes no rigorous historical periodization of the development of trade, but, precisely because he does not enter into historiography, his treatment of trade as a continuum across the whole of human history—indeed, on the premise that trade is what marked the end of prehistory and ushered humanity into the self-conscious phase of its existence—has the effect of casting business as we know it as a force of human nature. The unproblematized relationship of equivalency between Ridley's examples of objects of "trade"—from ancient obsidian tools to pencils, computers, and camera pills—culminates in a paragraph that portrays the defining characteristics of capitalism as the result of adaptive evolution, rather than as a contingently arising social system:

> Once human beings started swapping things and thoughts, they stumbled upon divisions of labor, in which specialization led to mutually beneficial collective knowledge. Specialization is the means by which exchange encourages innovation: In getting better at making your product or delivering your service, you come up with new tools. The story of the human race has been a gradual spread of specialization and exchange ever since: Prosperity consists of getting more and more narrow in what you make and more and more diverse in what you buy. Self-sufficiency—subsistence—is poverty.

In this view, capitalism is no longer a product of historical circumstance, and of class power and privilege, nor is it driven by ideology (this implicit position serves to affirm the assertion by Michael Hardt and Antonio Negri that capitalist "Empire" claims an atemporal status for itself: "this is the way things will always be and the way they were always meant to be" [xiv]). Divisions of labor become voluntary and intelligent, rather than exploitative and calculated. Prosperity (well-being) is definitionally correlated with a high capacity to produce and consume, poverty (ill-being—or at least a less than desirable state of being) with the inverse capacity, as though collective knowledge, innovation, new tools, and specialization and exchange could not possibly be destined—be content—to engineer, deliberately, a modest way of life. But the question of engineering—of deliberate intent, that is—does not enter into Ridley's manner of conceiving of the "collective enterprise." It is as if humans were programmed by nature itself to engage in capitalist trade as though on evolutionary autopilot: capitalism emerges as the structural behavior of the species. No executive function or higher power must intervene; simply by congregating as social animals, it seems, humans naturally interact in a way that constitutes collective intelligence and yields trade—for trade is cast as the practical expression of human thought. Foucault's "homo œconomicus," the social state proper to modernity, in which economics eclipse politics, takes on atavistic dimensions in Ridley's evolutionary argument. In other words, whereas in Foucault's vision homo œconomicus is a historically specific modality of social epistemology, in Ridley's, homo œconomicus becomes interchangeable with homo sapiens itself: the "knowing" that sets humans mightily apart from other species is that of trade.

Here the very manner of "knowing" experiences a shift in this new context of the collective. Although Ridley's insistence that ideas are what beget innovation and trade is in apparent consonance with the traditional view of knowledge and ideas as rational and consciously produced, it is essential to underscore Ridley's categorical treatment of the idea as something spontaneously arising in an unthinking fashion on the level of the collective. In other words, as a species there need be no deliberate determination to undertake this kind of trade-producing thought. That is, if we think of the species as a collective body, then trade is, in this view, the social behavior resulting from that body's autonomic system. Capitalism is tantamount to a parasympathetic social reflex.

The metaphor of the body of the species is mine, but its use is not gratuitous; on the contrary, it is intended to anticipate and make sense of the corporal imagery of Ridley's own rhetoric where, in the final resting point of his argument, trade is produced by the "sexual" relationship between ideas ("Trade is to culture as sex is to biology. . . . The rate of cultural and economic progress depends on the rate at which ideas are having sex.") Ridley may employ the catchy turn of phrase of ideas "having sex" for the sake of titillating his audience into captivity. It is, after all, far more engaging to say that ideas are having sex rather than to say simply that they are multiplying exponentially as a result of their contact. Indeed, Ridley entitled the TED-Global talk that this article would become in July 2010 simply, "When Ideas Have Sex," which has been viewed two million times.

But I would argue that there is more to his reproductive metaphor than sensationalist appeal. The concept of ideas having sex is one in which ideas—thoughts, the expression of Cartesian rationalism par excellence—assume affective dimensions, arising and combining by force of libidinous and carnal desire rather than by force of rational or intellectual compatibility. This is not to say that the latter scenario is not, in practical terms, a requisite for the fusion of disparate ideas into a singular composite idea constitutive of innovation or discovery. I seek to emphasize the discursive presentation of this highly rational operation in affective terms, as though ideas—as though avatars of their human authors—roamed the earth fornicating, driven by the affects. I do not mean to claim that Ridley's argument about the ways that ideas travel and culture reproduces itself is, in its structural aspects, new. Pierre Bourdieu's work on the reproduction of social class through cultural transmission in educational institutions is but one example of an exploration of how culture and society reproduce themselves (see, e.g., Bourdieu and Passeron, *Reproduction in Education, Society and Culture*). What I would like to emphasize here is not the novelty of Ridley's own ideas, but rather the rhetorical specificities with which he frames his meditations on an established theme. The notion of "ideas having sex" is not just a colorful ear bender; discursively, it insists on the biology of the metaphor to the point of rhetorically anthropomorphizing trade—as literal human intercourse—in which ideas interact affectively rather than rationally.

Ridley's intervention figures the longevity of capitalism as an inevitability tantamount to human reproduction. Nothing, arguably, besides the autonomic functions requires less thought, planning, foresight, rationalization, or conscious care than sex. Sex is impulsive, instinctive, automatic, desired, and, on a species level, unstoppable, and guaranteed—"inexorable," to employ the same term with which Ridley characterizes "progress," the long-standing teleological euphemism for capitalism, which, here, because of Ridley's references to global economy and technology (search engines, mobile phones, container shipping) effectively becomes neoliberalism: "There's a cheery modern lesson in this theory about ancient events. Given that progress is inexorable, cumulative and collective if human beings exchange and specialize, then globalization and the Internet are bound to ensure furious economic progress in the coming century—despite the usual setbacks from recessions, wars, spendthrift governments and natural disasters. . . . And things like the search engine, the mobile phone and container shipping just made ideas a whole lot more promiscuous still." If collective intelligence equals progress and progress equals neoliberal capitalism, then adding sex to that set of equivalencies imbues them all with the certitude and stability of visceral homeostasis through reproduction, as though the collective human body worked toward its own well-being and survival by generating—in a libidinal flood of pleasure—capitalist trade.

Ridley not only gives an affective characterization of capitalism by defining it as a product of "promiscuous" ideas but also invites his reader to evaluate his argument in similarly affective terms. In his introduction, Ridley claims that this "sex"-driven collective intelligence "holds out hope that the human race will prosper mightily in the years ahead"; in his conclusion he recapitulates this sentiment by asserting a "cheery modern lesson" in his argument. "Hope" and "cheer" are understandably called for at the historical juncture of global capitalist crisis in which Ridley writes, but they are more than moral states apt for the rallying of social morale; they are also the affective disposition with which Ridley expects his own ideas to be received. As readers, it is with an affective, rather than a rational, sensibility that we are meant to evaluate the long-term prospects of capitalism. In this model of reception, Ridley's argument presents itself as one that works curatively toward well-being. Accordingly, we are primed to receive this argument on the autonomic level, according to homeostatic criteria of acceptance or rejection. In other words, the affective treatment of capitalist trade as the result of unthinking visceral interaction mirrors the affective expectations that this conceptual content will be received unthinkingly and viscerally—and acritically—on the strength of having occasioned a positive emotional state in the reading public, thereby appealing to affective, rather than rational, criteria of acceptance.

Ridley's model of humanity as a species born for conceptual fornication of a variety that foundationally yields a capitalist social system echoes the notion of a mass of interstitial matter that provides organic integrity by gluing and communicating, and the idea that investigations conducted on a massive level of participation can produce the surest knowledge. In all three cases the collective functions discursively on the logic of the soma: a set of diverse and innumerable parts find organic integration within an overarching structure of unity; this organic integration functions through a flow—of information, in every case—that binds the parts together into a harmonious whole. Although it is information—data, neuronal impulses, ideas that spark trade—that flows like lifeblood through the collective, this information does not have the rational status that one might expect. That is, information does not appear here as the foundation of complex higher-order reasoning or intelligence; the kind of intelligence this information flow represents is markedly affective in the conceptual framework granted to the figure of the collective in these stories—affective insofar as the emphasis regarding the flow of information is on its transmission, which occurs through some force of affinity. For Ridley, this affinity is represented through the metaphor of sexual contact and reproduction; in the other cases, though such explicit rubric is not assigned to the mechanism of transmission, it is implicitly one that also follows an unthinkingly visceral flow—information converges and amasses as though carried through a bloodstream to nodes of mutual interest, ebbing and flowing in a way that maximizes knowledge by virtue of immanent and horizontal contact rather than transcendent and vertical reasoning.

Capitalist Uses of the Collective: *We Are Smarter Than Me* and the Harmony Prius Campaign

The model of collective social protagonism animated by an organic flow of information—capital for the global technological age—resonates strongly with the archetypal vision of the movement of capital. What has shifted since the classical model of capitalism in its inception is the size of the collective, which has experienced a dramatic expansion in scale toward the ahistorical and unquantifiable. We might comprehend this discursive gesturing toward infinity as a reflection of the triumph of Western capitalism that styles itself as universal in the post-Soviet era. Ridley's argument about capitalist trade as an adaptive characteristic takes the collective to the level of the species; unsurprisingly, this species collective is strongly echoed in neoliberal business methodology and narrative marketing strategy, as well as in the contestation of this global capitalist discourse.

The opening in 2006 of a Center for Collective Intelligence by MIT, its direction by a business management professor, Thomas W. Malone, and the fact of its first major project being a book about the possibilities of collective intelligence for business demonstrate the extent to which the notion of "group think"—once a derogatory term for conformist brainwashing—has become the model for inquiry across disciplines, but especially championed and driven by business. The book project migrated to an autonomous Wiki-based community at wearesmarter.org, where a community of four thousand participants developed from over a million invitations to cowrite the book extended to faculty and alumni of the Wharton School of the University of Pennsylvania and the MIT Sloan School of Management, as well as management and technology experts. The result, *We Are Smarter Than Me: How to Unleash the Power of Crowds in Your Business* (2007), stands as a testament to the current epistemological hegemony of the notion of collective intelligence. Its monumental stature at the cutting edge of business research and knowledge also suggests that business discourse is beginning to shape business practice. In other words, if there has been a disconnect between the two, with affective business discourse being at odds with rationalized business practice, then *We Are Smarter Than Me* may indicate—along with the countless business titles about harnessing emotional power for the purpose of increasing profit and efficiency—a decisive shift toward affect in the epistemological contest internal to business. Crowd sourcing as a method of interdisciplinary inquiry and the collective as the guiding concept structuring the parameters of that inquiry should be understood as symptoms of this shift across fields of knowledge and practice.

The self-promoting online description of *We Are Smarter Than Me* claims that the book "will help you transform the promise of social networking into a profitable reality" ("*We Are Smarter Than Me*: About the Book"). In an NPR interview, lead authors Barry Libert and Jon Spector cite one such "success story" as that of Goldcorp, a company that discovered untapped stores of gold worth three billion dollars by crowd sourcing its mining data online. Although Libert and Spector insist on the ostensibly democratizing practice of bringing all individuals associated with a business into the fold of its crowd—employees, customers, partners, distributors, investors—there is a deafening absence of any discussion of the equally democratic distribution of resulting profits. Business problems find solutions in the crowd, yet the crowd derives no benefit from its contributions to the profit-making machine. In this sense it would seem that crowd sourcing only serves to generate an even greater concentration of wealth in fewer hands than ever before, further increasing the asymmetrical distribution of capital that characterizes colonialist economic practice—whether proper to formal imperialism or informal neocolonialism. As a cultural text, the singling out of a gold company as the representative example of the profitability of crowd sourcing evokes the centuries-old history of exploitative colonialist extraction, a negative symbolism most recently and conspicuously updated for current cultural consciousness in the form of the "unobtanium" brutally mined at the cost of life and nature by the profit-driven and generically named RDA company in James Cameron's blockbuster film *Avatar* (2009)—a plot device that demonstrates the extent to which neocolonialism persists as a structure of oppression in our current cultural psyche.

Yet the emergent "we are smarter than me" mantra of capitalist discourse does not admit any relationship of asymmetry. It plays upon the idea of a perfectly democratic relationship between people in their pursuit of prosperity—a perfectly harmonious engagement among all the participants in this group that grows more intelligent and capable in the same measure as its limits go to zero. The perfectly intelligent "we," this model of profit-making suggests, encompasses all of humanity itself, if we are to take the imagery that supports this notion of a profit-generating group to its ultimate consequences. Libert, Spector, and their four-thousand-strong Wiki group of authors echo Ridley in their implicit core assertion that the species is tantamount to a single-minded collective driven to participate in the operation of capitalist moneymaking. I argue that it is more accurate to say that this is a single-*bodied* collective in that these visions of humanity treat the species as one large organism whose billions of internal actors all cooperate—collaborate—in perfect autonomic harmony with one another.

An example from advertising that builds its message on the conceptual foundation of this perfectly autonomic relationship among people figured as one limitless collective soma is the line of 2010 commercials for the Toyota Prius, arguably the world's premiere hybrid-energy car, whose global sales reached three million in 2011 and eight million in 2015 (Toyota, August 21, 2015).[1] The three commercials in the 2010 campaign—the aptly named "Harmony," "MPG," and "Solar"—show the third-generation hybrid-energy Prius driving through a landscape constructed exclusively of human bodies acting the part of nature. That is, hundreds of extras dressed as natural elements—rivers, tree trunks, leaves, stones, flowers, butterflies, clouds, the sun, Earth itself as seen from space—portray in synchrony the natural world. In each ad it is the coordinated movement of this human collective that produces the effect of rivers flowing, grass waving, flowers bursting open, trees growing, clouds floating, sun rays shining down. Just as in the case of "we are more intelligent than me," where the four thousand Wiki coauthors stand as a representative sampling of the larger pool of one million potential authors by original invitation, here, as we are told in the "Making of the Prius 'Harmony' Commercial," two hundred extras were used to generate over one million human elements in the final visual landscape. The human bodies that enact nature are not particular or individuated but general and interchangeable—that is, they are not meant to connote unique individuality, but rather generic interconnectedness. Each individual gestures toward a collective whole on a scale so large as to hint at the infinite, as we appreciate when the anthropomorphic depiction of nature culminates in the outer-space representation of Earth in "Solar."

The tagline of the Prius commercial series—delivered in a voice-over message at the close of each ad—is "It's harmony between man, nature, and machine." But the situation in these ads is one in which man and nature are not separable terms; as a category, nature is fully subsumed by humanity. This does not mean that humans are a synecdoche for the rest of the natural world, but that humans *are* their own natural world. The "world" in these Toyota commercials functions like one tremendous human organism comprised of countless constituent parts working seamlessly—organically, autonomically—to produce the basic stuff of natural life. Just as Ridley posited that out of the naturally occurring intercourse of humans comes trade, here, out of this human-made collective constitutive of its own habitat comes a product—the "machine," in Toyota's language—as though the Prius were the natural and causal result of the life-generating efforts of this collective. The theme song of these commercials, Petra Haden's 2009 a cappella cover version of the Bellamy Brothers 1976 hit "Let Your Love Flow," reinforces through both form and content the idea of an anthropomorphized habitat: in form because Haden creates all the song's lines of melody, harmony, and instrumentation with her voice alone, just as humans create all the elements of the "world" into which the Prius emerges; in content because the song's lyrics posit love as a metaphor for the homology between humanity and the natural world.

In the ads' theme song, love is the implicit reason for the very existence of the natural world—its reason for being—a world lyrically composed of the same main elements anthropomorphized within the visual content of the ads (the sun, mountains, birds). In the imagery of the song's lyrics, love is capable of feats of nature: love is what can flow, grow, fly, and shine, as though it were water, a living organism, a bird, or the sun. Within the commercials' diegesis, the lyrical protagonism of love as the creative agent of the natural world becomes homologous with the visual protagonism of humans as the creative agents of the natural world. A certain equivalency emerges: love is humanity. Love is the emotional manifestation of human agency, the force that unites humans and nature in a homeostatic relationship on the planetary, and even cosmic, level. Love flows like blood, connecting constituent parts, supporting life and promoting well-being. The song renders love as a kind of interstitial adhesive that creates one seamless unit of life out of the diverse elements of the natural world—including humans. Love has a status analogous to that of the interconnective tissue of glial cells or the ability to join all of humanity together in a relationship of trade on the strength of "sexually" reproduced ideas. Love is the ultimate expression of the human condition, the perfect synecdoche. Further, a humanity driven by love (or, to overlay Ridley's terminology, by ideas having sex) produces innovative products for consumption. In other words, a loving humanity is the natural agent of capitalist enterprise.

Born to Run: The Human Collective as Anticapitalist

The proposition that a loving humanity is the natural agent of capitalist enterprise could not be more anathema to the quietly anticapitalist thesis of the U.S. nonfiction bestseller *Born to Run* (2009), which, in its own way, also turns its gaze on all of humanity, even from an evolutionary perspective. Yet despite this difference of conclusion regarding the relationship between economics and human nature, the components of the anticapitalist argument in *Born to Run* do not differ from those of the Toyota Prius commercial. On the contrary, we find that the same basic figure of the single-bodied autonomic collective is in play, but instead of figuring this collective in the service of capitalism, the text uses the collective to discredit capitalist culture. Part extended anecdote of footraces and their colorful protagonists, part historiography of ultrarunning as sport and cultural practice, part disquisition into the role of running in human evolution, *Born to Run* ultimately sets forth the proposition that running may be the central adaptive characteristic of human evolution, the sine qua non of humanity that allowed for species triumph. Sports and war journalist Christopher McDougall builds toward this thesis through the optic of his research on the enigmatic and solitary Tarahumara of Northern Mexico, known in their native tongue as the Rarámuri—"running people."[2] McDougall exalts this tribe as the epitome of well-being, not only physiologically but also socially; their lifestyle predicated on ultra long-distance running (as much as hundreds of miles at a stretch) has, in his estimation, yielded a peaceful, fair, equitable community that lives in loving harmony without materialism or avarice:

Left alone in their mysterious [North Mexican] canyon hideaway, this small tribe of recluses had solved nearly every problem known to man. . . .

The Tarahumara geniuses had even branched into economics, creating a one-of-a-kind financial system based on booze and random acts of kindness: instead of money, they traded favors and big tubs or corn beer.

You'd expect an economic engine fueled by alcohol and freebies to spiral into a drunken grab-fest, everyone double-fisting for themselves like bankrupt gamblers at a casino buffet, but in Tarahumara Land, it works. . . . The Tarahumara are industrious and inhumanly honest. . . .

And if being the kindest, happiest people on the planet wasn't enough, the Tarahumara were also the toughest.

(14–15)

Once again, it bears repeating that the object of this analysis is not to ascertain the merits of McDougall's glorification of the Tarahumara, but rather to read that glorification as a cultural text idealizing a certain model of social behavior. McDougall's introductory elegy to the Tarahumara makes clear that his admiration rests in the tribe's peripheral relationship to global capitalist culture and its litany of discontents: Western disease patterns, social strife and crime, human-induced climate change, and selfish materialism. This last difference in the propensity to engage in capitalist consumption is what McDougall seems to privilege above all others as most illustrative of the cultural clash he is narrating. In one instance, McDougall tells of a Tarahumara runner who, on a fluke, enters and wins a California marathon; yet, marvels McDougall, "even though he'd found a surefire way to make cash, he'd never returned to race again" (28).

Conversely, a Tarahumara village by the name of Yerbabuena offers a cautionary tale about the impact of institutionalized capitalism—state-run and criminal alike. McDougall recounts this story of such noxious effects of "chabochis" (trouble-causing outsiders [29 passim]) on the Rarámuri way of life in the form of a dialogue between a Tarahumara schoolteacher and the guide whom McDougall has contracted in the U.S. Southwest. In this anecdote, the schoolteacher explains how the domino effect of "progress" did away with the traditional way of life in one village: the clearing and paving of a road, which permitted the introduction of a new food commodities market based around "soda, chocolate, rice, sugar, butter, flour," led to the Tara-humara entry into the local labor economy in order to be able to buy these commodities; they stopped running when their lives began to revolve around consumption and the low-wage labor necessary to engage in it (37–38).

Consumption—addiction to consumption, and, in particular, addiction to the sugar-salt-fat food additive triumvirate that has been recently decried as the profit-generating culprit of global obesity and disease[3]—is the face of ill-being; the autochthonous way of life as a running society that eschews it, the face of well-being. McDougall does not posit a direct connection between a life—and, specifically, a diet—of capitalist consumption and oth-er agents implicated in the literal paving of the way for that consumption culture. Yet his anecdote implicitly posits that the consumer culture that exploits paved roads, on the one hand, and the loggers, drug traffickers, and politicians who have a vested interest in their paving, on the other, are sim-ply different aspects of the same capitalist circumstance (38). The anecdote that McDougall selects to close his book underscores the protagonic role of consumer culture as the pernicious agent of capitalism. In it, a character called Caballo Blanco (White Horse)—a U.S. expatriate and honorary Tar-ahumara runner who serves as the cultural renegade vertebral to the entire narrative and embodying the possible salvation of the First World much in the way that the human-to-Na'vi convert Jake Sully does in *Avatar*—rejects the offer of a contract from the sporting goods company North Face, say-ing, in the words that close the book, "Running isn't about making people buy stuff. Running should be free, man" (287).

Throughout the text McDougall underscores the collectivist culture of the Tarahumara as the tribe's core characteristic that distinguishes it—and, to some degree, barring an onslaught of consumer goods or narcotraffick-ing interests, safeguards it—from capitalist assimilation. This collectivism is synonymous with antimaterialism in the economic sphere, as evidenced by the exchange system of "korima," the moral "obligation to share whatever you can spare, instantly and with no expectations," which McDougall calls the "cornerstone of Tarahumara culture" (37).

McDougall's description of *korima* evokes Evo Morales's credo of the indigenous way of life as "vivir bien" (live well) in opposition to the cap-italist "vivir mejor" (live better—connoting not self-improvement, but an unjust hierarchy among fellow beings). This same dichotomy is shown to be operative in the differing cultural conceptions of running itself. For the Tarahumara—whose indigenous name signals running as the foundational attribute of the people—running is a mirror for their *korima* "economy," and their collectivist antimaterialistic society. For the *chabochi* interlopers, on the other hand, running is an individualistic activity from which to extract personal gain. One passage of McDougall's text illustrates this opposition in particular clarity, during the discussion of how U.S. sports enthusiast and promoter Rick Fisher sponsored the entry of a group of Tarahumara runners for the first time in an annual one-hundred-mile race in Leadville, Colorado by treating the race as a divisive competition rather than as an exercise in unity, earning himself the nickname Pescador, a literal Spanish translation of Fisher's name that insinuates his greedy self-interest (75).

The Tarahumara treatment of running as a collective activity dashes McDougall's preconceived notions of running as a solipsistic exercise. The organization of his narrative suggests that this central hypothesis of running as a collective activity motivated him to investigate running as an atavistic behavior. This line of inquiry culminates in McDougall's exposition of biological theories of running as a physiological evolutionary adaptation that allowed humans to engage in persistence hunting—the running down of their prey over long distances that coincide with the length of a marathon (238)—and thereby to triumph as a species (see chapter 28, 214–44).

This species-level optic on the idea that "humans evolved to go running" (217) in order to become the most successful hunters resonates strongly with the dimensions of Ridley's perspective on trade as both motor and telos of human evolution. It is also significant that the ideological difference of perspective does not remit to a modernist primitivism-versus-civilization debate. McDougall considers running culture to be the basis of innovation—the same kind of innovation that Ridley prizes as the basis of trade culture. McDougall makes this case in the figure of Louis Liebenberg, a mathematician and physicist who ventured into the African bush in search of the answers to evolution's mysteries, which Liebenberg believed to have solved in the presence of a persistence hunt by the handful of Bushmen who had resisted assimilation within the cultural mainstream. According to Liebenberg, persistence running demands a set of skills (and develops "speculative hunting") including "visualization[,] empathy[,] abstract thinking and forward projection." Liebenberg muses, "Isn't that exactly the mental engineering we now use for science, medicine, the creative arts?" (235). Yet these attributes, McDougall's text suggests, are maximally developed in a collectivist society that stands outside their exploitative capitalist application. Whereas Ridley argues that humans use these competencies to produce a capitalist social system, McDougall argues that humans use these same competencies precisely to resist it—or, perhaps more precisely, that our capitalist culture beset by the ills that McDougall lists in his introductory pages would do well to heal itself on the model of the Tarahumara (much like the Na'vi of *Avatar*).

McDougall does not assert that humanity would have fared better had it forsworn technology for subsistence living; he argues—like Colin Beavan of *No Impact Man* (2009)—that the life of global capitalist-driven technology lacks heart. Like the Prius commercial in which love serves as the synthetic concept unifying what it means to be a species homologous with nature, and generative of technologically sophisticated consumer products that purport to protect that nature, love also makes a central appearance in McDougall's discussion of a species "born to run":

> The real secret of the Tarahumara [was that] they'd never forgotten what it felt like to love running. They remembered that running was mankind's first fine art, our original act of inspired creation. Way before we were scratching pictures on caves or beating rhythms on hollow trees, we were perfecting the art of combining our breath and mind and muscles into fluid self-propulsion over wild terrain. And when our ancestors finally did make their first cave paintings, what were the first designs? A downward slash, lightning bolts through the bottom and middle—behold, the Running Man. Distance running was revered because it was indispensable; it was the way we survived and thrived and spread across the planet. You ran to eat and to avoid being eaten; you ran to find a mate and impress her and with her you ran off to start a new life together. You had to love running or you wouldn't live to love anything else. And like everything else we love—everything we sentimentally call our "passions" and "desires"—it's really an encoded ancestral necessity. We were born to run; we were born *because* we run. We're all Running People, as the Tarahumara have always known.
>
> (92–93)

Once again, love is cast in the rhetorical position of representing humanity itself by virtue of constituting its deepest motivational—and even adaptive—drive ("everything . . . we love—everything we sentimentally call our 'passions' and 'desires'—[is] really an encoded ancestral necessity"). Love of running—love of "mankind's first fine art"—allows humans to "spread across the planet" in pursuit of all forms of love ("You had to love running, or you wouldn't live to love anything else") in an image evocative of the current global culture. McDougall does not enter into any sustained discussion of how love of running constitutes the core characteristic that allowed humans to become the citizens of global capitalist culture that we have become, but, like Ridley, his inference is that innovation stemming from the "first fine art" of running—coalescing in "science, medicine, the creative arts"—has propelled us toward our triumph as a species.[4]

Yet, whereas Ridley champions capitalist trade as the manifestation of innately innovative collectivism, McDougall devotes significant attention in his text to the discussion of the negative impact of capitalism on running. Not only does he pit the forces of commodification against the Tarahumara way of life; he also asserts that the same forces have adversely affected U.S. culture, specifically the culture of running. "American distance running went into a death spiral when cash entered the equation" (94), McDougall argues, because it lost its joyful collectivist aspect of a group given over to the love of running for the sake of running: "the American approach—*ugh*. Rotten at its core. It was too artificial and grabby . . . too much about getting stuff and getting it now: medals, Nike deals, a cute butt. It wasn't art; it was business, a hard-nosed quid pro quo" (93).

Nike is a particular target of McDougall's criticisms, not only for its role in turning running into an industry but also for having created a product—the cushioned orthotics-inspired running shoe—that duped runners worldwide into forsaking their own natural physiology for artificial commodity, yielding decades of chronic injury. "Blaming the running injury epidemic on big, bad Nike seems too easy—but that's okay, because it's largely their fault," McDougall alleges. "Before [the founders of the company] got together, the modern running shoe didn't exist. Neither did most modern running injuries" (179; extended historiography of Nike's running shoe research and development, chapter 25, 168–83). McDougall cites Nike cofounder Bill Bowerman himself as having become disillusioned with the company for "distributing a lot of crap" and effectively having abandoned its original mission of creating the best—and safest—athletics products for the single-minded objective of "[m]ak[ing] money" (182). Neoliberal critique takes shape as an indictment of profit making as working inexorably to the detriment of the consumer, effectively spreading ill-being on a global scale.

In its own marketing, Nike crafts precisely the opposite discourse, ob-scuring all reference to profit making and emphasizing exclusively the well-being of the consumer. This language of well-being does not limit itself to simple claims of specific health benefits of specific products, but rather extends, once again, into the sphere of species discourse, manipulating the same conceptual topoi that we have seen in play in other collectivist arguments. The annual "Nike+ Human Race," inaugurated August 31, 2008, and repeated October 24, 2009, is a worldwide ten-kilometer footrace whose name intentionally creates a double entendre through its evocation of the species itself. Billed as the "world's largest running event," the Nike+ Human Race coordinates registered participation on a single day across the globe (twenty-five cities in 2008, thirty cities in 2009), with remote participation through the digital upload of off-site running data from other locations. The Nike+ web page for the 2009 event features a world map constructed of photographed faces, with pop-up dialogue boxes indicating names of cities, numbers of runners, and average racing time. A bold caption spanning the width of the page—and therefore, also, of the visual representation of the globe—reads:

> Congratulations, Runners!
> Together the world ran 802,242 miles.

This cumulative number of miles run as a collective of untold proportions is only a fraction of the hundreds of millions of miles run day in and day out by the international members of Nikeplus.com, self-described as the world's biggest online running community. The self-reported goal of the community is for each of its members to "become a better runner," and the site purports to help with this goal by serving as an archive for each member's running data—distance, speed, and frequency objectives; calories burned in the process; and a coaching program. There is a group messaging board that seeks to build virtual relationships through the posing of running and fitness challenges among members. The website's claim of having logged over ten thousand "laps around the world" generates the image of the entire world population running in simultaneity—in conversation, in community—across the surface of the globe. Yet, in perfect opposition to McDougall's credo that "running should be free," the Nike+ community has a nonnegotiable price of membership. In order to join, the ineluctable "first step" is to "get the gear": a pair of Nike+ sensor-ready shoes, the

Nike+ Sensor that slips into the shoes, and the Nike+ SportBand (or Nike+ iPod Sport Kit) that reads the data from the sensor and uploads the information to Nikeplus.com through a detachable USB port. There is also an entry fee for any ten-kilometer run in a participating city on the day of the Human Race. Nike has commodified the discursive figure of the species affectively engaged in a collective drive toward its own well-being. In spite of detractors like McDougall who charge Nike with producing real-world effects that are the inverse of the company's discursive claims—that is, the delivery of ill-being under the guise of well-being—Nike has nevertheless successfully exploited the discourse of species consciousness for profit.

Technological Superorganism

If we attempt to assemble a composite portrait of this discursive protagonism of the figure of the collective in our current cultural production, we are able to distill recurrent motifs: interest in the fact of connectivity and the stuff of connectedness above and beyond the salient, the unique, the differentiated; democratic horizontality over hierarchical verticality; a dynamism generated by instinct and affect—love being the most frequent metonym of this motor; cultural activity on the order of the species; a concern for relative well-being versus ill-being, as though this cultural activity on the order of the species could be assessed by the self-governing homeostatic principle of the soma.

   Robert Wright, senior fellow at the New America Foundation, and sometime professor of philosophy and religion, speaks of this discursive figure of this soma of the species collective in ontological terms as a "superorganism," arguing that our global media and technology have brought humanity to a new stage of evolution: "Could it be that in some sense, the *point* of evolution—both the biological evolution that created an intelligent species and the technological evolution that a sufficiently intelligent species is bound to unleash—has been to create these social brains, and maybe even to weave them into a giant, loosely organized planetary brain? Kind of in the way that the *point* of the maturation of an organism is to create an adult organism?" Ridley tells us that humanity is born to trade, McDougall that humanity is born to run. Now Wright posits the hypothesis that we are born to create and then to corporeally inhabit—again, the metaphor of the soma—our own technology. If Ridley implicitly argues that humans are innate capitalists and McDougall that humans are innate antimaterialistic sharers (essentially commune-ists, but obviating the political stigma of communism), then Wright's political analysis of the superorganism frames the debate in terms that help to shed light on how the homeostatic principle of the collective may be related to the question of capitalism in the first place, as I shall argue here.

Wrestling with the position enunciated by the likes of Paul Virilio, who theorizes informatics as the new medium of social control and speaks of the "information bomb" as the new atomic bomb (1998)—a position seemingly affirmed by news reports of the need for increased "cyberwarriors" to protect U.S. (or any nation's) security in the global age (Gjelten) or by the vision of total human subordination to technology in the *Matrix* film trilogy—Wright rejects the notion that technology must be firmly associated with social control: "But at least the superorganism that seems to be emerging, though in some ways demanding, isn't the totalitarian monster that [George] Orwell feared; it's more diffuse, more decentralized, more reconcilable, in principle—at least—with liberty." Gently characterizing the technological superorganism as "demanding," but certainly not "totalitarian," Wright lays out an alternative set of concepts to be associated with its social hegemony: diffusion, decentralization, liberty. This latter conceptual imaginary resonates both with the flow of capital theorized by the neoliberal school as optimal—deregulated and free—and with Michael Hardt and Antonio Negri's vision of global-age empire as a circumstance of control brought about by the fact of capitalist globalization:

> Empire is materializing before our very eyes. Over the past several decades, as colonial regimes were overthrown and then precipitously after the Soviet barriers to the capitalist world market finally collapsed, we have witnessed an irresistible and irreversible globalization of economic and cultural exchanges. Along with the global market and global circuits of production has emerged a global order, a new logic and structure of rule—in short, a new form of sovereignty. Empire is the political subject that effectively regulates these global exchanges, the sovereign power that governs the world.
>
> (xi)

> Empire establishes no territorial center of power and does not rely on fixed boundaries or barriers. It is a decentered and deterritorializ-

ing apparatus of rule that progressively incorporates the entire global realm within its open, expanding frontiers.

(xii)

The construction of the paths and limits of these new global flows has been accompanied by a transformation of the dominant productive processes themselves, with the result that . . . priority [is] given . . . to communicative, cooperative, and affective labor.

(xiii)

The concept of Empire is characterized fundamentally by a lack of boundaries: Empire's rule has no limits. First and foremost, then, the concept of Empire posits a regime that effectively encompasses the spatial totality, or really that rules over the entire "civilized" world. No territorial boundaries limit its reign. Second, the concept of Empire presents itself not as a historical regime originating in conquest, but rather as an order that effectively suspends history and thereby fixes the existing state of affairs for eternity. From the perspective of Empire, this is the way things will always be and the way they were always meant to be. In other words, Empire presents its rule not as a transitory moment in the movement of history, but as a regime with no temporal boundaries and in this sense outside of history or at the end of history. Third, the rule of Empire operates on all registers of the social order extending down to the depths of the social world. Empire not only manages a territory and a population but also creates the very world it inhabits. It not only regulates human interactions but also seeks directly to rule over human nature. The object of its rule is social life in its entirety, and thus Empire presents the paradigmatic form of biopower. Finally, although the practice of Empire is continually bathed in blood, the concept of Empire is always dedicated to peace—a perpetual and universal peace outside of history.

(xiv–xv)

Wright's technological superorganism—diffuse, decentralized, and free— mirrors the vertebral description given by Hardt and Negri of the sovereignty of capital, wherein the question of the global collective also emerges ("the object of its rule is social life in its entirety") in the context of ahistorical atavism ("this is the way things will always be and the way they were meant to be"). Hardt and Negri's attribution of this landscape of cultural control to capitalist (neoliberal) empire itself allows us to glimpse and hypothesize a causal connection between global capitalist culture and the diverse expression of the metaphor of the species collective as a homeostatically managed superorganism. That is, if we admit Hardt and Negri's description of capitalist empire as a symptomatic cultural analysis—an analysis informed by the culture it diagnoses—then we may begin to entertain the notion that the recurrent image of the universal human subject (timeless, universal, driven by affect, adhered by communication, peaceful, and free) is given by capitalist discourse itself.

If we reflect on Lev Manovich's meditation on the rise of the World Wide Web (and adding to this the subsequent development of new media technologies) as the technology most adequately reflective of post–cold war political and economic sensibilities—which, properly described, are hegemonically capitalist—we might begin to ask if we should invert the directionality of our commonly held assumption of the relationship between capitalism and technology in which the technological advance simply propels capitalism without capitalism's having any influence over the direction of technological development. But if we consider capitalism as a source of epistemological narrative guiding and shaping the very ideation of what technologies would be desirable or even possible, perhaps we might hypothesize a connection between the discursive ideals of capitalism and the kinds of technologies that are developed to realize them.

Returning to Wright and his view of the technological superorganism as a monism—that is, as a singular entity of uncompromised integrity, whose homeostatic regulation is working successfully toward well-being—it is, from the perspective of a technology developing according to the dictates of capitalism and not vice versa, striking that Wright should ascribe an organic inevitability to that superorganism, casting it as essential for the fate of humanity; this perspective allows us to understand the fate of the superorganism as conceptually interchangeable with that of capitalism, if capitalism may in fact be posited as its originary epistemological author. Should the well-being of this superorganism reverse course toward ill-being—should the "fairly unified body" of the superorganism fracture into division and therefore divisiveness—the homeostatic harmony of the superorganism's parts will, Wright concludes, devolve into "chaos": "I do think we ultimately have to embrace a superorganism of *some* kind—not because it's inevitable, but because the alternative is worse. If technological progress grinds to a halt, it will be because chaos has engulfed the world; and if we don't use technology to weave people together and turn our species into a fairly unified body, chaos will probably engulf the world because technology offers so much destructive power that a sharply divided human species can't flourish."

Children of Men: Reproduction as the Salvation of the Collective

Children of Men (2006),[5] a film by the preeminent Mexican director and three-time Academy Award nominee Alfonso Cuarón, envisions precisely such a scenario of apocalyptic human affairs.[6] Although the film follows the intimate story of a handful of people, that small group represents the hope of humanity in its entirety against the backdrop of imminent species extinction. This circumstance of a gravely—and, apparently, terminally—imperiled human race has given way to the kind of chaos Wright imagines should the superorganism collapse. Here it is not because technological progress has ground to a halt, as Wright fears, but because humanity itself has suddenly and inexplicably lost the ability to procreate. The result is, nevertheless, tantamount to the dissolution of the superorganism—in the sense that people are no longer woven together into a fairly unified body—and the engulfing of the world by chaos. In this sense *Children of Men* is a negative portrait of the species collective, one that takes humanity in all its extension as its central topos but explores its demise and possible salvation. Although this is a collective in the throes of violent disintegration, the same constellation of associated concepts comes to the fore in the conceptual narrative framework: well-being and ill-being as the evaluative poles for a homeostatic assessment of the social state of affairs, the politics and products of capitalist commodification and their contestation as the target of this homeostatic assessment, and love as the emotional extract of the human condition—with sexual reproduction as the sole viable telos for the near-defunct species.

The central problem afflicting the human race is a sudden loss of fertility in the early twenty-first century, and the film is scathing showing how this unhappy pandemic has resulted in precisely the kinds of "global civil war" symptoms predicted by analysts of rising temperatures (this is the homicidal dog-eat-dog world of compatriot Alejandro González Iñárritu's 2000 film *Amores perros* brought to the edge of apocalpyse). A photomontage early on in the film shows in rapid-fire succession images of cities the world over that have succumbed to lawless violence: flames, death, and destruction give us to understand there is no longer any social compact of which to speak. At times we know that terrible and massive devastation has taken place simply by its elliptical mention, such as the cryptic but meaning-laden offering of condolences about people lost by virtue of their having been in New York "when it happened" or rueful lamentations about not being "in time" to salvage more than a handful of masterpieces from Madrid's Prado Museum before civil rule disintegrated into chaos. "The world has collapsed," propaganda advises and "only Britain soldiers on." The rest of the world has flocked in droves to Britain in the same kind of "large-scale migration" anticipated by the Nobel Peace Prize Committee when envisioning the effects of reduced resources on world demographics. At various points of the film, we see extended traveling takes that span the lengths of seemingly endless metal holding pens into which "refugees" from countries all over the globe are crammed, their hands spilling out and multilingual cries for succor falling on deaf ears of the indifferent British soldiers who coldly vigil their containment. And, later on, in full and unmitigated Abu Ghraib–style atrocity, we see these British soldiers debase, rob, torture, and summarily execute the illegal immigrants at will and on a seemingly infinite scale.

In this horrific imaginary circumstance in which "only Britain soldiers on," the status of illegality has been applied to the net sum of the remaining world population, while the British government maintains a perfect passivity toward their suffering. A recorded announcement played in public transportation urges British citizens not to view refugees as "my dentist," "my housecleaner," "my waiter," "my cousin"; "THEY are illegal," the public service message insists, breaking the bonds of first-person affective relationships in which all human beings are recognized as self-same and replacing affectivity with legality as the arbiter of the proper code of conduct with these distant third-person Others. Meanwhile, within the sphere of the British ruling elite, limousines of government functionaries divide the turbulent waters of the streets like sharks, lawn parties—albeit of tattered aspect—leisurely occupy entire stretches of green river bank in sharp contrast to the dense use of space in the containment of refugees, and a marble mausoleumlike edifice serves to amass and enshrine the world's cultural artifacts (the imposing "Ark of the Arts").

A security scanner submits the film's hero Theo (Clive Owen) to self-definition by what he carries in his pockets, echoing the moment in which the

Joker is likewise defined by the material belongings he carries on his person in the *Dark Knight*. Theo has a lighter, a package of cigarettes, a whiskey flask, and a foil-backed plastic sheet of pills—all of which make him the prototypical subject of ill-being. Indeed, Theo is self-professedly "hopeless" (Alfonso Cuarón describes his character as a "veteran of hopelessness . . . like a zombie" ["Theo and Julian," DVD special features]). When we see how a digital advertisement for the suicide drug Quietus serves as his alarm clock and when his morning coffee shoots out of his hand in a visceral reaction of fright to the explosion of the coffee shop he has just exited—and where, moreover, he has just watched a news report of the death by stabbing of the teenage "Baby" Diego (Juan Gabriel Yacuzzi), the world's youngest person—we begin to appreciate how Theo is given over to addictive self-medication. Like *WALL·E*, where ultimate dehumanization—lifelessness in the sense of no longer embodying the human condition—is represented by the inability to part one's attention from the screen that floats in front of the obscenely obese and perpetually reclined bodies, *Children of Men* gives an analogous portrait of life within the mainstream system in the form of Theo's office, where cubicles are defined not by physical walls but by the virtual walls of attention given over exclusively to the screen before each worker. Emotionally attuned only to the media output, and not to one another (the exchange between Theo and his boss is completely flat in contrast to the mediatic melodrama surrounding the youngest person's death), humans have clearly become alienated on a massive scale from the ability to form flesh-and-blood community. The adolescent son of Theo's cousin Nigel (Danny Huston), high-ranking government official and director of the Ark of the Arts, embodies this condition of lifelessness: clearly in the flush of youth—complete with a burgeoning whitehead pimple prominent on his cheek—Alex (Ed Westwick) is nevertheless riveted in absolute concentration to a video game that he plays by moving a set of wires hooked onto his fingertips, as though physiologically incapable of parting his mind or body from this virtual engagement. When Nigel successfully dislodges Alex from his video play by screaming his son's name at the top of his lungs from across the dining room table, it is only with the effect that Alex moves his hand—but not his eyes—to pick up and ingest the pills that his father is frantically commanding him to take. Are the pills keeping him alive or preventing him from living? Much like the futuristic dystopia of "peace" predicated on the collective injection of the sense-deadening drug Prozium in the film *Equilibrium* (2002), the dystopia of *Children of Men* seems to be succinctly and maximally summarized in the figure of Alex, whose apparent age places him, the spectator can surmise, in the general vicinity of the youngest people living. This youth is not the promise of the future, but the promise of death. And the behavior that represents this future-as-death is the absolute submission of self to medicated consumption.

The background detail of the film gives historiographical clues about how to formulate an interpretive periodization of this human apocalypse. One such moment is the commentary with which a pop radio disc jockey prefaces The Kills' "Wait" as a "blast from the past all the way back from 2003, that beautiful time when people refused to accept that the future was just around the corner." We know the film takes place in 2027, and that the last human birth was eighteen years prior, which we can calculate as 2008. So the choice of 2003 as a pivotal year, and one in which there was, as suggested by the radio personality's implicit cultural criticism, already a force of willful blindness about the death and destruction that lay ahead, seems pointed when one considers how strongly the year 2003 resonates with the other historiographical references made by the film. These references are most notably concentrated in an intense cluster that defines Theo's aging hippie friend Jasper (Michael Caine) and his catatonic wife Janice (Philippa Urquhart). This couple and their camouflaged house in the woods serve as a physical and emotional refuge for Theo and as the film's greatest symbol of all that stands in opposition to the extreme malaise that has overcome the human world. When Theo first enters their house seeking respite from those ills, the camera makes a slow pan over what we come to realize is a shrine of sorts to the couple's markedly leftist political commitment. Newspaper clippings, protest posters, professional awards, and photographs all combine to show what Jasper, as a political cartoonist, and Janice, as a photojournalist, have stood for in the public sphere. Their activism, as viewed in their chronologically ordered keepsakes and clippings, moves from opposition to the Iraq War to concern over declining births and, finally, to the defense of "foogies," the slang for illegal refugees in the era of full-blown infertility. This panoramic detail—later echoed by similar clippings pasted on the walls of the makeshift interrogation room maintained by the rebel group headed up by Theo's ex-wife Julian (Julianne Moore)—constitutes the single most sustained politico-historical commentary posed by the film. To it we may add Jasper's later recounting of how Theo and Julian met at an antiglobalization rally in what would have been the turn of the twenty-first century—perhaps a reference to the so-called J18 protests that took place around the world, one of them in London, on June 18, 1999. Our chronology becomes antiglobalization protests (1999), Iraq War (2003), infertility (2008), subsequent police repression of refugees. We see through the newspaper clippings that Janice became a leader in the public outcry against mistreatment of refugees, only to be tortured herself by the MI5, the British security service. Confined to a wheelchair during the film's present moment, impassive and motionless, Janice embodies the living-dead condition that afflicts the world: her moral paralysis registers the unbridled logic of homicide and its violent quashing of hope. Janice's body has been stilled by the violence that is just as much a part of the pandemic as infertility itself. Without new life, there can be no hope. Infertility, then, is the ultimate symptom and symbol of homicidal neoliberalism. (It is conceptually fitting, then, that Janice should meet her end with Quietus, administered though it may be by the loving hand of Jasper to prevent her from having to endure any further violence.)

The panoramic exposition of Jasper and Janice's lives is arranged in chronological order not only so we will understand them as characters, but, even more important, so that we will understand the world history that has led to their present moment, and most important, so that we will understand that world history as a sequence of events—as an evolution or, more precisely, as a devolving state, a disintegration. That is to say, this panoramic shot of newspaper headlines and keepsakes does not simply satisfy the need, in elegant shorthand, to provide the spectator with background information; it also suggests that world events have developed as though reaching a crescendo. Jasper tells Theo a joke about an Englishman at a dinner party who doesn't know the cause of infertility, but dines with gusto on stork; the lead-in to the punch line gives us background information that is analogous to the use of the panoramic shot. What has occasioned infertility?, the joke begins. There is apparently an established litany of possible causes: "genetic experiments, gamma rays, pollution, same old same old," recites Jasper. All these possibilities resonate with the culture of risk capitalism, of the harnessing of technology and science to further the interests of capital over humanity, of capital over the earth. The fact that infertility is never assigned a cause allows it to come into view as a cultural illness, as a moral illness (functioning in exactly the same as the loss of sight in Fernando Meirelles's *Blindness*). Neoliberal globalization comes to an apex in the bid to control oil resources—*Children of Men* presents the Iraq War as the last recognizable historical reference before the world succumbs to infertility.

(Director Kathryn Bigelow's perspective on the Iraq War in "The Hurt Locker" [2008] also adds warmaking to our growing list of addictions, as her *New York Times* reviewer Manohla Dargis attests in urging us to consider how the film "takes an analytical if visceral look at how the experience of war can change a man, how it eats into his brain so badly he ends up hooked on it.") The identification of 2003 as "that beautiful time when people refused to accept that the future was just around the corner" takes on a distinctly political resonance when we juxtapose 2003 as a transitional year with the timeline established in Janice's tabletop scrapbook: the Iraq War comes into view as the beginning of the end of the world. From the series of details presented to us about world events, we may infer a logic of causality between these social phenomena: the same neoliberal circumstances that inspired antiglobalization rallies also occasioned the Iraq War, before finally culminating in global infertility, the film grimly suggests.

Against this backdrop of homicidal capitalist hopelessness, Theo emerges as a chosen one to restore hope. His very name—"God," from the ancient Greek—resonates with other details as we approach his moral conversion from death to life. Along with the effects of destructive consumerism that Theo empties from his pockets in the Ark of the Arts, he also bears a set of keys. This last attribute proves to be a homonym for his messianic mission: Theo is asked by Julian to escort a "foogie" named Kee (Clare-Hope Ashitey) to the border, a trip that draws Theo out of his death-trap existence and thrusts him onto the path of an archetypal journey of individual purification and renewal with like implications for the species collective. When Julian is murdered on the road to the rendezvous point, Theo expresses his devastation by crumpling into tears rather than lifting his flask all the way to his lips—an emotional awakening is his first step toward countering his own culturally and commercially imposed ill-being. When he and the others arrive at their first safe house, the man who greets them remarks with surprise at that fact that the dogs, "who don't like anyone," nevertheless wag their tails without barking at Theo. It is here that we see Theo drink and smoke for the last time. The draft script includes a line cut from the final movie version in which the caretaker of the dogs rejects a swig from Theo's flask on the grounds that "alcohol is a tool of the government to numb the people," a claim that resonates conceptually with the structure of consumption embodied by Theo as zombie-addict. As Theo is led to the barn where he will behold the pregnant Kee in a state of epiphany, he stamps out his last cigarette. (Much later on in the film, an elderly man requests a cigarette from Theo, and we realize in hindsight that from this point forward he has no longer smoked.)

Summoned by Kee, Theo finds her in the barn surrounded by cows, and what follows is the film's most important stretch of dialogue:

> KEE: You know what they do to these cows, they cut off their tits, they do. Zzzt, gone, bye. Only leave four. Four tits fits the machine. It's wacko. Why not make machines that suck eight titties, eh?
>
> THEO: Is that what you want to talk about, cows and titties?
>
> KEE: Julian told me about your baby. Said his name was Dylan. You taught him to swim when he was two. He called you papa. She said anything goes spooky, I should talk to you. Said you'd help me. Said you'd get me to the boat.
>
> THEO: What boat?
>
> KEE: The *Tomorrow*.
>
> THEO: The *Tomorrow*? I don't know what you're talking about, but I'm sure your friends can take care of you.
>
> KEE: But Julian said only trust you. She said you'd help me.
>
> THEO: I don't know why she said that. Listen, I don't quite know what's going on.
>
> KEE: You can't leave!
>
> THEO: Kee, I'm in a lot of trouble myself. I'm sorry.
>
> KEE: Wait! (Kee starts to unbutton her shirt.)
>
> THEO: What are you doing?! Don't do that. (Kee takes off her shirt, covering her breasts with one hand and her underwear with the other—the "War, he sung, is toil and trouble" aria from Handel's opera *Alexander's Feast* starts again. Theo stares at pregnant Kee surrounded by cows.)
>
> KEE: I'm scared. Please help me.
>
> THEO: Jesus Christ.

On seeing Theo, Kee launches abruptly into a discussion of the cows and how they are milked. Disarmed by her offbeat overture, Theo is un-comprehending, but the meaning of Kee's comments lies in her implicit self-comparison to the mutilated cows—surrounded, as she is, by them as she speaks—and in her referencing of neoliberal capitalist practices as the starting point of her negotiations with Theo. Capitalism has no compassion, no empathy, doesn't care about the cows. Just as Quietus is the ultimate symbol of capitalist consumption, the four-nipple machine is the ultimate symbol of capitalist production. The four-nipple machine epitomizes risk culture: to turn a quicker profit, the cow is half-sacrificed with no thought to long-term effects. Capitalism functions against nature, against feelings, against health. When Kee has finished with her impromptu analysis of capitalism (which resonates with Sheriff Tom Ed Bell's discussion, between uneasy and mournful, of how cows are now slaughtered with air guns in the Coen Brothers' *No Country for Old Men*), she launches into an interpellation of Theo as a father. This seems at first like a non sequitur, but the movement Kee has made is from the threat that assails her and the life she carries—the future of humanity itself—to the force that can protect her from that threat: Theo as father. It is this part of Theo that has languished in half-dead internal paralysis—an emotional analogue of Janice's outward state—and it is this part of him that is capable of overcoming the four-tit machine of death. As he beholds Kee's bare pregnant belly in a sustained gaze of wonderment—accompanied by Handel's aria motif—Theo says, "Jesus Christ," here not only a banal expression of amazement but also a symbolic naming of the life in Kee's belly. The scene's biblical symbology suddenly becomes fully clear: Theo—God—beholds the savior of humanity in a stable. Theo's status as chosen one is reiterated by Kee, who reveals that she has inherited Julian's absolute trust in him.

In the following scene, the future of Kee's baby is debated by the Fishes. Julian's visually spectacular assassination by her own rebel group has already persuasively demonstrated the extent to which the political left has succumbed as much to corruption and violence as the political right that it opposes—in what tenuous sphere of coherent politics remains. This scene, in which the treacherous new Fishes leader Luke (Chiwetel Ejiofor) argues that the Fishes should appropriate Kee's baby for political leverage, confirms that politics proper has crumbled beyond salvation. Hope will not be found therein and can only lie elsewhere. In response to Luke's plan to use Kee's unborn baby as a political pawn, Theo argues before the full assembly of Fishes that what Kee needs is, above all, a doctor. As Theo speaks, a tiny kitten tries in a determined singularity of attention to claw its way up his pant leg. The attentions of the helpless kitten seeking protection from Theo signal him once again as a chosen one against the backdrop of broken politics. Theo will in fact become the very doctor for which he advocates, not only further abandoning vice but this time turning it into virtue by using and purifying the remaining alcohol in his flask to clean his hands as well as the newborn baby he delivers into the sick world standing on the verge of social death.

That this baby is an antidote to apocalypse is evident in the heart-stopping scene in which full-scale urban warfare between the police forces and the rebel uprising in the Bexhill refugee camp comes to a sudden and complete stop within the circumference of those who realize they are in the presence of a baby. The sound of the baby's wails leads instantly to the command to cease fire; the sight of the newborn baby brings awestruck soldiers to their knees against the audio overlay of the aria—once more—that symbolizes the power of love and life over hate and death. Theo is mortally wounded in the battle by the leader of the Fishes, who would use Kee's baby to galvanize antigovernment sentiment (and the same leader who has killed Julian because of her own commitment to humanity over politics), which only affirms politics—whether for or against a repressive government—as the enemy of humanity. In his role as a chosen one, Theo is neither fighter nor political activist. To underscore this pacifism, his character wears flip-flops through war zones; when Julian tells the story of their romance, Theo disavows its political aspect, saying he went to the rallies just to get her in bed, a sentiment he reiterates just moments before she is shot. For all his vice and hopelessness—the part of him that has succumbed to the zombifying effects of neoliberal risk culture—Theo is a father, a healer, a lover. Theo is the film's true revolutionary: he is the guardian of bare life. Theo is the fusion of Ernesto and el Chivo before him, a doctor and a father, like Bruce Wayne's father in Christopher Nolan's *Batman Begins* (2005), represented by the visual synecdoche of the stethoscope as the instrument capable of healing the sick body politic.

Children of Men ends on a note that brings the possibility of utopian redemption onscreen. This sequence begins with Theo's death, which is framed as a sacrifice for the sake of inspiring faith in Kee: Theo's last gesture is to rock his arms in imitation of what she must do to reassure her little girl Dylan (named after his own lost son, who represented his and Julian's hope, a "magical child," in Jasper's words, and thus represents the renewed possibility of the miraculous). Theo ends his life not as a cynic given over to ill-being, but as a father working selflessly toward the well-being of his adoptive family, rocking his arms and telling Kee that everything will be all right—for her, for Dylan, for all of humanity. As we watch in shock as our hero—our father-doctor, our messiah—slumps in death, the film takes us forward in time beyond the suspension of revolution-to-come and into the realization of our hope: in the final frames of the film the *Tomorrow* emerges from the fog—the clouded vision of humanity—to come into view. (The *Tomorrow*, incidentally, bears a striking resemblance to the Greenpeace boat *Esperanza*—hope—active since 2002.) Kee and her baby—our twenty-first-century Mary and Jesus—and, by extension, all humanity, are saved. Kee has, in fact, earlier joked that hers was an immaculate conception, only to confess that she does not know which of the "wankers" was the father, casting herself as more of a Mary Magdalene than a Mary yet nevertheless carrying a miraculously conceived and messianic child and opening the door for Theo to act as its symbolic father.[7]

Universal Morality, Perfect Democratization, Equitable Distribution of Resources

Health becomes the operative metaphorical measure of the status of the collective. Just as well-being—the product of an optimal homeostasis—indicates a healthy collective, ill-being—the breakdown in homeostatic function—indicates its potentially terminal imperilment. "If society fell apart, would you?" asks the Discovery Channel's reality show *The Colony*. This tag line signals the show's premise of social apocalypse, with the canonical handful of strangers from diverse walks of life "participat[ing] in an experiment that will test humanity's ability to survive." The show's doomsday scenarios and living conditions—biological disaster, pandemic, no power from the grid, no running water, no communication from the outside world—demonstrate a common concern with Wright and *Children of Men* over the fate of the human collective. In *The Colony* and *Children of Men*—also in *Blindness*, where the world struggles to cope with a pandemic loss of sight—the emergence of a small microcosmic community formed across social divisions of class, race, gender, and ideology constitutes the promise of human salvation. These works posit the rejection of the social hierarchy based on such divisive and segregating compartmentalizations as the first essential step toward redemption and social healing: a perfect democratization.

In contemplating the dissolution of the "technological superorganism," Wright muses that avoiding this chaos will require "morality." The implication that morality may be wanting in the current implicitly neoliberal landscape echoes the calls for capitalist reform by the likes of former British prime minister Gordon Brown, who at the G-20 Summit of 2009 declared the days of the so-called Washington Consensus—profit for profit's sake—to be over and urged the world to adopt a common set of "values" that do not cross "moral boundaries" ("Britain's Brown Urges Moral Values at G-20"). Brown urged the collective correction of what he called the "unsupervised globalization of our financial markets," including—to Brown's mind—the regulation of the "shadow" banking system and their hedge funds, credit rating agencies, tax havens, and corporate bonuses ("Old Washington Consensus Is Over: Gordon Brown"). But while the call to morality is meant to regulate and curb these neoliberal practices, which generate untold profit for a financial elite, Brown's discourse of morality—like Wright's warning that morality will be required to prevent the collapse of the superorganism or the moral awakening of the small reterritorialized communities in *Children of Men*, *The Colony*, and *Blindness*—does not contradict the classic discourse of capitalism itself. On the contrary, if we think back to the equivalency established across Adam Smith's works (*Theory of Moral Sentiments*, *The Wealth of Nations*) between morality and resources, both being guided by the invisible hand through the body politic in harmonious flow, we appreciate the notion that morality—as though an affective homologue of capital—is the blood of homeostatic capitalist dynamics.

Morality, democracy, the distribution of resources, and the human species are inveterate topics of inquiry and representation. What I suggest is that we consider the persistence with which they are arranged into a constellation of topoi that yields a certain vision of humanity consonant with the capitalist imaginary. This vision is neatly represented by the single image on the otherwise spare cover of the 250th-anniversary edition of Smith's *Theory of Moral Sentiments*: an origami heart shaped out of a one-dollar bill. The owner of this one-dollar bill heart is the species collective itself. If thus referenced in passing by Smith some 250 years ago, in the origins of modern-day capitalism, the notion of the species—and particularly of the species engaged in capitalist activity—has now exploded as a trope into the mainstream discourse of globalization. Moral humanity—love being its synecdoche and sexual reproduction its telos—is democratically interwoven in a shared and infinitely capacious body governed by its homeostatic tendency toward well-being. In place of politics articulated through the rationale of reasoned argumentation, this figure of the homeostatic species collective indicates a positive political position, with the language of health becoming the symbol of affirmative politics and the status quo; a negative political position is indicated by ill-being, connoting by homeostatic principle the urgent, life-or-death need to return to organic balance by reversing or otherwise reforming political course. In the formulation of inquiry across disciplines, the collective has begun to move toward epistemological hegemony both as the basis for the conception of what is knowable and for the scale optimal for the greatest, most sophisticated, and most accurate production of human knowledge. This knowledge may be rational in its substance and use, but it is produced unthinkingly through the shared heart that delivers a flow of capital to all its species constituents across the feeling soma.

2 We Are the World

Sentient People and Planet in Sustainability Discourse

　　The feeling soma has become a pervasive protagonist of cultural discourse, turning up as a conceptual underwriter of how we imagine social intercourse to be conducted and social action to be accomplished—both, as conceived in this affect-driven epistemological model, by an infinitely capacious group possessed of an intelligence that is fundamentally nonrational and synergistic. Notions of organicity and positive emotion are especially recurrent in these understandings—whether explicit or implicit—of social protagonism.

These concepts of emotional health, well-being, and a harmoniously unified human collective do not call attention to themselves as part of a larger discursive construct. They have been part of our Western politico-economic framework for so long that they are perceived, like the capitalist democracy they are pressed into the service of rhetorically naturalizing, as simply reflective of the human condition itself. We think that to speak of organicity and love is to meditate in the most elemental and even unsophisticated way on what it means to be alive.

A capacity for denaturalizing cultural vision like the one that guides Diamela Eltit's 2003 *Mano de obra* (Work Hand) shakes us out of any such
discursive complacency by holding up a novelistic—and fiercely critical—
looking glass to the feeling soma as an affective balustrade of the neoliberal
status quo. Eltit's cynical interrogation of the politico-economic use-value
of the concept of a loving collective peels back the affective wallpaper in
which democratic capitalism's most recent avatar of global neoliberalism has
covered itself in order to denounce a sinister and malevolent underside to
this seemingly benign and salutary rhetoric.

Having moved from the cultural margins of contestatory writing under
the Pinochet dictatorship to the forefront of the literary establishment in
Chile's recuperated democracy, in *Mano de obra* Eltit nevertheless fiction-
alizes a concept she has explored more explicitly elsewhere: that there is a
fundamental continuum in what she views as military-cum-neoliberal rule.[1]
Whereas Eltit's work has tended to focus on the political, *Mano de obra*
openly takes on the economic, figuring the supermarket as a microcosm
for contemporary neoliberal culture. The novel moves in two parts from
a portrait in the first-person singular of one supermarket employee whose
physical health progressively and inexorably deteriorates as a consequence of
his employment to a collective portrait in the first-person plural of a group
of supermarket workers who live together and whose lives are defined exclusively by their work status. A premise of perfect collectivity and horizontality
among the workers is belied by the value they place on wage earning, which
turns this horizontality into a cruel verticality of abuse when wage-earning
expectations are not met. A key aspect of the text that bears emphasis is the
language of love and respect Eltit places in the mouths of the collective we
to describe their relationship to money. In a mode of singsong repetition,
the *nosotros* of the novel equates love and physical well-being with strong
wage earning and promotions at the supermarket and, conversely, a lack of
love and physical dis-ease or ill-being with flagging income and decreased
shifts or work responsibilities. One character, for example, is beloved in the
same measure that she is tasked with the marketing of products: "Tres pro-
ductos. Tres empleos. Tres sueldos. Isabel tenía tres empleos y tres sueldos.
La queríamos y ella lo sabía" ("Three products. Three jobs. Three salaries.
Isabel had three jobs and three salaries. We loved her and she knew it";
79–80), avers the narrative voice. Yet, when this same character's exhaustion
compromises her performance and salary at the supermarket, the group
interprets her fatigue as an insulting loss of love: "Pensábamos que Isabel

nos había dejado de querer. La verdad es que sentíamos que ya no nos tenía cariño ni respeto" ("We thought that Isabel had stopped loving us. The truth is that we felt she no longer had affection or respect for us"; 131).

Eltit's evaluation of neoliberal culture may be scathing, but we may nevertheless distill from it a set of centrally defining characteristics of that culture. These key characteristics are the following: the idea that the neoliberal reality is one of perfect immanence extending its reach into every corner of everyday life; the idea that within this immanence there is a presumed relationship of horizontality and perfectly democratic equality among members of a group; the idea that, in fact, this group forms a single collective body defined by its participation in the neoliberal economic system; and, finally, the maintenance of order and power within that collective "we" as the net balance of an affective disposition that runs on a gradient from positive to negative emotion and, as a correlate, from somatic well-being to ill-being. In other words, it is through the negative optic of Eltit's ironic treatment of love and respect in the context of a collective bound by neoliberal logic that the figure of the feeling soma comes clearly into view as a discursive construct in the service of capitalist cultural order.

What happens when we turn the same denaturalized gaze on the discursive pillars of democratic capitalism? From the eighteenth-century revolutionary "life, liberty, and the pursuit of happiness" and "liberty, fraternity, equality" to the twentieth-century post–Berlin Wall "don't worry, be happy" and the twenty-first-century corporate consumerist "life is good," we begin to see a pattern emerge in which the true referent is not emotion as physiological experience, but that emotion is serving quite a different role as the key building material for our conceptual cultural edifice.

Sustainability Discourse and a Planetary Feeling Soma

If in the preceding chapter I gave a general pastiche-style presentation of the frequency with which the feeling soma informs cultural discourse in U.S. and Latin American media, in this chapter I would like to revisit the same theme in the more specific context of sustainability discourse. Specifically, I seek to demonstrate a single point that is quite spare in its simplicity: the extent to which a planetary iteration of the feeling soma—that is, a vision of the heretofore human feeling soma now extended to include the planet itself—defines our popular understanding of the fate of humanity on

Earth and, many argue, the fate of Earth itself. Sustainability discourse is particularly apt for the exploration of the role of epistemic affect because it represents a cultural platform for the working-through of capitalism's successes and shortcomings. It is a clearinghouse for twenty-first-century capitalism that both evokes its originary epistemic discourse of self-legitimation and critically evaluates its performance during the intervening centuries, with a particular focus on the current era marked by post-WWII U.S. economic hegemony and post-Soviet all-out globalization. In this current era, the logic of free-market capitalism has approximated the totalizing level of immanence on a planetary level that free-market capitalism has posited epistemically from the outset in the form of the feeling soma. Here, again, my objective is to call attention to the foundational role that epistemic affect plays—qua feeling soma—by gathering together a broad swath of cultural evidence from mainstream meditations on sustainability in the U.S. and Latin America, organizing this evidence into positions that mark the political differences of perspective across regions, but underscoring their common underlying epistemological refrain of privileging—and vying for discursive control over—the feeling soma, now of planetary dimension.

Sustainability discourse turns up persistently in hemispheric cultural production even where it is not explicitly announced as such, evincing the extent to which the foundational constellation of issues at play in the sustainability agenda—people, planet, profit—and their various discursive permutations are in fact the concise summary encapsulation of contemporary socioeconomic politics. If politics in general may be said to be affective in their representation, then the affective imperative of sustainability discourse brings that tendency into view in the context of what is fundamentally a sustained conflict about the direction of humanity. It is arguably the most salient repository for the teleologies purported to have categorically disappeared along with the failed isms of twentieth-century politics. If late twentieth-century postmodernism did away with teleology—with direction and purpose of grand social design—and submerged the political West in directionlessness and lack of ideology and master objectives, then the robust emergence of sustainability discourse at the outset of the twenty-first century reveals that what we believed to be "directionless" and "lacking in ideology and master objectives"—bare and putatively postpolitical capitalism—was invested precisely with direction, ideology, and a single master objective all oriented around profit. The most radical antiprofit strain of sustainability discourse throws the politics of capitalism into relief as social teleology by denouncing their abandonment of the social and the environmental for the sake of the economic. Pro-profit sustainability discourse—capitalism under a new green guise—responds with the discursive embrace of precisely the two elements with whose abandonment it is charged, strategically abandoning profit in the discursive realm that it may be recuperated without censure in the sphere of practice.

A survey of sustainability discourse in the United States and Latin America shows how both pro- and antiprofit variants inform cultural production in both regions, but with a significant difference between the antiprofit North-South discourses that reveals a contrasting view of self-empowerment in the global political theater. What is clear, in all variants across regions, is the epistemic status of affect in the construction of a politics of sustainability—which are, in essence, the master script for all contemporary politics.

Sustainability from the North

Sustainability is a concept born of the developed world, as the attenuation, precisely, of its development. Coined in the 1987 Report of the World Commission on Environment and Development of the United Nations charged with responding to a "concer[n] with the accelerating deterioration of the human environment and natural resources and the consequences of that deterioration for economic and social development," sustainability makes its first appearance as an adjectival modifier in the now well-known turn of phrase *sustainable development*. I emphasize the genesic placement of the concept in a subordinate position with respect to the central notion of development in order to underscore the persistent hierarchy operative between the two terms: development occupies the nominal category of permanence; it may or may not—in whatever measure it sees fit—adopt the contingent definitional nuance of sustainability.

In the intervening decade, the concept of a "triple bottom line" emerged to further define sustainable development. This now classic notion of a balanced privileging of the interests of people, planet, and profit—in scholarly terms, the social, the environmental, and the economic—is generally credited to John Elkington in his 1997 *Cannibals with Forks: The Triple Bottom Line of Twenty-First Century Business*. Again, a rhetorical analysis is instructive. In a retrospective interview with socially progressive magazine *Mother Jones*, Elkington recalls the process of terminological ideation:

It was 1994 that the phrase "triple bottom line" came to me. It wasn't an easy birthing because I'd been thinking for almost eighteen months, trying to come up with a term that would capture what to me was the full business agenda under the sustainability heading. At that time, with the best will in the world in many ways, people like the World Business Council for Sustainable Development were talking about ecoefficiency and basically seeing that as the royal road to sustainability. But I was, I think a number of people were, worried that if you just take financial and environmental, or at least resource efficiency (which is basically what they were doing with the ecoefficiency concept), you were missing out on large clubs of wider sustainability agenda. You were missing out on the economic impacts that companies and business generally have. And you were certainly missing out on the social agenda. . . . That wasn't totally accidental. I think quite a number of multinational corporations, in particular US corporations, were quite spooked by the whole social agenda and actively steering away from it. So "triple bottom line" was very consciously business language, trying to get under the guard of business people. It's almost a Trojan horse trying to give them a sense that this was something that they wanted to play with and subscribe to. Once they started to use the language and commit to it to some degree, we could then define it in ways that could stretch their imaginations a little.

(Finfrock)

The *triple bottom line* may be a "Trojan horse" for sneaking the social and the environmental into the domain of the economic, but it is critical to note that this sleight of hand functions only because of the conceptual primacy necessarily afforded to the "bottom line" as its anchor. That is, at the rhetorical level, the bottom line is the protagonist, restructured in a tripartite modality only adjectivally, in analogy to the 1987 adjectival redefinition of development as a sustainable enterprise. Development and the bottom line—the former connoting the successful execution of capitalist programmatics, the latter constituting the quintessential metonym for the corporate business world's primary preoccupation with profit—are the stable discursive elements enjoying an "always already" status of a priori timelessness, whereas sustainability enters into the conceptual equation only indirectly as a variable modifier. As rhetorical artifacts of broadly held cultural priorities, sustainable development and the triple bottom line reflect the unparalleled status of business in the now global West, where the capitalist imperative has no rival.

It is perhaps for this reason that there is a marked David-and-Goliath motif in sustainability narrative. In the animated children's feature *Fern-Gully: The Last Rainforest* (1992), a city kid working a summer job marking trees to be felled becomes a literally diminutive hero when he must single-handedly save the rainforest from destruction despite having been shrunk to the size of a fairy. In the real-life story of *Erin Brockovich* (2000), the eponymous heroine (Julia Roberts) is an unconventional bottom-tier legal assistant cum environmental researcher who achieves the impossible in bringing a national power company to ecological and social justice. Mumble (Elijah Wood), the CGI-generated penguin protagonist of *Happy Feet* (2006), must traverse the open ocean alone in an epic bid to reverse the deleterious impact of fishing practices on the penguin food supply and thereby save his community—and species. A deleted scene from *Happy Feet* included on the DVD provides a concise visual portrait of this recurrent dynamic of heroism against the odds: having embarked courageously but not without trepidation on his journey, tiny Mumble collides with a giant black object that fills the entire screen, conveying a sense of immensity to the spectator. Frightened, Mumble reels backward. His seagull friend explains that this is a whale. Mumble wonders if, big as he is, the whale might not be able to talk to the "aliens," but the seagull answers that "even the whale" doesn't have the power to change their course. During this last line the perspective draws back to show the whale becoming smaller against a broader horizon of water, framing Mumble's challenge visually as one that is so vast as to be virtually infinite and insurmountable. We might think of this imagery on the scale of the infinite as a visual representation of what French economist and philosopher Serge Latouche calls "la idéologie de la croissance" ("the ideology of growth").

We may be tempted to read these films as trafficking in the kind of archetypal storytelling intentionally exploited by the likes of James Cameron, who professes an absolute faith in the appeal of the David-and-Goliath structure and deploys it with a sustainability theme in *Avatar* (2009) to great commercial effect. But a further consideration of sustainability cinema provides a less utopian counterpoint by reaffirming the enduring power of Goliath as against so many would-be Davids whose story did not have a happy ending. In the adaptation of another real-life story in *A Civil Action* (1998), trial lawyer Jan Schlichtmann (John Travolta)—

the financially triumphant Erin Brockovich's less fortunate foil—loses his house, his law firm, and his savings in a quest to avenge families that have lost their children to contaminated public water; Jan settles the case for comparatively modest damages and finds himself penniless for his efforts. *The Garden* (2008) documents the story of a predominantly Latino Los Angeles community that fights unsuccessfully to keep its urban garden from the hands of a single outside owner who ultimately razes the land without developing it—to date, it lies fallow. The documentary *Crude* (2009) traces the herculean efforts shouldered principally by the young Ecuadoran attorney Pablo Fajardo to bring Chevron—formerly Texaco— to justice for its contamination of the Amazon and the resultant disease of its inhabitants.[2] Texaco's tactics of stalling and stymieing the trial in endless litigation are represented in the shot of a room stuffed floor to ceiling and wall to wall with paper boxes that the Ecuadoran judge must read before proceeding; this proverbial sea of paperwork serves as the real-life analogue of Mumble's nearly infinite sea as a gargantuan obsta- cle—here expressed as corporate legal muscle—to the project of achiev- ing sustainability.

   It should be clear from these examples that the Goliath in every scenario is a venture that seeks profit as a single bottom line in isolation from any concern for people or planet, calling to mind the moment in *An Inconve- nient Truth* (2006) in which Al Gore presents the image of a scale loaded with gold bars on one side and the planet on the other. Although Gore turns this image into an opportunity to affirm the obvious—that gold bars are a ridiculous desideratum in the absence of a planet on which to possess them—it is nevertheless absolutely essential to note that Gore does not speak in concrete terms about how the gold bars are driving the planet toward en- vironmental apocalypse; where the category of profit is concerned, he does not move beyond the field of metaphor. Gore's documentary ends with a call to individual activism in line with the reduce-reuse-recycle-renew credo, but it does not call openly for reform of profit. In its assiduous efforts to avoid antagonizing cultural capitalist supports, sustainability discourse thus has the odd effect of casting the environment as the source of its own ills by virtue of effacing their human culprit. If we return to contemplate the 1987 United Nations Brundtland Commission Report (as it is more commonly known for the surname of its chair), we appreciate how the introductory language of its very motivating concern—"the accelerating deterioration of the human environment and natural resources and the consequences of that deterioration for economic and social development"—has the rhetorical effect of isolating the environment in the passive voice as the de facto agent of its own deterioration and, consequently, the author of any resultant human impact. In other words, the environmental crisis is discovered in medias res, as though it were an already advanced case of illness that might yet only be palliated rather than fully remedied, and for which, moreover, it is itself responsible. *FernGully,* for example, stages precisely this logic: the devastation of the rainforest is ascribed to a Machiavellian relationship between a machine called the "leveler" that cuts down and consumes trees and Hexxus, the force of destruction that the leveler sets loose because of human error. In this scenario humans are the accidental and unwitting culprits—and not the agents or intellectual masterminds—of this two-pronged evil between nature and machine. Nature harbors the seeds of its own infirmity and will drive itself toward death if given the opportunity; ecologically enlightened humans—as the tiny protagonist Zak becomes—can prevent nature from going into its own tailspin. Humans are not the culprits of environmental disaster, but only the unwitting aiders and abettors of nature's own tendency toward entropy. The logical connection between the environmental crisis and its root cause of profit-driven environmental plunder is thus persistently debilitated to the point of severance—even in the very gesture of its assertion, as we have seen in the rhetorical analysis of the triple bottom line.

U.S. politics and culture are complicit with economics on this point. In the domain of politics, the Republican Party arguably harbors the staunchest political defenders of the single bottom line and development on the globe; in this capacity it has systematically stonewalled the question of the environment. From George W. Bush's notorious 2005 refusal to join the one 140 national signatories of the Kyoto treaty on climate change—on the grounds that it would have "wrecked" the U.S. economy ("Bush: Kyoto Treaty Would Have Hurt Economy")—to the March 2011 determination of the Republican contingent of the Energy and Commerce Committee of the U.S. House of Representatives to vote against acknowledgment of the international scientific consensus on climate change (widely interpreted as a vote "against reality"; Madison), the Republican Party has taken the discursive tack of denying environmental deterioration altogether as a means of protecting the imperative of profit.

In the cultural domain, the "golden arrow of consumption"—as Annie Leonard terms it in her partially animated online educational video short "The Story of Stuff"—dominates as the corollary of profit:

The golden arrow of consumption . . . is the heart of the system [of the materials economy, from extraction to production to distribution to consumption to disposal], the engine that drives it. It is so important that protecting this arrow has become the top priority for [government and corporations]. That's why after 9/11 when our country was in shock and President Bush could have suggested any number of appropriate things—to grieve, to pray, to hope—no, he said to shop! To *shop*?!

We have become a nation of consumers. Our primary identity has become that of being consumers. Not mothers, teachers, farmers, but consumers. The primary way that our value is measured and demonstrated is by how much . . . we consume.

And do we! We shop and shop and shop. Keep the materials flowing! And flow they do. Guess what percentage of total materials flow through this system is still in product or use six months after their date of sale in North America. Fifty percent? Twenty? No! One percent. *One!* In other words, ninety-nine percent of all the stuff we harvest, mine, process, transport, ninety-nine percent of the stuff we run through the system is trashed within six months.

This narrative establishes an extended mirror-image equivalency between production, consumption, and disposal. Our waste, which takes over the planet in the tragicomic Pixar film *WALL·E* (2008), and is shown to have become a perverse yet veritable habitat for Brazilian *catadores* (recyclables pickers) in the documentary *Waste Land* (2010), is the very image in the negative—an abject portrait—of profit-based consumer culture. If there were no trash, there would be no consumption; if there were no consumption, no profit. No profit, no U.S. economy.

It is little wonder then, that Colin Beavan, a New York City-based ecological blogger and entrepreneur of sorts who undertakes a year-long effort to reduce his environmental footprint to zero, receives what he describes as "a rather large amount of, well, hate mail. Someone wants to spray [wife] Michelle and I [sic] with an uzi and get [daughter] Isabella adopted by Angelina Jolie, for example" ("Today Is Answer the Critics Day"). Beavan's public—but intentionally nonevangelizing—program of graduated resource consumption and waste reduction for himself and his family shakes the national sense of consumer-and-profit-based cultural identity so profoundly that he is accused of being un-American (as he discusses in his documentary film *No Impact Man*). This same accusation is made against "Story of Stuff" ideator Leonard, who ripostes: "Can we put capitalism back on the table [in the United States] and talk about it with the same intellectual rigor that we welcome for other topics? Can we examine the failures of capitalism without falling into generations-old stereotypes and without being accused of being un-American? . . . The belief that infinite economic growth is the best strategy for making a better world has become like a secular religion in which all our politicians, economists, and media participate; it is seldom debated, since everyone is just supposed to accept it as true" (*The Story of Stuff* xxii).

One of the ways that agents of capitalism avoid having it put back on the table for debate is through the mastery of a discourse that responds to the ecological critique of unsustainable practices with a language of sustainability. It is thus, for example, that the Natural Gas Alliance effectively sidesteps the denunciation of its environmental and social devastation within the bounds of the United States by the likes of the documentary film *GasLand* (2010) and "My Water's on Fire Tonight," a YouTube rap video on fracking—the destructive and chemical-laden technique for natural gas removal—made and posted by New York University students in May 2011, simply by counterdefining natural gas as "clean energy to protect our health and the environment" ("Why Natural Gas?"). The continued news coverage of rural residents' reports of methane water contamination, a "defensive" industry that refuses to accept responsibility, and undeterred plans to drill "as many as 10,000 new wells in the next few years" (Joyce) all stand counter to the claim that natural gas is a "clean" energy that "protect[s] our health and the environment."

In this same vein, Chevron—the sometime exploitative villain of the Ecuadoran people and environment according to *Crude*—casts itself as just the opposite in a tag on its YouTube channel: "At Chevron, we are relentlessly focused on producing safe, reliable energy now and for the future. How are we doing it? By applying the energy we have most in abundance: Human Energy." A series of advertisements in this "Human Energy" campaign and branding effort painstakingly associates Chevron with people and planet, not only completely eliding profit but quoting ciphers in the millions and billions of contributions made to communities and ecologically minded research. This current publicity campaign contrasts sharply with the 1970s-era Texaco advertisement (as the company that would be subsequently acquired by Chevron) embedded in *Crude*, which figures the company as an adventuresome force bravely, boldly—even nobly—penetrating the rest of the world in search of the oil necessary to fuel transportation at home in the United States.

Yet the change in its public discourse has not been accompanied by a change in position in the ongoing litigation over contamination of the Amazon. Chevron has resisted assuming responsibility for the contamination of land and the disease of human life in Ecuador, fighting for ten years to remove the case to the United States so as to ensure a more favorable legal climate, spending an undisclosed but significant amount in legal fees because even that sizable expenditure is negligible compared to the $18.1 billion in pollution damages awarded in February 2011 to the plaintiffs by an Ecuadoran judge, even briefly filing a RICO (Racketeer Influenced and Corrupt Organizations Act) suit against the plaintiffs. In a *Bloomberg Newsweek* cover story the following month, Paul M. Barrett notes the contradiction between Chevron's determination to resist concession to the complaint of contamination and its public face of global advertising discourse:

> "We're going to fight this until hell freezes over," [Chevron] spokesman Donald Campbell said in May 2009. "And then we'll fight it on the ice." This strategy makes perfect sense in financial terms. Even if Chevron is spending tens of millions of dollars a year on legal fees—a conservative estimate on which the company won't comment—the expenditure doesn't approach the annual interest on a potential multibillion-dollar payment to the plaintiffs. (The prolonged legal fight doesn't exactly sync with Chevron's current cross-media advertising campaign—launched in October 2010—promoting common ground it shares with people around the world. "Oil companies should support the communities they're a part of," one of the ads states.)

Barrett's rhetorical use of a suggestive pair of parentheses to bracket out Chevron's "people and planet" double-bottom-line strategy of public discourse signals the logical incompatibility of this campaign with Chevron's legal battle, which signals the single bottom line as its real and sustained practical concern. We might also understand these parentheses as signaling a greater divide: by placing public discourse in brackets as an aside, the author—albeit perhaps unintentionally—suggests a fundamental disjuncture between corporate practice and discourse wherein discourse is understood as a game of smoke and mirrors that comes to bear on the central question of economic practice only as an idle and nonbinding exercise of moral fact-checking.

Setting aside the empirical and legal question of Chevron's guilt in the Ecuadoran case of alleged contamination, the fact remains that there is a discursive battle in which Chevron is accused by its detractors of privileging the single bottom line at the merciless expense of people and planet, an accusation that Chevron counters with the assertion that people and planet are its sole concerns, a discourse of self-promotion in which profit figures only implicitly as a mechanism by means of which to support the double bottom line. This strategy rewrites *Crude*'s narrative of big oil making money hand over fist as it sacks the environment and exploits the little guys by recasting Chevron as a philanthropic benefactor of communities the world over and an altruistic developer of new environment-friendly knowledge. In defining its stewardship of people and planet as a negative outflow of money, Chevron beats the Trojan Horse strategy of the triple bottom line at its own game by expressly championing the two elements that most "spook" corporations: it discursively renounces profit in order to espouse—in a tone of noble self-sacrifice—a double bottom line founded on the paramount importance of the social and the environmental. Chevron's advertisements include a recurrent establishing shot of a human crowd that almost completely fills the frame before moving into more intimate portraits charged with the emotional language of togetherness and well-being: a mother holding an infant tenderly in arms, a middle-aged father and adult son on a slow tree-lined walk ("Tomorrow"), a young father gazing through the hospital glass at his newborn baby ("We Are Chevron Latin America"), a farmer carrying hay at sunset ("Conservation") and myriad other human images framed by urban and natural landscapes while a poignant piano melody sounds in the background, linking all the commercials in the series. By appropriating the discourse of sustainability as a venue for self-definition—"We ask you to join us in one of our most important efforts of our time: using less. Will you join us?"—Chevron positions itself not as an unwilling subscriber to, but rather as a driving force of the sustainability initiative. Corporate self-definitional discourse portrays all of humanity and nature in harmonious interrelation and organic well-being as an inevitable consequence of capitalist enterprise. Publicity thus becomes the space in which the triple bottom line becomes a fait accompli through the channels of discourse without dislodging the single bottom line from the foundation of corporate practice and consumer culture. More precisely, we could assert that pro-profit sustainability takes a strategically algebraic approach to the embrace of the triple bottom line: in public discourse, it seemingly disregards the question of profit altogether in order to affirm people and planet; profit, disappeared from this discursive side of the equation as a testament to the moral character of the pro-profit entity, is thus liberated to reappear with absolute impunity on the other side of the equation that sums up real-world practice. A double bottom line in discourse—beating the Trojan Horse at its own game—exonerates a single bottom line in practice.

Sustainability from the South

Over the past decade, and especially in the past few years, the sustainability discourse of the developed world has been making its way south, finding greatest traction in the most economically developed countries—among them, Mexico, Argentina, Brazil, and Chile. In some respects, this discourse appears to be the mirror image of its northern counterpart: the agents of profit are most visibly heading up the cause as one focused on the environment, and in which these entities are the altruistic champions of a reform that is beneficent but entirely optional in the sense that "corporate social responsibility"—the practical notion born of the "triple bottom line"—is a good deed and not a requirement.

Brazil's Petrobras multinational energy company, ranked thirtieth on the 2014 *Forbes* list of the world's biggest public companies ("*Forbes* Global 2000 Leading Companies"), has made sustainability part of its branding. In 2011 Petrobras claimed on its website, "We lead [the] sustainability ranking" of major Latin American energy companies; in 2013 it boasted its ninth consecutive year on the Dow Jones Sustainability Index and the launching of the Petrobras Environmental Social Program with an anticipated budget of $1.5 billion reales from 2014 to 2018 ("Investor Relations"). Petrobras's publicity spot "Era de Sustentabilidade" ("Era of Sustainability") strongly echoes Chevron's "Human Energy" campaign, with a script about the company's commitment to the environment and the people of Brazil against the backdrop images of Brazil's verdant farmland and a sampling of ethnically diverse—though always smiling—compatriots. Mirroring Chevron, Petrobras's website lays rhetorical claim to the double bottom line—that is, the humble deference of the motive of profit to the moral motives of society and the environment: "Our company's growth is directly linked to respect for the environment and to commitment to the [sic] society. . . . Acting with social and environmental responsibility, to us, is a commitment to people and to the planet" ("Environment and Society").[3] Like Chevron and Petrobras, Endesa Chile, the country's largest electric company that achieved quarterly revenue in the range of a hundred billion in April 2011, has publicly adopted a sustainability agenda. In 2002 Endesa Chile outlined principles of "Sustainable Business Development" for itself ("Desarrollo Sostenible Empresarial"), and in 2004 joined the United Nations Global Compact; since 2002 it has produced an annual "Sustainability Report" ("Informe de Sostenibilidad") in which environmental respect and social justice are thematically foregrounded (e.g., "Informe de Sostenibilidad 2008 de Endesa Chile").

As in the United States, this corporate social responsibility finds in current Latin American cultural discourse a companion imperative for individuals to "do their part" to "save the planet"—in Brazil, "Sustentabilidade—faça sua parte!" Blogged and journalistic definitions of sustainability in Brazil and Argentina reinforce this idea, just as in the United States, of sustainability as a predominantly environmental issue, and one to be remedied principally at the level of the individual (Abreu, Herrera Vegas). *Waste Land*, which chronicles Brazilian artist Vik Muniz's project of making portraits of the *catadores* in the São Paolo landfill—the biggest in the world in terms of daily volume—features a spontaneous monologue by one of the oldest recyclables pickers in which he argues that keeping even a single plastic bottle from entering the stagnant build-up of trash in the Earth's land and waterways is worth the effort: "Ninety-nine is not one hundred," Valter concludes, with great feeling. This could be the mantra of the sustainability discourse as an apology for development as a fixed aspect of the human condition. This is so because the "ninety-nine is not one hundred" credo positions the besieging of the environment as a natural—read: naturalized—state of affairs; as a consequence, it interprets that environmental agony as a found object and recommends its postcare as an individualized practice—*faça sua parte!* This proposal for the care of the earth on an individual level is tantamount to the global socialization of responsibility for the corporate-driven profit-consumption loop that has the world in a vise grip.

Whereas in the United States the conservative political party has rejected the sustainability agenda as an affirmation of big business, conservative pro-profit Latin American politics have begun to embrace the sustainable development agenda. Mexico has led the way. In 2007 Felipe Calderón, the politically conservative and free-market-friendly president of Mexico and former secretary of energy under his predecessor Vicente Fox, released a six-year "Plan Nacional de Desarrollo" in which one of the points was "Sustentabilidad Ambiental." A businessman and former national bank director, Calderón has mounted a sustainability narrative that resonates with Chevron and Petrobras, arguing in a 2008 presidential address that "to live better" ("vivir mejor") is to protect environmental resources and create jobs—once again, rhetorically privileging people and planet above profit ("Mensaje del Presidente Calderón en el marco de su Segundo Informe de Gobierno"). Calderón claims intellectual authorship on Mexico's behalf for the World Bank's creation of the Green Climate Fund for developing nations, approved in the Cancún Agreements following the 2010 United Nations Climate Talks held in the same city.

But there is another sustainability discourse in Latin America, one represented, for example, in the assertion that the World Bank Green Climate Fund is neither green nor trustworthy because of its continued pattern of financing fossil fuels and its lack of institutional democracy, responsibility, and transparency, as well as its North-heavy mechanisms of administration. One such article, Marwaan Macan-Markar's "En el fondo, el Banco Mundial no es verde" ("Deep Down, the World Bank Is Not Green") suggests that the World Bank is only "green" on the face of it and that a deeper analysis shows otherwise. This perspective is disseminated in an online news venue called *Otramérica*—a play on "Otra América," or, Another America, "de Sur a Norte," from the South to the North, in a pointed inversion of the standard North-South directionality that connotes the hierarchy of power between the regions. It is worth examining the rhetorical mechanism by means of which Macan-Markar communicates this critique: whereas the charge of unsalutary fossil-fuel financing is made directly, the charge of an antidemocratic, irresponsible, and opaque North-heavy institutional character is made indirectly through the description of desirable institutionality, but in the hypothetical voice as an institutionality not yet having come into being:

"La financiación es parte de las reparaciones de la deuda climática que deben los países ricos e industrializados a los pueblos y países del Sur", dijo Ahmed Swapan, de Jubileo [Sur].

"La deuda climática debe ser reunida, administrada y entregada por una institución que sea democrática, responsable, transparente, y gobernada por una junta que tenga mayoría del Sur", añadió.

("The financing is part of the reparations of the climate debt that wealthy and industrialized countries owe to the peoples and the countries of the South," said Ahmed Swapan, of Jubilee [South].

"The climate debt should be gathered, administrated, and disbursed by an institution that is democratic, responsible, transparent, and governed by a board that has a majority from the South," he added.)

This rhetorical construction of an as yet unfulfilled but desirable alternative to reality may rightfully seem to be a common enough strategy of expression, yet I would argue that it is broadly symptomatic of Latin American political and cultural discourse, which, since Independence forward, could be characterized as having been in search of—but never achieving—social utopia, with cultural production in the earliest effervescent years of the Cuban Revolution constituting a sole and short-lived exception.

An explanation for this trope of an eternal—and eternally unsatisfied—utopia-to-come is to be had in the comprehension of Latin America as an economic neocolony from the moment of its very independence forward. The thesis of British informal imperialism—the "imperialism of free trade," as its ideators John Gallagher and Ronald Robinson termed it in 1953—holds that from the nineteenth century onward, in the wake of the first-wave independence movements and the coeval birth of free-market capitalism, British imperialism was informal and economic in the first regard and was only formalized when the cultural and political supports of a given region were not sufficiently strong to protect those economic interests. In this view Latin America's nineteenth-century relationship to Britain should be considered analogous to that of Asia and Africa. The formal colonization of the Asia and Africa should not, in the argument of this thesis, distract from the informal colonization that dominated Latin America in a fundamentally economic relationship common to all three continents vis-à-vis Britain. The logic of this tricontinental relationship was culturally salient in the revolutionary ethos of the 1960s, particularly in the form of Cuba's alignment in the broader name of Latin America with the decolonizing countries of Asia and Africa following its U.S.-driven expulsion from the Organization of American States in 1962 and in the subsequent founding of the "Tricontinental" journal and the corollary 1966 Havana convention by the same name. But, in the ensuing decades of military intervention and neoliberal economic politics, this logic of a common intercontinental circumstance between Latin America, Asia, and Africa was lost.

It has only been in the past decade that this sensibility has resurfaced in the new rubric of the *Global South,* a term meant to denote, precisely, Latin America, Asia, and Africa as regions suffering from a comparative underdevelopment with respect to their Northern continental counterparts. This nomenclature seems to have been born of United Nations discussions in the mid-1990s in its Dialogue with the Global South program, for example, in which it establishes relationships with universities in the "developing countries" of Asia, Africa, and Latin America. The Indiana University Press journal by the same name, the *Global South,* echoes this geographical understanding of a bipolar North-South world, defining itself since its appearance in 2007 as "concentrat[ing] on the literature and cultures of those parts of the world that have experienced the most political, social, and economic upheaval and have suffered the brunt of the greatest challenges facing the world under globalization: poverty, displacement and diaspora, environmental degradation, human and civil rights abuses, war, hunger, and disease" (Project Muse, "Global South").

In the 1960s the binding force of the "tricontinental" relationship between Asia, Africa, and Latin America was a common struggle against imperialism, with Asia and Africa struggling against the fact of formal colonization and Latin America struggling against neoimperialism by the United States, as expressed, for example, in Che Guevara's famous final call from the Bolivian jungle for Latin America to rise up as "two, three, many Vietnams" ("dos, tres, muchos Vietnam"). Now, the contemporary rubric of the *Global South* recuperates that continental triumvirate from the point of view of the global distribution of wealth and resources. Jubilee South, a nonprofit organization founded in the same years that the United Nations began to speak of a Global South, had as its central mission the cancelation of third world debt by the year 2000, the organization's name referencing the biblical concept of a fifty-year Jubilee cycle in which slaves were liberated, debt forgiven, and land reappropriated. The aforementioned critique of the World Bank's Green Climate Fund by a representative, precisely, of Jubilee South takes the position that these monies should be conceived of as tantamount to such reparations, on the dependency theory–minded premise that the developed countries of the North have been submitting the developing countries of the South to the sustained pillage of their resources—"our stuff on someone else's land"—for decades and even centuries.[4]

If there is, as seen in the examples of Calderón, Petrobras, and Endesa, a pro-profit Latin American sustainability discourse, then this alternative antiprofit Latin American sustainability discourse is best understood as the contemporary avatar of the dependency theory of old—a contemporary platform for the agenda of mid-century revolution. This perspective helps to elucidate why an online Chilean magazine devoted to the blog-style exposition of "green" product design and consumerism, would nevertheless be entitled "Greenade," a set of energy-efficient lightbulbs topped with grenade caps serving as its homepage banner.

If it is tempting to dismiss this example as the facile co-optation of subversive discourse by commercial forces, then we might consider the political evolution of a contestatory figure such as Fernando "Pino" Solanas. Codirector with Octavio Getino of the classic New Latin American Cinema documentary *La hora de los hornos* (The Hour of the Furnaces, 1968), part didactic exposition of the theory of neocolonialism—the informal economic domination of Latin America first by Britain and then by the United States, with the complicity of the native Creole dominant class—and part open exhortation to guerrilla revolutionary violence, Solanas traces this neocolonialism to the influence of the IMF- and World Bank–driven economic neoliberalism of the intervening years first in military dictatorship and then in the Carlos Menem years in *Memoria del saqueo* (2004). Now Solanas heads up an alternative leftist Argentine political party, Proyecto Sur ("Project South"), whose name extends beyond Argentina to echo in its unadorned privileging of the South as a symbolic geography the Jubilee South call for South-South alternatives to economies dominated by the North.

Solanas defines Proyecto Sur as "una fuerza verde, y, como tal, la protección del medio ambiente es uno de nuestros pilares fundamentales" ("a green force, and, as such, the protection of the environment is one of our fundamental pillars"; InfoSur). The protection of the environment in this context is linked directly to the industry that creates the crisis—in sharp contrast to the Northern trope of environmental devastation as a found object—with Solanas's central objections being to the destruction of Argentina's glaciers for the extraction of precious metals by the Canadian company Barrick Gold and the deforestation produced by the expanding monoculture of genetically modified soy and its attendant pesticides, over both of which the agribusiness giant Monsanto has a monopoly. With respect to the latter, Solanas has made his battle cry "ni un metro más de soja" ("not another meter of soy"; "Ni un metro más de soja"]), and Proyecto Sur has adopted the slogan "Por un programa agrario que armonice producción, población y medio ambiente con equidad y distribución" ("For an agrarian program that harmonizes production, population, and environment with equity and distribution"). Solanas takes the triple bottom line (production, population, and environment) and adds two further terms (equity and distribution) that gesture toward the horizontal redefinition of profit as a benefit to the lowest, rather than the highest, agents in the chain of production. Under the new guise of sustainability, Solanas most fundamentally retreads the old notion of nationalized resources as a hemispheric patrimony of ecology, thereby completing the conceptual concatenation of dependency theory with sustainability discourse as its new iteration.

This equation of mid-century dependency theory with the contemporary sustainability agenda achieves its most explicit Latin American political expression in the discourse of Evo Morales, the first indigenous president of Bolivia and one of few in all of Latin American postindependence history. In his first major address to the United Nations in 2006, Morales outlines the difference between *vivir bien* ("living well") and *vivir mejor* ("living better"; "General Debate Statement"), which he has since developed conceptually into a "doctrine" and a "practice" that positions itself squarely as an alternative to capitalism, as the title of a 2011 edited scholarly volume on the same theme, inspired by Morales's politics, makes clear: *Vivir bien: ¿Paradigma no capitalista?* (Farah H. and Vasapollo). In this light, Felipe Calderón's definition of *vivir mejor* as protecting the environment and creating jobs comes clearly into view as a defensive response to Morales's original definition of *vivir mejor* as the capitalist way of life. In stark contrast to the pro-profit position of sustainability propounded by Calderón, Morales outlines an antiprofit countermodel, a model of sufficiency as against prosperity:

> Mientras los Pueblos Indígenas proponen para el mundo el "Vivir Bien", el capitalismo se basa en el "Vivir Mejor". Las diferencias son claras: El vivir mejor significa vivir a costa del otro, explotando al otro, saqueando los recursos naturales, violando a la Madre Tierra, privatizando los servicios básicos; en cambio el Vivir Bien es vivir en solidaridad, en igualdad, en armonía, en complementariedad, en reciprocidad. En términos científicos, desde el marxismo, desde el leninismo dice: socialismo-capitalismo; y nosotros sencillamente decimos: el vivir bien y el vivir mejor.
>
> [Whereas the Indigenous Peoples propose "Living Well" for the world, capitalism is based in "Living Better." The differences are clear:

living better means living at the expense of the other, exploiting the other, pillaging natural resources, violating [raping] Mother Earth, privatizing basic services; in contrast, Living Well is to live in solidarity, in equality, in harmony, in complementarity, in reciprocity. In scientific terms, from the point of view of Marxism, or of Leninism, [this binary is referenced as]: socialism-capitalism; we say, simply: living well and living better.]

(Farah H. and Vasapollo 9)

Like Venezuela's Hugo Chávez, who, on his first meeting with Barack Obama in 2009, gave the U.S. president a copy of Eduardo Galeano's *Las venas abiertas de América Latina* (*Open Veins of Latin America*), the classic 1971 exposition of dependency theory, Morales's definition of terms makes clear his vision of *vivir bien* as the conceptual heir apparent to the Marxist dependency theory of old, coinciding with Chávez in signaling the continued relevance of dependence theory, yet opting for a new terminology.

What is to be gained in Morales's terminological passage? It is striking that Morales should so vertebrally cast the political opposition in the affective terms of a relationship—between self-aggrandizing self and abject other, in the case of capitalism, and, in the case of "living well," the simple community of an undivided "we." Morales overwhelmingly characterizes the profit-driven behavior of the self-aggrandizing capitalist self as behavior that is reprehensible because it is hurtful (living at the expense of the other, exploiting the other, violating Mother Earth); he goes on to call agents of capitalism "los señores de la muerte" ("the lords of death"; Farah H. and Vasapollo 10). In contrast, the program of *vivir bien* is idealized in terms that connote systemic health and well-being within a single yet collective—multitudinous—organic whole (harmony, complementarity, reciprocity); it is this model and only this model that can, Morales avers, "salvar a la humanidad" ("save humanity"; Farah H. and Vasapollo 10). Political judgment also becomes affective in its fundamental mechanism of collecting evidence through sensory perception and performing analysis through feeling: "Nuestros ojos y corazones lo ven y lo sienten . . . : el capitalismo es el peor enemigo de la humanidad" ("Our eyes and our hearts see it and feel it . . . : capitalism is the worst enemy of humanity"; Farah H. and Vasapollo 10).

The political language that Morales favors for the expression of dependence theory in the era of all-out neoliberalism is one that is rooted in the epistemic logic of homeostatic affect: of ill-being (*vivir mejor*) versus well-being (*vivir bien*). This is the logic that comes to the fore in Morales's act of terminological translation; this is the epistemic angle privileged by the translation, the conceptual vocabulary that, for Morales, has the greatest relevance and resonance. Morales himself may not reflect in these terms on his own discourse and might argue that it is simply the most adequate expression of indigenous life. But the present study seeks to show that this same epistemic anchor of a homeostatic contest between ill-being and well-being is what unites sustainability discourse across regions and across circumstance. Pro-profit sustainability discourse defines itself as an agent of well-being, treating ill-being as an exogenous and contingent reality; antiprofit sustainability discourse accuses pro-profit capitalism of inflicting ill-being on people and world, and positions itself to recuperate that compromised well-being. Where regional difference comes into play, as we shall see, is in how North and South represent their own potential to defeat what they diagnose as capitalist ill-being and to inaugurate a functional—real—model of sustainable well-being.

Affect and Un/Happy Endings to North-South Antiprofit Sustainability Narrative

In their 2005 music video "Madre hay una sola" (There Is Only One Mother), the well-known Argentine rock group Bersuit Vergarabat gives us just such an example of antiprofit sustainability discourse, which we may fruitfully analyze in the affective dimension. Founded in 1989 and active in the intervening two decades, Bersuit Vergarabat—whose nonsensical name online Argentine rock lore explains as a declaration of musical freedom—initially positions itself as a critic of democratic culture and its neoliberal bent. Their defining 1992 song "El tiempo no para" (Time Doesn't Stop), a cover of the 1988 "O tempo não pára" by the Brazilian artist Cazuza, posits the meaningless repetition of history, the futility of resistance, and the faceless pillage of the nation. Like Solanas's work and politics over the years, Bersuit Vergarabat's music asserts an equivalent national historiography of destruction and theft, effectively suggesting a seamless continuum between their initial resistance to postdictatorial neoliberalism—that is, neoliberalism as another aspect of dictatorship—and their subsequent critique of the devastation of the earth.

"Madre hay una sola" is a veritable manifesto of sustainability from the South inflected by the reverberations of dependency theory, but also by affect. In the video of "Madre hay una sola" the members of the Bersuit Vergarabat appear wearing oxygen masks and funereal expressions while playing their instruments in the clearing of a forest. A concept-establishing close-up of unnaturally dark sap oozing down the side of a tree gives the impression that the trees are crying black tears of toxicity. A subsequent shot of a young personification of Mother Nature nursing a baby in a madonna-and-child pose reveals a tear of milk running down her face as the wailing baby falls off the—again, unnaturally—nippleless breast; Mother Nature has been rendered incapable of nurturing life. A red cloud passes above the trees and rains as though the sky were bleeding, covering the people below in its blood. A princely figure reminiscent of East Asian myth, adorned with a gold crown and a necklace of flowers—perhaps further evidence of the contemporary current of South-South solidarity—stands in saddened harmony with the forest only to be pictured later lying in death, his eyes covered with coins, an impotent lover of the earth laid to rest. An angel of nature unfurls beautiful black wings against a vibrant dress only to be shown naked and wingless thereafter, with freshly sutured incisions where her wings were; some moments later, where the lyrics reference gluttony, an unapologetically lascivious man crouches over her, rubbing his hands together as he contemplates her nude, defenseless, and virtually lifeless form, in a stance of predatory pleasure and insatiable greed. These archetypal characters are theatrically stylized in their symbolic attire or high-contrast coloring, but there is also another set of characters in quick gray-tone succession that would seem to represent, together, a composite everyman from young to old enveloped by sorrow: several bury their heads in their hands; one wanders through the forest speaking to himself, his eyes wide in shock and his palms outstretched as though in grieving disbelief.

Although there is one image of a chainsaw being swung violently toward a tree, in clear reference to deforestation, the video does not make further accusations—much less create a full inventory—of concrete ecological ills. Rather, the representation of the environmental crisis assumes almost entirely metaphorical dimensions. This extended image of nature in its death throes is the visual counterpart of the song's central assertion that progress and prosperity run counter to vitality. In using these two terminological pillars of capitalist ideology to indicate the primary cause of the environmental devastation, the song suggests—echoing Morales—that the death of the natural world is the direct and ultimate consequence of capitalism. In the simplest terms, the fundamental denunciation of the music video is that capitalism drives inexorably toward death. This view of capitalism casts it as a neocolonial force of linear and vertical greed and plunder, dispossessed of empathy and perfectly immoral, in resonance with the characterization and analysis in the 2003 Canadian documentary film *The Corporation* of corporate capitalism as psychopathy according to the standards established by the World Health Organization and in the American Psychiatric Association's *Diagnostic and Statistical Manual of Mental Disorders. The Corporation* alleges the following about the "personality of the corporate 'person'" (for the corporation has enjoyed the legal status of personhood under the Fourteenth Amendment since the late nineteenth-century era of post–Civil War Reconstruction): "it is self-interested, inherently amoral, callous and deceitful; it breaches social and legal standards to get its way; it does not suffer from guilt, yet it can mimic the human qualities of empathy, caring and altruism. . . . The institutional embodiment of laissez-faire capitalism," the film's online written synopsis concludes, "fully meets the criteria of a 'psychopath.'"

The public discourse of corporations indeed performs—mimics—the human qualities of empathy, caring, and altruism by creating, as we have already seen, a "double bottom line" that disingenuously masks the question of profit by selectively focusing on humanity in the environment. This portrait depicts humanity in robust health and thriving, interconnected with one another and with the earth through the corporation as a facilitator of that well-being. The critique of the corporation, then, is to posit, in the same conceptual vocabulary, precisely its failure to produce well-being. The denunciation of neoliberalism as a force that sickens, renders infirm, takes life, plunders, and destroys, effectively alleges that capitalism is a bearer only of ill-being.

What is critical to note is that this denunciation makes a crucial—though apparently unconscious—distinction between agent and discourse of capitalism. That is, the critique damns the capitalist agent but does not reject—through deconstruction, demystification, or any other form of conceptual skepticism—the epistemological discourse foundational to capitalism itself as a model of knowledge of self and world. Just as neither the Jubilee South representative, quoted earlier, nor Morales rejects democracy as a political category, but only its aberrant Northern iteration, neither—in all rigor—rejects capitalist discourse in its epistemic dimension. This is not a conscious rescue; in fact, it is, on the face of it, completely antithetical to their contestatory positions. Yet if we accept the view of homeostatic organicity as the epistemic vehicle of both capitalism and liberal democracy as economic and political counterparts, then we appreciate that nowhere in their critique is this epistemic vehicle challenged. On the contrary, the harmonious self-regulation of the body on the nonrational principle of affective order—or, to put it more simply, order as somatic-affective well-being—is overwhelmingly reaffirmed with full credence in the fundamental vision of human order as one derived from the principle of well-being. The most radical sustainability discourse—South-on-South sustainability discourse—posits itself as the antithesis of capitalism, but unwittingly assumes the discursive position of the true steward of originary free-market epistemology. In other words, sustainability discourse takes capitalism to task for failing to fulfill its originary promise—for betraying that promise in the adoption of a counterdiscourse of kleptocratic neocolonial expansionism in a practice of massive theft and deception—and proposes to make good, itself, on that originary model of well-being. There is an epistemological premium on well-being such that all competing discourses battle one another for the power of legitimacy to define it. The present intervention argues, simply, that it is not on empirical or ontological terms that well-being is at stake in this discursive contest. That is, it is not the reality of well-being that makes it such a prize, but rather its discursive status as the conceptually synthetic synecdoche of capitalism itself. To control the discourse of well-being is to intervene decisively, definitively, into the very history and fate of capitalism.

Returning to the comparative analysis of North-South sustainability discourse, we might summarize by arguing that each region engages in profit-friendly (pro-capitalist) and profit-averse (anticapitalist) sustainability discourse. The difference between the profit-friendly discourses of the North and South seems to be negligible, although if we were to put a fine point on the analysis we would have to inquire in greater depth about the embrace of sustainability from the corporate-state sector in Latin America, largely free of the pro forma conservative ideological resistance to sustainability that marks U.S. politics. Does the U.S. political resistance to sustainability secure freedom of profit for the rest of the free-market world by ensuring that the double bottom line will never move significantly beyond the bounds of discourse to threaten the practical reality of a single bottom line? Or does the lack of a conservative antisustainability Latin American analogue suggest that even the pro-profit Latin American sector shares, to an extent, sympathies with the South-South agenda of resistance? Mexico's resistance over the past five years to pressure exerted by Monsanto to penetrate the national corn industry with its genetically modified seed, all in the face of a persistent shortage and the annual importation of millions of tons of corn, may signal that even a neoliberal presidency harbors some sensitivity to what a more radical news source calls a question of "soberanía alimentaria o dependencia" ("nutritional sovereignty or dependency") in an adjectival adaptation of the notion of economic neocolonialism to the contemporary circumstance of global agribusiness (Acedo). Regardless, the discursive expression of a double bottom line that strategically represses the reality of profit and lays claim to the conceptual category of well-being is common to corporations and free-market-friendly governments in both regions and overwhelmingly the norm. Despite geography, sustainability lays claim to the epistemological position of capitalist discourse and its basic principle of homeostatic well-being.

Antiprofit sustainability discourse also shares a fundamental commonality across regions. This common gesture is the foundational critique of capitalism's ill-executed practice of its ideals—the accusation that a practical reality of ill-being underlies, and thus gives the lie to, capitalism's discursive claims of well-being. Again, we must note in our analysis that this corrective does not abandon those ideals themselves, but rather positions itself—even if not self-consciously—to recuperate an originary model gone awry.

There is, on the other hand, a significant regional difference between the profit-averse discourses. Their point of divergence is that Northern discourse tends to build toward a triumphalist salvation from that ill-being in the form of sustainable well-being, whereas the South tends toward the formulation of such a utopia as a deferred or even extinguished possibility, contemplating instead a proximate and inexorable reality of the full and definitive triumph of capitalist ill-being as social, environmental, and planetary death.

"The Story of Stuff," for example, in spite of its unflinchingly bleak portrait of ill-being, nevertheless ends with a surge of optimism around the idea of reversing cultural course to achieve sustainable well-being. The audiovisuals of this final upswing are the greening and dynamic circular rendering of a black linear materials economy along with the upbeat percussive music and an emphatic optimism in the tone with which Annie Leonard delivers her closing exhortation to join the ranks of sustainable activism in the last minute and a half of her twenty-minute exposition:

So you see, it *is* a system in crisis [in the background, a linear five-part graphic representation of the materials economy: extraction, production, distribution, consumption, disposal]. All along the way we are bumping up against limits, from changing climate to declining happiness. It's just not working. But the good thing about such an all-pervasive problem is that there are so many points of intervention. There are people working here [signals drawing of the planet] on saving forests, and here [signals factory symbol] on clean production, people working on labor rights and fair trade and conscious consuming and blocking landfills and incinerators, and—*very* importantly—on taking back our government so that it really is by the people and for the people.

All of this work is critically important, but things are really going to start moving when we see the connections—when we see the big picture. When people along the system get united, we can reclaim and transform [linear system moves into pattern of circular connected by arrows, its color changing from black to green as it makes this change] this linear system into something new, a system that doesn't waste resources or people. Because what we really need to chuck is that old school throw-away mindset. There's a new school of thinking on this stuff and it's based on sustainability and equity, green chemistry, zero waste, closed-loop production, renewable energy, local living economies. It's already happening. Now some say it's unrealistic, idealistic, that it can't happen. But I say that the ones who are unrealistic are those that want to continue with the old path [energetic percussive music begins]. *That's* dreaming. Remember, that old way didn't just happen. It's not like gravity that we've just got to live with. People created it, and we're people too! So let's create something new [drums and funk guitar kick in full swing to accompany credits].

("The Story of Stuff")

In opposition to the bloated corporate model of the profit-driven linear materials economy, Leonard creates the rhetorical first-person plural category of a "we" whose ideal dimensions are implicitly on the scale of humanity itself. This collective protagonist on a grand scale will be guided by the operative principle of the internal harmony of an interconnected system as embodied in the rerendering in vital green and dynamic movement of the materials economy. This model is akin to Serge Latouche's notion of *décroissance* ("degrowth"), except that where Latouche insists on the status of *décroissance* as a slogan—but not yet a concrete alternative—for rethinking a postprogress model that may yet save the South ("Et la décroissance sauvera le Sud . . . "), Leonard asserts a more Northern point of view: that sustainability is not just an idea; it is a fact and a plan *already* in effect. On the epistemic level, the representation of this claim in the language of homeostatic capitalism itself has the effect of legitimizing its discursive power of substitution. By casting capitalism in its linear, pro-profit aspect and appropriating its discourse of homeostatic well-being, "The Story of Stuff" casts sustainability as a cultural politics of well-being that can outdo capitalism's pretensions of the same not only in the utopian mode of counterfactual idealization, but in reality itself.

In contrast, the lyrics and audiovisuals of "Madre hay una sola" do not build upward toward any solution of sustainability but rather descend deeper and deeper into the inevitability of neoliberal-driven death—of humanity, of the planet. To be sure, the song and video evince a conception of social protagonism in totalizing dimensions of collectivity analogous to "The Story of Stuff"—the song references a shame to be part of this "species" that destroys the earth; the video creates the composite everyman already discussed. Yet here there is no hope for the restoration of well-being; only the steady accusation, as though in a downward spiral, of its toxic and ultimately fatal lack. Whereas "The Story of Stuff" ends on the note of what we might consider, for the sake of contrast, a percussive heartbeat—the audio connotation of life and health—"Madre hay una sola" ends with a spare melancholy guitar melody in the minor key and frames its extended lamentation with the image of disease and death. In addition to the symbolic use of oxygen masks by the band's members and the signs of decay of the trees and Mother Nature herself, the video also opens and closes with the image of a blood-red heart impaled on a pole and abandoned to the elements in a literal rendition of the "mortal attack on the center of [Mother Earth's] heart." Thus, although "Madre hay una sola" adopts the same critical position as "The Story of Stuff," there is no redemption of the homeostatic principle of well-being through sustainability as a viable—much less real, in the sense of already extant—alternative to capitalism. In a cynical helplessness that mirrors the neocolonial subject position of terminally compromised sovereignty, the Southern antiprofit perspective on sustainability discourse does not signal any escape from the fate that pro-profit capitalist development has imposed on the world. The song and video cast that fate in the very terms of capitalist discourse by turning them on their head. Whereas capitalism promises well-being for the species—and, in sustainability discourse, for the planet—this critique asserts species and planet as a dying co-organism (indeed, the oxygen masks appear to connect the humans to the earth) whose internal homeostatic system has been mortally overrun by forces of plunder and consequent disease.

Sustainability Is All Heart and No Brain

A statement written for the Guggenheim Museum on the theme of "progress" by Colin Beavan, our unlikely protagonist of the self-ideated and self-executed experiment in leaving no environmental footprint for a full year—no meat, no electricity, no trash—in the middle of Manhattan, gives us perfect grist for our theoretical mill of affect and its relationship to sustainability discourse. Beavan's statement redefines progress as a function of people over "stuff," as Leonard would call it, arguing that advances in technological gadgets like cell phones is not "progress," but rather advances in technology for humanitarian ends, like producing clean drinking water:

> I would give up my secondhand Blackberry [sic] and any other cell phone I've had or will have if it would mean no one died of thirst. I think most people feel that way. People have big hearts.
> . . . What would be real progress?
> When we find a way to put our brains where our hearts are. When we find a way to use our big brains to facilitate the desires of our big hearts.
>
> ("How Is the Idea of Progress")

Beavan's characterization of the sustainability dilemma as a clash between two different applications—indeed, vertices—of technological research and development resonates, most likely unintentionally, with the Latin American revolutionary discourse of the 1960s influenced by and often coterminous with dependency theory. An example that brings us back to the origins of the film director turned political hopeful who has now gone "green"— understanding the sustainability platform as the most authentic and viable expression of leftism for the twenty-first century—is the canonical New Latin American Cinema manifesto published by Solanas and Getino in 1969, "Hacia un Tercer Cine" ("Toward a Third Cinema"). In this manifesto they argued that disciplines of knowledge—technologies—had to be wrested away from capitalist ends and redirected to the broader social good. This is exactly the argument that Beavan makes by casting the obstacle to achieving sustainability as an excessive dedication of technological research and development to the objective of making better cell phones for the relative few rather than to finding a way to give clean drinking water to the many.

There is, Beavan suggests, a moral application of technology toward human well-being on a planetary scale and an immoral application of technology toward the advancement of cell phones. Beavan does not spell out his intended symbolism of the cell phone, which grants him the safety of the same profit-neutral stance of which Gore avails himself in *An Inconvenient Truth*. But Beavan's audience readily understands the greater whole symbolized by the cell phone to be that of Leonard's culture of stuff, the unending consumption-profit matrix that is unendingly vertical in the sense of being a ceaseless quest for more—in Morales's words, "la obtención de más y más ganancia por sobre todas las cosas" ("the obtaining of more and more profit above all else") and "el consumo sinfín [sic]" ("endless consumption"; Farah H. and Vasapollo 10). Against this consumption-profit matrix stands the well-being of the rest of the world, in an echo of Gore's scales balancing gold bars against the planet itself. The ill-being of the rest of the world—the death from thirst and diarrhea for lack of clean drinking water that Beavan evokes—may not be caused by the relentless quest to improve cell phones, but the idea is that it is perpetuated by a misguided focus of attention and energies of the developed world. A misguided set of priorities that may not set out to be immoral, but becomes immoral even if only through ignorance, recalling the message in *FernGully* that humans can save nature (from itself) through an ecologically oriented self-reeducation.

This reeducation would allow people to comprehend the production of cell phones as a luxury fetish, and, in stark contrast, the production of clean drinking water as a basic human right and necessity. Beavan's statement brings the populous Global South into view, arguing that its fate depends on the contest between consumerism and sustainability, and, by speaking in the first-person plural, implicitly indicating that the fate of the preponderant minority is the fate of humanity itself. Once again, human survival— life over death—is the central concern here. The impediment to choosing sustainability over consumption lies in the rationalized valorization of the wrong technology ("The people we are proud of for having the smartest brains work, not on water, but on bringing us still better cell phones."). Having "big hearts," being "good," and choosing clean drinking water are all equivalent terms in Beavan's moral mathematics. "Big brains" and cell phones lie on the opposite end of the moral spectrum, yet Beavan does not assign blame. The adjectival recrimination that logically completes the comparison is not forthcoming; no one is "bad." Beavan gently diagnoses the problem as one of misguided priorities by essentially good people who have allowed their hearts to be eclipsed by their heads. In repurposing the code word of capitalist modernity—progress—Beavan suggests internal reform rather than extrasystemic revolution, echoing the rhetoric of Gore and, especially, the Obama administration, where they advance a vision of the same economic structure with new content—that is, throwing out the neoliberal baby in exchange for a sustainable one, but keeping the bathwater of capitalism.

Beavan's statement brings to the fore the rhetorical postulation of sustainability as heartfelt and collectivist altruism as against rationalized and selfish capitalist materialism. The alignment of our brains with reason in what is, in the final analysis, the rational pursuit of consumption-driven profit—"looking for a way to bring better TV reception to our cell phones"—satisfies the intellect and the desire to possess, but it does not satisfy the heart. The heart here has not the slightest association with whimsy or caprice, but rather carries all the gravitas of life and death, insofar as Beavan defines a "big heart" as one that would willingly sacrifice its cell phone to ward off the untimely demise of the world's children. The alignment of our brains with affect rather than reason is what will usher in the era of sustainability, here a morally charged category. Wresting the concept of "progress" away from its steeped cultural signification of capitalist accumulation and production in order to reemploy it in the discursive service of global sustainability, in which the only "profit" is better health and longer life, Beavan concludes that we will arrive at "real progress"—a qualification that implicitly denounces our standing ideologically informed notion of progress as false—when we accomplish an epistemological shift— "[w]hen we find a way to put our brains where our hearts are. When we find a way to use our big brains to facilitate the desires of our big hearts." To achieve moral sustainability, we must, in Beavan's formulation, achieve sustainable morality: we must give the brain—the organic agent of rational progress—over to the heart.

This downward movement of the brain constitutes a new iteration of mind-body dualism that does away with the association between brain and transcendent rational mind and instead imagines the brain as part of a somatic continuum dominated by feeling. But this is not simply soft feeling of the private and sentimental variety; it has the semantic teeth of full politicization. The heart represents a morally charged political position of support for the survival of the Global South over the material gluttony of the developed Global North and a determination to work consciously and deliberately—rationally—against the fatalities of poverty. This rational determination, however, is decidedly packaged and transmitted in affective terms. Politics emerge as an entirely organic matter in which emotion is cast as the ultimate judge of morality and, therefore, of principled—rational—social action.

Beavan's substitution of heart for brain as the basis for developing a new social compact based on altruistic empathy rather than selfish intellectualism effectively updates the eighteenth-century utilitarian discourse for the twenty-first century. In *A Treatise of Human Nature* (1739), David Hume makes an analogous claim privileging affect ("the passions") over reason as the primary motor of human action:

> Nothing is more usual in philosophy, and even in common life, than to talk of the combat of passion and reason, to give the preference to reason, and assert that men are only so far virtuous as they conform themselves to its dictates. Every rational creature, it is said, is obliged to regulate his actions by reason; and if any other motive or principle challenge the direction of his conduct, he ought to oppose it, till it be entirely subdued, or at least brought to a conformity with that superior principle. On this method of thinking the greatest part of moral philosophy, antient and modern, seems to be founded; nor is there an ampler field, as well for metaphysical arguments, as popular declamations, than this supposed pre-eminence of reason above passion. The eternity, invariableness, and divine origin of the former have been displayed to the best advantage: The blindness, unconstancy, and deceitfulness of the latter have been as strongly insisted on. In order to shew the fallacy of all this philosophy, I shall endeavor to prove first, that reason can never be a motive to any action of the will; and secondly, that it can never oppose passion in the direction of the will.

Hume goes on to explain that it is only the passions that can affect the will through the "prospect of pain or pleasure," generating a "consequent emotion of aversion or propensity" that becomes an impulse to action; it is only here that reason enters on the scene to guide that impulse toward realization. Reason alone, Hume argues, does not give rise to action. It is in this context that Hume makes his famous assertion that "reason is, and ought only to be, the slave of the passions, and can never pretend to any other office than to serve and obey them" (II.iii).

Forty years later, in the opening lines of *The Principles of Morals and Legislation* (1780), Jeremy Bentham dispenses with Hume's apologetic preamble and launches straight into a decisive recapitulation of the same thesis:

> Nature has placed mankind under the governance of two sovereign masters, *pain* and *pleasure*. It is for them alone to point out what we ought to do, as well as to determine what we shall do. On the one hand the standard of right and wrong, on the other the chain of causes and effects, are fastened to their throne. They govern us in all we do, in all we say, in all we think: every effort we can make to throw off our subjection, will serve but to demonstrate and confirm it. In words a man may pretend to abjure their empire: but in reality he will remain subject to it all the while. The *principle of utility* recognises this subjection, and assumes it for the foundation of that system, the object of which is to rear the fabric of felicity by the hands of reason and law. Systems which attempt to question it, deal in sounds instead of sense, in caprice instead of reason, in darkness instead of light.
>
> (1–2)

This radical philosophy of the affects as the source of human action arises contemporaneously with the birth of free-market capitalism as a function of the emergent bourgeoisie and the age of revolution as its first triumph. Utilitarianism is suggestive as a philosophical—indeed, epistemic—counterpart of bourgeois capitalism: it undercuts established vertical hierarchy from below, privileging precisely that which was rendered abject under the old model of human behavior. The power struggle between reason and the passions mirrors the power struggle between colonial monarchy and its subject bourgeoisie. Reason is the episteme of colonial rule by the cultured elite over the vulgar, the uncivilized, the savage, the masses driven by emotion—colonialism being a paradigm for the rigidly hierarchical relationship of power between monarch and subject as well as for the bottom-up economic flow between the two. The vindication of the passions over reason inverts this hierarchy not by displacing the hierarch of rational colonial monarchy but by rendering it irrelevant. Reason cannot *do* anything—cannot *act*—without the passions as a primary driver of action. As an allegorical system for human affairs, the philosophical contravention of the hegemony of reason is tantamount to declaring a bourgeois revolution—understanding the bourgeoisie in context not as the cultural elite, but rather as the most powerful representative of the nonmonarchical as a residual social category. In spite of its abject status with respect to the monarchy, the mercantilist bourgeoisie is nevertheless the economic support of colonialism. The affirmation of the passions says: the passionate body is not ipso facto inferior to the thinking head. On the contrary, the thinking head has no autonomous capabilities, no reason for being, without the passionate body as a sustaining force. Indeed, in *Passion Is the Gale*, Eustace argues that it is this very philosophical current redefining the status of the emotions as a universal—and not subaltern—category that underwrites the American Revolution by allowing for what I would term an epistemic reconceptualization of social power from the colonial to the democratic mode.

In its epistemic origins, free-market capitalism and democracy—the economic and political modalities of the bourgeoisie—are horizontal and inclusivist in a universality that breaks with vertical and exclusivist colonial elitism. The passions do not, in all rigor, require reason; on the contrary, it is reason that is dependent upon—a "slave" to, in a turn of phrase that makes clear the perfect inversion of power—the passions. The passions may be directed by reason, but this is a concession to the persistence of reason that does not detract from the primacy of the passions; indeed, it is the passions that occupy the new "throne" of the human condition, the passions that are the "sovereign masters [of mankind]."

This philosophical redefinition of the emotions saves the passions—and the bourgeoisie, as part of the nonmonarchical body politic—from the inferiority assigned to them from on high by colonial-monarchical reason. It is this model of a universally passionate body politic—whose emotions are now the masters of reason, and no longer the other way around—that serves as the epistemic foundation for free-market capitalism and democracy.

If this passions-over-reason model is proper to capitalism, why should sustainability discourse be accusing capitalism of the opposite—that is, of exercising reason over the passions? Why should capitalism need the corrective of feeling with its heart instead of thinking with its brain?

Sustainability discourse effectively assumes the epistemic posture originary to capitalism and regards capitalism as capitalism once regarded colonial monarchy. Treating capitalism as a neocolonial force, sustainability discourse argues for its decapitation. Reformist sustainability postures gently encourage capitalism to self-correct—and accept any and all gestures from the capitalist corporate ranks, including the discursive double bottom line, as a sign of compliance with the need to reconnect with heart over brain and tolerate the persistence of profit as the vertebral driver of capitalist practice. Radical sustainability postures want to do away with capitalism altogether and disavow profit and progress in the name of a self-contained system motored by the heart and attentive in exclusivity to the well-being of people and planet.

The Affective Imperative to Claim the Well-Being of People and Planet

In both the North and the South there are pro-profit and antiprofit versions of sustainability discourse that mirror one another in their strategies: pro-profit sustainability discourse elides the question of profit and focuses only on people and planet. This is true as much of corporate sustainability discourse, which adopts the double bottom line discursively in order to give carte blanche to the single bottom line in practice, as it is of noncorporate—yet not categorically opposed to profit—sustainability discourse, which, in tending toward a profit-neutral position, has the same net effect of exonerating profit for lack of open critique, let alone indictment. In the North this is the variant that prevails on the whole. In the South, on the other hand, the variant that has the loudest voice is the one that is also present in the North, but in quieter tones: the antiprofit sustainability discourse that accuses capitalism of ill-being produced by its blind fidelity to the single bottom line, which seeks to reclaim the category of well-being for the people and planet much maligned by that single-minded ideological privileging of profit as master pursuit and objective. In the end, what we see is that in the field of discourse the triple bottom line is a chimera; there is really a double bottom line of people and planet used either to redefine and sanction—to "greenwash"—or to indict and discredit the continued cultural hegemony of the single bottom line. We also see, across regions, the difference in representation of outcome that reflects a sense of relative power within the global grid of economic hierarchy between neocolonizers to the North and neocolonized to the South—although, of course, this neocolonization requires complicity from the dominant Southern class.

We may think of Solanas indirectly accusing the leftist president Cristina Kirchner of such complicity in the claim that "Argentina is an occupied and colonized country" by virtue of the foreign mining industry to which she granted national access ("'Argentina es un país ocupado y colonizado'").

All sustainability postures share their fundamental discursive strategy of diagnosing the current state of environmental, economic, and social state of affairs in affective terms. As a cultural problematic, sustainability is articulated in a system of signification—as much audiovisual as linguistic—rooted in emotional meaning. Happiness and sadness become far more than transitory physiological states; they are synecdoches for well-being and ill-being, these in turn representing two full—and fully opposed—political positions with respect to global capitalist practice. The homeostatic principle of the world as an organism harmoniously and lovingly ordered through the natural flow of its interconnected component parts—people and environment—is the prize concept for which capitalist and anticapitalist agents of sustainability discourse fiercely compete, since this notion of affective well-being confers an epistemic legitimacy to whatever project may successfully claim it for its own. Yet, as an epistemically derivative discourse of capitalism, sustainability—even in its antiprofit guise—should be understood as a narrative of global capital. Capitalism may acquiesce to reform itself—if not practically, then at least discursively—according to sustainability's precepts because they are capitalism's own. It is a logical aporia, however, that sustainability should ultimately unseat capitalism, because they are born of the same epistemic model—and that model posits as its life force the homeostatic flow of capital through its veins. On a discursive level, how can sustainability present a radical challenge to capitalism if they share the same epistemological structure?

But beyond this conjecture in regard to the fate of world economic systems and resources, what is significant and incontrovertible about this discursive debate over their definition and control is the extent to which every party that intervenes in it defines the current cultural subject in the same way, namely, as a double bottom line of people and planet. In other words, sustainability discourse evinces a subject of universal proportion and affective dimension defined through its organicity—the whole of life itself, as a single and affectively self-regulated entity, becomes the cultural actor in a politics of sustainability. It may seem like an inevitability that this should be so. After all, are not the planet and its inhabitants uniform and equal shareholders in a common ecological fate? Perhaps. But, even so, discourse about that fate might take many forms—an epistemically rational argument might assert a taxonomy and categorization of affected regions and peoples, for example. It has been my objective in this study of sustainability discourse to achieve a denaturalization of the cultural subject sufficient for the dual purpose of suspending assumptions about its inevitability and thus of permitting a clearing for analysis in which to consider the epistemic patterns of its construction. Some may argue, as does the prolific Argentine fiction writer and cultural critic Martín Caparrós in his 2010 critique of climate change provocatively entitled *Contra el cambio* (Against Change), that the organic oneness of cultural subjectivity posited by the current discourse of ecological crisis is little more than a tool wielded by powerful first world states and corporations to maintain infrastructural power and dominance of global resources while making fortunes through the inspiration of fear. But if this is true—as might other allegations of the political uses of the global affective monosubject be equally true—what I seek to trace in the present study is the *epistemic* explanation for the traction of that subject. Without the viability of the feeling soma—that is, without its firm insertion in the cultural imaginary—it would have no susceptibility to interested political manipulation. I suggest, simply, that the conceptual power of the feeling soma in our current cultural imaginary derives from the epistemological self-legitimation of capitalism itself. It is our epistemic faith in this organic model of subjectivity as a single feeling soma that permits its political uses in all their ideological diversity.

II *Homeostatic Dynamics*

3 "Becoming well beings"

Homeostatic Dynamics and the Metaphor of Health

I have charted how the feeling soma comes into view in global cultural texts in every medium, from literature to publicity to the politics of human and planetary futurity. Of dimensions equally capacious as imprecise, this flexible body is predicated on an organicity that posits a fundamental indistinction of scale, thus allowing the same model of protagonism to be applied to the individual organism or all of humanity or life in all its kingdoms or the planet itself. This notion of protagonism channels democracy in its most perfect and idealized form: the smallest part is interchangeable with the whole; any and every representative of the body is qualitatively equal and significant. There is fluid conceptual movement between the individual and the grand collective of life, all embraced within this model of nonrational sentience.

At this juncture I would like to turn my attention to the organizational dynamics of this body, focusing on the persistence with which it is represented as being governed by the logic of its own feelings as a model of order. This model diverges sharply from the traditional model of rational subjectivity. In the classic Cartesian framework, the subject constitutes itself through the engagement of reason to affirm the existence of the self, establishing a critical self-reflexive distance in which there is a doubling of the self between the rational observer and the nonrational observed—the mind and body, respectively. It is the rational mind, as distinct from the body, that analyzes, makes plans for action, and executes those plans, guiding the nonrational body down the path laid out by the advance strategy of the reasoning mind. In the epistemically affective model, this dualism disappears. All analysis, plans, and execution of action are nonrationally performed. This does not mean—to evoke Ruth Leys's concerns about the same (see note 12 of the introduction)—that we may not speak of self-awareness, cognition, analysis, or deliberate action, but we must entertain the possibility of rediscovering—and redefining—those concepts so strongly associated with Cartesian rationalism in the context of the "affectivism" of the feeling soma.

Leys establishes a kind of conceptual lobby on behalf of affect in order to safeguard against what she views as an overdetermined separation between reason and affect in which affect is therefore circumscribed from the Cartesian attributes of reason. Leys protects what I would call the epistemological potential of affect insofar as she defends the possibility of understanding affect as being capable of doing all that reason does, with a particular emphasis on cognition.

Whereas Leys approaches this issue empirically, shouldering the burden of ontology and sifting through physiological evidence, I approach the same issue representationally. I identify how the feeling soma is portrayed as a conceptual model in any kind of text, placing science on a par with film in my discursive analysis of cultural storytelling. Rather than argue for any kind of scientifically verifiable status of affect in the cognitive, decision-making, and action-taking processes, I look at how these processes are narrated. In the aggregate these diverse cultural texts reveal a recurrent formulation of what we would traditionally consider the purview of reason—cognition, judgment, principled action—at the level of affect. That is, cognition, judgment, and principled action become nonrationally informed.

Analysis of the representation of the feeling soma, I argue, points to homeostasis as the mechanism for the accomplishment of these erstwhile rational tasks. Terminologically, I employ *homeostasis* to denote the body's automatic self-regulatory tendency toward well-being measured in somatic and emotional terms. In originary free-market tracts, as in the most current of arguments espousing a radically laissez-faire view, capital traverses the global body politic without the slightest need for rational intervention, following its own wisdom, which inevitably brings happiness to each and all the world over in its all-encompassing flow. It is the homeostatic principle that underwrites this view, which evinces a belief in the capacity of the feeling soma to guide itself toward healthful and happy equilibrium on the strength of its nonrational internal operations. In the texts I will examine as evidence of this belief, the nonrational internal operations of the feeling soma assume the logic of an emotionally coded flow. Health—the net balance between ease and disease, happiness and unhappiness—becomes a central metaphor for the state of affairs within the feeling soma. The cognitive powers of the feeling soma are rooted in the ability to self-diagnose, with discernment between well-being and ill-being constituting the fundamental analytical operation in determining action needed in response to the net disposition of the feeling soma along the continuum of health, from the positive pole of well-being at one end to the negative pole of ill-being at the other. In this chapter I will consider the persistent cultural concern over and representation of health and I will analyze the homeostatic dynamics of the feeling soma in cultural texts that posit the balance of health as an index of cultural politics. In a back-and-forth alternation between U.S. and Latin American texts, I will consider how cultural ill-being is denounced as a function of capitalist consumerism and materialism and how a distancing from that capitalist culture is posited as a curative remedy for the restoration of well-being on both the individual and cultural levels.

Health on the Cultural Horizon

Health has become a persistent media issue over the past decade—not because ours, collectively, is perceived to be good, but because of fears that it may be under cultural assault, in jeopardy of decline. Reports of the increasingly global affliction of obesity, expanding in tandem with the influence of Western culture and diet, are perhaps the most salient example, hence inspiring Michelle Obama's national campaign to end childhood obesity in the United States. Therapy of all kinds, including self-help literature, yoga, and alternative medicine, have become booming industries (the National Institutes of Health expanded in 1991 to include complementary and alternative medicine). Healthcare has been a heated political issue in the United States, which resulted in the passage of so-called Obamacare;

premiere and ever controversial U.S. documentary filmmaker Michael Moore's *Sicko* (2007) anticipates this debate, framing the lack of socialized medicine as a symptom of greater cultural ills in the United States. Third Cinema ideologue and preeminent Argentine director Fernando "Pino" Solanas,[1] likewise, foregrounds sickness and the even more widespread lack of healthcare in Argentina in *Memoria del saqueo* (Social Genocide, 2004) and *La dignidad de los nadies* (The Dignity of the Nobodies, 2005) as a symptom of economic neoliberalism.

Television is replete with doctors—to name only a metonym of the many shows staged around hospitals, *ER* (1994–2009) is the second-longest-running serial drama in U.S. television history. Doctor figures are also a recurrent motif of recent film. Christopher Nolan's blockbuster film *Batman Begins* (2005), updating the canonical WWII superhero for the global age, places emphasis on the vocation of Batman's father not as a businessman, but as a doctor; though the family's mansion burns to the ground, Batman pulls his father's scorched stethoscope from the ruins, a symbolic reminder of the notion that corporations are meant to serve the well-being of their communities rather than spawning poverty, disease, and death. In the same way that the primacy of medicine makes business secondary in *Batman Begins*, the primacy of medicine makes social revolution secondary in not one but two portraits of the legendary revolutionary Ernesto "Che" Guevara: Walter Salles's *Diarios de motocicleta* (*Motorcycle Diaries*, 2004) and Steven Soderbergh's *Che* (2008) both cast Guevara's revolutionary identity as derivative of his foundational commitment to being a doctor and a healer. Prominent Brazilian director Fernando Meirelles's *Blindness* (2008), adapted from Portuguese Nobel laureate José Saramago's eponymous 1995 novel, makes an ophthalmologist and his wife the central protagonists of the eponymous plague that is at once physiological and moral; the ophthalmologist's wife leads her husband and their diverse microsociety back to health by forging a new community based on love and the equal distribution of resources across all lines of social division. These filmic examples, all of which enjoy high—and global—visibility because of the prominence of their directors, the cultural cachet of their subject matter, particularly in the instances of Batman and Che Guevara, and their broad distribution, all manifest a significant coincidence in locating their leading doctors at the epicenter of a crisis of social health of dimensions that tend toward the universal. Well-being and ill-being represent broad social models in conflict; in the aforementioned filmic examples, ill-being constitutes the undesirable status quo associated with capitalist culture—either explicitly or as a culture of greed—that the doctor works to remedy as the architect of cultural well-being, designing a social model that ranges from a "kinder, gentler" corporate capitalism in *Batman Begins* to informal socialism in *Blindness* to declared anticapitalist revolution in the Che Guevara films.

Contemporary narrative diagnoses the cultural landscape as though it were a soma. It no longer comprehends long-winded rational discourse about rights, justice, equality, exploitation. It does comprehend those concepts—it understands what rights, justice, equality, and exploitation are; they just don't resonate in their old packaging. An example of such affective repackaging of rational political discourse is to be had in Avi Lewis and Naomi Klein's film *The Take* (2004), in which the young antineoliberal-globalization-activist Canadian couple travel to Argentina in search of an economic alternative to profit-driven neoliberalism. Since its disastrous economic and political collapse of December 2001—including an IMF default and the seizure of national bank deposits—Argentina has been attractive to the postneoliberal gaze not only because the collapse marked the end of Argentina's decades-long neoliberal experiment but also because it unexpectedly revived the political left in a continental domino effect. Even beyond this revival, Argentina has, in the aftermath of its crisis, produced what Klein and Lewis view as a radical break with the neoliberal model in the form of the hundreds of factories abandoned in the massive flight of capital that have since been reoccupied and returned to operational productivity not by their owners but by their former workers. *The Take* chronicles the struggle of one such group of workers—in this case, of the steel plant Forja—to organize in solidarity as a collective in order to take over the abandoned means of capitalist production and to participate in the capitalist market as a quasi-socialist producer of goods. The film's express intent—as manifested in an interview between a free-market apologist and Klein, whom the former accuses of having no viable alternative—is precisely to find such an alternative to neoliberalism. Yet the film does not produce analytical language describing that alternative—i.e., not in the way that I have provisionally attempted. Instead, the film lets the workers' emotions bear the brunt of the storytelling. A central scene in this regard is one in which a small group of Forja representatives are waiting outside a judge's chambers to learn her decision about whether they will be made to evacuate the premises or permitted to continue their operations. When they hear that the judge has decided in their favor, the emotion is overwhelming. One middle-aged man calls his father to tell him the news and breaks down in tears on the phone. The camera stays unabashedly trained on that expression of sentimentality, those tears of joy and relief, because therein lies the story of rights, justice, equality, and exploitation. The film speaks in the language of that explicit political metanarrative only to the extent that is necessary to frame the story; the rest is told in the affective terms of a collective feeling soma whose joyful release of sadness marks the turning of a political tide away from serving as the supports of neoliberal exploitation and toward serving as the supports of the heretofore exploited.

Like Mel Gibson's hyperbolically bloody Christ, Rodrigo Bellott's collective vomit, or McDonald's love-as-hamburger, *The Take* adopts a narrative strategy that places more faith in the power of a visceral, rather than rational, presentation of information. And this visceral narrative is not simply telling a story about the body, but is using the body to tell a story about the world, a story that should be understood as a fully articulated social critique. It is in the language of the emotions and the soma that feels them that this critique is articulated, yielding what, in effect, we might with some poetic license call an epidemiological optic in the sense that it is principally attuned to the question of (dis)ease. Diagnostics of health are affective analogues for the political in which well-being represents the positive pole of analysis and ill-being a negative critique.

Epidemiological Narrative: Diagnosing Ill-Being

In public health initiatives, as in the cinematic examples explored in the previous section, the feeling soma undergirds an understanding of the social; in the case of the nonprofit organization U.S. Healthiest, dedicated to making the United States—as it claims on its website—the "world's healthiest nation" by promoting "healthy communities," "healthy workplaces," and a "healthy you," there is also an explicit homology between the emotional and economic homeostasis of the U.S. public. With a board of directors composed largely of corporate executives from retail, healthcare, and investment companies, as well as governmental functionaries, it is not surprising that the homepage mission statement should read: "We understand that health is the key to not only physical, emotional, and intellectual well-being *but also to economic strength.* Our members are committed to making health and well-being a priority *in industry and government*, but also for individuals, families, and communities" (emphasis added). As though reviving eighteenth- and nineteenth-century utilitarian philosophy—which prescribed the calculation of social good in "utils" of benefits and detriments—and recasting it in the language of health, U.S. Healthiest posits health as the basis of a robust social order in which there is a seamless interconnection between individuals and economy.

In an audiovisual declaration of intent, a video short entitled *Healthiest Nation*, U.S. Healthiest takes as its point of departure the assertion that the United States is not in good health ("1 in 2 children is likely to develop type 2 diabetes/ by 2025 chronic disease will affect half the population/for the first time our children will have shorter life expectancies than ours/ . . . healthcare[:] / our nation is more interested / in the 'care' part/ than in the 'health' part") and tries to convince its audience to join its movement to remedy that infirmity. The way in which the video short frames that remedy reveals the homeostatic principle at work: well-being is a phenomenon of dynamism ("let's create a movement / that creates movement") that is all-encompassing, reaching into every aspect of life, from transit to shelter to inner life ("walking / carpooling / demanding bike lanes / smoke free public places / supporting local farmers / and farm to school programs / building LEED certified structures and community gardens around them / turning off the T.V./ (so we can rest)/ (so we can dream)" and across all social sectors, in the spirit of democracy ("a movement that connects / cities states businesses neighborhoods human beings / a movement that gives the people the power / to change how they: eat / commute / shop / play / feel"). In this "power-to-the-people" list the rights of old are replaced by the simple operations of a work- and consumption-based culture—eating, commuting, shopping, playing, and, underscored by the largest font and screen size of all these items, as though its conceptual apotheosis, *feeling*—are advanced as the territory of democratic intervention (for the people, by the people). Like the tears in *The Take*, the theme of health in *Healthiest Nation* video is politically charged; it is a call to well-being that is inseparable from the context of liberal democracy and free-market capitalism not only because of the overt references to their foundational principles, but because the entire vision of the meaning of health evokes the model of homeostatic affect, from its premise of the interconnectedness between individual and globe ("your health and global health are connected" being the key realization to launching the "movement"), the dynamic movement that organizes the parts of that collective whole, and the definition of those parts as "not just being well / but becoming well beings / physically / emotionally / environmentally / healthy healthy healthy." It is worth noting here that this last definition of health as that which is proper to the individual—physical and emotional—and to the planet—environmental—expands the collective subject to all of nature itself. What the health of this collective subject ensures is an organic structure through which capital may find easy transit, producing profit in the capitalist model of well-being. Placed in the context of the mission statement of U.S. Healthiest, which stresses economic health as its furthest-reaching concern, the video suddenly seems less about well-being for its own sake and more for the sake of preparing a collective organism sufficiently fit on a structural level to accommodate the fact of the economy. Yet, even as it makes upbeat and cheery recommendations for achieving greater well-being on a national scale, it also cannot help but signal a marked anxiety over the diagnosis of U.S. ill-being that has prompted the intervention in the first place.

Mad Men: Capitalism as Ill-Being Masked by Well-Being

If the United States is sick, then we find an attempt to diagnose that illness in *Mad Men* (2007–2015), an original AMC cable television series with a viewership in the range of several million, consistently ranked in the American Film Institute's top ten television shows and boasted a litany of other award nominations and wins to its credit. *Mad Men* reads as an extended epidemiological narrative—that is, a narrative focused on the diagnosis of (dis)ease, which is figured as a net balance between well- and ill-being. This period series about the Madison Avenue advertising world of the early 1960s goes back in time to the moment when the United States was heady with postwar affluence and global influence, the moment when this new capitalist superpower in the bipolar cold war was establishing its hegemony through the aggressive birth of consumer culture. Indeed, citing the *New York Times*'s introduction to *Mad Men* as historiography,[2] Goodlad, Kaganovsky, and Rushing paraphrase this reception of the series: "Don Draper [i]s not fiction but biography; *Mad Men* [i]s not television but a repository of the past" (1). Indeed, the preponderance of *Mad Men* scholarship takes this historiographical tack, approaching the series first and foremost as a period piece and plumbing its content largely for issues of gender, sexuality, class, and race in the 1960s.[3]

I would argue, however, contrary to what the period aesthetic of *Mad Men* most immediately invites us to contemplate in the preterit, that this biographical repository of the past is most deeply about the cultural present; as Gary R. Edgerton avers, *Mad Men* "capture[s] and express[es] the [current] zeitgeist" (xxi). An interpretive optic that focuses on the show's content in the context of capitalism and advertising come closest to its deepest pulse and relevance for our cultural present. If *Mad Men* puts its finger on any cultural wound, it is the consumerism that has come preponderantly and unapologetically to define our lives. Michael Bérubé expresses this to a tee in a poetic meditation on the way *Mad Men* interpellates us as consumers: *Mad Men*, Bérubé muses, "is a good series about good advertising that advertises itself well while calling advertising into question. Structural irony, *Mad Men* style. You'll love, and at the same time you won't love, the way it makes you feel" (359). It is precisely in this capacity to make us feel both good and bad that *Mad Men* is most relentlessly about the twenty-first century and most urgently begging interpretation. The reason for being of this analysis—of this entire study as a whole—is to argue that our zeitgeist turns on the precarious balance between well-being and ill-being, between ease and disease, between joylessness and happiness, between love and its lack, all against the social fabric that vacillates between consumerism and consumption, between freedom and unfreedom, and the understanding of consumerism as that which promises freedom only to yield unfreedom as the ineluctable consequence of consumption.

Mad Men is notoriously lush in its aesthetic, representing the opulent excess of Madison Avenue and the unapologetic materialism of the suburbs that were emerging in complementary fashion at the same moment. But beneath this lavish mid-century surface of well-being, the characters of Mad Men are mired in a social and interior landscape of malaise—enveloped by clouds of cigarette smoke, plagued by chronic illness, wracked with bouts of nausea, tormented by deep-seated emotional damage. These motifs of ill-being—dirty undershirts, uncontrollable spasms of muscular atrophy, violent vomiting—lying just below the surface of glamour, high-powered competence, and success constitutes a representation of affluence and malaise that it is not one or the other, but both. *Mad Men* portrays a system in which affluent well-being is only a surface-level phenomenon of appearances, existing only in the upper levels of the chrome-and-glass high-rise buildings that house advertising firms whose executives script social "happiness"—which the show's protagonist Don Draper says was "invented by guys like me"—while the reality underneath it all is one of supreme and physical unhappiness. *Mad Men*'s characters smoke, drink, and fornicate their way into momentary bliss, a bliss that is not only always fleeting, but, moreover, only works to aggravate their underlying ill-being. In this sense, *Mad Men* presents an unflinching portrait of consumerism as toxic addiction.[4]

As a series, *Mad Men* is predicated on the tension between Don Draper's outward charisma and impossible success, on the one hand, and his internal instability and emotional emptiness, on the other, with the effect of positing that the subject of consumer culture bears a relationship of analogy to the product it consumes—that is, dressed in an illusion of well-being that hides a reality of inner ill-being. The opening credits show the prototypical "Madman" (a play on the "adman" of Madison Avenue) falling down, down, down into the seated black silhouette of a suited businessman whose outline conceptually resolves into the opening shot of the series in which we see Don Draper from behind in an after-hours club as smoky as it is swanky.[5] We learn that the circumstance of this silhouette—that is, what is engrossing Don Draper as the first shot of the series captures him in thought—is a profound anxiety about how to market cigarettes now that research links cigarettes to cancer. Draper has a meeting the next morning with the entire Lucky Strike family, and he's "got nothing," as he confesses to his lover, to whom he pays an impromptu late-night visit following his unsatisfying brainstorming on the proverbial cocktail napkin. "Next time you see me," he tells her, "there'll be a bunch of young executives picking meat off my ribs." Don Draper's elegant dress and confident mien suggest that this is a man of infinite success, but it is significant that we should meet him precisely in this moment of self-professed creative flatline. In spite of his robust exterior, we see that, internally, he is a subject in crisis. His is a constant vertigo, a constant fear of falling. Normally, we intuit, he is able to save himself with his signature savoir faire. The fact that we meet him under threat, at the precipice of failure—whose irreversibility we infer from the scale of his anxiety—with nothing in his head, filled with quiet panic and dread, yet performing—to himself, to others—as though absolutely nothing were wrong, epitomizes his existential landscape: outward well-being, inward ill-being.

If we think about Don Draper's past and present on the level of social metaphor, we can appreciate how he might be seen to represent the derivation of U.S. affluence from the tragedy of war and depression. A decorated war veteran (or so the purple heart medal in his office drawer would lead us to believe), Don Draper is nevertheless reticent about his past. His junior executives joke that no one knows anything about Don Draper ("He could be Batman, for all we know," one quips), a sentiment that his own wife shares with far less mirth, breaking the ice with his new secretary with the plaintive remark that Peggy probably knows him better than she. Slowly, we find out that Don Draper is trying to hide another identity. Even his name—the name we see embossed on his purple heart medal—is not his own. He has a different name, Dick Whitman, one that emerges in shadowy association with a childhood of rural poverty, an emotionally gray history dominated by emasculating ridicule and the lack of love: a prostitute mother dead in childbirth, a blood father who died some years later after remarrying a callous stepmother who deprived him of a mother's love, an "uncle" (the husband of the unloving stepmother) who ribbed him for being "soft." One by one these characters have died, we learn; his younger half-brother is Draper's only remaining connection to his past—and he commits suicide midway through the first season. It is as though the agricultural, prewar past of the nation dies away in the figure of these estranged relatives who disappear into oblivion, leaving nothing to contradict the ascendant—but false—reality of Madison Avenue.[6]

Draper's service, we eventually learn, was during the Korean War. But the biographical uncertainty of the initial episodes has the effect of casting mid-century war simply as a point of contrast, a circumstantial foil, for the gleaming Madison Avenue offices to which Draper has risen. The sudden catapulting of the United States into global hegemony on the heels of World War II constituted a sharp turn up and out of the lingering aftershock of the Great Depression. Market values finally returned to their precrash levels in the mid-fifties and then began to surpass them on the strength of a new economy based on consumerism. Along with the astronaut—and, indeed, a stranger at a bar asks a sleepless Don Draper if that's what he is ("The Doorway," season 6, episode 1)—the adman is an archetypal character of these times, populating the U.S. national imaginary in the form of Darrin Stephens (Dick York, Dick Sargent), the advertising executive who marries a witch on the 1964–1972 television series *Bewitched*, for example.

Draper refuses to honor his past—he leaves his long-lost half-brother at the table of their anticlimactic reunion, saying on his way out the door that their meeting "never happened"—in the same way that the U.S. also began anew in the wake of war. If we may take Draper as an avatar of the postwar U.S. culture of affluence, then this postwar identity is profoundly amnesiac and disconnected from its prewar history. The baby boom begins U.S. history anew with the U.S. at the arrogant helm of world domination. Superheroes were born for the new superpower—Draper might well be considered Batman in the sense that he represents the pinnacle of this new U.S. powerhouse. But the comparison also suggests that superhero status may only belie an equally great hidden trauma: Draper's outward character embodies an unbridled power and disdain for any authority other than his own, but his lost self, his disavowed name and past signal that this success is built upon the precarious foundation of willful social amnesia. Just as Draper spins slogans out of thin air—generating "happiness" and prosperity out of nothing—so does the rise of Madison Avenue constitute the birth of affluence from a cultural void. On the surface, Draper is the picture of success, wealth, and happiness. The underbelly of his hidden past is the negative image of failure, destitution, and depression.

Draper's first female client and budding love interest shakes Draper visibly by suggesting that he may well know what it means to be "disconnected" from the world, to reside in a chronic state of alienation—a perfect countermodel to homeostatic well-being. As the episodes progress, we learn that Rachel Menken's mother died giving birth to her. Likewise, Don Draper's past is characterized by the absence of a mother; we soon learn that he had a stepmother who "never let him forget" that he was not her son, and later the deaths of his biological parents is confirmed. If the attraction between Rachel Menken and Don Draper represents the union of the corporation and its public face, the composite picture and basis of a new era of wealth, then it is clear that this new era has come into being with neither history nor love. This generation has to create both for itself; it has to fabricate the well-being that is foundationally absent in its being born motherless and without the name of the father. For just as Don Draper is orphaned by his father, Rachel Menken effects a self-orphaning by supplanting her out-of-touch father as the new head of their business. She introduces herself as the steward picking up the reins of her store following its "worst sales year ever," asserting that it is her opinion, and not her father's, that now matters. American consumer culture is, the series suggests, the orphaned—and therefore utterly brazen—love child of economic and cultural rock bottom. From the ashes of prewar U.S. depression, Don Draper and Rachel Menken rise up on the wings of postwar affluence to define a new era of economic prosperity based on capitalist consumerism.

But their depression and underlying ill-being only seem to grow in the same measure that their success and putative well-being grows. At-large consumer culture critic Annie Leonard posits the same in her online exposition of the materials economy in "The Story of Stuff," where she argues that our consumerism functions on the basis of a negative desire: on the basis of feeling bad about ourselves, we rush out to make ourselves feel better with a purchase, only to have the negativity renewed by the news that now we need a new thing to feel good. This is a pursuit of happiness that has no finality and no true catharsis; it is simply a chase of what cannot ever be attained because the well-being that is pursued is always already—and ever—an illusion. What *Mad Men* adds to this model of consumption is the notion of ill-being as a fundamental underlying condition, a reality in the sense of the Lacanian dimension of the real—the unrepresentable horrors that our ego tries to cover over with a patchwork of imaginary narrative. Advertising—the symbolic language of consumption—is the narrative through which our poor beleaguered ego tries to reconstitute itself in the imaginary terrain of idealized well-being, to cure its primordial subterranean state of abjection, misery, ill-being.

Mad Men is born of cigarettes: the pilot episode situates itself in the advertising crisis provoked by the Surgeon General's report linking tobacco to cancer. At Sterling Cooper, the firm where creative director and rising star Draper is making a name for himself, tobacco is not just one product of many; Lucky Strike is the bread-and-butter account that brings in more than half its annual revenue. In the same way, we might interpret the episode's foregrounding of tobacco as anything but arbitrary. The choice of tobacco as the signal product to begin a series that is, in turn, about the birth of consumer culture suggests that, in its genesis, that culture is fundamentally rooted in ill-being, promoting an addiction that leads inexorably toward death.[7]

Yet, when confronted with such scientific evidence, Draper's response is to throw the surgeon general's report in the trash, not only obscuring but also rendering abject—that is, making what should be edifying an undesirable knowledge—the fatal truth of addiction and, in its place, creating a slogan for Lucky Strike that reassures, comforts, gives the appearance of stability, denotes nature and nurture at once: "It's toasted," he proposes to say of the erstwhile carcinogenic cigarette. (Draper's "brainchild" slogan dates back to 1917, making the show's commentary on the perverse advertising strategy of Lucky Strike—and consumer capitalism in general—all the more profound.) The consumer does not want to be reminded of ill-being, says Draper; the consumer wants only positive affirmation:

> Advertising is based on one thing: happiness. And do you know what happiness is? Happiness is the smell of a new car. It's freedom from fear. It's a billboard on the side of a road that screams with reassurance that whatever you're doing is OK. You are OK.
>
> Advertising thus creates the patently false illusion of well-being, an illusion that is, nonetheless, entirely credible on the strength of desire, a desire for pleasure, freedom, and happiness.

The consumer engages in addiction but maintains the illusion of autonomy, self-determination, freedom of choice, prosperity of purchasing power, wealth in happiness stemming from the pleasure that comes from consumption. All the while, the product that confers an intentionally ephemeral pleasure—in order to encourage addiction and a permanence of consumption—only increases a subterranean reality of ill-being that can only be alleviated by consuming more of the same in a pattern of escape that is short-lived and noxious, digging the consumer deeper and deeper into ill-being with every cycle of consumption, every desperate bid—gambling, risking one's life—in the quest for refuge. Thus health—not only the health of the planet robbed of its resources and equilibrium but the health of the individual—becomes the Achilles' heel of consumer culture: health is not linear and infinite; eventually the ill-being resulting from a lifestyle predicated on unhealthy addiction will reach a point of terminal unsustainability, bursting asunder the illusion of happiness.

When Draper arrives at his office for his big Lucky Strike meeting unshowered, underslept, and unkempt, he pulls from his drawer a brand-new white button-down shirt still in its wrappings and puts it on over his dirty undershirt. This is the operative image and metaphor for U.S. consumerism as an infinite cycle of a reality of dirty ill-being underlying the illusory appearance of well-being. The button-down shirt is an opaque cover-up of bravado, charm, narrative brilliance—this top shirt is the one associated with Draper's coup in the world of illusion: the simple tagline "It's toasted" to cast Lucky Strike cigarettes as the epitome of natural growth, home cooking, health, comfort, happiness—well-being in a package. The undershirt constitutes the repressed memory of the anxiety of the abyss of creative death, the general precipice over which the entire world of affluence hovers, built, as it is, without foundation; it is the secret depression and malaise of the suburban world that has not yet admitted to itself that its happiness is illusory, sheer image and no substance. The undershirt is also the memory of the medical report linking smoking to cancer that Draper has relegated to the trash can—the suppressed knowledge that cigarettes are, in truth, death for sale in a well-advertised box.

This first and foundational episode of *Mad Men* thus invites us to view cigarettes as a synecdoche for the entire market of consumer products, the ultimate symbol of consumption as a cultural phenomenon. The episode not only talks about cigarettes; it contextualizes them in use—a heavy and self-medicated use. The opening shot of the pilot episode, "Smoke Gets in Your Eyes," begins with Draper's silhouette, establishing him as the proto-typical Mad Man, and then travels through a Manhattan bar where Draper and his elite advertising colleagues let off steam from the workday. The bar is clouded with smoke—as the camera pans, we see that everyone, without exception, is laughing, talking, drinking, with a lit cigarette in hand. Draper initiates an impromptu conversation with his black waiter—a conversation proscribed by the racist norms of the era, which circumstance makes the conversation all the more truthful for its universality of sentiment across the deepest of social divides—in which the two men effectively define cigarettes as the true love of every man, an affective relationship underscored by the background song about a "band of gold" that plays upon the name of the waiter's favorite cigarettes, Old Gold, to suggest a marital relationship be-tween man and cigarette. Draper—along with everyone else, but especially Draper, as the epitome of both master and subject of consumer culture—smokes his way through the episode. A master of consumer culture, Draper reveals the fabrication of the illusion of well-being by throwing out the medical report and promoting a false sense of pleasurable security in its place; as its subject, he reveals how the pursuit of happiness is a flight from unhappiness whose aftereffects only serve to exacerbate this fundamental ill-being. The cycle of consumption digs its subject further and further into the trenches of ill-being with every attempt to consume a happiness that is not only illusory, but noxious, to the consumer's health. Consumption promises health and well-being, but delivers sickness and ill-being.

Draper's Madison Avenue office is the domain of illusion: "Who could not be happy with all this?" Draper asks with a broad smile, sweeping his arm around the bright luxury executive accommodations that surround him. Yet, when left to his own devices beyond those reassuring confines, Draper's deeper unhappiness leads him to pass out, drunk at the wheel, under a dark bridge. Acutely aware of his own malaise, and trapped in the social structure corresponding to capitalist consumption (urban desk job; suburban home, wife, and two kids), the fantasy of a liaison with Rachel Menken obsesses Draper to the point of self-medicating his way into the quick fix of happiness he is craving with can after can of beer. This use of alcohol is analogous to cigarettes, one more aspect of the same cycle of consumption.

Draper's boss lectures him about the way he handles his "daily friendship with [the] bottle":

> ROGER STERLING: You don't know how to drink. Your whole generation, you drink for the wrong reasons. My generation, we drink because it's good, because it feels better than unbuttoning your collar, because we deserve it. We drink because it's what men do. . . . Your kind with your gloomy thoughts and your worries, you're all busy licking some imaginary wound.
> DON DRAPER: Not all imaginary.
> ROGER STERLING: Yeah, boo hoo.
> DON DRAPER: Maybe I'm not as comfortable being powerless as you are. ("New Amsterdam" 1.4)

Draper's accusation of a collective "powerlessness" seems at odds with the prestige of their circumstance as successful admen. But this is a moment when the underbelly of the real is rearing its head, a reminder that, from below, the real is always conditioning the imaginary on high. The specific reminder that Draper's real is bringing to bear on his world of imaginary well-being is the foundationlessness of this well-being, a reminder of the sickly feeling of free fall that visually characterizes the entire series in the introductory sequence in which an adman in black silhouette (a generic Draper—Draper rendered as cultural structure) falls from the heights of a Manhattan skyscraper, passing billboard after billboard on the way toward a demise that miraculously never comes to pass because of the cushion—toxic though it may be—of self-medication, from the false happiness of advertising and wealth to the fleeting highs of cigarettes and alcohol. Toward the end of the first episode, Don Draper himself recognizes advertising as a mask of well-being for a profound and bottomless ill-being: "The reason you haven't felt [love] is because it doesn't exist. What you call love was invented by guys like me, to sell nylons. You're born alone and you die alone and this world just drops a bunch of rules on top of you to make you forget those facts. But I never forget. I'm living like there's no tomorrow, because there isn't one" (1.1).

Spanish poet Federico García Lorca saw in the New York of 1929–1930 a dichotomous world divided between the culture of finance on high, which Lorca represents in the depersonalized abstract mode of offices and ciphers ("multiplicaciones," "divisiones," "sumas" ["multiplications," "divisions," "sums"]), and "la otra mitad" ("the other half"), which Lorca characterizes as "un río de sangre tierna" ("a river of tender blood") that flows sacrificially below the numbers (240). The world of financial success and power, Lorca argues, is a cold abstraction at a vertical remove from the masses below whose constant sacrifice—death in blood and abjection—is the unsung price that has to be paid to keep this affluence afloat. Lorca made this argument at the moment that the Roaring Twenties came abruptly to an end; *Mad Men* likewise came into being just before the 2008 credit crisis, at the moment that neoliberalism, having produced spikes in wealth not experienced since the 1920s, was on the verge of crashing down on itself into what analysts will characterize as the worst recession since the Great Depression. Whereas Lorca posits a separation between the illusory world on high and its abject real down below in this hierarchical social landscape—in other worlds, two worlds that are systemically interconnected but don't touch each other—*Mad Men* internalizes this divide within the somatic landscape of the individual. The world on high, *Mad Men* suggests, always already contains its own river of grease and blood.

Consumption as a cultural way of life is an internalized schizoid state. But, it must be emphasized, not an arbitrarily schizoid state; on the contrary, a programmatically cyclical schizoid state continually revolves in a loop of consumption that seeks well-being and begets ill-being, a cycle that is designed to awaken, harness, channel, and exploit desire without ever fulfilling it, so that desire, even when disappointed—*especially* when disappointed—comes back full circle, time and again, for more, in an unadulterated addiction to the process. This cycle is not just about consumer products; it is about emotions. Because consumption is coded affectively, defining positive emotional states in illusory terms (happiness is a pair of pantyhose, love a diamond ring), homeostasis itself is thrown out of balance by being realigned along an axis of false emotional definition. If homeostasis constitutes the body's autonomic self-regulation in the direction of wellness—well-being being the objective of every body—then the capturing of that basic, primordial, homeostatic category by consumerism confuses the body. According to the three thousand commercials we see daily, well-being is what we buy: things and more things we don't need (many of which remake our natural environment in artificial simulacrum just to sell it back to us with a profit, from bottled water to human breast milk now being produced through genetically modified cows), clothes we can't fit into, cars we can't afford, fast food for breakfast, lunch, and dinner (in *Super Size Me* [2004], Morgan Spurlock's doctors were warning him he was putting his life at risk after some twenty-odd days of eating exclusively at McDonald's, still nearly ten days shy of fulfilling his thirty-day commitment to a fast-food-only diet).

In *The End of Overeating: Taking Control of the Insatiable American Appetite* (2009), former Food and Drug Administration commissioner David Kessler examines how, since the eighties—the onset of the neoliberal years—the advertising and food industries have exploited the body's desire-based and pleasure-seeking reward system, overloading the body's cravings and drowning out the homeostatic drive to maintain an energy equilibrium, creating a nation of overweight eaters addicted to sugar, fat, and salt. An interview with Kessler is worth quoting at length for his succinct discussion of the physiological mechanisms of addiction associated with consumption—we can view this as an explanation of the obesity aboard the spaceship *Axiom* in *WALL·E*, where the passengers spend all day gorging themselves on reward-center foods, as well as a conceptual tie-in to our contemplation of cigarette advertising in *Mad Men* as a synecdoche for consumer culture itself:

> Fifty years ago, the tobacco industry, confronted with the evidence that smoking causes cancer, decided to deny the science and deceive the American public. Now, we know that highly palatable foods—sugar, fat, salt—are highly reinforcing and can activate the reward center of the brain. For many people, that activation is sustained when they're cued. They have such a hard time controlling their eating because they're constantly being bombarded—their brain is constantly being activated. . . .
>
> For one gentleman I spoke with, the hardest thing for him every day is to get home past the newsstand at the train station because of the Kit Kats. For him, it was Kit Kats, for someone else, it's chocolate chip cookies, but one of the key core features is sugar, fat, salt. Once

your behavior becomes conditioned and driven, you get into this cycle and you get cued. When the neural circuits get activated, it focuses your attention. There's a bit of an arousal as you have increased attentional focus, and then the only way to get it out of working memory is to consume the product. The next time you're cued, you eat again, and you're in this cycle. Every time you do it you strengthen it. . . .

Not only is there amplified neural activation in the anticipatory phase with people with conditioned hypereating, but as they're eating, the stimulation stays sustained so it's very hard to stop. It isn't until the food's gone—considerably later—do you feel full because the reward circuits are overriding the homeostatic circuits. . . .

Putting sugar, fat and salt on every corner, that's been the business plan. You make it not only accessible, but you make it socially acceptable, you create the social norms, you add the advertising, the emotional gloss.

(McCready)

The wisdom of what has happened in the food industry—creating (and deriving massive profits from) foods that are, Kessler says, analogous to addictive drugs—gives us our operative model for consumerism in general, a concept further supported by recent research on compulsive buying disorder linking shopping to other addictive behaviors like gambling that are governed by the reward center and its dopamine release.

(Black)

Kessler's view of consumerism as addiction further elucidates the central premise of *Mad Men*: we should think of consumer culture as having rewired the body at the homeostatic level, hooking us on the addictive releases of the reward center (whether eating, shopping, or smoking), rendering us viscerally insensitive—somatically blind, so to speak—to our own well-being and responsive only to those emotional prompts that promise happiness in a package, plenitude through the use of a credit card, which behavior only mires us in ill-being. The cyclical lure of false well-being as a short-term high from consumption that only exacerbates real long-term ill-being would prompt the reconceptualization of Visa's slogan, for example—"Life takes Visa"—as its inverse: "Visa takes life."

Blindness: Implosion of the Reward System and
Return to Communal Homeostasis

Fernando Meirelles's *Blindness* (2008),[8] adapted from Nobel laureate José
Saramago's eponymous novel (1997 English translation; original *Ensaio sobre
a cegueira*, 1995), brings the world of *Mad Men*—of idealized consumption
compensating for underlying ills—to the brink of social apocalypse. The
plot is simple: an urban center—filmed in São Paolo, but meant to be any
global city—is afflicted with a pandemic of blindness. For a time, the afflicted are quarantined; later, once the pandemic reaches universal proportions,
the quarantine no longer has surveillance and the inmates take to the streets
only to discover that the social fabric has been decimated by the pandemic.
Within this broad narrative frame, the film maintains a smaller focus on a
core group that moves from affliction to quarantine to postapocalyptic social existence. The real story lies in the shifting quality of life of this group
whose contours are defined by the first man both to lose and to regain his
sight, for it is this interpersonal experience of the pandemic that helps us
to understand its significance as a somatic metaphor for the journey from
ill-being to health in which physiology is a mirror for morality.

The film begins with close-up shots of red and green lights that alternate
with blurry images of cars in motion at short range. This visual constriction
gives way to medium-length shots that allow us to comprehend that we are
seeing a grid of rush-hour traffic obeying stop-and-go traffic-light signals. It
is at the corner of one such intersection that we see the first man go blind
(Yûsuke Iseya); a volley of car horns and a small throng of onlookers marks
the aberration from the normal flow of transit. From here, taking the first
blind man as a point of departure, the story follows in a contiguous manner
a constellation of characters with whom he comes into proximate contact:
a good Samaritan (Don McKellar) who drives him home, his wife (Yoshino
Kimura) who finds him there, the ophthalmologist (Mark Ruffalo) in his
office and later at home with his wife (Julianne Moore), a woman wearing
sunglasses (Alice Braga) whom we have earlier seen consulting with the
ophthalmologist turning a trick in a hotel. In quick succession, each of these
characters—and those with whom they have come into contact—go blind
in the same mysterious way that the first man has lost his sight in his car.

These introductory scenes seem to serve little purpose other than that of
presenting the major characters at the juncture of the blindness outbreak.
Their settings—the street, domestic interiors (living room, kitchen, study),

doctor's office (waiting room, examination room, office), pharmacy, and hotel—are completely average, and their behavior cleaves to a predictable routine in an urban context. At first glance there is nothing exceptional or noteworthy about this introductory sequence or the portrait of urban life that it presents.

What is significant in this social portrait becomes clear only by way of eventual contrast, as we see the order of normal life disintegrate. It is in this context of an extended exercise in contrast—particularly in the arena of interpersonal dynamics—that the set-up sequence becomes so important. When we revisit this sequence, we appreciate the extent to which low-grade negativity, isolation, and even violence predominate in every interaction, from the public to the private. As the film opens, the sounds of cars screeching to a halt and honking establish the qualitative tenor of urban life; one of the first medium shots shows cars and pedestrians each trying to beat the other out at a light, the cars lurching forward in premature motion before the light changes, but having to jerk to a halt as pedestrians strike out from the pavement in a mad dash to cross before the traffic resumes. This brief shot encapsulates the urban pathos as that of an unempathic and literally breakneck competition over resources—here, of time and public space—in an attempt to assert the self over the other. Self and other coexist in a dynamic of constant and unrelenting antagonism and separation no matter how numerically abundant or intimate the contact.

The quality of interaction in every scene of the introductory sequence builds a composite picture of distance, tension, and conflict as the default way of life. Once the good Samaritan has gotten the blind man home, a remark about the upscale interior is enough to make the blind man instantly and visibly nervous about the presence of his visitor, whom he ushers out abruptly. When the blind man's wife comes home to find a broken vase on the floor, she complains about the loss and reproaches her husband that she is not his "maid." Once the couple realize that the good Samaritan has in fact stolen their car, the blind man lashes out in recrimination: "What kind of man steals from a blind man? He should go blind." At the doctor's office, the mother (Fabiana Guglielmetti) of a young boy (Mitchell Nye) vents her frustration that the blind man is admitted ahead of her son. The subsequent conversation between the blind man and the ophthalmologist is charged with tension, including the careless expression of doubt by the doctor as to the veracity of his patient's claim of blindness and the blind man's angry retort in self-defense.

Later, when the woman from the ophthalmologist's office who has been granted orders to wear her sunglasses except when bathing or sleeping is playfully asked by a flirtatious store cashier (Mpho Koaho) what she is "hiding from," she coldly replies, "Jerks like you," causing his face to freeze up with the pain of insult. It has been clear from the woman's earlier exchange with the ophthalmologist that she desires, more than needs, permission to wear her sunglasses—we don't know what medical reason motivates their use. Her ensuing disposition of icy distance and hostility—in a store ironically called Harmonia—and the emotional disengagement with which we then see her inform her sex-work client that she will turn her trick with her sunglasses on ("doctor's orders") embody the emotional status quo as one of chronic detachment from the other in which only self-interested absorption—in one's own needs, in one's own affairs, in one's own feelings and experiences, in one's own best interests—is possible.

Yet this self-absorption does not stem from a positive feeling of self-love, but rather from a negative feeling of insecurity that must be mitigated by unbridled narcissism. Indeed, Christopher Lasch's 1979 diagnosis of narcissism as the central affliction of Western bourgeois capitalism describes the social state of affairs that *Blindness* depicts as the dominant paradigm: "the culture of competitive individualism, which in its decadence has carried the logic of individualism to the extreme of a war of all against all, the pursuit of happiness to the dead end of a narcissistic preoccupation with the self" (xv). Lasch regards unfettered narcissism as the swan song of this "culture of competitive individualism"; as though to render that prediction of demise in narrative form, *Blindness* stages social apocalypse in the form of pandemic illness. The body politic is afflicted as though—again—it were a single organism whose ill-being had reached a tipping point toward terminal unsustainability. Both Lasch's *Culture of Narcissism* and *Blindness* diagnose capitalist culture's moral condition in the language of the feeling soma.

The moral character of the physiological affliction in *Blindness* comes into view during a conversation between the ophthalmologist and his wife, whom we meet for the first time following her husband's examination of the first blind man. As the doctor muses aloud about a possible diagnosis of his patient's inexplicable blindness, it is his wife who proposes the true nature of the pandemic, though the codependent pattern of his condescension and her self-deprecation prevent them both from appreciating the import of her hypothesis:

OPHTHALMOLOGIST: It could be something neurological, like something we call agnosia, which is an inability to recognize familiar objects.

WIFE: Agnosia?

OPHTHALMOLOGIST: That's right. It's as if a man sees, I don't know,
a fork; he looks at it and says, "What is this? I've never seen anything
like this before."

WIFE: Is that related to agnosticism?

OPHTHALMOLOGIST: In what way?

WIFE: You know, agnosia, agnosticism . . .

OPHTHALMOLOGIST: Etymologically speaking?

WIFE: Yeah, didn't you take Latin?

OPHTHALMOLOGIST: It's actually Greek, dear.

WIFE: Well, I bet it has something to do with ignorance or lack of belief.
There's a lot of judgment in that word. Oh, never mind. Never mind.
You want some more wine?

OPHTHALMOLOGIST: No, but are you sure you do?

In an extended excerpt of Lasch's *Culture of Narcissism* reprinted in
its May-June 2011 issue, the alternative press *Utne Reader* calls narcissism
a pandemic—describing Lasch's text as "so spot-on and even prophetic
that it could have been written this year" ("Enough About You")—in a
characterization that resonates strongly with *Blindness*'s premise. The oph-
thalmalogist's wife gestures toward the understanding of what her husband, once afflicted, will call the "contagious" nature of the blindness as a
moral, rather than physiological, contagion. Indeed, all the characters we
first meet are afflicted in the same order in which they come into contact.
The introductory sequence concludes with a quick montage of newly blind
characters that signifies the inevitably universal character of the affliction—
as though one collective soma, the entire body politic will fall victim to the
blindness. But, contrary to what the ophthalmologist assumes, the spectator is given no cause to surmise that that contact must be physical, because
several of the characters in the montage of successive blindness have had
only proximate contact; they have been in each other's presence, but have
not touched onscreen. This ambiguity of contagion only further develops
the idea of blindness as moral affliction, as an illness derived more from
a common way of life than from a physiological transmission—although
the fact that the film never resolves the limits between the moral and the
physiological creates a conceptual collapse of any difference between the

two that is important to note, for, once again, there is no epistemological transcendence of the somatic. The morality of social systems is represented as an emotional-physiological state of health—more precisely, at the outset of *Blindness*, a lack thereof.

If the film's insistence on the normalcy of its depiction of capitalist city life gives its representation of the associated narcissistic malaise a subtle quality at the outset of the story, then that subtlety quickly gives way to hyperbole once the initial cast of characters finds itself confined by the government to a crude quarantine shelter that is "staffed" only by armed guards in sentry boxes outside the building who shoot down anyone attempting to leave. As the afflicted arrive in greater numbers at the quarantine, access to resources becomes contentious. One group—Ward 3—tyrannizes the other inmates under the leadership of a self-proclaimed "king" (Gael García Bernal). This exclusively male ward replicates the logic of the urban city we have seen in the introduction in a perverse magnification that renders the patterns of its ill-being explicit and unmistakable. In the hands of Ward 3, a single gun and the building's public address system are sufficient to impose a reign of violent coercion over the entire quarantine. The "king" and his henchmen commandeer all the boxed rations that the government delivers to the quarantine and make their distribution contingent upon payment. The exaction of valuables becomes the first method of payment; we see the sacrifice of such prize possessions as wedding rings, crucifix pendant necklaces, and watches in exchange for food. A man blind long before the epidemic (Maury Chaykin) and versed in Braille mathematics keeps a tally of goods and foodstuffs, becoming the accountant of greed. Once the glorified theft of valuables is exhausted, Ward 3 extorts a new form of payment: female prostitution. Desperate to survive, the other wards reluctantly acquiesce. In keeping with the pattern of escalating demands, bartered rape becomes increasingly violent. The inevitable comes to pass: a woman dies while performing this brutal sex work in Ward 3. Once the line of respecting life has been crossed, the ophthalmologist's wife leads a principled mutiny by stabbing the "king" to death, inciting a chaotic stampede toward the outside only to discover that the sentry posts have been abandoned; the interns are free to go.

All the while that the reign of terror by Ward 3 has intensified capitalist cultural logic—with its contextually nonsensical but unshakable faith in the eternal exchange value of luxury items that are also markers of social status, with its self-arrogated function of hoarding and "selling" resources needed even for the most basic survival, with its disregard for others so radical as to exploit to the points of rape and death—the ophthalmologist's wife has represented an alternative model of social organization. If in "normal" life she neutralized herself with wine and self-doubt, the outbreak of the epidemic forces her to find her strength. With the sole and brief exception of a black man with an eye patch (Danny Glover) who counsels empathic generosity to the mother frustrated when the first blind man is seen before her son in the ophthalmologist's waiting room ("Miss, let him go; he's worse off than we are"), the ophthalmologist's wife is the only character who demonstrates compassionate affection and care. Whereas other victims have been treated with skepticism and abuse, the doctor's wife embraces her husband when he discovers he can't see, comforts him, kisses his eyelids, pretends to be afflicted in order to accompany him into quarantine. For a time, she manages to instill a regimen of equity and respect among the interns. When the rule of Ward 3 takes shape in stark contrast to her paradigm of kindness and reciprocity, it becomes clear that the quarantine is a kind of social crucible in which normal life on the outside is distilled to a contest between its elements of well-being and ill-being, with the latter reified to the point of implosion. Yet the ophthalmologist's wife does not give up; once having reclaimed freedom, she leads her small group to safety, first procuring food for everyone—in contrast to the hordes who only pillage the remains of grocery stores to satiate their own hunger—and leading them to the safety of her home.

This final extended scene of the film represents the realization of the alternative social order modeled by the ophthalmologist's wife. First, the rigid compartmentalizations by race and professional hierarchy operative in the normal society of the introductory sequence—and also into the experience of quarantine, where individuals are identified by profession and race—completely disappear. In addition to her husband, the ophthalmologist's wife shelters the black man with the eye patch, the prostitute, the first blind man and his wife, the son of the woman in the waiting room, and a dog: the classic sociological differences of class, race, and gender are (with the curious exception of homosexuality) fully represented and resolved within this utopic group. As soon as they enter the house, the opthalmologist's wife offers clean clothes; when the opthalmologist asks if she is talking to him, she clarifies that she is addressing "everyone." These first words in the house underscore her vision of the group as a collective—as a de facto family—where only the plural way of thinking makes any sense. "I want you to feel at home here, because this is your home now too," she announces.

The entire group sheds its dirty clothes and bathes, with the camera focusing on the mirth of communal cleansing and lingering on the shimmering contours of wet flesh in a symbolic act of rebirth that is joyous. No longer are there sharp words or gestures exchanged as at the outset of the film, but rather gentle words and caresses. The rebirth is followed by what we might consider a "first supper" in which all share equitably the bounty that the ophthalmologist's wife has managed to secure for them. It is in this context that the first man to lose his sight is also the first to regain it; as he marvels amid the smiles and excited laughter of the others, he exclaims, "I love you guys, you guys are so beautiful!" Overcome with emotion, the ophthalmologist's wife walks onto her balcony and looks upward. The screen shows a sky of pure white. A shot of the wife's face registers her fear: perhaps she, too, now has finally succumbed to the epidemic. But a traveling perspective shot of what she sees as she lowers her head immediately counters this fear with the contrary emotion of hope: the white resolves into a colorful city skyline standing tall and proud behind a swath of trees. This final shot of the film contrasts profoundly with the first shots of green and red lights in disorienting close-up. Where those lights were rigidly and mechanically segregated, obeying a logic of isolated compartmentalization and emotional indifference toward others, here, in the final vision of the ophthalmologist's wife, the cityscape has become reintegrated into a single collective whole, colorful and verdant. Once everyone regains their sight in the reverse sequence of how they lost it, this ending implies, they will not only have recuperated the faculty of vision but also the well-being that comes from the inner vision of mutual empathy—having come to "know," as the eye-patch man remarks while falling in love with the prostitute en route to final refuge, "that part inside us that has no name."

The meaning of the film's extended trope of knowledge and ignorance thus finally comes into view as a function of the relationship to objects of love. If agnosia is the inability to recognize familiar objects, and agnosticism the lack of belief, then the blindness epidemic is the physiological manifestation of a moral condition of narcissistic and ruthlessly acquisitive capitalist culture. This is so, the film's conclusion shows, because the familiar objects that the capitalist "blind" cannot recognize are their loved ones—others, understood as a broad moral and affective category—and the lack of belief is in the power of love to bind self to other in a bond that is not any less powerful for its namelessness. The sight and faith that are regained on the strength of the collective journey through blindness are firmly rooted in the fact of loving companionship, of antimaterialistic and interconnected togetherness.[9]

In *Blindness*, then, the faculty of sight exercised by people in a society visually described as compartmentalized along class-race-gender lines, profoundly unempathic, and frozen in a grid of hierarchical institutions that perpetuate acquisitional greed, is tantamount to blindness. This physiological symptom acts as a somatic manifestation of the fundamental condition of ill-being in a collective soma whose homeostasis is off-kilter, interrupted by the false divides of hierarchy—based on race, class, gender—but also, and most significantly, on the endemic and reified inability to bridge the veritable chasm that isolates self from other. As in *Mad Men*, the principle of homeostasis has been overpowered by that of the reward system; self-interest, self-absorption, and acquisitiveness have suppressed the balance that comes from moderate consumption and the modest satiation of appetites in a model of sufficiency rather than greed. This ill health represented by the synecdoche of blindness contrasts sharply with the inner capacity for true vision that the inhabitants of this rat-racing modern cityscape develop once they lose their sight in a pandemic of moral overtones. In proposing a remedy for the toxicity of the capitalist lifestyle, *Blindness* rejects the contemporary iteration of capitalism but embraces its epistemological principle of homeostasis. The inner—and profoundly emotional—vision that the small group of pioneers led by the ophthalmologist's wife develops as an affective form of knowledge of self and world serves as the basis for the moral cure of learning to live in a loving and collectivist community that works against excess and toward the communal harmony of common needs and shared goods. The paradise-as-commonwealth of this new social order is predicated on the power of love to overcome myopic capitalist vision and to inspire an existential condition of deeper collective insight that guides all component beings in a perfectly equitable relationship governed by empathy and love as the drivers and safeguards of resource allocation by necessity rather than greed.

Portraiture of the Homeostatic Principle: Neoliberalism as Ill-Being (*No Country for Old Men*), Revolution as Well-Being (*Diarios de motocicleta*)

This struggle between ill-being and well-being—the critics of neoliberalism denouncing neoliberalism's noxious effects, neoliberalism countering with the assertion of its salutary effects—revolves around the fundamental conceptual framework of homeostasis. The body's self-regulating mechanism takes place on the autonomic level and embraces sensory perception, sensation, emotion, and feeling. This autonomic sequence has become the aesthetic—and, indeed, epistemological—language in which to represent social and political meaning, a sequence organized, more precisely, into the cycle of addiction defended by neoliberal symbology as one that gives well-being and life and assailed by its critics as one that yields ill-being and death.

If *Mad Men* and *Blindness* represent, respectively, the genesis and apocalypse of capitalist addiction—fundamental ill-being masked by an illusory well-being provided by addictive consumption—then the Coen brothers' *No Country for Old Men* (2007) and Walter Salles's *Diarios de motocicleta* interrogate in narrative form the homeostatic principle of capital flow. Echoing *Mad Men*, *No Country for Old Men* posits a pathological iteration of that flow as one that takes, rather than supports, life. *Motorcycle Diaries*, on the other hand, resonates with *Blindness* in that it reasserts the vitality of the homeostatic principle in an economy based on love rather than capital.

No Country for Old Men:
"I got here the same way the quarter did"

Made by Joel and Ethan Coen, a team of brothers at the forefront of U.S. auteur and independent filmmaking, *No Country for Old Men* is among the most highly celebrated of their long list of films, nominated in 2007 for the Palme d'Or at the Cannes Film Festival and for eight Academy Awards, winning four for best film, best director(s), best screenplay adaptation, and best supporting actor for the Spanish cinematic wunderkind Javier Bardem. The film constitutes a slow and painful pathologization of contemporary culture for its addictions to violence and money. In the end, the title suggests, the only futurity in this vicious cycle is death, a death meted out in a flow of ill-being that goes against nature in turning homeostatic logic back on itself.

No Country for Old Men stages the lengthy and fruitless attempt by Sheriff Ed Tom Bell (Tommy Lee Jones) to capture psychopathic killer Anton Chigurh (Javier Bardem) while simultaneously protecting Vietnam veteran Llewelyn Moss (Josh Brolin) from the killer. Moss has come into Chigurh's deadly sights when, on a hunting trip in the desert, he makes off with a briefcase full of money that he lifts from the body-strewn scene of an illicit hand-off gone awry; this act of monetary possession makes Moss Chigurh's target in an unrelenting hunt. It is key to note that Bell and Moss are presented as takers of life alongside Chigurh, in a landscape of total death. The narrative begins with a voice-over recollection by Bell of a young man whom he has sent to the electric chair; we meet the war veteran Moss looking at gazelles through the crosshatching of his rifle. Although the film ostensibly posits Chigurh as the villain in opposition to the civic morality represented by Moss and Bell, the reality is that together they constitute a triumvirate of killers. Father, son, and holy ghost of a common cultural logic: Bell is bent on affording Moss fatherly protection, but his imaginary son inevitably falls prey to the merciless and almost supernaturally omnipresent and omnipotent Chigurh.

Chigurh is relentless, but not unprincipled; even Bell concedes, with a certain tone of respect for his nemesis, that Chigurh operates according to a certain moral code. The terms of this moral code are most explicitly articulated in the conversation that Chigurh sustains with a middle-aged gas station proprietor (Gene Jones), in whom Chirgurh incites a terse retrospective reflection on his life's path. This scene in a forlorn Texas town is framed by a long camera shot that foregrounds the Texaco sign marking the station, in which the logo is disproportionately large in comparison to the surrounding dusty wasteland, calling attention to the status of gas as a commodity to be bought and sold. Inside the store, Chigurh asks the sunken man behind the cash register how he came to operate the gas station and nearly chokes on a peanut in dismay when he finds out that the attendant has willingly and knowingly married into this life, inheriting his dismal and barren line of work from his wife's father. In what is a non sequitur for the proprietor, Chigurh then offers him a choice of heads or tails; the latter protests that he "didn't put nothin' up [as a bet]." Suddenly possessed of an animated but quiet indignation, Chigurh sternly corrects him: "Yes, you did. You've been putting it up your whole life; you just didn't know it." The still unwitting gas station owner is saved by the toss; Chigurh tells him to keep his lucky quarter separate from the others, as though the fact of setting money in circulation would cause its luck to sour.

The meaning of this scene becomes clear in a second discussion of a coin toss later in the film, this time between Chigurh and Moss's widow Carla Jean (Kate Macdonald). After Moss has met his demise with an inexorability that we now begin to surmise is related to the inevitable and inescapable ill effects of trafficking in money, and after her mother has succumbed to what she calls "the cancer," Chigurh comes for Carla Jean. When Chirgurh offers to attenuate the certainty of her death by substituting the coin as arbiter of her fate, she plaintively asks him to act autonomously from the luck of the toss—to separate his morality from that of chance: "The coin don't have no say; it's just you," she asserts. Chigurh responds, with a roll of his eyes at once exasperated and mournful, "I got here the same way the coin did." Carla Jean assumes that Chigurh possesses an autonomy independent of the quarter; she presumes, in a word, his possession of a free will that he deliberately elects—and immorally so—not to exercise. But what Chigurh attempts to convey in this otherwise nonsensical statement—"I got here the same way the coin did"—is that he has no freedom apart from the quarter, and, consequently, no logic he can obey other than that which it dictates: the certainty of homicide attenuated only by the chance of dumb luck.

At no time does *No Country for Old Men* explicitly define what Chigurh means when he unequivocally affirms that the gas station proprietor—as a capitalist everyman—has been "betting [his] whole life" or that he himself "got here the same way the quarter did"; these concepts hover in abstraction. The epigraph of Luc Boltanski and Ève Chiapello's *The New Spirit of Capitalism* (2005 [1999]), taken from French essayist Charles Péguy's *L'Argent* (*Money*, 1912), resonates uncannily with the theme of chance and life-long betting so central to *No Country for Old Men*:

> We have known, we have had contact with a world (as children we partook of it), where a man condemned to poverty was at least secure in poverty. It was a kind of unspoken contract between man and fate, and before the onset of modern times fate had never reneged on this contract. It was understood that those who indulged in extravagance, in caprice, those who gambled, those who wished to escape poverty, risked everything. Since they gambled, they could lose. But those who did not gamble could not lose. They could not have suspected that a time would come, that it was already here—and this, precisely, is modern times—when those who do not gamble lose all the time, even more assuredly than those who do.
>
> (xxx)

Like Ulrich Beck, who calls modernity a "risk society," Boltanski and Chiapello signal from the very outset of their tome on contemporary capitalism, with this single quotation, that gambling—risk taking, betting, riding on chance—may be understood as the single most emblematic characteristic of capitalist culture. For his part, Beck calls "chance and danger" the "two faces of risk" in a culture that depends upon decision making—not coincidentally the reason for being of a new interdisciplinary field of investigation called neuroeconomics—"decisions which play off positive and negative aspects against one another, which connect progress and decline and which, like all things human, are bearers of error, ignorance, hubris, the promise of control and, ultimately, even the seed of possible self-destruction" (*World at Risk*, 4).

In the figure of Chigurh, *No Country for Old Men* creates a cinematic poetics of capitalist gambling, understanding risk society only in the negative register, taking the "seed of possible self-destruction" to its full-blown aspect of a self-destruction that is assured and imminent as an existential state of capitalist affairs. In this sense we might consider Chigurh the perverse holy spirit of capitalist risk culture in which the foundational practice of risk taking is distilled to its starkest terms as a wager between life and death. This wager, furthermore, is predicated upon the pursuit of money—inscribed within money in its material aspect, we might even interpret the film as suggesting, since the path of the quarter is the path of chance, chance being understood no longer in its old valence of disinterested luck, but now in its new valence of dangerous—almost invariably fatal—risk. *No Country for Old Men* anthropomorphizes the cultural pathos of risk culture in the form of Chigurh, thus creating a villain for the age of global capitalism who embodies chance as a wager against death, a wager expressed as a function of the lethal transit of capital.

More of a grim reaper than a holy spirit, Chigurh's morality consists of bringing his victims—all participants in risk culture—face-to-face with the ultimate consequences of their lifestyle of get-rich-quick schemes and Walmart consumerism: all die or are marked for death. Chigurh, meanwhile, is the only real survivor. He is also the only character able to therapeutically regenerate himself—we see Chigurh perform a minor surgery on himself at one point after elaborately robbing a drug store for supplies with sophistication and knowledge, whereas an injured Moss must pay for a doctor's services. Chigurh is indestructible. At the end of the film, we see Chigurh walk away from what should have been a fatal car crash; the driver of the other car expires on impact. "The crime you see now, it's hard to take its measure," says Bell in voice-over as Chigurh first comes into view in the opening scene of the film; Chigurh represents the measureless, the infinite. And yet it is not, as Bell would hope, an aberration that Chigurh represents, but rather the central and reigning logic of capitalist culture.

Chigurh's weapon of choice is an air gun used to kill cattle, as Bell describes to Carla Jean in a seemingly disconnected musing about how vulnerable her husband Llewelyn is to Chigurh. The point is that Llewelyn is hunted down like an animal by Chigurh, but we should also take away the idea that the air gun is a metaphor for capitalist culture, whose operational logic has become one of murder by means of the very elements that should give life. Air does not give life; it kills.[10] As Chigurh limps away from the scene of the car crash, he bribes two young boys into silence about his whereabouts—"you didn't see me," he instructs them as he hands one of them a hundred-dollar bill. Immediately, the boys, who just before have offered to help the wounded Chigurh out of altruistic compassion, now lean down toward the bill—seeing only the bill and nothing else; having eyes, so to speak, only for the money—and literally don't see Chigurh exit the frame. The youngest generation is thus ushered into the logic of capitalist risk culture: they have earned easy money on the gamble that it is better to accept the grim reaper's terms than to follow their moral compass—in fact, the hundred-dollar bill substitutes itself instantly for that moral compass. The boys' initiation into the logic of capitalism demonstrates that there is no longer any choice; there is only chance: chance that they will stay alive even though they have given themselves over to the permanent risk of death for the sake of accumulating wealth. The hundred-dollar bill that Chigurh gives the boys comes from the case stolen by Llewelyn and recuperated by Chigurh, as though it were simply returned to the hands of its rightful owner: death. Indeed, Chigurh earlier asserts that he knows "to a certainty" where the satchel of stolen money "[is] going to be": "It will be brought to me and placed at my feet," he says, claiming perfect omniscience in matters of money. Chigurh is the spirit of money—the perverse holy spirit of the trinity formed with Bell as god the lawman and Moss as the sacrificial son martyred by his innocent faith in the virtue of chasing the dollar in his own failed pursuit of happiness.

Bell calls Chigurh a "phantom," and, in fact, he is literally represented as such in a sequence at the film's conceptual climax that exploits cinematographic discontinuity to metaphoric effect when the expectation of Chigurh's presence is followed by his inexplicable absence. After Moss is killed by the drug runners whose money he has stolen—in a death sentence dictated by Chigurh though executed by others—Bell returns to the scene of the crime to confront his nemesis, whose presence he expects with certainty. As Bell crosses the police tape to approach the motel room door, we see that it has in fact been blown out, as predicted, by Chigurh's signature air gun blast. Indeed, the camera cuts to a shot of Chigurh pressed up against the wall behind the door holding his air gun; we see two perspective shots of the empty lock cylinder in which we can make out distorted wavering reflections, one from inside the motel room (as though Chigurh were looking at Bell in the reflective metal) and one from outside (as though Bell were looking at Chigurh), but when Bell finally throws open the door, it hits an incontrovertibly bare wall. As Bell registers the room, there is evidence that Chigurh has entered and taken the money from its hiding place; however, contrary to our expectations, there is no Chigurh. A shot of the closed and locked bathroom window—which at first glance might seem gratuitous—along with the other shots of Bell registering the room, confirms the impossibility that Chigurh might have found a quick escape route before Bell threw open the door. Where there should be two men, there is only a double shadow of Bell against the wall.

Chigurh is Bell's conflicted internal twin, his force of ugly anagnorisis: Bell not only recognizes in Chigurh something that he calls a moral code; he seems to understand and even to admire Chigurh's morality. The spectator is given the opportunity to comprehend this moral affinity, for example, in the fact that Bell is repulsed by a news report of the base avarice and cruelty of a couple who tortures and kills the elderly to collect their social security checks, in the same way that Chigurh is disgusted by the wheedling attempts of bounty hunter Carson Wells (Woody Harrelson) to bribe his way out of death ("You should admit your situation; there would be more dignity in it"). Bell seems to understand that Chigurh is a pure and unadulterated force of moral justice over whose path he is absolutely powerless: Chigurh brings the world to summary trial and execution for its participation in the capitalist culture of constantly risking death; Bell is part of that world. Bell is, by his own admission, "overwhelmed" by what he perceives to be a new kind of crime in which ordinary people—kids—are driven to kill with pleasure and no remorse. Speaking of a young man he sent to the electric chair, Bell says in the voice-over that opens the film and defines its central theme of death: "He killed a fourteen-year-old girl. Paper said it was a crime of passion, but he told me there wasn't any passion to it. Told me he'd been planning to kill somebody for about as long as he could remember; said if they turned him out, he'd do it again. Said he knew he was going to hell. Be there in about fifteen minutes. I don't know what to make of that." And yet Bell's final lesson is also the impromptu family history delivered by his reclusive brother—who has rejected the human world for a family of felines—that the criminal order Bell faces is no different than what his predecessors faced and that to live by the sword is to die by the sword. In this sense, Bell is complicit in the same violence he seeks to quell, part of the same homicidal logic that drives capitalism.

What is so disturbing about Chigurh is that he destabilizes all complacency and myths of sovereign moral exception that Bell might cherish: anyone complicit in the logic of capitalist homicide—epitomized by money, which is always already blood money, the film suggests—must face the consequences of their own choices, which are always gambles. There are no decisions that do not involve wagers; everyone participates in immoral risk culture. Even Bell goes out on a limb of uncertain chance in falsely, at it turns out, claiming to be able to protect Llewelyn from Chigurh. Llewelyn may be likable, but he is not innocent, and it is the knowledge of the unsparing and unforgiving nature of Chigurh's mortal judgment that gets under Bell's skin and leaves him nervous and unsettled. Though Bell retires from duty after Llewelyn's murder, his final dream connotes riding to his death in a repetition of family—and, more broadly, capitalist—history. There is no innocence, only luck—the only way out from neoliberal immanence is on its own terms of risk. The flip of the coin, Chigurh urges Carla Jean to understand, "is the best [he] can do" to mitigate her hour of reckoning. Chigurh is the pathos of risk culture, the psychic internalization of its spirit of death that underwrites all possibility of prosperity and plenitude. Set in 1980, just before the onset of the Reagan years, and released in 2007, just before global economic recession, *No Country for Old Men* leaves us with the image of Chigurh limping off toward the horizon of imminent full-blown neoliberalism to collect gambling souls in abundance: he is the unyielding grim reaper of neoliberalism, a pure social mirror that reflects the capitalist social order as a constant wager with death, an implacable killing field.

Like capital is its purist theorizations, Chigurh is unsusceptible to borders and boundaries of any kind. As though possessed of divine powers, he seems to have unfettered access to any point in the collective soma he traverses. Chigurh assumes metaphysical dimensions of impossible ubiquity and circulation within the bounds of the social—he is anywhere and everywhere, in endless flux, never fixed or static, never ruled by the laws of inertia, but rather in constant movement throughout the social order that holds the characters together as though he were the perverse embodiment of homeostatic capital flow within it. Chigurh's is the logic of the luck-riddled quarter, whose path he travels to collect the souls condemned to death by its transit, as though tracing the path of a love for—or at least an addiction to—money that always proves fatal because its pursuit can never be more than an act of hubris, setting in motion a wager against death that can never be won except by dumb luck.

Diarios de motocicleta: *An Economy of Love for the Open Veins of Latin America*

Diarios de motocicleta (*The Motorcycle Diaries*), directed by Walter Salles, preeminent in Brazilian cinema and nominated for dozens of awards the world over, counters the fatalistic resignation of *No Country for Old Men* with the rejuvenation of revolution. Whereas *No Country for Old Men* presents a social portrait of ineluctable addiction to the deadly logic of capital flow, *Diarios de motocicleta* methodically dismantles the supports of this portrait, and, like *Blindness*, posits another in its place. If *Mad Men* travels back in time to identify the origins of contemporary cultural ills, then *Diarios de motocicleta* revisits the same time period in order to recuperate a model for their correction—a correction that is framed, significantly, as healing.[11]

The agent of this cultural therapy is none other than the young Argentine medical student and future revolutionary icon Ernesto Guevara (Gael García Bernal). Adapting Guevara's travelogue to the screen, *Diarios de motocicleta* recreates the well-known journey that he and his friend Alberto Granado made across continental Latin America in the early 1950s, during which Guevara's political conscience was progressively awakened. Like Mel Gibson's *The Passion of the Christ*, *Diarios de motocicleta* retells the story of a towering cultural icon, arguably the greatest in twentieth-century Latin America, who since his death has even become popularly canonized as "San Ernesto de la Higuera" in the Bolivian region of his execution. What is significant about this particular Che story is its emphasis on a personal journey from sickness to health as a narrative through line that we might say runs parallel to the story of his political awakening, but even more accurate would be to say that the film represents this movement from sickness to health as what underwrites his political awakening—what makes his revolutionary metamorphosis possible. In other words, politics *are* physiological disposition. Strongly echoing Gibson's treatment of Christ, Guevara's story under Salles's direction becomes a function of the feeling soma.

The very first shot of the film is a close-up of Ernesto's inhaler as he packs his bags for the famously transformative trip. During the establishing sequences, we see him using his inhaler while playing rugby, a sport inherited from British neocolonialism that signals Ernesto's well-to-do social status. Even in the blush of health, the film suggests, Ernesto is fundamentally unwell. As he leaves for his journey, his mother (Mercedes Morán) wraps a scarf around his neck with an anxious brow and tells him that as long as he uses his inhaler he will be fine. The film's chronicling of Ernesto's metamorphosis into the revolutionary Che will, in fact, adopt the same definitional axis of Ernesto as an asthmatic, and, as though his asthma were a marker of his bourgeois background, he will fight to overcome his asthma in the same measure that he struggles to reject bourgeois culture. Every time Ernesto confronts a major juncture in the development of his social conscience and principles, the film makes the challenge somatically manifest in relation to his asthmatic condition.

Ernesto thus begins his journey as a subject of illusory well-being who is really sick inside—in an echo of the blindness pandemic, his asthma represents the social sickness of privilege that is blind to the suffering of others. The bourgeoisie is ill, rotting from the inside out (a concept affirmed in floridly gothic style for the global age by Lucrecia Martel's *La Ciénaga*), though it clings hard and fast to the ultimately false appearance of well-being. This is also a cycle of dependency: Ernesto is addicted to the crutch of the inhaler just as he is emotionally addicted to his bourgeois lifestyle, most patently in the form of his ultrarich girlfriend Chichina (Mía Maestro), who entrusts him with what becomes, for the two travelers, a small fortune of fifteen dollars for the indulgence of buying her a bathing suit once he reaches the United States.

Ernesto's first challenge comes when he and his companion Alberto Granado (Rodrigo de la Serna) seek food and shelter from a provincial couple of means living comfortably in the countryside. The man of the house (Fernando Llosa) assents to host the pair for the night and, when he finds out they are medical students, asks that they examine a large protrusion on his neck. Ever the opportunist, Alberto says with a smile and a shrug that it is nothing but a harmless cyst; Ernesto more soberly tells his would-be host that it is most definitely a tumor and that he ought to seek proper medical treatment immediately. Stunned with disbelief and fear, the man angrily turns the pair away: he is the film's maximum example of the sick bourgeoisie that refuses to acknowledge its own cancerous condition. Grumpy and ill-humored, Alberto chides Ernesto for having cost them their food and shelter. Self-possessed and unwavering in his convictions, Ernesto replies, in his first exposition of principle, that every person has the right to know the truth in order to have the best foundation for action. Alberto rewards Ernesto for this first step toward political consciousness with the task of procuring their dinner; Ernesto must brave the cold waters of a pond to retrieve a fallen duck. In the next sequence, Ernesto suffers his first onscreen asthma attack. The contiguity of the scenes suggests a relationship between the development of his conscience and the relative strength of his body: the categorical privileging of truth over comforts is his first moral test; the ensuing asthma attack demonstrates that his body is not yet strong enough to shoulder the consequences of his emergent value system.

In spite of this serious episode, and in spite of the letter that Ernesto receives from Chichina ending their relationship, the companions continue on to enjoy a light-hearted and even mischievous trip until they cross paths with an indigenous couple (Brandon Cruz and Vilma M. Verdejo) in the Atacama Desert of Northern Chile whose dependence on travel for work and survival—the man is an itinerant miner—sets into sharp relief, particularly for Ernesto, the luxury of travel for the sake of travel. Both he and Alberto are clearly chastened by the contrast between the couple's dire necessity and their own comparative frivolity. As they sit talking late into the night around a fire about the difficulties of finding work, the loss of a home, and political persecution, the change that this self-proclaimed Communist couple works in Ernesto is written in the empathic gravitas of his face. But it will not be until later on in the film—significantly, on the heels of his second and even more extreme asthma attack—that we learn that Ernesto has secretly given Chichina's fifteen dollars to this couple. In reallocating these resources, Ernesto accomplishes the realignment of his affections from the bourgeois elite to the masses of Latin America; the currency of bourgeois capital is, in the process, redefined as a currency of affective solidarity. This symbolic redistribution of wealth inaugurates an economy of love as the currency of revolution.

The desert encounter with the mining couple has been made possible by the final demise of "La Poderosa" (The Powerful One), Alberto's motorcycle, which, like the tumor-addled provincial landowner and possibly the asthmatic Ernesto himself, turns out to suffer from a debilitating—and finally terminal—illness. The loss of this vehicle has forced the travelers to move through the body of Latin America on foot, abandoning the remove of bourgeois status and entering into an intimacy of unrestrainedly democratic encounter that has led them to the couple that changes Ernesto's heart.

This friendship leads Ernesto to witness the couple's exploitation—and the exploitation of a continent—at the hand of a foreign-owned mining company (Anaconda Mining Company) whose abusive Latin American overseer refuses to give the miners water, much less fair pay. Ernesto hurls a rock at the side of the truck as it pulls away with its selection of dayworkers, including his newfound friend; Ernesto's gesture seems small and purely symbolic in contrast to the metal casing of the truck, which represents the long reach and nearly invincible grip of foreign companies—echoing Glauber Rocha's Explint (Company of International Exploitation)—on the Latin American people and resources. At Machu Picchu, when Alberto gives voice to hedonistic fantasies of realizing political change by marrying into Inca nobility and spearheading a pacific revival of the Tupac Amaru revolutions of centuries before, Ernesto bluntly and laconically replies that a revolution *sin tiros* ("without gunshots") will have no effect. These few words constitute Ernesto's sole explicit meditation on the theme of revolution, but they indicate that the experience with the mining couple has irrevocably altered his political outlook. Within the film's economy of meaning, however, Ernesto must ready his body for revolution before he is able to shoulder the truths that his heart and mind are learning; it is thus that we must see Ernesto undergo hand-to-hand combat with his own internal ill-being and emerge victorious before he can openly reveal himself to have become the righteous lover of all of Latin America.

At this juncture, the film enters into its only explicitly pedagogical cycle: a sojourn at the house of liberal Peruvian doctor Hugo Pesce (Gustavo Bueno), who exposes Ernesto to José Carlos Mariátegui's *Siete ensayos de interpretación de la realidad peruana* (Seven Interpretive Essays on Peruvian Reality, 1928). Mariátegui was the founder of the Peruvian Communist Party and argues in his *Siete ensayos* that the indigenous way of life is fundamentally Communist and should be looked to as a model for a more just society. In keeping with the minimalist treatment of political metadiscourse—its rendering instead in affective terms—none of this background information is explicitly communicated in the film. The way that the spectator sees this important text take shape in Ernesto's consciousness is simply through a series of living stills that seem to interpellate him. That is, we see Ernesto absorbed in his reading, and as he turns the pages the onscreen image cuts from one full-body tableau vivant to the next with a powerful percussive beat, each frame featuring an indigenous figure gazing steadfastly at the camera—at Ernesto, we understand, calling him to social conscience through the simple act of eye-to-eye recognition.[12]

Armed with his two guiding principles of speaking only the truth and helping others, Ernesto arrives with Alberto at the Peruvian San Pablo Leper Colony, a visit the film figures as the apotheosis of Ernesto's revolutionary tutelage and transformation—the narrative climax in which Ernesto will finally embody his nascent political principles. From the outset, Ernesto refuses to be an accomplice to any of the supports of the hierarchical division between the lepers, on one side of the Amazon River, and the doctors and nuns who live on the other. First, he refuses the "purely symbolic" gloves that are required of the doctors by the nuns. Observing that leprosy under treatment is not communicable through skin-to-skin contact, Ernesto breaks with this institutionally imposed hierarchy of division, instead extending his hand in greeting to the first leper he meets on the "other" bank, a patient who can scarcely contain his surprise.

Although Ernesto and Alberto give the lepers medical attention, the bulk of the screen time in San Pablo is spent showing how their most significant "medicine" is the fortification of community and vitality: they build houses alongside the lepers, organize soccer matches fully integrated between the lepers and the medical staff, and break bread at the same tables. When Ernesto and Alberto refuse to attend mass, and therefore forfeit their right to be served food according to the nuns' dictates, the affectionate solidarity they have inspired in their patients leads the lepers to defy institutional repression by secretly preparing and serving two plates of food to their new friends, thus committing their first act of principled—protorevolutionary—insubordination. In a sequence that recalls the "first supper" of *Blindness*, this nutritional seed of revolution is figured as an act of affective communal care.

As the young students' stay comes to a close, a final celebration is organized on the "high" side of the river on the occasion of Ernesto's birthday. It is here that Ernesto delivers his only political sermon of the entire film in the form of a terse toast to his friends and to the *mestizo* Latin America that he has realized they all, together, form:

> Creemos—y después de este viaje más firmemente que antes—que la división de América en nacionalidades inciertas e ilusorias es completamente ficticia. Constituimos una sola raza mestiza desde México

hasta el Estrecho de Magallanes. Así que tratando de librarme de cual-
quier carga de provincialismo, ¡brindo por Perú y por América unida!

[We believe—and this journey has only confirmed this belief—that the
division of America into unstable and illusory nations is a complete
fiction. We are one single mestizo race from Mexico to the Magellan
Straits. And so, in an attempt to free ourselves from narrow-minded
provincialism, I propose a toast to Peru and to a united America!]

Leaving the doctors and nuns, Ernesto wanders down—in symbolic descent—to the river's edge in search of a way to cross in order to continue
the celebration of his birthday on the other side, with the lepers. It is nighttime and he can't find the rowboat, so Ernesto launches into the water,
swimming with strong and determined strokes. This, we understand, is the
somatic equivalent, and, in fact, the very foundation, of the words he has
just uttered. This attempt to cross the river on the strength of his bare life
puts the exorcism of his bourgeois ill-being to the ultimate challenge in
favor of a classless well-being.

As he swims, Alberto and the doctors and nuns cry out to him from their
bank of institutional privilege that he is crazy, that he will kill himself, that
he can't make it, to come back. Simultaneously, the lepers begin to gather
on the other side of the bank and encourage him from the very seat of abjection with great smiles and cheers of encouragement—he can do it, they
shout. This is the coming alive of the interpellative stills we have seen—the
tableaux vivants that have gazed on him in wordless expectancy. The lepers
represent the vital awakening of the downtrodden that Ernesto is meant
to help. We realize that the truly ill are the doctors and nuns who live in
their unhealthy and static world of vertical institutional normativity, like the
other bourgeois symbols of profound ill-being under the illusion of well-being we have seen in the film (and recalling Don Draper's dirty undershirt
beneath the whitewashing appearance of the brand new button-down),
whereas the putatively ill are, in truth, emotionally and spiritually robust,
full of hope and faith in this miraculous feat of self-renewal that represents
the potential of revolution to heal an entire continent. The lepers' illness is
the scourge the bourgeois world has assigned them, within which it confines
them as an abject support for the comparative power and authority and os-
tensible well-being of the bourgeois order itself—in other words, leprosy is
figured as nothing more or less than a bourgeois narrative. This dangerous

and physically grueling swim should have occasioned a third—and, perhaps, fatal—asthma attack, yet it does not take place. This time Ernesto's body does not give out. As he uses this new strength to cross the river, Ernesto simultaneously crosses into well-being and revolution—not only for himself, but for the entire colony as a microcosm of Latin America.[13] In the act of purging himself definitively of the limiting and debilitating stranglehold of his asthma, Ernesto liberates the entire community—high and low—from this cycle of foundational ill-being. It should be emphasized that Guevara's journals and biography show that he suffered from asthma to the end of his life. The contrast of this biographical fact with his filmic "cure" only underscores the intensely politicized symbolism ascribed to the well-being associated with the well body.

In the sequence that immediately follows Ernesto's triumphant arrival on the lepers' bank, the entire colony bids him and Alberto farewell. This scene affirms in its visual composition the revolutionary principles that Ernesto has spelled out with his symbolic swim: the nuns, doctors, and lepers stand together in admixture on the "low" bank, all waving goodbye to the pair of travelers in an unrestrained display of love and enthusiasm—even touching his clothing as though he were a Christ figure. This shot serves as the synthesis of Ernesto's emergent revolutionary activities: adhering to his moral principles, which have coalesced in his vision of a single *mestizo* Latin America free from division, he has bridged the social divide, eliminating hierarchies predicated on ill-being and establishing an egalitarian community held together by mutual respect and affection in place of the petrifying and asymmetrical rules of old. The integrity of Ernesto's body affirms his definitive shedding of bourgeois ill-being and the capacity to embody, finally, his new ideal of unified continental well-being.

In the closing scene of the film, Ernesto reflects—again, in terse simplicity—on all that he has seen: "Tanta injusticia" ("Such injustice"), he remarks to Alberto, with a brow furrowed in the pain of empathy that speaks volumes more than his words, before boarding a plane home to assimilate what he has experienced. The film thus brings us to the very edge of Ernesto's transition into Che, the last moments of Ernesto as Ernesto before he becomes the guerrillero that history remembers. The tagline of the film urges, "Let the world change you, and you can change the world"; this return to the revolutionary before he is a revolutionary exhorts the spectator to return to the time before the armed struggle in which he participated in Cuba, Angola, and Bolivia. Yet his is a story of struggle that history has since condemned to failure: the Bolivian military captured and executed Guevara with the clandestine training and assistance of the United States government, Africa has fallen into cycle after cycle of genocidal civil war, Cuba has slowly shriveled up into a shell of its former revolutionary self under four decades of economic embargo and extreme material privation, and Bolivia remains the poorest and most malnourished country in all of Latin America. Yet Salles's presentation of Che as Ernesto encourages us to wipe clean the otherwise fated slate of history, to begin anew, to take his transformational journey as a starting point for the initiation of a new revolutionary campaign for the global age. Salles brings us to the edge of this transformation and stops short: we are invited to fill in the blank page of revolution that he leaves pending as an off-screen promise. The representation of Ernesto's metamorphic travels in the era of full-blown global neoliberalism invites the revival of a revolutionary antidote for the ill-being of the twenty-first century.

In Salles's rendition the budding Che is not a fighter, but a healer. He does not take life; he gives life. The revolutionary for the global age is not a violent fighter, but a healer and a lover, a figure who makes the world better with the body rather than with a gun. This is not simply a return to the likes of John Lennon and Yoko Ono's "love-in" hotel room protests, for current cultural production emphasizes a full physiological engagement with the politics of love—with politics of all stripes—in an epistemic terrain that, in the intervening era of increasingly hegemonic capitalism, has borne the articulation of social interventions steadily toward an extreme of somatic expression. In *Diarios de motocicleta* the contestation of that capitalist hegemony of alleged ill-being is figured in the same conceptual terminology as a struggle to achieve well-being through a process of healing. As in *Blindness*, there is little distinction between the curative healing of self and other—the process of healing categorically breaks down those very divisions as mechanisms of unhealthy separation associated with capitalist hierarchy. Social health becomes the extension of individual health as Ernesto's self-healing positions itself as the first in an outward wave of propagations that will extend that therapy of the self outward to all of society as though in an organic ripple effect.

Moreover, this internal healing and movement toward well-being finds its outward analogue in Ernesto's movement through the "soma" of continental Latin America. Significantly, this is not a portrait of the elitist revolutionary "vanguard" that Guevara himself posited in his writings, but rather that of a revolutionary in no way at a vertical remove from the people. In *Diarios de motocicleta* the future Che emerges as one with the people in a horizontal model of revolution that resonates with the homeostatic principle of democracy and free-market capitalism—of the people and by the people. Ernesto circulates through the soma, meeting an eclectic diversity of non-professional actors who are meant to represent Latin America as a *mestizo* amalgam, achieving a ubiquity and omnipresence that recalls *No Country for Old Men*'s Chigurh, for whom we might think of Ernesto as an antidote. Whereas Chigurh travels through the moribund body politic as a grim reaper of capitalism, Ernesto restores that body to vitality as an anticapitalist agent of revolutionary solidarity. Ernesto's journey through the open veins of Latin America establishes an economy based on love rather than capital in which interconnectedness derives from affective rather than exploitative bonds and resources obey the flow of horizontal solidarity instead of vertical profit.

Although Ernesto and Chigurh are narrative antidotes, they are never-theless built on the same underlying conceptual model: both are figured as a kind of "blood" or vital energy that travels as though by superconduction through the body politic as a collective feeling organism—Ernesto giving life in love, Chigurh taking life in sorrowful resignation.

Homeostatic Subjectivity

A simple and recurrent pattern emerges across continents, across media: cultural subjectivity—the cultural body politic—is figured as a feeling soma, and the political agency of that feeling soma is figured in terms of its health as a struggle between ill-being and well-being. This struggle represents the contest between competing cultural models—a contest rooted principally in their relationship to material resources—and the balance between ill-being and well-being signals the status of that contest on the spectrum between the respective poles of failure and success.

The cultural narrative considered here ranges from the critical identifi-cation of the pattern of capitalist ill-being (*Mad Men*, *No Country for Old Men*) to its dissident—or even revolutionary—contestation (*Blindness*, *Diarios de motocicleta*).[14] In the narrative critical of U.S.-driven capitalist culture from within the United States, that culture is epitomized by consumption, which is represented as a loop of addiction—or, alternately, narcissism—in which a fundamental state of ill-being is only aggravated by the effects of ever increasing dependence on consumption as a drug that provides a well-being as illusory as it is fleeting, activating the reward center to override the body's natural equilibrium and causing the body to consume more in pursuit of a temporary surge that feels like wellness but only leaves an aftermath of toxicity. In the narrative contestatory of U.S.-driven capitalist culture originating within Latin America, that culture is represented as an asymmetrical and unjust—neocolonial—force of exploitation in which the exploitative asymmetry creates a somatic imbalance in the cultural subject where ill-being predominates over well-being; the dissident cultural subject rejects that ill-being on the level of the feeling soma and strives toward well-being with the health of the individual being represented as the health of the whole, as though there were a perfectly interconnected communicativity between the individual and the collective soma.

Underlying every representational iteration of the health of the feeling soma is the same basic principle of affective homeostasis—that is, an automatic self-regulation of the organism toward the maximization of well-being, with the results of that self-regulation being visible in the net balance of emotion. The affirmation of happiness constitutes a status quo; the accusation of unhappiness requires remediation. This homeostatic principle is epistemologically hegemonic, serving as the blueprint for how we assess—whether affirmatively or critically, whether elegizing or disavowing—our range of possible social structures and as the basis of the imaginary from which we derive the parameters of our possible social intervention.

4 Legs, Love, and Life
The Affective Political Actor as a Well Being

In the homeostatic logic of the epistemically affective subject, love becomes both a catalyst and a synecdoche for organic health. The preponderant role of love in narratives about overcoming ill-being to achieve well-being has the cumulative effect of coronating love as a "king" emotion that catalyzes this process; love is overwhelmingly cast as the curative mechanism through which a homeostatically challenged body achieves a plenitude that is manifest both physically and emotionally, in a perfect homology between these two dimensions. The flow and balance of nonrational emotion is thus posited as a kind of moral superconductor that determines the disposition of the soma: if the body experiences a wash of positive emotion, it will outwardly manifest signs of health; if the body experiences a wash of negative emotion, it will outwardly manifest signs of disease. Within this conceptual matrix, love is the champion positive emotion that dynamically secures a net balance of well-being throughout the soma and, therefore, is the agent of health.

Love does more than cure the individual body. Because love establishes a bridge of empathy and care between self and other in which the very boundary between self and other disappears, love has the effect of what we might call establishing community, which, in the affective lexicon, we could equate as synonymous with expanding the feeling soma to embrace this plurality of self and other newly enjoined in a state of emotional and healthy singularity. It is love, in other words, that brings affective subjects into organic unity, whether as a community of two or of humanity at large. Moreover, in narratives that participate in what we might call an affective sustainability script (whether explicitly or implicitly treating issues of social, ecological, or planetary longevity), love underwrites the feeling soma in its most capacious planetary guise. That is, love is represented as bringing all sentient beings—humans, animals, nature—into organic unity.

This chapter will explore how contemporary cultural narrative persistently stages this "love story" as one in which the internal homeostatic equilibrium of the protagonist is recuperated for the better after a period of struggle with ill-being and disease. The restoration of good health is accompanied by a restoration of bodily integrity—what disability studies calls "able-bodiedness"—that is, in turn, accompanied by the integration of that body within a larger sentient community in which the individual and the collective are interchangeably represented as part and whole of the same feeling soma.

In the diverse narratives gathered together here in this chapter, the return to health is represented as a getting of legs, both literally and figuratively. Ill-being is recurrently represented in connection with the physical handicap of disabled legs, which is correlatively figured as an emotional stagnation due to negative emotions or sheer disaffection. The recuperation of able legs—and emotional mobility—occurs on the strength of a flood of positive emotion headed up by love. The recuperation of legs through love reaffirms the life force of the sentient individual—the protagonist—and has the effect of relocating the protagonist within a set of collective coordinates embracing, in concentric outward circles, the beloved, a new community, and all of nature itself. In this regard I would argue that the love story in the cultural context of epistemic affect tends more often than not toward the sustainability script. That is, whether the love narrative intentionally inscribes itself within sustainability discourse or not, its self-fashioned parameters nevertheless evince an understanding of homeostatically defined subjectivity as one that embraces all of life itself.

The final aspect of the sustainability love story I would like to underscore before entering into several such analyses in the U.S. and Latin American contexts alike is its political dimension. The being that is unwell—the ill being—is often initially located within a context of political adversity. A system of abuse and injustice, which is emotionally coded as cold—unfeeling, unempathetic, and even hateful—is thus assigned responsibility for the ill-being of the protagonist. The pivotal juncture of the love encounter is thus staged as a moment of revolutionary transformation, and even subversion, in which the immobile ill being becomes a mobile well being capable of critiquing, denouncing, and even resisting the politics of ill-being from a subject position now defined by a politics of well-being asserted by a system of care and justice, which is emotionally coded as warm—sentient, empathic, and loving. The politics of ill-being are represented as a homeostatics gone awry in which negative emotion and disease have perversely come to constitute a point of equilibrium, maintained through violence or repression; the politics of well-being are represented as a homeostatics recuperated and realigned with a point of equilibrium resting on positive emotion and health maintained by love and freedom.

The homology between the physical and the emotional therefore takes on a further dimension: the political. Within the feeling soma, political action is figured as being a function of healthful well-being. Since love confers this latter disposition, it is love that serves as a catalyst for political intervention. Without love and health, political subjectivity cannot come into being; the sentient being suffers in a state of compromised health—disease—that denotes political abjection, which makes political plenitude impossible. Political participation is thus figured, simply, as the ability to form part of the feeling soma—to count oneself within the singular subject of limitless component heterogeneity. The lack of homeostatic equilibrium precludes participatory affective subjectivity. The denunciation of ill-being is thus the maximum political critique, for it effectively accuses a governing system of preventing its constituents from internal participation by incurring disease as a physical, emotional, and political condition that atrophies robust homeostatic function and truncates subjectivity. The assertion of well-being, in contrast, is the ultimate affirmation of a governing system as one that includes all its constituents within internal participation by fostering health as a physical, emotional, and political condition that optimizes robust homeostatic function and maximizes subjectivity. Love, as the superconductor of well-being, and health, as the requisite condition for political subjectivity within an affectively epistemic culture, therefore become the prize conceptual topoi for whose control a discursive battle is waged. Being well is participation within the body politic of the feeling soma; it *is* political participation in the democratic–free market complex.

The Organic Love Story

Although the close readings in this chapter will focus largely on texts that approach the planetary feeling body—and the sustainability script of a loving expansion of that collective body toward well-being—from a perspective critical of capitalism, there is arguably nowhere other than consumerist discourse itself that love and nature have been more strategically linked. The multinational Japanese electronics company TDK, for example, has created an internal certification process by which environmentally conscious products are rated as "Eco Love" or "Super Eco Love" based on their comprehensive assessment scores. The products thus certified are marked with logos that bear a gridlike globe out of which grows, as though on a delicate stalk that has the effect of softening the lines of the grid, a heart that rests gracefully atop the globe.

If TDK's logo constitutes a minimalist visual representation of the planetary feeling soma operating on the strength of love, then Stonyfield Farm's "organic love story" campaign literally and figuratively fleshes out the loving soma by creating a digital collective of consumers whose love for Stonyfield's products is woven through their testimonial storytelling into their love for the earth and community. One of the first mainstream organic food producers, yogurt maker Stonyfield Farm distributed its products in 2011 with foil lids that asked, "What's your organic love story? Visit stonyfield. com to tell us how you and organic got together." An inset picture of a woman pressing a red cut-out heart onto her chest and looking away with dreamy eyes and a smile completes the label. The company website hosts a seemingly vast archive of "organic moment" stories in writing and on video, from citizens to celebrities. The portal page to these stories that establish a wordplay on the so-called magic moment of falling in love is a patchwork grid of icon-sized faces in the visual trope of multitudinous collectivity that has become ubiquitous as a means of representing "everyone" in recent years. The Stonyfield campaign patently responds to CEO Gary Hirshberg's view that customer loyalty—and the willingness to pay more for an organic food product—comes from "building an emotional relationship with the consumer" (Gunther), which would seem, simply, to signal Stonyfield Farm's strategic integration within the affective groundswell in advertising that both cultivates and exploits affective cultural subjectivity.[1]

The Stonyfield campaign also resonates distinctly with an "organic moment" of romantic epiphany in a natural setting that recurs in films that stage intercultural Romeo-and-Juliet-star-crossed love stories whose central conflict revolves around whether to treat nature as a home or as resources for plunder. Three films in particular, *FernGully: The Last Rainforest* (1992), *Pocahontas* (1995), and *Avatar* (2009), are both love stories and sustainability scripts. Their narrative axes are so similar that a bevy of YouTube mash-ups pairs the audio of one with the video of another in varying permutations of all three films to demonstrate their interchangeability. The fundamental plot line of each stages the aggressive penetration of a native nonwhite culture by white Westerners in search of wealth through the extraction of native resources, which leads to a confrontation in which the native culture triumphs and protects its land and natural habitat. In each instance a white Western male protagonist emerges early on as a natural leader by virtue of his virility and adventuresome independence, at first in consonance with the established leadership of his kind and eventually in a moral dissonance that leads to political dissidence and revolt when he changes loyalties to side with the natives and lead them to justice over the invaders, either through diplomacy or warfare. The mechanism by which this shift of loyalties occurs in the Western hero is also always the same and is a prominent feature of the mash-ups: the Western hero meets a native maiden—always the most important and powerful of her kind—who educates him in the ways of nature, grants him entry into her native culture, and chooses him over a native suitor. The magic—and organic—moment that consolidates this process is one in which the Western hero and the native heroine couple romantically before the witness of nature. In each case this romantic bonding happens at the foot of a tree inhabited by an ancient feminine Mother Earth spirit and in each case—before, during, or after the coupling—the presence of seeds serves to signify nature's approval of the union, which formalizes the Western hero's invitation to transculturate, which he accepts by standing his ground against Western invasion and in defense of the native culture.

This transcultural and organic "getting together" of narrative film also finds its documentary counterpart. *Crude* (2009) and *The Garden* (2008) foreground the legal struggles, respectively, of Ecuadoran Amazonians against the contamination produced by Texaco-Chevron's oil drilling and of predominantly Latino Los Angeles residents against the expropriation of a public garden by the city in league with a private developer. In each case, it is Western celebrity intervention that garners media attention and broad-based international support for the aggrieved parties: in *Crude*, the support of singer Sting and his wife Trudie Styler—through their non-profit Rainforest Foundation—and in *The Garden*, the support of a small group of Hollywood stars, including Darryl Hannah and Danny Glover, have the effect of magnifying the power of the underdog—either a non-white native or ethnic minority—against the profit-seeking Western invader. Unlike the narrative films, neither documentary story has a utopian ending, but the publicity resulting from the media attention does work to level the otherwise vastly uneven David-and-Goliath playing field. The support of the Hollywood stars in *The Garden* has the effect of allowing the Latino gardeners to raise the $16.2 million required to save the city plots, and, though their offer of purchase is rejected and their garden razed, they are nevertheless able to relocate and establish a suburban garden on the outskirts of Los Angeles. In the case of *Crude*, the global public support for the Amazonians has led to the establishment of clean drinking water in affected areas and arguably provided the cultural clout needed to bolster the Ecuadoran court in its February 2011 decision levying an $18 billion fine against Chevron for its pollution of the Amazon.

In each film the arrival of the Western media star—here a white blond-haired and blue-eyed woman (for Daryl Hannah is the focus of the celebrity intervention in *The Garden*, eclipsing that of African American male Danny Glover)—is figured in a way that echoes significantly with the "organic love story" of *FernGully/Pocahontas/Avatar*. In *The Garden* Daryl Hannah is shown gardening alongside the Latinos and joining forces with the native gardeners to prevent their land from being razed (ultimately being forcibly removed from a tree and arrested, though this is not shown in the film). In *Crude* Trudie Styler's arrival in Ecuador is represented as an extended affective encounter over a series of meetings between Styler and Amazonian natives, the last and most emotional of which takes place with a family afflicted by cancer, with whom Styler is granted an off-camera session for the sake of privacy, as though this were the emotional equivalent to a bedroom scene. It is after this intimate tour that Styler's commitment to the cause is cemented and the money- and awareness-raising efforts begin on a massive scale, including a stadium-sized benefit performance by her legendary rock star husband. The deeply political commitment to cross cultural—and economic—lines in order to help those rendered subaltern and abject by one's own culture is represented as being driven by a kind of falling in love.

Posthuman Interspecies Love

This notion of ecolove, thus far studied as a love of the planet for the sake of fellow humans, expands to further dimensions of interspecies love between human and animal. This figuring of a love relationship between human and animal posits the animal as the new radical Other of the human being. In other words, the most conceptually—and, more important, emotionally— remote Other is no longer constituted by other humans beings themselves (i.e., along the lines of race, class, and gender canonical in academic social analysis since the advent of cultural studies); radical alterity is marked, instead, by nonhumanness.

An advertisement for the fully electric Nissan LEAF (Leading Environmentally friendly Affordable Family car, 2010) takes this human-animal love motif as its central concept. A written legend below the one-minute video embedded in the company website characterizes this encounter as one between car and planet: "100% electric. No tailpipe emissions, and for that matter, no tailpipe ("Innovation for the Planet"). The Nissan LEAF has arrived as a true innovation for the planet. And the planet is glad it's here." The advertisement takes this car-planet relationship further by allegorizing it as one between a human owner of a LEAF and a polar bear. The ad begins with a close-up of a drop of water falling from a melting block of ice. The camera pulls back to show an avalanche from the side of an iceberg plummet into the water as a lone polar bear watches on from his seat atop an even smaller strip of ice. A poignant and swelling piano melody plays as the polar bear swims through the water, arrives onshore, traverses a forest, seeks shelter from the rain beneath a freeway, walks down railroad tracks and along a highway, arriving at a city at nighttime. From a pause to contemplate the moon above the lights of the cityscape, the polar bear crosses a bridge, continues on across a city avenue, startles a raccoon as he laps water from a puddle in the cement, and, as day breaks, comes to a residential neighborhood. Here the bear makes a gentle roar, and the camera cuts to a driveway where a man in a suit, with a briefcase in one hand, and, with the other, reaching for his keys, walks briskly toward his Nissan LEAF. Stopping short, and frowning in a mixture of disbelief and fear, the man turns his head to behold the polar bear whose approach he senses from behind. The bear rears up, roars gently again as though in greeting, and gingerly places each of its paws over the man's shoulders in an embrace. His face transformed into a broad and heartfelt smile, the man puts his arms around the bear as the camera pulls back to show the two locked in a steady embrace at the side of the car. A voice-over sounds—"The 100 percent electric Nissan LEAF. Innovation for the planet. Innovation for all"—as a final shot of the sun in the sky morphs into the company's round logo.

Referenced simply as "Polar Bear" in online posts, the advertisement evokes what has become one of the most reified symbols of the climate change debate ever since Al Gore included an animated sequence in *An Inconvenient Truth* (2006) depicting polar bears swimming to their death in an open sea, with rising temperatures having deprived them of any and all remaining ice on which to rest. This image struck a chord in the cultural mainstream; after seeing the film in the theater, Princeton physicist and climate-change critic Freeman Dyson, for example, is said to have had to defend his views at close range when his wife, "with visions of drowning polar bears still in her eyes, reproached him: 'Everything you told me is wrong!' she cried" (Dawidoff 2). The Nissan LEAF advertisement thus strategically takes as its point of departure precisely the possible extinction of the polar bear as a tropological synecdoche for planetary devastation, giving the polar bear a mise-en-scène as a profoundly emotional subject in crisis.

As though drawn by an internal compass of the heart, the polar bear moves deliberately, with decision and determination, toward its object of loving gratitude. At the end of this journey is a human whose ecofriendly consumption has worked to save nature. It is important to note that this man is not styled as a rebel or dissident but as a squarely participating member of capitalist culture: he sports a matching two-piece suit and a button-down shirt, carries a briefcase, and wears a wedding ring—as we see when he lifts his arm to return the polar bear's hug—and lives in a typically American ranch house with a grassy front yard and open-air concrete driveway. The smallest of details—the lack of necktie, the bulky style of briefcase—code him as a somewhat offbeat capitalist professional, but a capitalist professional nonetheless. He expresses his commitment to the environment—to the polar bears of the world—as an act of consumption; the polar bear, in turn, has an innate comprehension and valorization of that gesture, as though there were a metaphysics of consumerism appreciable by the animal kingdom as the supreme expression of sentient life. The advertisement thus proposes that, where scientists, politicians, and activists have tried and failed to ensure planetary survival, the profit-consumption matrix prevails in yet another representation of the double bottom line, this time with planet and people bound together, no less, in interspecies love.

A discussion of what philosophical currents have coined as *posthumanism* is useful in unpacking interspecies love. As a conceptual current, posthumanism is proper to the post-Soviet era, making it contemporary with the epistemological watershed of affect. The *post* in *posthumanism* denotes not a point beyond humanity itself but rather an optic analogous to that of postmodernism or postcolonialism in which humanity as a concept is critically interrogated; the *post* signals that the conceptualization of humanity has moved toward a new definition. Although there are multiple denotations of the *posthuman*,[2] the definition that I wish to explore is the one that takes the vertical axis of the animal kingdom and flips it on its side to a perfectly horizontal position; in this new vision, humanity no longer presides over the rest of life from on high; rather, it humbly takes its place alongside every other species, with no distinction of hierarchy or privilege. That is, posthumanism reframes the hierarchy of the animal kingdom by viewing homo sapiens as one species among many instead of claiming sovereign exception, to make a posthuman application of Giorgio Agamben's terminology for human politics.

My pointed periodization of the emergence of posthumanism in the globalization era is meant to anticipate the observation of its conceptual affinity with the feeling soma of free-market democracy, since it posits a democratizing, egalitarian organicity of interspecies interconnectedness, an interconnectedness figured overwhelmingly in the postulate of emotion as a shared faculty. As mentioned in the introduction, the work of Charles Darwin (1998 [1872], and, a century later, Paul Ekman (1980), hypothesizes emotion as being universal among humans. But it is also hypothesized as being common across species. A spring 1999 article in *Emory Magazine* entitled "Why Do Voles Fall in Love?," for example, bears as its epigraph a line from Robert Palmer's 1985 hit song, "Might as Well Face It, You're Addicted to Love," an interspecies comparison that anticipates the furthest-reaching— and as yet speculative—conclusion of Thomas R. Insel's research, namely, that there may be a biochemical basis for love as common to humans as to the prairie voles whose female oxytocin and male vasopressin hormonal activity seem to be responsible for their mating for life.

Insel's colleague at the Yerkes Primate Center, the preeminent biologist Frans de Waal, argues for "putting the altruism back into altruism"

(2008)—countering the three-decade reign of the notion of "altruism" as selfishness established by Richard Dawkins's theory of evolution as genetic self-interest in *The Selfish Gene* (1976)—and in the process yielding a portrait of natural selection based not on the ruthless survival of the fittest but rather on what de Waal calls "empathy-induced altruism" that "derives its strength from the emotional stake it offers the self in the other's welfare" (279).[3] Whereas de Waal analyzes empathy from an intraspecies standpoint in the book-length version of this study, *The Age of Empathy: Nature's Lessons for a Kinder Humanity* (2010), extrapolating lessons for humanity from the animal kingdom, in *The Bonobo and the Atheist: In Search of Humanism Among the Primates* (2013) de Waal argues for the biological basis of morality along an evolutionary continuum from primates to humans.

De Waal's intervention thus mirrors in the sphere of scientific investigation the horizontality between humans and the rest of the animal kingdom that is posited in what might be considered the "animal" or "posthuman" turn in poststructuralist theoretical currents. Jacques Derrida is arguably most visible—and the most cited—among them: in "L'Animal que donc je suis (à suivre)" ("The Animal that Therefore I Am (More to Follow)," 1997), for example, Derrida revisits the question of the radical frontier with the Other interrogated in decades past as being between races, genders, social classes, or ideologies—but always an intrahuman Otherness—and relocates Otherness at the boundary between species, between humans and animals. In contemporary cultural theory—whether derived from poststructuralism, postcolonialism, or cultural studies—the Other poses the consummate moral challenge: knowing that the self-Other divide is untraversable, the self must yet attempt to traverse it for the sake of establishing a horizontal understanding that works to counter repressive hierarchies of power. The location of this Other at the level of the interanimal signals a marked shift in the conceptualization of the human self, which is no longer fundamentally anthropocentric. That is, the self-Other divide is no longer posited as human-human, but rather human-animal. Donna Haraway, for example, the erstwhile champion of a subversive cyborg-humanity (1985), has since redirected her attentions to the animal Other (e.g., *The Companion Species Manifesto: Dogs, People, and Significant Otherness* [2003] and *When Species Meet* [2007], the latter of which features on its cover a romantic-film silhouette of a dog's face and outstretched paw embracing a human hand).

I argue that the *post* in this strain of the posthuman impulse refers to a moving beyond the anthropocentric vision of the animal kingdom. To return to the discussion of Foucault's epistemic periodizations discussed in the preface, does this variant of posthumanist theoretical discourse also, therefore, suppose a moving beyond what Michel Foucault calls the epistemic reign of "man" (*The Order of Things*)? I would like to pause here to consider this question, because I have located its terms at the conceptual center of my study. Given that I have, on the one hand, posited a homologous relationship between Foucault's "birth of man" and the emergence of epistemic affect and, on the other, identified animal posthumanism as a symptomatic subset of epistemic affect, the apparent contradiction between Foucault's birth of man and animal posthumanism bears further consideration.

Foucault carefully periodizes the emergence of the "birth of man" in the late eighteenth century, arguing that this epistemic modality—that is, a way of apprehending the world and self—is a fundamentally "organic" mode of knowledge, organic in the sense of being conceptually modeled on the mechanisms internal to a living organism and no longer on the exogenous mechanisms of order prevalent during what Foucault calls the reign of the "classical" epistemic mode. I accept Foucault's periodization insofar as his study of Western epistemicity spanning the sixteenth to nineteenth centuries posits a single major tear in the age of revolution. I differ from Foucault in the terminological definition of these two epistemic periods that result: where Foucault refers to the early modern European period as being governed by a "classical" epistemic modality (based on a taxonomic, gridlike ordering principle), I would call it colonial reason; where Foucault refers to the postrevolutionary age of industrial revolution as the "invention of man," I would call it free-market affect. I propose this terminological difference with a double intent: first, to distinguish between reason and affect as epistemic vehicles—because for Foucault, it is an a priori assumption that all epistemes are intrinsically rational. Second, to attach socioeconomic modes of power to their epistemes in order to add a political dimension to the gesture of epistemic periodization, that we may turn our analysis intently on the question of fleshing out how each epistemic modality arises in a mutually supporting relationship with the predominant socioeconomic model of the era.

To return to the issue of posthumanism, it is significant to note that Foucault's "invention of man" is, in the lens of the present study, homologous with free-market affect. Yet Foucault also remarked that, as he wrote—in the late 1960s—he felt the rumblings of epistemic tremors on the same scale. To summarize what I discussed at greater length in the introduction, I argue that following the birth of free-market affect, reason and affect enter into a hybrid period in which free-market affect and colonial reason become fused, yielding the imperialism of free trade: during the nineteenth century, formalized in Europe as the "white man's burden" and *la mission civilisatrice* and informally represented in the United States as Manifest Destiny; during the twentieth century represented in the cold war division of the globe between neocolonial liberal democracies and occupied Communist states.[4] Formal decolonization—happening at the time Foucault was writing—coincided with the neoliberalization of the neocolonial West and culminated in the fall of the Soviet Union, and with it any further ideological obstacle from the history of the colonial West (the issue of the obstacle posed by the Arab world being another issue altogether, but one that is currently finding resolution in what appears to be the liberalization of the Arab world analogous to the liberalization of the Soviet Union in the early 1990s). This program of neoliberalism proposed a radical return to free-market principles: the penetration of all sectors of human affairs—economic, political, social, cultural—by market logic.

As a topos both theoretical and scientific, posthumanism emerges concurrently with affect as episteme in the wake of decolonization and the end of the cold war. Does posthumanism, in seeking to dethrone man from the center of the animal kingdom—from his self-arrogated monarchical position from which to colonize earth and beyond, as far as he can reach—seek to correct the neocolonial bent of the culture defined by free-market capitalism and liberal democracy, or does posthumanism unwittingly derive from and contribute to its epistemic foundation? In the sense that posthumanism essentially extends the concept of political subjectivity across species and planet—expanding the social compact to include the full animal kingdom and its habitat—it yields the most radical and penetrating reach of affective epistemicity, this analytical lens sharing its perspective of the immanence of the free-market project with Michael Hardt and Antonio Negri, for example, where they posit a constitutional inclusivity as the mode of interpellation of what they call contemporary empire—that is, one that always already imagines that it can embrace and comprehend everything; nothing, always already, lies outside; inherently, in accordance with its own logic, it has no outside. In answer to my question about the relationship between the birth of man and posthumanism, then, I would argue that posthumanism moves away from the delimitations of the episteme given by Foucault as "man" by expanding those limits to embrace sentient life itself. On the other hand, if we consider this expansion to be an intensification of the epistemic premise of the birth of man as that of organicity, then posthumanism is perfectly consonant with the epistemic paradigm Foucault seeks to signal with the "birth of man" and that I, in turn, seek to understand as the birth of epistemic affect.

Is posthumanism the discursive apology to a capitalist democratic system with pretensions of total global conquest? Or is posthumanism its ultimate discursive denunciation and contestation? In the sense that posthumanism challenges the anthropocentrism that underwrites the capitalist-democratic paradigm of imperialist growth and expansion, it levies a harsh critique. On the other hand, in the sense that posthumanism also takes the capitalist-democratic feeling soma and expands it to embrace all sentient life on a perfectly democratic and horizontal plane, posthumanism only works to perfect the affective epistemological underpinnings of the capitalist-democratic complex.

Returning to the question of sustainability discourse, which is both a critique and an epistemological affirmation of capitalist-democratic logic, posthumanism might be considered the discursive analogue of sustainability discourse—or perhaps even one of its conceptual variants or components. Bolivia's 2011 legislative "granting all nature equal rights to humans" by making Pachamama (the indigenous Andean term for Mother Earth) equal before the law (Vidal) would seem to resonate strongly with both posthumanist and sustainability discourses, and equally to work against the personhood granted to the capitalist corporation under U.S. law in the late nineteenth century. Does this gesture work to expropriate free-market epistemicity from free-market cultural politics? Or does it work, counter to all intentions and expectations, to reify its power?

The Nissan LEAF advertisement either deploys or exploits (depending upon the politics of interpretation) both posthumanist and sustainability discourses in the service of consumption—an ecoconsumerism, to be sure, but a consumerism nonetheless. What is critical to note is the extent to which all these diverse perspectives converge in narrating the same model of empathy-driven interspecies and planetary cohabitation in which emotional knowledge of the somatic experience generates pivotal action. Ill-being, whether outright illness or lack of ease, but always consciously registered by the body at the level of feeling, propels that feeling agent to move toward well-being, a state of health and ease. This movement takes place on the basis of affective and nonrational knowledge, planning, and execution. In this movement between the poles of ill-being and well-being, the individual and the planetary collective constitute perfect mirrors of one another—the micro and the macro are perfectly continuous, as though part of the same unbroken organic chain of a continuous systemic whole. The individual is the collective; the collective the individual.

The drop of water from the melting ice and the avalanche from the side of the iceberg in the first frames of the Nissan LEAF commercial establish as their point of departure an environmental ill-being that is reflected in the sad piano music and the melancholy way in which the polar bear is positioned with its back to the spectator as it solemnly beholds these signs of environmental devastation. The depressed stasis with which the polar bear apprehends ecological ill-being—his head on his paws with sorrowful eyes in one shot, his back stooped in dejection in another—establishes a continuity between bear and environment, yet this imperiled state contrasts sharply with the ensuing burst of activity the polar bear demonstrates in embarking on its energetic journey. Although the bear seems to know where it is going, the spectator does not, creating a suspense in which the definition of the journey's character antecedes the definition of its telos. As a result, the narrative focus rests on the journey itself and, most specifically, on the bear's disposition throughout—his dynamism, his self-determination and perseverance, his self-possessed movement toward a goal. From a mute and sad countenance on departure to robust roars as he nears his destination— with these vocalizations serving as much as an affirmation of the persistence of the self in the face of adversity as an affective overture—the bear moves toward well-being. Against the image of a polar bear reduced to a fatal degree of ill-being, then, the advertisement restores its agency and well-being, these latter being represented in the polar bear's anthropomorphized determination to cross the face of the earth in order to communicate an expression of love. The ad gives the polar bear back its legs, so to speak, a point on which the advertisement itself insists with several sustained close-ups throughout of the polar bear's legs in motion, both in the water and on land, in which the locomotion of putting one paw in front of the other is the central focus of the camera. Salutary self-determination—well-being— finds physiological representation as the ability to walk, to travel, to self-direct, to stay alive; infirm incapacity—ill-being—as a depressed stasis before the fact of environmental ruin, and with it, physiological death. Well-being is tied to planetary and interspecies survival and to a politics of sustainability; ill-being is tied to planetary and interspecies death and is the direct result of unsustainable practices.

Well-Being as a Love Story of the Able-Bodied

Here is where, finally, all these seemingly disparate threads come together: sustainability as love story, the extension of that love story to planetary—and posthuman—dimensions on the strength of a politics of empathy, and the definition of a politically enabled protagonism in the physiological vocabulary of able-bodiedness. To put this more simply, the representations of who may engage in a felicitous love encounter as a function of nature identify the characteristic of physiological integrity and fitness as a requisite for any candidate for organic romance. Not only does the Nissan LEAF camerawork emphasize the polar bear's physical prowess, exertion, and integrity; if we revisit the *FernGully/Pocahontas/Avatar* triad, we see that from the time of first encounter between Western hero and native love interest to their eventual coupling, the Westerner undergoes a rigorous and extensive process of physical training by the native love interest. Here the proverbial "going native" is rendered somatically in a pedagogical sequence that emphasizes physical dynamics as a primary course of engagement with, and point of entry within, the native environment: Jake must learn to swing from vines, to navigate the forest, to ride winged creatures—in short, to match her own boundless able-bodiedness in the context of the natural domain—before Neytiri will consent to a mutual declaration of love.

I have presented this set of films as though they were all equivalent in their status as sustainability texts, but only *FernGully* explicitly associates itself with sustainability discourse by treating the highly publicized theme of rainforest conservation. If it seems at this juncture to be a given that *Pocahontas* and *Avatar*, two films that share the same storyline to the point of evoking popular charges ranging from unoriginality to plagiarism, could equally be considered sustainability narratives, then I would argue that the affectively rendered triple bottom line—most frequently represented as the double bottom line of people and planet, with the elision of profit—and its central figures of well-being and ill-being as the extremes of political signification permeate contemporary cultural production, even that which does not cast itself as an argument about sustainability. Regardless of rubric, what I seek to underscore is the pervasive nature of what we might consider a sustainability script in which corporations occupy the position of the "bad guy," with profit for profit's sake identified as the central pathos that vexes—threatens, destroys, sickens—

the "good guys," who are indeed presented overwhelmingly in the plural (echoing the dimensions of the feeling soma) and whose ethos is one of interconnective love and native harmony with nature. I understand the recurrent dramatic antagonism of corporations versus nature (the latter understood as people and planet—the planetary feeling soma) as the inverse narrative rendition of the central concern of sustainability as a political project: how, as the Brundtland Commission proposed, to achieve maximum development (corporate growth and profit) while minimizing environmental degradation. The good-and-evil fairytale genre of cultural production—overwhelmingly produced to achieve the growth and profit of the companies that make them—nevertheless turns this desideratum on its head by proposing to minimize corporate growth and profit while maximizing environmental integrity.

I have gathered a set of U.S. and Latin American texts that stage a contest between well-being and ill-being as a function of able-bodiedness—specifically, as a function of the use of legs. James Cameron's high-tech U.S. blockbuster *Avatar* (2009) and Pixar's animated *WALL·E* (2008) represent antiprofit sustainability discourse from the North, Nike's 2008 Beijing Olympics "Courage" campaign its pro-profit analogue, and Salvadoran director Víctor Ruano's low-budget independent short *Ever Amado* (2007) and Mexican director Carlos Reygadas's critically acclaimed debut feature *Japón* (2002) the antiprofit counterpart from the South. In these film and advertising narratives, leglessness symbolizes the ill-being directly resultant from the neocolonial condition of profit-as-teleology and, as such, is correlated with death and the lack of human interconnectedness—cold isolation, at best; at worst, violence and hate. The recuperation of legs, on the other hand, is correlated with the surmounting of profit-as-teleology in a return to nature that proposes nature as the source of an organic and sustainable human social model in harmony with the environment as an organically arising alternative to capitalism and, as such, a source of love and life. One loses one's footing in capitalist culture; one can "get one's legs" in nature. Although all these narratives evince a common understanding of well-being and ill-being as politically empowered and disempowered positions, respectively, the difference between North and South once again emerges as a function of their endings: narrative from the North tends toward a final empowerment (well-being); narrative from the South toward disempowerment (ill-being).

Avatar: From Neocolonial Leglessness to Sustainable Legs

Avatar—the highest-grossing U.S. domestic release of all time with a lifetime worldwide gross of almost $3 billion[5] and plans for three sequels (Vijay)—displaces to the fictional planet of Pandora the conflict between capitalist and ecological concerns. Staging what *New York Review of Books* critic Daniel Mendelsohn calls its "apparently anticolonial, anticapitalist, antitechnology message" (1), *Avatar* effectively updates dependency theory for the twenty-first century: neocolonialism has become interplanetary neoliberalism; the third world has become Pandora; Native Americans and Africans are rendered as the native Na'vi; extractive commodities like timber, sugar, charcoal, rubber, coffee, tobacco, and beef are conceptually distilled as the fantastically valuable "unobtanium"; covert CIA operations have become overt mercenary operations; and the state has ceded without a trace to the Resources Development Administration (RDA), an omnipotent and faceless corporation that echoes Glauber Rocha's "Company of International Exploitation" (*Terra em transe* [Land in Anguish], 1967).

If, as Mendelsohn charges, the plot, characters, and themes of *Avatar* seem "highly derivative, if not outright plagiaristic" (1), then we might well consider that it is because all of the major twentieth-century conceptual variants of antiexploitative cultural discourse find composite representation therein. *Avatar* represents the full slate of anticolonial complaints against capitalism, but now passed through the conceptual filter of ecological concerns. That is, the plot politics of *Avatar* constitute a compendium of denunciations that updates the categories of colonialism and counterculture for the twenty-first century: now colonialism is synonymous with corporate capitalism; countercultural resistance to it with ecological activism. The film at once epitomizes and brings to the fore of our cultural consciousness the contemporary tendency to discursively approach the problems of asymmetrical global power through the rhetoric of the environment. Sustainability becomes politically vested as the vehicle for the countercultural position and message of old.

What is striking about how *Avatar* updates the category of colonial resistance is the way in which it defines sustainability. Contrary to what Mendelsohn characterizes as an "antitechnology" (2) posture, it is more accurate to say that *Avatar* pits one kind of technology against another. The natives' technology of sustainability goes head to head with the military technology of the human invaders. One might, for lack of an established term, call the natives' technology an antimaterialistic oneness of being (this linguistic lack only serving to deepen the conceptual opposition between native and human cultures, evoking the psychologically inflected theoretical opposition between the symbolic and presymbolic orders). The fact that this native technology resembles the internet in form and function—fiber-optic-like "bonding" between natives and other life forms, an exponential capacity for the storage of cultural information—evokes Michael Hardt and Antonio Negri's assertion that resistance for the age of immanent empire (tantamount to the corporate capitalism represented as the new colonialism in *Avatar*) will consist of the expropriation by the "multitude" of the technological instruments of their own oppression. Given that the Internet was developed as a vehicle for state and military communication, the triumph of fiber-optic bonding over military informatics in *Avatar* is not at all a rejection of technology but rather the casting of revolution—if we may agree that this term as yet has a place in twenty-first-century parlance—as a self-determined struggle of native technology (of the people, of the multitude) against military technology (of the colonialist, of empire). The triumphant native technology of sustainability serves the function of what we might call interconnective circulation, in stark contrast to how the human technology of war stands in the service of the static and isolated accumulation of capital.

This human and bellicose accumulation of capital is characterized as lifeless, driven toward death, in sharp opposition to the dynamism and vitality assigned to the native culture of circulation. Human culture is cold, given only to fear and unmitigated aggression directed toward any obstacle to accumulation in the expression of a violently exclusionary logic; native culture is warm, alive—in a word, loving—and inclusive on every level, from the emotional to the physiological. The Na'vi have a profoundly somatic—"grounded," in the current terminology of cognitive psychology—form of cognition, a form of cognition that also has a collective distribution as social memory (maximally represented by "Eywa," the Na'vi Mother Earth who resides in the matrix of life and its organically stored memory). Embodied intersubjectivity—or a kind of somatic communication—becomes both the hallmark of the Na'vi people and the mechanism that evokes and channels the audience's sympathy toward their cause. In other words, both the representation of affective—somatic, embodied, emotional, physiological—communication of the Na'vi (as opposed to the terse and unfeeling linguistic bark of military orders) as well as the participatory and experiential reception of this affective communication by the audience are what define and create a sympathetic identification with sustainability as a contestatory political platform.

The way in which this sustainability script becomes prescriptive and activist—even revolutionary, one might say, looking back to the mid-century language of the countercultural and anticolonial left—is to enact a shifting of loyalties. The figure for this cultural defection is Jake Sully (Sam Worthington), an ex-Marine rendered paraplegic in battle (in Venezuela, we are told—a current instance of the putatively hostile and dangerous third world),[6] who ultimately forsakes his human form altogether for his native Na'vi avatar designed for strategic cultural reconnaissance. Why is it that the pivotal character of this sustainability epic should be assigned—and defined by—disability in the form of nonfunctional legs? As the film's central symbol, Jake's legs efficiently and economically signify an affective equation and moral judgment: the human community as profoundly cold and uncaring, sacrificing the physical integrity of soldiers like Jake without compunction or recompense in their battles of greed; the Na'vi community as one of full-bodied vitality in which bodily integrity represents the unequivocal commitment to the embodied experience of life rather than the disembodied and lifeless accumulation of wealth. One of the most significant moments of the entire film is the brief sequence in which the audience sees Jake begin to run in his avatar body: we see his face and limbs in close-up, hear the happy rhythm of his respiratory exertion, see his human eyes flicker in delight behind closed lids, watch his avatar lips spread into a broad smile of boundless joy as he breaks past the stasis of human constraints and into dynamic unity with nature. The motif of Jake's disabled legs is conceptually foundational to the film's political narrative, and equally indispensable to the development of an affective identification with Jake that guides the audience toward moral support for his political decision to renounce colonialist capitalism for sustainable community. And toward the audience's willingness to throw over its own self-definition as human—and "White," one reviewer on Iranian.com says, applying the racialized category of colonial domination—in favor of an identification with a hybrid subaltern—and blue—Other. To opt for the third world circulation of love in place of the first world accumulation of capital, and thereby to save the first world from its own demise. For this is, as many have quite rightly charged, a myth of the white savior (e.g., Annalee Newitz's "When Will White People Stop Making Movies Like 'Avatar'?"). But it is not a white savior of the third world blue natives per se, but rather of the first world itself. If *Avatar* traffics in third world glorification, it is ultimately to show how the capital-driven first world may yet thwart the fate of death it has already meted out to its own mother—as the film has it—through a redemptive identification with the sustainable Other.

As a culture, we do not seem prepared to embrace this message in *Avatar* any more than we did in *Pocahontas*, Disney's ill-received attempt to capitalize on anticapitalist sentiment and the weakest link in the so-called princess industry that saved the company from financial ruin in the early 2000s, notwithstanding the comparative unpopularity of the Native American "princess." Internet mash-ups overlaying *Pocahontas* and *Avatar* audio-visuals in the wake of the latter film's release clearly seek to take the sting out of the analogous politicized storylines by rendering them trite and risible. *Avatar*'s fate at the March 2010 Academy Awards echoes this reluctance to take its narrative content seriously: though nominated for nine awards (best art direction, best cinematography, best directing, best film editing, best original score, best picture, best sound editing, best sound mixing, best visual effects), *Avatar* won only three (best art direction, best cinematography, best visual effects), in categories that solely valorized its technologically mediated aesthetic. *Avatar* received no wins in the directorial or picture categories, and did not even have a single acting nomination of which to speak, a treatment that marks *Avatar* as lacking in the serious human interest these awards traditionally affirm.

Yet we are clearly drawn to the subject matter of *Avatar*, if we may judge by the awarding of the Oscar for best director to Kathryn Bigelow for *The Hurt Locker* (2009), the story of a U.S. Army bomb technician in the current war in Iraq. Unlike *Avatar*, *The Hurt Locker* has been billed as being politically neutral—ultimately refusing to settle on a "moral frame" for, or judgment of, its war content (Orr)—and even accepted as a dignified portrait of military service by right-wing critics (e.g., Debbie Schlussel's blog: "About 'The Hurt Locker': Yes, It's a True Story; No, It's Not 'Left-Wing'"). Yet *The Hurt Locker* is also the "story of an addict" (Orr), as its opening epigraph, a quotation from journalist Chris Hedges's *War Is a Force That Gives Us Meaning* (2002), reads: "The rush of battle is often a potent and lethal addiction, for war is a drug." The caption fades out strategically, turning the last clause into a stand-alone assertion—"war is a drug"—and allowing this message to remain alone for several seconds as the only image on the otherwise black screen. Despite this seeming indictment of the military enterprise, the film itself manages not to stand in explicit political judgment of its protagonist, thereby skirting the pitfall of *Avatar* by maintaining an apparent political neutrality. Yet the fact that the film's heroic bomb technician ultimately chooses to begin a new tour of service instead of staying safely at home with his wife and infant son, though presented as the result of a profound soul-searching about his life's purpose, is a decision that nevertheless may be read as the ultimate condemnation of the war machine: it produces addicts who cannot be fathers, leaving the next generation rudderless, without guidance or direction.

If we understand Bigelow's film as a searing commentary on the pathos of military service—and indeed, of military heroism—then we might grant it the conceptual status of backstory to *Avatar*'s symbolic characterization, via Jake's war-inflicted paraplegia, of modern-day military service as a source of social ill-being. *Avatar* suggests that the military is a broken and joyless system: the de facto leglessness of Jake, who represents that system, is compounded by his heavy despair at always having to wake up from dreams of flying and by the inveterate cynicism of his wards on the shuttle that bears him to Pandora. When the servicemen arrive on the hostile planet, Jake, in voice-over, dryly notes that they are well paid to be there. Although this reference to monetary gain is quick and unglossed, we understand that the soldiers are trapped in a ludicrous cycle of desire for the accumulation of wealth that leads only to their death—for one of the first things we hear upon their arrival is the assurance of Colonel Miles Quaritch (Stephen Lang), in a second and now fatalistic appearance of cynicism that gives us to understand it as part of the fabric of military culture, that he will surely fail in his mission to protect them. But although *Avatar* paints an unflattering portrait of the military in corporate service (and it is as though there is no longer any other kind of service), this portrait is two-dimensional; it does not give a complex diagnosis of the social illness at play. *The Hurt Locker*, on the other hand, explores the structural pathology of military service, and zeroes in on its psychology and emotional landscape, concluding that war is a moral addiction. *The Hurt Locker*'s soldier protagonists are emotionally paralyzed; Jake's disabled legs may be viewed as the physical representation of their moral wounds.

So it is not that *Avatar* is off target in its characterization of human affairs as "legless"—wounded, death driven, caught up in a myopic and ultimately fatal attraction to materialism—but rather that it does not go far enough, deep enough, in exploring that pathos. Or maybe, in rendering that pathos in the two-dimensional terms of mythical archetype, it goes *too* far by proposing a truth about the neocolonial state of our contemporary global economic and cultural affairs we would rather not acknowledge. What is more objectionable: admitting that we share more values than we would like to say with the colonel, or admitting that we do not want to become the Other as a remedy for our excesses? That is, we do not want to be the Na'vi any more than we want to be Pocahontas. A blog critique of *Avatar* (@mazsa) makes this point succinctly in the representation of a terse dialogue between users:

> BIBOR.ORG: 'Would you rather be a Na'vi than a Man?'
> MAZSA.COM: 'Er . . . No.'

Yet the box office sales of *Avatar* give a popular lie to its dismissive critical reception. The film evidently strikes a cultural chord, and, since we do not seem to want to give a neocolonial name to what it touches, we instead fetishize its technology.

Rather than defend his film on the merits of its politics—though this is a Canadian director who canceled his application for U.S. citizenship when the neoconservative George W. Bush was elected president (Goodyear)—Cameron instead argues that the "heart" of the film is neither its politics, nor its technology, but rather its love story: "Too much is being said about the technology of this film. Quite frankly, I don't give a rat's ass how a film is made. It's an emotional story. It's a love story. They're not expecting that. The sci-fi/fantasy fans see the trailer, and they think, Cool—battles, robots. What you really need to get to is, Oh, it's that [meaning a love story], too" (Goodyear).

Avatar's love story can only take place because Jake recuperates his legs in the body of his blue hybrid Other-self (half his dead brother's DNA, which matches his own, and half Na'vi genetic material). The scene in which Jake wakes up in his Na'vi body is critical to the development of his love story, for it is an affective awakening in which he falls in love with his own new body that predisposes him to fall in love with another. As Jake comes to life in the form of his avatar, his excitement leads him to disregard all rules of safety and protocol that belong to the human side of affairs. The Na'vi Jake moves at will amid the shouts and reprimands of humans who unsuccessfully attempt to subject him to rational control. Na'vi Jake instead bursts past all such rationalized strictures on his freedom of movement and experience, crashing through the doors that seek to keep him within the bounds of the physical analogue of these rationalized constraints. Na'vi Jake is clumsy at first, but quickly finds his legs in an extended traveling close-up of his face and body as he begins to run. His face registers the movement beyond an initial disbelief into pure exhilaration as the realization dawns on him that, in this new body, he is no longer disabled.

The world of freedom and lush nature (these being synonymous conditions in the film's conceptual economy) is represented as physical integrity, completion, plenitude. The positing of Jake's recuperation of his legs as a liminal event—the event that marks his crossing of the threshold from one world to another—establishes a fundamental and essential opposition between the human world of wounded leglessness in aggressive pursuit of material riches and the native world of therapeutic physical full-bodiedness in peaceful harmony with immaterial wealth. As a second stage in this crossing over, Na'vi Jake meets his Na'vi love interest, Neytiri (Zoë Saldana), when she rescues him from predators—"thanators," agents of death—and simultaneously schools him in an unconditional respect for life. Among the first scenes we saw in the human world was the unceremonious, sterile, and undignified cremation within a glass chamber of Jake's brother's body in a cardboard box as Jake looked on impassively, with a dry-eyed and empty sadness. Here, in contrast, this foundational scene in the Na'vi world has Neytiri lamenting in an open display of emotion over the dead beast that Na'vi Jake has killed in self-defense and unapologetically outraged over what she teaches him to view as the unnecessary taking of life.

Two constellations of opposing terms come to define humans and Na'vi, respectively. On the human side: disability as ill-being, cynical lack of empathy and self-centered isolation, the linear will to destroy nature and kill other beings, all for the blind ambition of accumulating material wealth. On the Na'vi side: physical integrity as well-being, open-hearted empathy and outward-reaching interconnectedness, the will to protect nature and honor the life of other beings, all for the insightful participation in a web of sustainable being. Upon entry into the Na'vi world, the emotionally and physically paralyzed Jake gains legs, life, and love.[7] His own nascent self-love will be externalized as love for Neytiri in an affective flow that links beings within the Na'vi world—which is postulated as its own complete and viable alternative cosmos—in an endless circuit of interconnective communicativity.

Technology is not something outside this constellation of legs, life, and love; it is literally the fiber of vitality and affect and of their circulation in the currency of social memory. The natural world of Pandora is outfitted for participation in cosmic oneness: the superconductor unobtanium naturally occurs in highest concentration under the "Tree of Souls" that serves as the gateway to the Na'vi Mother Nature; life forms on Pandora, including the Na'vi people, are physiologically endowed with ports and cables—anemonelike tails with fiber-optic tentacles called "neural queues"—with which to "bond" with the receiving modules on other beings and with the very Tree of Souls and thereby to achieve a neural plug-in with the communicational web of this cosmic oneness. Technology on Pandora is not man-made or bought and sold as a commodity; it arises biologically and is immanent to the natural world. Technology is not a cold and rational death machine, but rather the operating system of love—a love that flows through the channels of a perfectly interconnected life field to converge in the central hub of Mother Nature herself.

The invading human population on Pandora prizes precisely the superconductor of this love, yet without being able to understand its function as such. RDA CEO Parker Selfridge (Giovanni Ribisi) speaks reverently of its staggering worth in dollars, at twenty million per kilogram. Later, countering with her own set of figures, scientist Dr. Grace Augustine (Sigourney Weaver) asserts that its worth lies not in the price tag of the material but in the incomprehensibly extensive network the material sustains:

> GRACE AUGUSTINE: I'm not talking about some kind of pagan voodoo here, I'm talking about something real, something measurable in the biology of the forest.
>
> PARKER SELFRIDGE: Which is what, exactly?
>
> GRACE AUGUSTINE: What we think we know is that there is some kind of electrochemical communication between the roots of the trees. Like the synapses between neurons. And each tree has ten to the fourth connections to the trees around it. And there are ten to the twelfth trees on Pandora.
>
> PARKER SELFRIDGE: Which is a lot, I'm guessing.
>
> GRACE AUGUSTINE: It's more connections than the human brain. Get it? It's a network. It's a global network and the N'avi can access it. They can upload and download data. Memories! . . .
>
> PARKER SELFRIDGE: What the hell have you people been smoking out there? They're just goddamn trees! . . .
>
> GRACE AUGUSTINE: The wealth of this world isn't in the ground; it's all around us.

The conversation comes to rest on the contested status of trees: Grace—as her name symbolically suggests—argues that trees are sentient archives of social memory; Selfridge is quiet for a moment, contemplating this possibility, but then bursts out laughing at the radical proposition that any material could be valorized on any scale other than its exchange value ("They're just goddamn trees!"). The brief hush of wonderment that had taken over the entire room as Grace explained the complexity of the natural web of social memory on Pandora thus gives way instantly to the neocolonial paradigm of exploitative greed in which—as Selfridge's name symbolically suggests—egotism eclipses community. In the sense that *Avatar* posits the collective as a category ultimately held together by love—love of the forest, of the native way of life—then love is also implicitly the driver of the trees' archives of social memory. Love, then, is what is bigger than the human brain; love is what makes sentient beings synergistic, more than the sum of their individual selves. Yet this is the computation that humans willfully refuse to comprehend. Within the narrative economy of *Avatar*, therefore, humans blindly covet a material superconductor without comprehending the power of what is being conducted, which is no more or less than love itself.

WALL·E: From Sedentary Consumption to Active Farming, via Love

Avatar is not alone in positing the alienation between humans and their capacity to love as a symptom of unsustainable estrangement from the natural world. *WALL·E* finds humans held hostage by the most extreme consequences of their artificial consumerism. Like the humans of *Avatar*, who have "killed their mother"—recalling the Bersuit Vergarabat accusation of the same—the humans of *WALL·E* have likewise rendered earth uninhabitable with the trash and toxins of a consumer capitalism represented by "Buy 'n' Large," a Walmart-inspired megastore that has—in the same neocolonial spirit of *Avatar*'s RDA—taken over every human institution: commerce and industry, the media, government, and the military. In the face of the literal trashing of the planet, humans are evacuated to space at the behest of the CEO/president of Buy 'n' Large (Fred Willard). Long after the death of this maximum human agent of neoliberalism, the neoliberal spirit soldiers on in the form of the spaceship's central computer system AUTO—an unthinking "self" analogous to Avatar's CEO (it is telling that in both films the neoliberal corporation, though characterized as vast, is nevertheless pointedly represented by a single man). The spaceship's name, *Axiom*, would, in turn seem to refer to that of blind allegiance to the cultural precept of consumption. Humans, having been held captive to consumption for seven hundred years, have lost their humanity. They have grown so obese on their diet of computer-generated fast food and from their confinement to mechanized lounge chairs that they have lost the bone density necessary to stand and walk.[8] Moreover, they are so bound in their attention to the digital screens atop their lounge chairs that they no longer speak directly to their neighbors. Like Jake Sully, the humans aboard the *Axiom* are, in effect, both physically and emotionally paralyzed, their physical and emotional integrity compromised by the prison house of neoliberal culture. And, like the humans of *Avatar*, the humans of *WALL·E* face the threat of species extinction because of this cultural-cum-physiological addiction to consumerism.

As in *Avatar*, *WALL·E* stages a David-and-Goliath battle of technology against technology. Here, the giant is the effectively neoliberal AUTO, who has enslaved humans to their own consumption. The tiny hero is a small trash compactor, the last functioning "survivor" of a now defunct army of such machines left behind to clean up the planet for eventual human reoccupation. But WALL·E (Ben Burtt), as he is called (short for "Waste Allocation Lift-Loader, Earth-Class"), is a rebel of love: when the spirit moves him, he defies his "directive" in order to rescue from oblivion those objects that tug at his robotic heartstrings. Within his garage to rival all garages, with endless shelves of neatly organized knickknacks and cultural curios, we quickly learn that WALL·E's favorite piece of "trash" is a videocassette of the film *Hello, Dolly!* When we see WALL·E play back this classic 1969 Barbra Streisand musical, we perceive his humanity of sentimental desire as he imitates with his own two metal pinchers the onscreen hand-holding that seals Streisand's final triumph in her labored quest for love. Like Dolly—whose syllable rhyme with his own name playfully underscores their moral homology—all WALL·E wants is a companion. Love, intimacy, a community of two: these are the desiderata of this diminutive and unlikely rebel hero.

The film's action is set in motion when WALL·E makes his greatest find: a single seedling, fragile and vibrantly green. Enter EVE (Extra-Terrestrial Vegetation Evaluator, Elissa Knight), a sleek white female robot sent to Earth by AUTO to seek out and retrieve any plant life that would evidence planetary habitability by humans. For WALL·E, it is love at first sight, though the trigger-happy EVE nearly singes him to death in keeping with her impulse to deliver a fatal blast to any unknown entity. In this sense, her standing protocol of visiting the Other—any Other—with wanton death and destruction makes EVE a comedic incarnation of the neoconservative military strategy of "shock and awe" and a light-hearted analog to the darker logic of *Avatar*'s Colonel Quaritch. But this logic, we learn, is not that of EVE, but of AUTO. Like Jake Sully, EVE will have a change of heart—here, literally, for the chamber into which she secrets away WALL·E's plant throbs with a red glow as though it were just such an organ, and her change of heart is motivated as much by her love for WALL·E as it is for the plant, which constitutes evidence of the viability of terrestrial life. When EVE realizes that AUTO does not intend to nurture the plant but to destroy it, thereby consolidating his reign by eliminating the evidence that humans need to return to Earth, she will finally abandon her directive in order to protect the seedling, following WALL·E's lead in rejecting the logic of the neoliberal oppressor for the cause of love and environmental sustainability, here inextricably intertwined, as in *Avatar*.

It is EVE's defection not only from her directive but from its (im)moral position of cold destruction—just like Jake's defection from human self to Na'vi Other—that catalyzes human salvation: as EVE and WALL·E dance through space in an expression of mutual love, two inhabitants of the Axiom who sit watching them through the windows of the spaceship turn away from their lounge chair screens to smile at one other and, in what is figured as the ultimate affirmation of their inevitable recuperation of humanity, to join hands. This simple gesture engenders a spirit of rebellion: the couple find their legs, rising up from the cells of their lounge chairs in an act of self-determination that is conceptually homologous with the reclaiming of their physical integrity as a function of love. Thus freed from colonizing mechanization by AUTO, the humans' desire to play together, walk together, swim together, touch one another in a sequence of Adam-and-Eve flirtation mirrors that of the emotionally anthropomorphic robotic couple that has inspired their own amorous insurrection. In a climax that is far less devastating than *Avatar*'s apocalyptic battle, the humans aboard the *Axiom* take back the contested plant as their birthright in a gesture of spontaneous solidarity that is synonymous with the affirmation of love and community. Just as *Avatar* ends with Jake's opening of his eyes as his Na'vi counterpart, signifying the beginning of a new era in which humanity is reconfigured as a sustainably loving collective, so does *WALL·E* conclude as though human history were starting anew. Following the triumphant return of the *Axiom* passengers to Earth, WALL·E's closing credits are overlaid against hieroglyphs of their subsequent efforts, executed with loving tenderness and togetherness, to relearn the ways of farming in harmony with nature.

As incarnations of technology, WALL·E and EVE may not constitute the natural Internet of *Avatar*, but their love has an analogous rhizomatic communicativity. Their amorous sentiment spreads "virally" through the human population in a ripple effect of social contagion that mirrors the interconnectivity of the natural world collective in *Avatar*, creating a web of affect. WALL·E may not be a ten-foot blue native with a somatic connection to the social "Internet," but his triumph of love over the cold and calculating AUTO signals a similar conceptual privileging of back-to-nature primitivism over posthuman—and, therefore, postnatural—artificial intelligence. AUTO is intent on sacrificing the sole promise of natural life on Earth in order to maintain in perpetuity his thoroughly nonnatural environment. In this sense the tiny seedling that AUTO schemes to eradicate is a miniature version of the Na'vi Hometree mercilessly blown apart by Colonel Quaritch in the neocolonial service of capitalist culture. For AUTO and Colonel Quaritch there is no sacrifice too great or sacred in obeisance to the materialist status quo sustained by an endless quest for profit. Their technologies of power are destructive, hierarchizing, their method annihilating. This Goliath technology seeks to maintain a triumphalist separation from nature in which the wielder of technological power rules supreme as the ruthless plunderer of the surrounding world(s)—all that is Other. WALL·E and the Na'vi, in contrast, revere and honor all that is Other, bringing it, by force of affective bond, into the sphere of the self, always working toward community—that is, always moving toward horizontal and interconnected togetherness on the strength of love.

WALL·E moves away from the artificiality of AUTO through his anthropomorphized soma of expressive eyes and yearning hands and moral character maximally expressed in his practice of affection-driven recycling. Like el Chivo in Alejandro González Iñárritu's *Amores perros*, who proposes to turn over a moral leaf by subsisting entirely from what he finds in the trash, or Marla in David Fincher's *Fight Club*, who adopts, loves anew, and even implicitly heals a second-hand prom dress she has bought for a dollar—which she tenderly describes as something "that someone loved for a day and then threw away like a sex crime victim left bound in electrical tape by the side of the road"—WALL·E practices what we might call "rescue consumption: not just pragmatic recycling, but recycling with heart. This is a form of recycling that turns waste into want, thereby reversing the harmful footprint of consumerism one object at a time. The desire motivating rescue consumption is not one of greed, but one of love. In all three of these films rescue consumption serves as the moral practice with objects that paves the way for the establishment of a sustainable and sound relationship of love between sentient beings: el Chivo determines to resume his role of father to his abandoned daughter; Marla becomes the "Eve" of an Edenic couple in a postapocalyptic landscape in which what has been destroyed is the neoliberal system of social enslavement by credit; WALL·E rescues hand-holding from where humans have unwittingly thrown it out with the trash, thereby catalyzing the rekindling not only of affective bonds but also of the autonomous self-determination and the relationship with nature that are posited as the moral and practical outgrowths of this capacity for love regained.[9]

To help us understand this anthropomorphization of consumer waste and its investiture with a democratizing love that restores lost subjectivity, we might consider such analyses of the political as Wendy Brown's "wounded attachments" (1993)[10] or Martha Fineman's "vulnerable subject" (2010). If a postmodern politics of identity has come to replace the modern politics of ideological teleology, then, Brown argues, this politics of identity is centrally defined by "*logics of pain*" (390) in which identitarian groups constitute themselves as political subjects through a discourse of "wounded attachments" (391 et passim) that posits its agency and demands rights on the basis of what Brown posits as a Nietzschean "ressentiment." Whereas in Nietzsche's formulation, ressentiment "produces an affect (rage, righteousness) that overwhelms the hurt . . . a culprit responsible for the hurt, and . . . a site of revenge to displace the hurt" (401), Brown views subject of late modernity as "an utterly *unrelieved* individual" (403) who "seethes with ressentiment" (402) but never experiences the Nietzschean catharsis because, "buffeted and controlled by global configurations of disciplinary and capitalist power of extraordinary proportions" (402), this subject ultimately "becomes invested in its own subjugation" (403). Fineman approaches the contemporary body politic in much the same way, conceptualizing it as "vulnerable" and calling on the state to respond therapeutically to this vulnerability. Brown would say that the state is responsible for perpetuating the very vulnerability to which Fineman would have it respond, yet a much more optimistic Fineman considers that this practice of a therapeutic "responsiveness to vulnerability" by the state would yield "a more self-conscious and aware egalitarian political culture[,] one that more robustly adheres to the All-American promise of equality of opportunity and equal access to the American dream" (41).

In the composite, what these two political analyses have in common is a vision of the body politic as one foundationally marked by suffering, fragility, precarity (this last term being one also used by Lauren Berlant to characterize the effects of neoliberalism on the subject, as earlier discussed). To return to the filmic formulation of what I am calling a rescue consumption, we see the anthropomorphization of consumer waste as "wounded" and "vulnerable": waste becomes a mirror of the consumers who do the wasting. Here the act of rescuing and healing consumer waste "heals" not only the discarded object, but—more important—the rescuer by breaking the cycle of engagement with a consumerism that inflicts wounds and hurt.

Here it is the rescue consumer who responds to wounded vulnerability, not the state. Yet the rescue consumer is figured as the basis of a democracy capable of healing the wounds inflicted by corporate capitalism. In this sense the films parse the capitalist-democratic complex into its two components, directing their harshest critique at capitalism and reserving the possibility of utopic rehabilitation for democracy as a conceptual category, thus associating pain with capitalism and love with democracy.

In *Avatar* and *WALL·E* alike, the split between hurtful capitalist hierarchy and loving native democracy is represented by two kinds of technology. The putatively "lesser," more primitive technology is cast as such for lack of the capacity to assist in practices of neocolonial military subjugation and social control. The Na'vi shoot arrows at aerial tanks while Colonel Quaritch sips coffee and laughs in derisive disbelief from inside the protective hull of the master aircraft; WALL·E, a small and pitiful Frankenstein of retread parts, cowers, defenseless and impotent, before the deadly rounds that the sleek and powerful EVE—as the minion of AUTO—initially shoots at will, literally blazing her path and leaving a trail of fire in her wake. The patent unsustainability of this destruction mirrors the less visible unsustainability of the linear logic of the neoliberal consumer culture that the Goliath technologies support. In contrast, the natural Internet of Pandora and WALL·E's rescue consumption form the basis of sustainability, understood—in keeping with its increasingly canonical threefold definition—as a social, economic, and ecological phenomenon. In *WALL·E* the economic critique of unsustainability is less pointed than in *Avatar*, where the lure of substantial remuneration is posited as the major draw for enlistment in the RDA's service on Pandora and where Selfridge takes patent pleasure in quantifying the astronomical value of the prized unobtanium. Yet both omit capitalism from their positive representations of sustainable culture: at the close of *WALL·E* Buy 'n' Large and its logos are markedly absent in the scenes of community farming; in *Avatar* the circulatory—as opposed to accumulative—social logic of the Na'vi has no trace of money or material ownership (possession, if it may even be termed as such, is strictly affective). In both instances love is the circulatory social force that orients the collective toward ecological conscience and robust vitality epitomized by the restoration of legs—this is the conceptual constellation that constitutes the discursive definition of antiprofit sustainability.

Nike, Purveyor of Legs: "Everything you need is already inside"

Given these recurrent anticapitalist tropes, one would think that this discourse of love-as-sustainability is proper to a position of resistance. The cold capitalist humans in *Avatar* (corporate profit mongers and their mercenary muscle) would seem analogous to a global powerhouse like Nike, denounced by critics for keeping a slave-driving production line calculated in hundredths of a second (*The Corporation*) while maintaining sweatshop conditions of labor as recently, some claim, as 2009 (one activist website calls Nike the "King of Social Injustice" [@freedomrebel]). Its practices of rationalized capitalism liken Nike to the exploitative RDA of *Avatar*, yet Nike's publicity strongly echoes none other than the discourse of native Pandora.

Take, for example, Nike's "Courage" campaign, launched in summer 2008 for the Beijing Olympics. In the face of slowing revenue during what was then taking shape as a serious recession, Nike increased its advertising budget in early 2008 by 50 percent over its $190 million budget in 2007. Joaquín Hidalgo, the vice president of global brand marketing, called this campaign an investment in "demand creation" to cement Nike's "brand strength" and "drive growth." Interestingly, Hidalgo also uses a turn of phrase that evokes the trope of communicativity associated with the Na'vi world when he identifies a major desideratum of the campaign—and therefore a principal driver of growth—as the ability to "connect with [the] consumer" (Hein). Yet Hidalgo's statements contrast with the advertisement itself in that, no matter how conceptually resonant they may be with antiprofit sustainability, they nevertheless serve principally to assert the advertisement's function as a vehicle for increasing profit, whereas the advertisement itself—like Chevron and Petrobras—elides the question of profit altogether, as though the company's only concerns were, once again, the double bottom line of people and planet.

The one-minute commercial that defined Nike's "Courage" campaign features several dozen athletes from nearly as many nations in quick MTV-style succession. These sports figures are of varied fame; during the time that this commercial was posted on the Nike website, a scrolling legend of names underneath the video lit up in synch with the images to indicate which athlete was onscreen as the ad progressed.[11] Some, like Michael Jordan or Lance Armstrong, were immediately recognizable to a global audience; others had more local renown in their countries of origin. Each name was hot-linked to a brief biography that explained the rationale for inclusion in the campaign. While the stories differed wildly, the motif of struggle against the odds came through as a unifying theme. Some of the athletes were indeed champions or medalists, but it also became clear that victory was not the narrative thread that Nike wanted to privilege. Biographies like those of Henry Marsh, who ran an Olympic steeplechase event with a fever and lung congestion to finish fourth and be carried off the field on a stretcher, or Julie Moss, who dragged herself after collapse through the last hundred yards of the Ironman Triathlon, suggested that this commercial was celebrating a triumph of inner strength and of the will rather than victory for victory's sake. In spite of the preeminence of some of the figures in the commercial, the general tenor of the ad was not the coronation of champions, but the celebration of the unsung heroism of underdogs fighting to achieve their personal best. In this sense, the Nike athletes—understood in the context of this style of presentation—were far closer to a Jake Sully who selflessly bets his life on the taming of the grand Toruk dragon for the sake of saving the Na'vi than to a Colonel Quaritch who fights brutally and senselessly to the death because he is unable to let go of his egocentric power and cultural "crown."

In keeping with this underdog status, the Nike commercial's athletes—even those who are from developed countries—are not associated with the first world. On the contrary, a running subtheme of the commercial links them to predominantly African-looking landscapes and cultures through the splicing of wildebeests and cheetahs and dark-skinned people with tribal face painting between the shots of athletes as well as Asian art. This insertion of African and Asian images alongside the athletes suggests an affinity of these underdog competitors with the third world. Indeed, the ad first aired in Asia and Latin America before making its U.S. debut, in a poetically symbolic third-to-first-world movement, as though to affirm that it had a greater resonance with those regions on the lower end of the global economic and political power differential.

The commercial's other two subthemes are mirror images of one another. On the one hand, a series of visual references to the inner body: the progressive firing of a neuron, red blood cells, the insemination of an egg by a sperm, an embryo in utero, a brain scan. On the other hand, a series of images of outer space. The visual similarity of the two sets of images, and their juxtaposition—in one instance, of an explosion inside the body with an explosion in space—have the effect of making the micro and the macro conceptually and imagistically continuous with one another. The inside of the human body *is* the galaxy, the ad suggests, resonating strongly with the continuity of life on Pandora, where all beings are part of a bigger pulsating collective of organic experience. The images of human life from conception to embryonic development to toddling child emphasize the somatic and physiological aspect of life—life as feeling, as embodied cognition, rather than as rational thought.

The fast tempo of the commercial does not invite contemplative thought; it interpellates its audience on the level of feeling and sensory perception, imitating in both its audio and visual tracks the fast adrenaline-raising pace of a pounding heartbeat, echoing the scene in which Jake Sully first finds his running legs in the body of his avatar. Indeed, in a finale that bears an uncanny parallel to the theme of leglessness in *Avatar*, the closing image in the Nike commercial shows Oscar Pistorius, aka "Blade Runner," a double amputee who styled himself the "fastest man with no legs," sprinting down a track on a pair of prosthetic lower limbs. Nike will not be the RDA or the Marines, who take legs as a sacrificial casualty of the neocolonial pursuit and then concede to give them back only in a ruthless quid pro quo arrangement that exacts the ultimate betrayal of love and life; Nike will instead position itself rhetorically as a giver of legs. Nike will be Mother Nature herself—Eywa incarnate—aligned again here with "good" technology that therapeutically brings the compromised body back into a state of organic integrity and harmonious alignment with the rest of the natural world. "Courage" privileges the knowledge, and not the power, derived from technology. In terms of this discursive presentation and positioning, the technology that allowed Oscar Pistorius to sprint down a track is not the technology of war—not the technology that allows humans to blow up the natural world of Pandora for its unobtanium. It is rather the technology of love, we might say, in that its application is destined for the immaterial betterment of lived experience within a social collective, since peaceful and absolutely horizontal social collectivity is the imagined community of athleticism—a cross-cultural togetherness that the Olympics, the venue for which the Nike commercial was expressly prepared, quintessentially symbolize.

The Nike commercial implicitly engages, then, in the good technology/bad technology divide postulated by *Avatar* as a cultural measure, but elides all reference to the bad technology except that which is proposed already in the negative mode—as a repudiation—by the chorus of the soundtrack, which repeats throughout the ad as its sole audio message: "I've got soul but I'm not a soldier" (The Killers, "All These Things that I've Done," 2004). This chorus stages and resolves, in one efficient assertion, the contest between the two technologies and their respective social orders. The turn of phrase "I've got soul" has been a part of mainstream U.S. speech for decades, yet this expression nevertheless still bears the vestigial connotation of celebratory subversion associated with the black "soul power" counterculture of the late 1960s and early 1970s. Someone who has "soul" is not only someone who has heart, but is, more specifically, someone who has heart enough to challenge a repressive system, someone who has enough inner fortitude to define what it means to be a cultural subject in his or her own iconoclastic terms: to sport an afro, to wear flamboyant clothing, to dance in a style of aggressive, provocative, and often sexualized self-expression, to break all the social rules—this is "soul power." The song's chorus, therefore, further affirms the visual alignment of the Nike athletes with the nonwhite third world through this implicit affinity with cultural "blackness" as the critical subtext of this repeated assertion of core identity. On the other side of this statement is the disavowal of military service and bellicose politics—also in keeping with the countercultural ethos of the 1960s. The refusal to be a soldier is as symbolically charged as the claim to having soul, especially in the context of the 1960s—the time period the song's chorus evokes—when the military was firmly associated with Vietnam and demonized as neoimperialist, a sentiment that has been reawakened in the context of the U.S. war in Iraq (which many have dubbed the new Vietnam). Like *Avatar*, this Nike ad brings 1960s discourse full circle into the twenty-first century by making an oblique but unmistakable gesture of reasserting the contemporary relevance of the old "make love, not war" cultural zeitgeist.

The Nike commercial may not thematize love or sustainability, but it does privilege the fusion between technology and the natural world and makes the same kind of substitution of heart for brain that Beavan propounds as a vertebral concept of sustainability discourse. If the audio track proposes the notion of "soul," then the visual material of the ad fills this notion with the semantic content of the organicity of lived experience, the interconnectivity of life and deep emotion. This emotional information is conveyed by the extremely and diversely expressive faces of the athletes: the story of moral and antimaterialist triumph is one of feeling. The use of the emotive face as the kernel of narrative meaning recalls the pivotal scene of Jake's first run in the body of his avatar where the camera focuses on his face and on his breathing, as if to affirm the truth of the written message that initiates the Nike "Courage" commercial: "Everything you need is already inside." This slogan (attributed on the website to Nike cofounder and track coach Bill Bowerman) echoes the notion of affective immanence, returning us to Pandora, where, as Jake discovers, love, life, and technology are already "inside."

The Affective Imperative Belongs to Both Sides

The real-life equivalent of *Avatar*'s RDA, merciless in its acquisitions and infinite in its material greed, is more on the order of Goldman Sachs than Nike. A recent exposé of the gargantuan investment bank by Matt Taibbi in *Rolling Stone* alleges that Goldman Sachs bears tremendous—if not exclusive—responsibility for the greatest economic upheavals and downturns in the twentieth-century United States by "behav[ing] recklessly for years, weighing down the system with toxic loans and predatory debt, and accomplishing nothing but massive bonuses for a few bosses" (8). Regarding public consciousness of this persistent exploitation, Taibbi gives an explanation that, once again, uncannily resonates with the motif of capitalist-occasioned leglessness:

> It's not always easy to accept the reality of what we now routinely allow these people [like Goldman Sachs investment bankers] to get away with; there's a kind of collective denial that kicks in when a

country goes through what America has gone through lately, when a people lose as much prestige and status as we have in the past few years. You can't really register the fact that you're no longer a citizen of a thriving first-world democracy, that you're no longer above getting robbed in broad daylight, because *like an amputee*, you can still sort of feel things that are no longer there.

(8, emphasis added)

Taibbi suggests that the once firm boundaries of the first world have been eroded by the capitalist incursions of what many hail—or decry—as the most powerful financial firm on the planet, incursions designed to "pick the American carcass clean of its loose capital" (7), thereby turning the broader U.S. populace—its multitude—into so many legless victims of this exploitative extraction, victims who are, as yet, blind to their own cultural leglessness. Ours "should be a pitchfork-level outrage," yet, as Taibbi notes, "hardly anyone sa[ys] a word" (7). Perhaps this is because the politics of rational denunciation lose their power in the face of the cultural discourse of affective identification.

In other words, if the RDA of *Avatar* were allowed to develop its own advertising campaign, chances are it would mirror Nike's in its appropriation of the affective imperative of sustainability. Or, we could view it in the reverse: that companies like Nike are driving the aesthetic discourse adopted in turn by their very critics. Our serious consideration of this latter possibility—that capitalism is dictating the terms of social meaning—allows us to understand how sustainability discourse (and it is important to distinguish between discourse and practice), though revolutionary in regard to its slate of goals, is nevertheless not self-avowedly so; it cannot adopt the rubric of revolution because it does not operate outside the playing field of social meaning established by its discursive adversary (again, it is crucial to distinguish between capitalist discourse and practice). Antiprofit sustainability discourse is reformist—which we appreciate in Beavan's statement, insofar as it does not discard the concept of "progress," but rather seeks to rework it, which is a guiding sentiment of the Obama administration as it seeks, likewise, to rework, rather than abandon, the capitalist system in the direction of sustainability. Perhaps this is why, within the so-called first world, we cannot take *Avatar* seriously either in its demonization of the human race or in its suggestion that we all become members of the Na'vi race: because our social discourse—mainstream and contestatory alike—is held firmly captive within a shared conceptual terrain dictated by capitalism, and, as a result, the idea of turning our backs on its neocolonialist practices and siding with the neocolonized dissipates as soon as we leave the theater and catch a glimpse of the likes of the Nike "Courage" ad during a commercial break from the Olympics. Nike is Eywa, not the RDA; the Nike world is Pandora, not the devastated Earth. This affective discourse of capitalism and the stranglehold it maintains on the constellation of *positive* affects (legs, life, and love) prevents its users—the general Western public—from perceiving its own amputee status.

Regardless of the direction of causality we are willing to accept in the matter of this common discursive adoption of an affective aesthetic and imperative, we ought to pause to contemplate its implications. What this commonality of opposed political signs suggests is that the soma—and, specifically, the feeling soma—has become the predominant vehicle for the communication of social meaning (as much its representation as its reception, for as viewers we receive the affectively encoded message in kind). The expressive face, the sound of the heartbeat, the affirmation of heart and soul: these are the very epistemic brick and mortar of our contemporary social—and, not least, political—language.

Ever Amado: "¡Levántate y camina!" ("Get up and walk!")

In *Avatar* principled and self-sacrificing—revolutionary—contestation of the RDA and its abusive exploitation is embodied by one individual who rises up to distinguish herself from the neocolonial rank and file. Trudy Chacón (Michelle Rodríguez), as this moral dissident is called, is the only character in the military panoply guided by the principle of legs, life, and love without even needing the catalyst of romance. We appreciate this capacity when she breaks rank to spirit Dr. Grace Augustine's avatar lab away to safety following the discovery that Colonel Quaritch is using Jake as an RDA spy. As Trudy flies the scientific team to the floating Hallelujah Mountains, we see the seed of her ultimate alliance with the Na'vi in her acknowledgment of her passengers' awe as they behold this sublime expression of the natural world: "You should see your faces," she says with a quiet smile. Later, it is Trudy who withdraws her helicopter from the firing line in front of Hometree rather than participate in its bombing ("I didn't sign up for

this shit"), Trudy who rescues Jake and the scientific team from imprison-
ment by the RDA's military, Trudy who paints her face with Na'vi war colors, and Trudy who sacrifices her life for the cause of liberating the natives
from their human oppressors. Once the Na'vi have won their improbable
victory, we see a handful of "good" humans policing the definitive exit of all
the rest from the planet, but this dissident subject position is represented,
during the conflict itself, exclusively in the figure of Trudy Chacón.

Is it accidental that the conscience of the humans in *Avatar*, this lone
pilot who turns away from her mission to destroy Hometree, eventually to
martyr herself in battle on the side of the Na'vi, bears a diegetic Hispanic
name and is played by a Latina? The casting choice of Michelle Rodríguez,
a high-profile and immediately recognizable U.S.-born actor with a Dominican mother, a Puerto Rican father, and stereotypical Latin looks—café au
lait skin, smooth dark hair and dark eyes, full lips, curvaceous figure—gives
a certain cultural connotation to her character's will to defy an authority
that has become morally bankrupt. The white American Jake Sully has to
learn to recognize and repudiate injustice; the brown Trudy Chacón knows
it when she sees it and doesn't waver in her immediate and steadfast resistance of it. The narrative positions her as the locus of objective discernment
between good and evil; it is no wonder that an entry on the online *Avatar*
forum calls her "the most heroic of all" (@ToKatz).

Trudy Chacón represents a dissenting minority perspective on the dominant majority constituted through economic and military might. This perspectival rift in which the brown Hispanic is marked as having a knowledge—
pure, certain, intimate, unencumbered by doubt—of white regimes of power
resonates strongly with the representation of the Salvadoran civil war in *Ever
Amado* (*Ever Loved*), a 2007 film short by Los Angeles-based Salvadoran
director Víctor Ruano. This short, which has traveled the international film
festival circuit (Germany, United States, Latin America, Canada),[12] narrates
the clandestine flight of its eponymous protagonist from war-torn El Salvador
to the United States. Ever Amado's search for refuge goes horribly wrong:
though he miraculously survives deep waters without knowing how to swim,
he loses his wife in the crossing, only to be beaten so badly himself by a pair of
racist white Americans who stumble upon his hiding place ("It's a Spic!" they
exclaim in disgust) that, when he finally regains consciousness in a border
clinic, he finds he is an amputee, having lost his legs and his sight.

The film's vertebral storyline may be simple and easily summarized, but
its imagery is more complex and experimental—as one might expect from

an artist whose cinematic craft is only part of a larger studio practice (Santasombra [Shadowsaint]) that also specializes in motion graphics, animation, and graphic design. A running theme of religious iconography against the grain in the form of two virgins appears at intervals throughout *Ever Amado's* journey. One, dressed in white and of impassive facial expression who inspires fear in Ever in a voice-over mental dialogue with an imaginary mother, is called "La Perra de Hielo" (The Icy Bitch); a second, clad in veils of black lace, who succors the wounded Ever and even mounts him sexually in his hospital-bed fantasies, is the "Mamá del Pueblo-Niño" (Mother of the Child-People). These two virginal characters are intertextual references to a lyrical debate by two prominent Salvadoran poets, David Escobar Galindo and Roque Dalton, over the proper interpretation of the massive violence of civil war. In "Duelo ceremonial por la violencia" (Ceremonial Mourning of Violence, 1971), Escobar Galindo categorically condemns violence as a Communist plague and, along with it, the *perra de hielo* as a kind of perverse patron saint of the violence that should always be damned. Roque Dalton—a member of the Ejército Revolucionario del Pueblo (People's Revolutionary Party)—answered Escobar Galindo with "La violencia aquí" (Violence Here, 1974), a utopian vision of leftist violence as a means to a liberational end for the lower Salvadoran classes and made *la mamá del pueblo-niño* its apologetic agent.[13]

In Ruano's film both virginal figures appear, but there is no longer a counterpoint between them in the sense of hope or lack thereof; both form part of an equally hopeless equation. It is true that La Perra de Hielo strikes fear into Ever, whereas La Mamá del Pueblo-Niño brings him comfort and copulation, but the latter is no longer capable of utopias. In one scene cascades of milk stream from the breast of La Mamá del Pueblo-Niño over Ever's bandaged head and torso while a recurrent shot of a baby crying alone, flailing its arms and legs about in defenseless grief, suggest that nature has lost its compass, in a strong echo of Bersuit Vergarabat's nippleless Mother Nature. In a scene after La Mamá del Pueblo-Niño has sex with Ever, she takes an infant from the shadowy arms of Flor, only to leave him alone to cry on the floor, driving home the idea that this distortion of nature is epitomized by maternal abandonment. Another—not discordant—way to interpret this abandonment would be as an abandonment by life itself, since the baby is effectively either born into death or its very life robbed by death, being that Flor, the baby's mother or would-be mother, is a phantom. In this sense the insistent trigenerational imagery of the baby, Ever, and a generic older man also confined to a wheelchair who shares Ever's hospital room conveys the idea that across generations only disfigurement and death await.

The film argues, thus, that it is not only Ever who is abandoned by the virgin, but all of fratricidal El Salvador (the inclusion of a fragment of Archbishop Oscar Romero's homily of March 23, 1980, the day before his assassination, in which he pled that brothers not turn against brothers, iden-tifies the struggle as such within the narrative economy of the film). Aban-donment by the virginlike figure—which, in the Latin American context, is tantamount to being forsaken by the collective cultural birthright—is also posited as homologous with abandonment by nature itself insofar as the film develops a visually metonymic relationship between the treacherously craggy surface of the desert Ever treads and the ominous appearances of the virgin clad in black. In the face of the atrocities committed by broth-ers against brothers, nature itself has symbolically reversed course to work against life and toward death.

The film insists on the shadowy status of humanity—at least that born of La Mamá del Pueblo-Niño—as being damned from the start, reiterating the image of the lone baby boy crying in desperation, without comfort or solace. Here the "organic moment" of romantic union in nature as an expression of well-being has gone fatally wrong. Ever's sexual fantasies as he lies bandaged from the loss of his legs and sight are violent and sterile instead of loving and fecund: in one sequence he imagines pushing Flor down and forcing himself on her on the cracked earth; in another, when masturbation gives way to sex with La Mamá del Pueblo-Niño, only the fact of being born into pain and death results.

This abandonment by the virginlike figures seems at odds with the title of the film, which attributes to Ever in the form of his very surname, Amado (Beloved), the contrary status of enjoying a steady and uninterrupted source of love. Yet the synopsis of the film available on the websites of Santasombra and of those film festivals where it has gained entry affirms that, "[u]ltimate-ly, as Ever confronts his physical pain, he discovers a life-changing spiritu-al revelation" (Santasombra). It would seem that this spiritual revelation is what affirms the truth of his name: that he is "ever loved." The moment of revelation comes when, after losing his legs to unfettered violence, he finds them again in obeisance of the command whispered by his wife's apparition, "¡Levántate y camina!" ("Get up and walk!"). Ever resolutely drags himself on his stumps toward a window, where the divine white light of religious iconography shines through, opening up like clouds parting to reveal a still photographic image of a family: mother and father above three young children. The spectator's speculation that the photo may represent Ever's family (the image is sepia-colored and the style of dress outmoded, suggesting that it could date to his childhood) quickly gives way to the realization that such specificity is irrelevant. What this "revelation" posits is that the simple fact of the persistent integrity of the family as a cultural—and, as the film has it, "spiritual"—category in the face of fratricide is, in and of itself, miraculous. This image of the family as a kind of godhead goes hand in hand with the image of the blue and white sky, the classic image of the natural sublime. The opposite of war and death is thus figured as the homologous integrity of nature and family, together constitutive—once again—of legs, love, and life.

Yet it is difficult to affirm that the film comes to rest on the strength of this utopian moment; the sequence immediately following the family photo in the sky emphasizes cruelty and solitude and segues into the narration of Ever's disfigurement, which is announced by a long trail of blood. The final sequence before the credits begin to roll shows a new group of Spanish-speaking immigrants discovering Ever and carrying him together to safety. During the credits, the camera focuses in on the dark contours of an old man's face in barely illuminated close-up—we don't know if this is the same old man we have seen before or if this is a representation of an aging Ever—and finally shows him moving toward the window. The same soft light of the earlier family revelation shines through the window, possibly offering hope, yet Ever rests in darkness, and we hear the intermittent sound of a single water drop that has characterized the clinic from the beginning as though suggesting it as the terminus of a gradual process of drought that represents the death of nature and, with it, love and life. Though Ever's revelation gives him a glimpse of legs, love, and life, the film's diegesis insists on the opposite state of ill-being—that is, on leglessness, loveless abandonment, and death, against a backdrop that witnesses not the affirmation of nature but its contravention.

Ever Amado opens and closes with footage of the Salvadoran civil war. The first such images show throngs of civilians screaming, ducking, and running for cover in a crowded plaza as shots are fired in the background. A caption reads "September 11, 1980." Although 1980 was a year of conflict in El Salvador, there is no historical event associated with September 11. Indeed, Ruano explains on his website that "the date given at the beginning of this film is mere poetic license" (Santasombra). The attribution, then, seems best interpreted as a symbolic comparison to the two September 11s of note within the Latin American cultural conscious: that of the 1973 Chilean coup against Salvador Allende and that of the 2001 attacks on the World Trade Center in New York—the former having been revived as a subject of public discussion in the wake of the latter as the "Southern" September 11.

To a North American audience, the September 11s of 1973 and 2001 may seem unconnected. But it has been argued from the Latin Americanist perspective that the September 11s of Santiago and New York serve to bookend a period of U.S. history: the rise and fall (or at least deep crisis) of the United States as a violent neoliberal hegemon. That is, the covert U.S. economic and military support of the coup against democratically elected socialist president Allende that ushered in the neoliberal-friendly dictatorship of Augusto Pinochet and his economic advisers trained by Milton Friedman and known as the "Chicago Boys" is understood as one of the most pronounced events marking the beginning of a "neoimperial" era in the political life of the United States (Coronil) whose reality of violent imposition at the expense of the well-being of the rest of the world is patently revealed as a "desert of the real" when terrorists from the aggrieved global periphery willingly give up their lives to destroy the world's most symbolic financial center (Žižek, "Welcome to the Desert of the Real"). Naomi Klein analyzes the Chilean coup of 1973 as an instance of what she calls "disaster capitalism," which preys, vulturelike, on massive social upheavals, installing itself within the vacuum before there is time to recover from the damage. Greg Grandin takes this perspective even further, arguing that the United States gave the neoliberal-military imperialism that would achieve full-blown expression in the current Iraq War a preliminary test drive in the indirect military interventions in Central America during the 1980s. In Grandin's analysis, the civil war of El Salvador is part of the "empire's workshop." The "poetic license" that Ruano claims in labeling the public repression by U.S.-backed Salvadoran forces as "September 11, 1980," thus gestures to both 1973 and 2001 as historical moments whose commonality is as much a tragic loss of life—at least seventy thousand Salvadorans are said to have died in the civil war (*Enemies of War*)—as it is the affirmation of a hybrid form of economic and military dominance on a global grid of repressive verticality in which the Latin American elite dovetails into the U.S. military-industrial complex (in El Salvador, big landowners—2 percent of the population owning 95 percent of the wealth [*Enemies of War*]—joined with the U.S.-backed national military to quash the leftist opposition).

Within the narrative economy of *Ever Amado*, the unseen agents of violence—figured principally as the U.S.-supported Salvadoran military and right-wing paramilitary—are implicitly equated with the two young American men who beat Ever to the edge of his life. When a group of three Spanish-speaking men—presumably the newest arrivals in an endless wave from the South—discover Ever's bludgeoned and near-dead body, it is by following a hyperbolically long and twisting—riverlike—stream of blood that has flowed from Ever's wounds. A telltale river of blood thus flowing symbolically from North to South may be read, on the strength of the same poetic license invoked by Ruano, as serving to identify the United States as the implicit author—or at the very least as a perpetrator on the same continuum—of the Salvadoran atrocities from which Ever sought to escape.

The final set of images from the footage of the Salvadoran civil war shows a series of gruesome cadavers, some intact but bullet riddled, some partially skinned, and still others decapitated or otherwise dismembered. A relationship of analogy between Ever's amputations as a consequence of his beating in the United States, on the one hand, and this fatal dismemberment by U.S.-backed right-wing Salvadoran forces, on the other, is expressly imputed by a montage sequence in which Ever's discovery of his own amputated legs as he attempts to rise up from his bed is visually juxtaposed with the decapitated torso of a Salvadoran victim of war. *Ever Amado* brings the leglessness of *Avatar* and *WALL·E* out from the safe confines of imaginary cultural narrative and into the life-and-death domain of the political real. The RDA Corporation, Colonel Quaritch, and AUTO are joined in their ranks of violent exploitation by the real-life U.S. and Latin American military and economic elite.

Ever Amado posits the love of family as the cure for violent and implicitly neoliberal fratricide, the ultimate triumph of social sustainability over its opposite condition, though this revelation does not restore Ever's legs or deliver him from the shadowy confines of his remote hospital room.[14] Should we nevertheless be tempted to view this aesthetic rendering of a political concept of love as the cultural manifestation of Hardt's philosophical attempts to identify a political concept of love for use by the left in combating the kind of violence that inflicts "leglessness,"[15] we would do well to remember Nike's parallel claim to life, love, and legs. Keeping our sights on the likes of the "Courage" commercial even as we analyze the unforgiving cultural condemnation of a film such as *Ever Amado* compels us to consider that there may not, in fact, exist any ontology of love as a human and humane phenomenon standing outside the reach of the market and military forces so frequently denounced as inhuman and inhumane by contestatory de facto sustainability discourse, but that the two sides are, rather, constructing opposing social messages from the same symbolic fabric.

Japón: "Mejor arreglar y no tirar" ("Better to fix than to throw away")

A film that elegantly threads together these politically charged topoi of well-being and ill-being without exiting its own abstract poetics is Mexican director Carlos Reygadas's debut feature, *Japón* (*Japan*; 2002). An unflinchingly experimental director who has been equally feted and panned on the festival circuit and in independent film criticism, Reygadas is nevertheless one of the most discussed and important young Mexican filmmakers. Paul Julian Smith calls Reygadas a "controversial auteur" (32) of "purist 'festival films'" (24), known for "explicit scenes of sexual acts" (25) and "unaesthetic [nonprofessional] casting" (26). Ignacio M. Sánchez Prado more lightheartedly calls him the "Lone Ranger" of Mexican cinema, a "director whose illegibility and irritating nature is precisely the condition of possibility of his impact and genius" (196).[16] Though Reygadas may be difficult to place within the landscape of Mexican film—indeed, Sánchez Prado reports that "part of the critical consensus regarding *Japón* tends to assert that the film is an 'exception' in the Mexican and Latin American context, based on its purportedly unique use of cinematic form for the transmission of emotions and narrative" (199)—I would contend that his filmography, and *Japón* in particular, has much to say about the "siege of political division, social inequality, and unprecedented violence" that Sánchez Prado believes most centrally characterizes neoliberalism and Mexican society's experience of it (226).

In regard to his choice of title for *Japón*, Reygadas says it is intentionally nonreferential to open up multiple interpretations, citing Terry Gilliam's choice of title *Brazil* for his fantastic Kafkaesque narrative study of bureaucratic totalitarian dystopia ("Entrevista con Carlos Reygadas"). One reviewer, in fact, comes independently—and plaintively—to that very comparison with the remark that "*Japón* . . . seems as arbitrary and willfully absurd as Terry Gilliam's *Brazil*" (Tobias), leaving the reader to infer that, like its more famous counterpart assigned by the comparison, *Japón* also

creates an allegorical aesthetic that is unconventional and difficult to interpret. This may be so, but I argue that that the structure of well-being and
ill-being as an affective language of cultural critique elucidates its otherwise
cryptic symbolism.

The fundamental plot is easily summarized: an unnamed male protagonist (Alejandro Ferretis) travels a hundred miles from Mexico City to the
countryside in the state of Hidalgo with the intention of committing suicide
and accepts a modest room and board in the lean-to farmhouse of an oc-
togenarian widow named Ascención (Magdalena Flores). The relationship
with Ascen, as she is called, spurs a spiritual catharsis in the man, who,
instead of taking his own life, asks for and receives sexual intercourse from
his elderly hostess. Shortly after this encounter, and in spite of the visitor's
disapproval, Ascen's nephew Juan Luis (Martín Serrano) comes to remove
the stones that serve as the foundation for her house whose ownership was
bequeathed to him by her dead husband. Leaving the man behind, Ascen
accompanies her nephew and his men down the mountain where she lives,
riding atop the flatbed truck overloaded with stones. Unable to bear the
weight of its cargo, the truck topples over and delivers death to all when
it strews its content—human and inanimate alike—across the valley below.

One point of first-level access to the film is the longstanding city-country
divide in Latin American letters. Best known of all such interventions is
political essayist and sometime Argentine president Domingo Sarmiento's
nineteenth-century dichotomy between desirable *civilización* (civilization)
and undesirable *barbarie* (barbarism), which he maps conceptually onto the
city and the countryside—the Argentine *pampa*, specifically, positing what
was to become a culturally hegemonic value system whereby the city was
positively coded as the seat of Eurocentric civilizing forces conducive to the
development and consolidation of the newly independent Argentina, and
the countryside as the negative source of barbaric autochthonous tyranny
obstructive of that end. But in spite of the fact that Sarmiento's is arguably
the most canonical such formulation, the theme of the relationship between
city and countryside is a persistent one in both nineteenth- and twentieth-century Latin America—and Spain, for that matter—which is unsurpris-
ing given the fact that both regions' economies were agrarian, concentrated
in the hands of a landowning elite. Another equally preeminent contemporary of Sarmiento, Chilean writer and statesman Andrés Bello, recognized,
in the wake of the independence movements, that the countryside held the
key to the economic future of the fledgling sovereign nations and urged

the virile youth of Latin America to make haste for the countryside, there to find work and prosperity and to leave behind the city, which he cast as a den of pernicious in-fighting, sloth, and vice.[17]

Reygadas does not replicate any of these city-country arguments per se, but *Japón*'s point of departure—its opening mise-en-scène—works precisely to evoke this tropological dichotomy around which grand statements of ideological and social critique have historically been fashioned. *Japón* begins with an extremely brief but absolutely fundamental sequence of urban traffic in which the camera hovers in the slow crawl of cars locked in a multilane grid. Only the shells of the cars are visible; there is no human protagonism, and the camera behaves as one more car among the many wedged together in the visual representation of urban life as a teeming mass of impersonality and congestion that impedes human activity from achieving any transcendent meaning. This is virtually the only direct information that the film gives us about city life, and the only definition of the provenance of the protagonist, who, being nameless throughout the film, therefore functions as a pure metonym for his urban origins. It is as though the protagonist represents Western culture in its most skeletal form: he brings with him orchestral music in a digital audio player, paint and canvas, a gun, and a fully developed death wish. His limp, which requires the support of a cane, goes diegetically unremarked (deriving from a real-life case of childhood polio) but offers itself for interpretation as the physiological manifestation of civilization and its discontents. In this regard the protagonist is the generic embodiment of urban—civilized—ill-being, already signaling that the position of the film will be to formulate a critique of that "civilization" from the vantage point of the country.

Indeed, in an interview, Reygadas characterizes the protagonist—whose character Reygadas claims is inspired by the longtime friend of his parents' who would, in the end, play the role onscreen—as part of a general pattern of "gente como [Alejandro Ferretis] que es muy cultivada, con muy buen gusto y muchas ideas acerca de la vida, pero que a la que al final [sic] de cuentas le falta cierto *savoir-vivre*" (people like [Alejandro Ferretis] that are very cultured, with very good taste and a lot of ideas about life, but who, in the final analysis, lack a certain *savoir-vivre*" ("Entrevista con Carlos Reygadas"). This lack of a "knowing how to live" is endemic, the film suggests, to city life, whose "culture" seems oriented more toward death than toward life. Just outside the city but not yet outside its logic—for the film seems also to propose that this civilized death logic pervades well beyond the bounds of the city in holding forth as a generalized cultural rule—the protagonist finds himself in the company of a small group of hunters of some status and means; when the protagonist communicates his avowed mission of suicide in response to the elder's inquiry into the motive of his trip, the latter replies, simply, "Entendido" ("Understood"). The protagonist knows how to kill a small bird by wringing its neck into decapitation, which, moreover, is staged as a pedagogical exercise by a young boy looking on, presumably the son or grandson of the senior hunter; he is also versed in—and claims to enjoy—shooting a gun. Having spent his first night outside the city at a midway point in a town called San Bartolo, the protagonist awakens to the blood-curdling squeals of a pig being slaughtered off-screen, with a wash of blood emerging from the door of the makeshift slaughterhouse visible from the protagonist's window. Later, the protagonist is visually compared to a dead horse as they lie in poetic juxtaposition at the edge of a mountain cliff, while the camera draws back into the sky to reveal how close they are to one another and yet how small both are against the rest of the comparatively immense natural world. The role of horses—and of animals in general—in Reygadas's film has most frequently been compared to what one reviewer calls Andrei Tarkovsky's "unacceptably harrowing treatment of a horse in *Andrei Rublev* [1966]" where an agonizing horse falls down a stairway to its death. Setting aside for a moment the general question of animal cruelty, the eviscerated horse in *Japón* readily recalls the symbolism of the dead donkey in the surrealist avant-garde short *Un chien andalou* (1929), where codirectors Luis Buñuel and Salvador Dalí use the animal corpse to signify, along with a heavy cargo of other cultural artifacts—tablets, monks, pianos—the enervating weight of bourgeois decadence. In *Japón*, then, the protagonist, as the representative of civilization, is the embodiment of the death of nature.

In an interview Reygadas expresses indignation at the intolerant reception of his representation of what he considers reality—including sex and violence—an intolerance that reaches the level of official censorship in the case of *Japón*'s animal cruelty:

> What you find in my films you see any ordinary day: a gas station, a hunter killing an animal, people making love. I'm not trying to impress anyone with those images; they make sense in the context of my films. People feel uncomfortable seeing a beheaded pigeon. What's the big deal? . . . Whoever thinks I'm depicting something

shocking is a hypocrite who thinks that what he or she would prefer not to see simply doesn't exist. For me the real is beautiful. Blood is beautiful if it's real, but a beautiful woman and a beautiful house are horrible to me if they're not authentic. All those *feel-good* things to me feel *really bad*—their falsehood is depressing. I can't believe that in England, the country that birthed democracy, *Japón*, to this date, is censored: they cut the scenes in which the pigeon is killed and the village's veterinarian tickles a little dog. The country with the most infamous colonial history thinks that by censoring my film they've paid for their sins!

(Castillo)

I would like to call attention to the subtle references to ill-being and well-being, on the one hand, and to colonialism, on the other, as a means of entering further into what we might consider Reygadas's anticolonial critique on a par with that of the films thus far discussed. First, Reygadas rejects a prepackaged aesthetic of "a beautiful woman and a beautiful house" on the grounds that their "falsehood is depressing"—"All those *feel-good* things to me feel *really bad*," he avers. This would give his reader/spectator to understand that his representation of brutality forms part of what truly feels good for the fact of its authenticity, yet his comment equating the censoring of his film with the payment of colonial sins presents a new piece in the conceptual puzzle that will not permit such a facile equation. Reygadas accuses England not simply of democratic hypocrisy—that is, the failure to adhere to its own principles of cultural freedoms of expression and representation, etc.—but that England's hypocrisy is actually a question of the pot calling the kettle black: in other words, this hypocrisy turns on the question of mutual recognition in which England cleans its own historical conscience by condemning its likeness elsewhere.

To be sure, Reygadas's representation of "colonial" violence does not—as his protest implicitly asserts—approach the scale of empire. But it is worth reflecting on the ways in which a violence, acquisitiveness, and lack of empathy are all clustered together in the regions affected by city logic. The disposition toward hunting and violent animal deaths already described happen en route to the protagonist's final destination of Ayacatzintla. The town of San Bartolo wherein transpires the audial brutality of the pig slaughter also harbors the unmitigated greed of Ascención's nephew Juan Luis, who we learn has also spent time in jail for undisclosed reasons. Though having accepted his aunt's care while in jail, including images of the virgin, to which he masturbated, we are told, Juan Luis subsequently responds with the singular determination to tear apart her house for its raw materials. This succinct representation of a neocolonial economy of extraction is accompanied by a relationship of vertical disdain and disrespect toward the other whose resources are being pillaged. Instead of expressing gratitude, Juan Luis and his sons ridicule their aunt as a *pendeja* ("dumb-ass") for letting her house be dismantled without offering the slightest gesture of resistance. Fully aware that he will render his aunt homeless, Juan Luis nevertheless imperiously declares that he will not rest until every last stone from the foundation of her house is in San Bartolo, callously asserting his legal privilege to the letter of the law.

In the film's sole reference to the United States, the protagonist disparagingly communicates his instinctive aversion to the nephew by calling him a "cara de marrano que nunca se quita la gorra de gringo" ("pig-face who never takes off his gringo baseball cap"). Indeed, Juan Luis's unempathically gluttonous project of the static accumulation of capital—the large stones of Ascen's house serving as the quintessential representation thereof—embodies the posture ascribed to the United States as the cold and relentless neocolonial hegemon symbolically represented in Colonel Quaritch and the RDA, AUTO, and, historiographically, in the ruthless violence of the Salvadoran Civil War sponsored by the United States' most conservative factions determined to deliver "freedom" in the form of a neoliberal government. Juan Luis's commitment to the project of capital accumulation reveals itself to be pathological in the sense that his inability to allow practical considerations to attenuate his greed leads to terminal dis-ease in the form of death and destruction. Determined to take his aunt's stones in one single trip down the mountain, Juan Luis disregards warnings that the load will be precariously heavy. Although the film elides the moment of upheaval, a final panoramic camera shot travels the extensive circumference and long diameter of the predicted wreckage, revealing body after body amid a field of large stones. Like Al Gore's gold bars with no planet, the stones lie eternal but useless—stripped of their value—in the wake of perfect carnage. Death, *Japón* posits, is the ultimate and inevitable externality of unbridled materialism.

Ascen, on the other hand, represents all of nature. Without knowing that she is what he seeks, the protagonist comes to her at the figurative and literal nadir of his life and journey—which is a long descent down the side of a mountain to the town of Ayacatzintla. Once there, the town representative gives the protagonist a formal speech of welcome in which he claims a state of exceptionality of his town as one that is unlike all the rest in that it is safe and he need not fear coming to harm; Ayá—as it is called in colloquial shorthand—is cast as a singular oasis of communal harmony against an otherwise homogenous backdrop. Everywhere else, that is, is the same; only Ayá is different. This claim of exceptionality has the effect of coding everywhere else as culturally continuous, which resonates with the notion that capitalist city culture is not limited to urban confines but has rather become hegemonic in its immanence—its totalizing "resting within" with no outside, no transcendence.

As the extractive incursion by the Juan Luis demonstrates, even Ayá is not unsusceptible to this culture of capitalism. Yet, on the village mountaintop—the high point of the nadir—and the inevitability of this incursion notwithstanding, Ascen embodies a contrapuntal logic of uncontestatory resistance. Hers is a practice of seemingly bottomless generosity and self-sacrifice not unlike Shel Silverstein's "giving tree" (1964) who allows the little boy she loves to swing from her branches when he is a boy, to harvest her apples to sell when he is a young man, to cut her branches to make a house when he is a grown man, to take her trunk to build a boat when he is middle aged, and to rest on her stump when he is an old man. Ascen, likewise, endlessly and unquestioningly offers: shelter, food, drink. She becomes the source of the protagonist's nourishment, and though at first he is loathe to eat—in keeping with his self-conceived proximity to death—he does eventually acquiesce, and his meals grow more robust in sustenance and content as his stay with Ascen progresses. For her part, Ascen asks for nothing in return. She cares for the protagonist without invading his privacy—when cleaning his room, she finds his gun hidden inside his wool jacket; she simply wraps it up again, leaving it exactly as she found it. In the morning, she leaves him a note saying, simply—giving the spectator to understand that she has intuited its intended use—that she is happy to see him again and that she has left him breakfast.

Ascen, whose first act upon meeting the protagonist is to correct his error of address by clarifying that her name is not the more common Asunción (Assumption), but rather Ascención (Ascension). The difference, she goes on to explain, is that the former refers to the heavenly ascension of the Virgin Mary, for which she required the help of angels, whereas the latter refers to that of Christ, which he was able to accomplish on his own. Ascen does not gloss this explanation further, but her cumulative actions show that she is indeed a free spirit content to live and let live, seemingly without judgment or taboos, completely dispossessed of any impulse to control others. She readily smokes the protagonist's marijuana, "no más para probar" ("just to give it a try"), takes swigs of pulque, seems entirely unfazed by her nephew's use of her gifts of religious iconography for masturbatory purposes, and, in a dreamscape fantasy of the protagonist, in which Ascen appears alongside a younger conventionally attractive woman of slim build and large breasts dressed in a scanty bikini, Ascen leans forward to give her a peck on the lips, with a furtive sideways glance at the camera that acknowledges an awareness that her curiosity of desire that may be perceived as transgressive, but that she is predisposed to obey it all the same. Ascen adds a diminutive to most things she names, including her *difuntito* ("'little' dead [husband]") and the *animalitos* ("'little' animals") on her small farm. Modest and economic of emotive expression, Ascen nevertheless demonstrates a limitlessly expansive care and affection—Christlike in its unconditional character—for the world that surrounds her.

The greatest proof of this unconditional love takes the form of her total submission to Juan Luis's plans to destroy her house. The protagonist becomes increasingly agitated by these plans once he learns of them, and one last attempt to persuade Ascen to stand against them produces one of the most significant sets of exchanges in the film. In the face of the protagonist's insistence that her nephew is tricking her into forfeiting her legitimate right to her house, and, moreover, making fun of her behind her back, Ascen gently counters with her own philosophy: "Es que no soy aferrada" ("It's that I don't cling [to things]"). When they next reconvene, the protagonist uses her phrase in a way she doesn't accept, serving to round out the definition of her outlook:

EL HOMBRE: . . . Se necesita mucha serenidad para dejar muchas cosas a las que estamos habituados pero que en realidad ya no queremos.

ASCEN: Ajá.

EL HOMBRE: Hay que saber tirar lo que ya no sirve.

ASCEN: Ajá. Mejor arreglar y no tirar, ¿o no?

EL HOMBRE: Sí, pero hay ciertas cosas que no se pueden arreglar y es mejor tirar que vivir aferrado a ciertas cosas sólo por costumbre.

ASCEN: Ajá. Creo que sí lo entiendo, joven. Pero sabe, joven, que aunque a mí no me gustan mis brazos viejos y enfermos, pero aun así no me los cortaría.

THE MAN: . . . One needs a great deal of serenity to leave behind many things to which we have become habituated but which in reality we no longer want/love.

Ascen: Mmm-hmm.

THE MAN: One has to know when to throw away what is no longer useful.

ASCEN: Mmm-hmm. Better to fix [things] and not throw [them] away, isn't it?

THE MAN: Yes, but there are certain things that cannot be fixed and it is better to throw [them] away than to live clinging to certain things only out of habit.

ASCEN: Mmm-hmm. I think I understand you, young man. But you know, young man, that even though I don't like my old and sick arms, even so I wouldn't cut them off.]

These two conversations turn on the use and definition of the term *aferrado/a,* the past participle of the verb *aferrar,* from *ferrum,* the Latin for iron, meaning to clutch, to hold, or to anchor, and which here makes most sense to think of in its reflexive form as *aferrarse a algo*—to cling onto, to hold fast to something. Both Ascen and the protagonist coincide in the view that to be *aferrado/a* is undesirable, but they do not define the term in the same way. When Ascen says she is not *aferrada,* it is in the context of being willing and able to let go of her stones, and her house along with them, for, as the protagonist reminds her in frustration of what she herself has earlier said, without the stones the house will not resist the winds. Ascen simply remarks that her nephew needs the stones more than she does and asks the protagonist not to speak further about her decision. When the protagonist says—implicitly referring to himself, though assuming the pedantic and prescriptive voice of the general third-person singular—that one must learn to throw away what cannot be fixed rather than to live *aferrado* to those useless things, he is, though he does not acknowledge as much, referring to his own life as that which no longer has use value. Ascen intuits this in her response (though this response is also informed by the passing by at that moment of a young girl who is the daughter of a man with deformed and useless hands) when she says that she would not cut her hands off even if "old and sick." Ascen defends life and the body as its vehicle, marking an essential difference in the category of "things" to which to cling or let go between these—life and the body—and material objects, no matter how dear. In contrast, the protagonist is willing to put life and the body along with material objects into the same category of "things" to be discarded when useless. In his view life and the body hold the status of commodities among many; having been reduced to a state of ill-being by the capitalist city, his solution is to throw them away. Ascen, on the other hand, assigns an absolute value to life and the body even in the face of their ill-being.

Ascen's commitment to protecting life and the body—of working toward their well-being—achieves its maximum expression in her final act of generosity toward the protagonist: when she decides to ride down the mountain atop the cargo of stones; before leaving she asks the protagonist for his jacket—in only the second instance during the entire film in which we see her ask anything of anyone, the first having been to ask the protagonist to bring water to the house. The protagonist willingly drapes his jacket over her shoulders, acknowledging that the ride will be chilly. But when we recall Ascen's knowledge of the jacket as the place where the protagonist has stashed his gun, we realize that she did not so much wish to borrow his jacket as to take away what it contained. She knows that her departure—even, perhaps, foreseeing her own death—will leave him alone at the mountaintop. Her last gesture toward the protagonist, then, is to dispossess him of the instrument of capitalist death. In this way Ascen's two requests resolve into a single impulse: toward the protection of life.

The protagonist's story ends in suspense; we don't know whether this dispossession of the instrument of death will effect a disintegration of the desire for death, which would be a necessary condition for him to take Ascen's place as he stands poised to do. Self-sacrifice for the perceived well-being of others—the willingness of the liberal position to accept a Christlike martyrdom—which is how we may interpret Ascen's death, stands in contrast to the self-destruction the protagonist holds as an objective on arrival in the town. We may not know what his fate will be, but the fact in which the narrative has situated him, the transformative position of the Western outsider who "goes native," throws into question the certainty of his eventual suicide.

The key shift that has occurred in the protagonist as a consequence of his arrival at Ascen's house—what her caretaking of him has occasioned—is the awakening of his libido. The first proof of this awakening comes a few days of Ascen's caretaking—she has fed him repeatedly and concertedly, cleaned his room, beaten the dust from the blanket on his bed, accompanied him in conversation, and accepted his offer of marijuana. After this last encounter, in which Ascen recounts her nephew's lascivious behavior with the iconography she once sent him in jail—which produces a soft smile of pleasure in the protagonist, the first we see on his face—he makes his first onscreen suicide attempt. Lying in bed, he presses his gun into his bare chest between the sides of his shirt. The camera cuts to find him in the same position, but now entirely unclothed, with his hand having moved from his chest to his penis, which he is slowly masturbating. The visual analogy between his hand holding the gun and then holding his penis instead suggests a relationship of equivalence between the two: the erection has taken the place of the gun, with the desire to satisfy the libido being stronger and more urgent than that of satisfying the death wish.

Sex is further developed in association with vitality, as against death, in the scene of equine sex witnessed by the protagonist after his conversation with Ascen in which she defines herself as not being attached to material things (*no soy aferrada*). Immediately after this animal voyeurism, the protagonist takes out his gun for a second time at the edge of the mountain cliff, holding it to the sky. Without pulling the trigger, he suddenly lowers it and makes haste to move away from the precipice, gasping for breath as though having narrowly escaped danger and dropping down on safe ground next to the dead horse in the scene earlier discussed; it is unclear whether the landscape of which dead horse is part is real or symbolic, but a steady rain falls on his face as though in purification, and the camera pulls up and out to reveal a vast expanse of nature that subsumes both protagonist and animal corpse, reproducing in visual terms the protagonist's experience of a natural sublime that leads him to submit to its dictates—which are the privileging of life and of sex as its affirmation. In effect, his next act is to rejoin Ascen and to make a first reference to the proposition he would like to make, which, we will eventually discover, is that he would like to have intercourse with her. Ascen assents, in keeping with her boundless generosity of self, and, during their sexual encounter, the protagonist begins by placing her on all fours and trying to mount her from behind in a clear visual echo of the horses. On climax, the protagonist bursts into heaving sobs and accepts the comfort of Ascen's stroking hand and embrace. From this moment forward, the protagonist evinces no further impulse toward death; it is as though the sexual act has created an affective catharsis of emotional bloodletting, so to speak, in which the protagonist has begun to shift his internal equilibrium away from ill-being and toward health.

In this regard, *Japón* may stage the curative process of healing Western ill-being through loving contact with the earth—for Ascen is just as much Mother Nature as Christ—but it does not stage the utopian finale of salvation for nature at the hands of the transformed Westerner. On the contrary, this Westerner, transformed though he may be, must look on helplessly as the forces of extractive urban capitalism carry his love—Mother Nature—to her death. The detail of the placement of her body, as the camera travels the extent of the wreckage, is significant: hers is the last to be found in the camera's eye and lies squarely between a set of train tracks. The ultimate symbol of technological advancement in the service of capitalist progress, here train tracks instead serve the purpose of a coffin, recalling Bersuit Vergarabat's assertion that progress has been a failure and Evo Morales's claim that capitalist progress is responsible for the devastation of humanity and the natural world.

Eco-Love and Legs: The Political Agency of Well-Being

In all these narratives the cultural protagonist arrives on the scene as a stand-in for the rest of humanity—or of the entire animal kingdom—and, indeed, always on behalf of the natural world. A love interest presents itself, whose felicitious or infelicitous outcome serves as code for the political potential of the cultural protagonist to champion and achieve his program of social-natural harmony based on empathy. This "ecolove" is only achievable by the able-bodied. Those who have had the ability to recuperate their legs—to overcome ill-being with renewed well-being—may oversee the triumphant rise of a new people-and-planet-friendly community; those whose legs are irrecuperable—for whom well-being cannot surmount ill-being—must witness the death and destruction of humanity and nature.

Across hemispheres, and across dispositions with respect to the question of profit, these instances of cultural production derive their narrative from the same set of plot points, as though they shared a common puzzle and differed only in the arrangement of its pieces. *Avatar*, *WALL·E*, Nike's "Courage" campaign, *Ever Amado*, and *Japón* construct narratives predicated on an ecolove on the scale of humanity that seeks to reestablish a natural well-being over a neocolonial ill-being. In Northern examples—*Avatar*, *WALL·E*, Nike's "Courage" ad—ecolove triumphs over neocolonial capitalism and its imposition of ill-being (with a perfect and ironic indistinction between anti- and pro-profit-consumption models). In Southern examples—*Ever Amado, Japón*—ecolove makes an appearance as an ideal, but cannot triumph; there is no countering neocolonial circumstance, and ill-being holds forth to the end. In both hemispheres we find the same fundamental valorization of well-being as a desideratum, but the characterization of its attainability express differing political realities that register the vertical power differential distributed between North and South America. The same episteme is at work in both places, coding political possibility in the same way: as a function of homeostatic health denoted by somatic integrity—legs as able-bodiedness—and love as the conditions of life. All narratives (including corporate advertising) stand against neocolonial capitalism, yet all narratives (including anticapitalist narrative) reaffirm the epistemic principles of capitalism.

Conclusion

Affective Biopower

"As if by the nod of some invisible conductor"

In December 2010, still in the thick of U.S.-driven global recession, the *New York Review of Books* published a review of books dedicated to a consideration of economic recovery. One of these texts is British financial reporter Anatole Kaletsky's *Capitalism 4.0*, which reviewer Jeff Madrick characterizes as espousing a "hopeful economic agenda" in which Kaletsky "relies heavily on his faith in the ingenuity of capitalism as an adaptive mechanism" (1). Madrick goes on to quote Kaletsky on this point: "'Hoping that "something will turn up" may sound like deluded wishful thinking,' [Kaletsky] writes, 'but it is really just an extension into politics and macroeconomics of Adam Smith's arguments about the self-organizing dynamics of the capitalist economy'" (1). I intentionally break from scholarly convention to cite Kaletsky indirectly in order to underscore the reach of such ideas through concatenated mass-media repetition and also in order to point out how, in spite of the fact that Madrick begins his review with a cynical recognition of the "rarely recognized" structural weaknesses of the U.S. economy and a resultant skepticism about its possibilities of recovery, his article is nevertheless titled, "How Can the Economy Recover?" The title itself echoes Kaletsky's posture of faith in the persistence of the economic fact and its capacity for self-healing; it is not a question of whether, but how. Adam Smith's invisible hand and the model of somatic homeostasis it represents—the organic and autonomous tendency toward well-being—turns up as a conceptual source of hope for the longevity of the capitalist fact. Why do we think our culture will continue to be capitalist? Because we believe in the persistence of the self-same, and that self-same is intrinsically—epistemically—founded in the homeostatic logic of capitalism. The epistemic feat of the "invention of man" was to make human homeostasis capitalist.

Six months later, also ruminating on the economic crash of 2008, and giving a blog preview of his own coauthored book on the subject, Greek political economist Yanis Varoufakis departed from the opposite premise that no economic school is to be regarded as having the silver bullet remedy: "The simple point is that, as economists (of almost all persuasions), we have been barking up the wrong tree." In the face of the "most spectacular privatisation of money in the 1990s and beyond," Varoufakis writes, "our petty squabbles between 'monetarists' and the so-called 'Keynesians,' between those favouring inflation targets and those against the fans of zero inflation; between advocates of microeconomic reform in the labour markets and others paying more attention to the credibility of central banks" were all "pointless." Instead, Varoufakis makes the ludicrous—but, seemingly, not disingenuous—proposal that the economy should follow the example of the U.S. National Football League, where "socialist planning lives in sin with unbridled competition." In justifying his model, Varoufakis draws from British literary critic Terry Eagleton (2007) in another embedded representation of homeostatic principle disseminated through mass-media circuitry:

> In his little book, *The Meaning of Life,* Terry Eagleton faced a similarly daunting task [analogous to the drafting of what Varoufakis calls the New Global Plan]: to capture, in brief, the . . . meaning of life. His answer was: A band like the Cuban Buena Vista Social Club; that's the meaning of life! Eagleton's point was that such a band illustrates the dialectic at its best. A "community" with a clear, unifying tune toward which each "individual" contributes by . . . improvising. Its members do not mechanistically play from some given score, writ-

ten by a despotic musical mind (however brilliant that mind might be), but, rather, integrate their own private freedom into a collective pursuit which enhances the experience of each of its members. Their improvisation confirms their private freedom not by having each not whimsically selected by autonomous players but, rather, when all the various pieces of improvisation fall into place, *as if by the nod of some invisible conductor.*

(emphasis added)

Varoufakis's rejection of economics as an established disciplinary source of knowledge nevertheless circles directly back to free-market epistemicity as a source of knowledge that is not only naturalized as supremely legitimate but is also cast as being at the crux of the human condition itself. The search for the new global plan is tantamount to the search for the meaning of life, and both searches reach their conceptual apotheosis in the reiteration of the figure of free-market homeostasis—in which "private freedom" results from collective integration within an organic whole whose "various pieces of improvisation fall into place" in a process of self-organization that is not top-down and autocratic, but rather markedly democratic of spirit and, as such, spontaneous and unregulated, yet communicated through a harmonious collective sensibility "as if by the nod of some invisible conductor," a reference that implicitly evokes what was explicit in Kaletsky, namely, Adam Smith's invisible hand.

In the same way that the Christ narrative dominates Western ideals of social comportment, the capitalist homeostatic principle has come to dominate Western ideals of social structure and to condition the possibilities of knowledge and imagination that those structures support. It is not simply a model of commerce and exchange in the economic dimension, but in the intellectual and moral dimensions as well. Things work best, we believe, when structured as a collective free flow that obeys only the natural laws of organic integrity that work toward the equity, harmony, and happiness of homeostatic well-being. This homeostatic principle of how things work serves at once as the foundation for thought and its highest proof; it is a point of creative departure as well as a legitimizing force with the power of self-institutionalization.

In a set of posthumously published and instantly classic lectures (*The Birth of Biopolitics*, 2007), French philosopher Michel Foucault meditates on this very question of the epistemicity of free-market capitalism, which he calls *homo œconomicus*—now a more refined epithet for his earlier "invention of man"—as the power to define the knowable:

> Since the eighteenth century, has *homo œconomicus* involved setting up an essentially and unconditionally irreducible element against any possible government? Does the definition of *homo œconomicus* involved marking out the zone that is definitively inaccessible to any government action? Is *homo œconomicus* an atom of freedom in the face of all the conditions, undertakings, legislation, and prohibitions a possible government, or was he not already a certain type of subject who precisely enabled an art of government to be determined according to the principle of economy, both in the sense of political economy and in the sense of the restriction, self-limitation, and frugality of government? Obviously, the way in which I have formulated this question gives the answer straightaway, but this is what I would like to talk about, that is to say, *homo œconomicus* as the partner, the vis-à-vis, and the basic element of the new governmental reason formulated in the eighteenth century.
>
> *Homo œconomicus* is someone who can say to the juridical sovereign, to the sovereign possessor of rights and founder of positive law on the basis of the natural right of individuals: You must not. But he does not say: You must not, because I have rights and you must not touch them. This is what the man of right, *homo juridicus*, says to the sovereign: I have rights, I have entrusted some of them to you, the others you must not touch, or: I have entrusted you with my rights for a particular end. *Homo œconomicus* does not say this. He also tells the sovereign: You must not. But what must he not? You must not because you cannot. And you cannot in the sense that "you are powerless." And why are you powerless, why can't you? *You cannot because you do not know, and you do not know because you cannot know.*
>
> (282–83, emphasis added)

This losing battle of the sovereign to *homo œconomicus* is succinctly recounted in the review—to circle back to Kaletsky's reviewer—of Jeff Madrick's *Age of Greed: The Triumph of Finance and the Decline of America, 1970 to the Present* (2011) by U.S. economists Paul Krugman and Robin Wells. Madrick explains how the increasing deregulation of finance gave rise to cycle after cycle of deepening greed, extreme risk taking, and dubious legality in banking from the 1970s to the present, creating "so many [villains] that by the end of the book," Krugman and Wells aver, "we were, frankly, suffering from a bit of outrage fatigue" (2). In their review of Madrick's book, Krugman and Wells say they "get a lot of the what, but not much of the why"—"why have villains triumphed so repeatedly?" (2), they ask. "If the problem was lack of oversight, that leads to another question: Why did the regulators abdicate—and keep abdicating despite repeated financial disasters?" "There's another book to be written here," Krugman and Wells aver, "one that gets at the forces that made the reign of financial villains possible" (2). Yet, throughout their review, Krugman and Wells make reference to a deepening ideological naturalization of the free-market ideal, beginning with how Ronald Reagan, on the strength of Milton Friedman's radical free-market paradigm, "made unchecked greed and runaway individualism not only acceptable, but lauded, in the American psyche" based on the conviction that "financial markets could do no wrong" (1). Krugman and Wells even give their own term for this, in a pithy definition of the conceptual backbone of the neoliberalism that Reagan and Friedman spawned: "greedism," the "creed . . . that unchecked self-interest furthers the common good" (1). If free-market capitalism was born in synchronicity with liberal democracy as its political avatar, then neoliberalism has constituted the radical expression of free-market capitalism by forcing its political counterpart to obey its epistemic principle of self-regulated horizontality to the letter of the law.

In Krugman and Wells's economical turn of phrase—the creed that unchecked self-interest furthers the common good—we have a concise summary of the fundamental epistemic operation of neoliberalism: the fusion of the model of neocolonial growth (unchecked self-interest) with that of free-market homeostasis (the common good). This is why, as a culture, we cannot set limits on profit: because to do so is tantamount, we believe (we *know*, in the epistemic sense of free-market hegemony), to short-circuiting our own well-being—in a word, to committing suicide. And so the argument rages about the definition of well-being and ill-being, with free-market apologists claiming that to limit profit is terminal ill-being, with free-market antagonists like Varoufakis warning that humanity is on course to "[end] up like a dim, self-defeating virus," both sides engaging organic metaphors of well-being or malaise to stake their claims, each claiming the epistemic privilege of invisible somatic self-orchestration that only works to reaffirm the originary free-market model.

Biopower: Affective, Epistemic

> *Homo œconomicus* . . . tells the sovereign: You must not. But what
> must he not? You must not because you cannot. And you cannot in
> the sense that "you are powerless." And why are you powerless, why
> can't you? You cannot because you do not know, and you do not
> know because you cannot know.
>
> (Foucault, The Birth of Biopolitics, 283)

In the face-off between models of power that this passage enacts, it is the
sovereign—the ruler that presumes to govern by exception when the homeostatic principle of immanent democracy has categorically precluded
such power—who is now visited with the powerlessness of not knowing
and not being able to know. The sovereign is categorically barred from the
knowledge of *homo œconomicus* (because the sovereign is the rational head
that has been disavowed—disowned—by the feeling soma of *homo œconomicus*); only the perfectly democratic constituency of that feeling soma
may *know*, in the intransitive rendering of that normally transitive verb Foucault employs to denote an epistemic access to the limits and possibilities
of knowledge.

But beyond their function of tracing a logic of epistemic inclusion and
exclusion, Foucault's words also hold a more general import, to which this
entire study is dedicated: simply, that free-market capitalism—*homo œconomicus*—has its own epistemic modality, its own ways of knowing. (I like
to imagine that it was this rumbling of the tectonic cultural plates—"the
deepest strata of Western culture" [xxiv]—that Foucault claimed to feel
as he finished *The Order of Things* in the mid-1960s, a historic moment
when global decolonization would spell the end of epistemic reason, the
beginning of free-market triumph, and the ascendance of epistemic affect.
"It is the same ground that is stirring once more under our feet" [xxiv],
he wrote, though he himself left that rumbling ultimately undiagnosed and
unnamed.) If Foucault's free-market *homo œconomicus* claims an epistemic
monopoly that translates into absolute power, then it is of the essence to
comprehend the terms of that monopoly over the structure, sign, and play
of knowledge.

From the time that Thomas Jefferson formulated political autonomy
as the right to "life, liberty, and the pursuit of happiness" (1776), there-

by declaring a state of sovereignty for the body politic from the colonial crown, that last phrase—"the pursuit of happiness"—defined the resultant headless body as a feeling one. If reason and its tropes of order and control performed by a thinking head to the effect of subjugating the body constituted the epistemic imaginary of colonial power, then affect and its central trope of well-being—for which happiness, along with love, is the ultimate metonym—now emerged to constitute the epistemic imaginary of democratic power. The feeling soma's claim to happy well-being is synonymous with its claim to sovereignty: it is the ability of the feeling soma to generate and participate in, simultaneously, its own self-arising and self-justifying mechanism of power that makes it its own sovereign master. In this model of affective sovereignty, the homeostatic criteria of that system of order—and knowledge of that system—are not only organically immanent to that feeling subject but also, as Foucault astutely observes, exclusively accessible to that feeling subject. The rational apparatus may perceive and even appreciate well-being, but its physiological experience, and therefore its authorship and ownership, are proper to the nonrational homeostatic affective pathways of the soma.

Current research in psychology holds that, as a medium of knowledge, affect functions through a mode of communication that is organically monosemic and involuntary. In other words, as a sign—a signifier denoting a given signified—affective information is neither arbitrary nor polyvalent, but rather constitutes a signification that is organic and of a meaning both singular and unequivocal.

As previously mentioned, Charles Darwin's *The Expression of the Emotions in Man and Animals* (1872) argued for the universality of the expression of human emotion. This hypothesis languished in oblivion for almost a hundred years; Darwin's twentieth-century editor Paul Ekman believes that his universalism was politically unacceptable to scholars who viewed their own commitment to cultural relativism as an ethical imperative for countering fascist politics and atrocities.[1] Ekman himself professes to have set out to prove Darwin wrong with an experiment comparing Western and non-Western cultural identification of emotional expressions, which yielded data that unexpectedly corroborated Darwin's belief that humans are programmed to experience and display the same emotional sets (1980). Of interest for the question of epistemic affect is Darwin's claim, sustained by Ekman, that as humans we are not only programmed as a species to express emotion, but that we are programmed to react to each other's expressions.

In analogy to how Noam Chomsky contends that infants are universally and innately equipped to generate linguistic grammar, even in isolation from fully developed language, Ekman proposes the affective equivalent, arguing that humans are born with the ability to communicate universally in what Darwin called "the language of the emotions" (360). This means that the interpretation of the face of the other—which Darwin and Ekman believe is simply the outward manifestation of an inner physiological state—is a hard-wired and involuntary act.[2]

Perspectives informed by the cultural relativism that has dominated the Western academy—especially the humanities—with particular intensity in the wake of decolonization and the resistance of imperialist politics in any guise will object to this universalist characterization of emotion on the grounds that it is essentialist, foreclosing the possibility of contestation and autonomy in the form of emotional variation across cultures or of the sovereign performance of emotional states as distinct from the construal of their performance as involuntary experience. In defense of the universalist point of view, Ekman answers that, while there are many second-order corporeal communicative signals that are learned (rather than innate) and arbitrary (rather than organic), there is nevertheless a basic set of human emotions—anger, disgust, fear, happiness, sadness, and surprise—that are common to the species and, when felt, are expressed involuntarily on the face in what may be considered the true and organic sign of an internal physiological state. Even when these emotions are imitated for the sake of performance, Ekman argues—as he himself has done for the sake of cataloguing thousands of emotions—the effect is to generate the physiological experience of the emotional state being imitated; in this sense, there is no difference between performance and experience as a catalyst for emotion and its expression. Just as emotional experience produces a matching emotional expression, emotional expression also matches—and produces—emotional experience.

Let us return to Foucault in order to recall his characterization of modernity as a political epoch that exerts far more control over the body of the subject than ever before. In contrast to the "ancient right to *take* life or *let* live," Foucault argues in his earliest formulation of biopower, modern politics wields the "power to *foster* life or *disallow* it to the point of death" (*The History of Sexuality* 138). That is to say, modern political systems have an unprecedented ability to interfere with the quality of life, to regulate not only birth and death, but, more important, all that lies in between. This is precisely the power of *homo œconomicus*: to maximize control over the most intimate bodily livelihood. In this model of subjectivity cognition operates at a visceral level that bypasses both the second-order process of reason and the polysemy of verbal language; the language of affect—to render Darwin's original formulation in epistemic dimensions—is direct and unappealable. Whether in the service of a politics of fear or love, or of a consumption of health or toxicity, this is biopower at its most potent. It is no wonder that anticonsumer culture activists like Sut Jhally warn that we are "advertising at the edge of apocalypse."

"Estás aquí para ser feliz"
("You are here to be happy")

Since 2006, Coca-Cola—a company that boasts the total consumption of 1.7 billion servings per day—has developed the global branding campaign of the "Coke side of life," which its central concept of "happiness in a bottle" clearly defines as the side of affect, with the imperative to "Open Happiness" (in Spanish, "Destapa la felicidad"). In developing the campaign, Coca-Cola researchers "learned that what loyal Coke drinkers love most about the brand was the physical and emotional uplift they got when drinking the product" (Macarthur). Constructing the representation of a global affective subject on these terms, the Coca-Cola website hosts an interactive feature called the "Smile-izer" in which users are invited to record their laughter and to search by name for other users' recordings. The image of a studio microphone hovers against a backdrop made to look like the brown liquid of Coca-Cola, with bubbles floating to the top of the screen conveying the idea of Coca-Cola as the medium of happiness. Coca-Cola figures its consumers as the expression of their positive emotion—whether in aural disembodiment as a representation, precisely, of the feeling body or in the throes of somatic response to consumption—defining subjectivity on both an individual and collective scale as tantamount to happiness and, most critically, laying claim to the very physiological experience of happiness.

Indeed, an advertisement from the "happiness in a bottle" campaign deepens this claim to the physiology of happiness. In "The Library" (developed in 2009 by Weiden+Kennedy, Amsterdam) a teenage boy and girl seated across a table experience a wordless communion that is silent not so much because they must observe the institutional norms of learning as because they find another more powerful mechanism of communicating and sharing the experience of life that does not require words or the rational edifice they support. The boy draws a bottle of Coca-Cola on his forearm; the girl draws a glass with ice cubes on hers. The Coca-Cola on the boy's forearm comes to life as a substance that flows from his arm and into her glass. They are joined in a physiological encounter in which the product becomes indistinguishable from the body of the consumer; they merge into a homeostatic loop in which the product-cum-lifeforce circulates as though it were blood. The two seem to fall in love—an idea reinforced by the title of the theme song, "Strange Love" by the Swedish jazz duo Koop, for which the advertisement won a CLIO award—yet even this concept falls short of conveying the intense intimacy that this somatic-affective communion creates. Happiness, love, community—here in the intimacy of a couple—and the physiological substance of vitality itself are all collapsed into the bottle of Coke. Coca-Cola positions itself as the purveyor of homeostatic well-being, the motor that drives life itself.

This communion has taken place not only without breaking the rules of the library but without engaging the library's attention or entering into its sphere of consciousness. This kind of communication passes completely unperceived by the surveilling logic of reason. The library is powerless because it does not know; it does not know because it cannot know. How can a library think beyond institutionality, borders, words, rules? The control of institutions built on a model of rational control—discrete, compartmentalized, panoptic—gives way to a new model of order that is based on organic interconnectedness, shared knowledge rooted in a common affective experience, and self-regulated.

Another Coca-Cola advertisement goes even further in its claim to well-being and, as such, life itself—understanding life, according to Foucault's definition of its modern variant, as all that lies between birth and death. "Encuentro" ("Encounter"; also developed in 2009, by McCann Erickson, Madrid—a firm, incidentally, that is one of Don Draper's fiercest competitors) stages the meeting in Madrid between the 102-year-old Mallorcan Josep Mascaró and hours-old newborn Aitana Martínez, likely making them the oldest and youngest actors in the world as well as encompassing the full spectrum of human life and experience. Throughout the running time of the ad, a message from Josep to Aitana sounds in voice-over as he shares with her the wisdom of his years: that times of adversity and "crisis" aren't what really matter; what matters is what makes us happy. The visuals paired with the audio track chronicle the story of Josep's trip and Aitana's delivery:

Aitana's mother in a taxi going to deliver her baby, Josep's trip by car to the airport; Aitana's mother's preparation for delivery, Josep's first ever airplane ride from Mallorca to Madrid; Aitana's mother's labor and delivery, Josep's arrival at the hospital and entry into Aitana's room; the expectant tenderness of Aitana's mother as she watches Josep approach Aitana in her bassinet, Josep's expression of great-grandfatherly care and wonderment as he beholds this new little life and touches her tiny fingers with his. The commercial closes with Josep amid a gathering of loved ones, wherein, finally, the brand makes its appearance as a small sea of Coke bottles rise above smiles in a toast that punctuates Josep's last axiomatic words: "Estás aquí para ser feliz" ("You are here to be happy").

Coca-Cola moves beyond artificial representation and toward narrative forged from the reality of bare life, penetrating the most private points of human existence. Though in excellent health, Josep's delicate physique nevertheless evokes compassion for his proximity to death—his face and hands are a mass of softly knotted wrinkles; his walk has the halting and jerky rhythm that comes with age. The camera likewise shows Aitana at her most vulnerable, in the very instant of her birth, raised up from between her mother's legs and placed on her mother's chest as the medical staff rub her vigorously to bring color to her body and to induce a first cry. As an extended part of the advertisement, Coca-Cola arranged with the hospital to allow webcams to be installed with family consent above the cribs of babies so that websurfers might view them in real time and post their own messages of optimism to the website.

"Encuentro" crosses all established boundaries of intimacy, of the division between public and private, between the virtual and brick-and-mortar world, joining even those who don't know one another in a togetherness predicated on a universal sentiment of humanity. This common humanity should be understood in the qualitative terms of principally emotional experience—that is, what it means to inhabit the human condition—but also in the quantitative terms of population. The bringing together of Josep and Aitana is a gesture symbolically representative of a single and vast human race; their pairing works as a cross-section of the present moment, each occupying the extremes of extant human life, but their pairing also connotes the unending cycle of life, therefore standing in for humanity in all its diachrony, in timeless perpetuity. The two become connected as though one by pathways of common experience and sentiment and of emotional communication that knows no borders, but rather travels in a free flow just as easily between perfect strangers as between family and lifelong friends. In "Encuentro" Coca-Cola constructs humanity as a single organic network powered by the vital flow of emotion; it delivers as its message—in a bottle—the emotional knowledge of the human condition.

Reactions to "Encuentro" register the receipt of this message along an analytical axis of markedly emotional criteria. A Spanish advertising blog site commends the spot's power to communicate feeling: "Muchos directores de cine les gustaría hacer llegar parte del sentimiento que hace llegar Coca-Cola. Felicidades" ("Many film directors would like to convey even part of the emotion that Coca-Cola conveys. Congratulations"; "Anuncio Coca-Cola"). U.S. advertising blog sites echo this perception: one such intervention titles itself—even in its URL—"Coke ad from Spain has grown men falling to their knees crying" (Wasserman); another begins with a descriptive account of personal feeling in reaction to the commercial, and, on this basis, segues into broadly prescriptive advice on emotional behavior: "[Josep's advice] seems so genuinely heartfelt and honestly-meant that I let myself go and went for the emotional ride of it. And you should too. Sometimes, it just feels good to feel good" ("Coca-Cola: Encounter"). These bloggers affirm the wisdom that emotional narrative is received in kind: viscerally, nonrationally, and mimetically. We uncritically accept as a truth the emotional maxim of the ad along with its implicit imperative: we are here to be happy (we will buy Coke).

Zombies and Human Consumption

If the most powerful companies in the world seek to bind our happiness, from life to death, to the consumption of their products, then I argue that the most devastating—and terrifying—critique of that consumerism is to be found in the now culturally iconic zombie. The zombie itself has certainly become a fetishized commodity, starring in a full-fledged film genre that is typically traced to George A. Romero's *Night of the Living Dead* (1968), gracing crowdsourced T-shirt designs like those sold by Threadless.com, topping bathroom reading piles with books like *The Zombie Survival Guide: Complete Protection from the Living Dead* (2003), or serving as the enemy in some hundred video games that have sold millions upon millions of copies worldwide. With this proliferation of mass-produced imagery, pulp literature, and screen presence, the zombie seems to have become the reigning monster of popular global culture. Even Cuba boasts an officially sanctioned zombie thriller, *Juan de los muertos* (2011), which, in its English translation "Juan of the Dead," rhymes playfully with both the second film in Romero's classic zombie trilogy, *Dawn of the Dead* (1978), and its successful British comedic parody, *Shaun of the Dead* (2004).

Why does the zombie resonate so strongly within our cultural imaginary? The growing corpus of zombie criticism suggests many themes—contagion, migration, surveillance, warring populations, religion, suburbia, and militarism, among others. But I argue that what we find so compelling—and disturbing—about the zombie is how profoundly it speaks to the power of consumption.

Although the zombie has its roots in Haitian voudou and the idea that through magic a dead body is awakened to do the bidding of another, the zombie's contemporary iteration does away with this power dynamic of third-party intercession. Since Romero's *Night of the Living Dead*, in which a horde of the undead attack a handful of the living sheltered in a Pennsylvania farmhouse, zombies have been treated as a found object, with no history or backstory for how they came to be; they simply—always already, in an Althusserian kind of way—exist.

Zombie mechanics are simple to the point of monotony. Their singular drive is to consume live human flesh, which is the only substance that will retard their decomposition. Penetration of the living by zombie teeth induces death, which, in turn, is followed by reawakening as a zombie. Zombies have no character, no individuation, no higher faculties; they rely on sensory detection of life and move inexorably toward their prey. Only mortal wounds to the head can kill zombies. The fact that these prototypical dynamics have been so spare and static for fifty years, yet have steadily occupied the cultural imaginary—and with a prominence that has only been on the rise—should alert us to the likelihood that something about the zombie is tapping deep into our contemporary psyche.

What are zombies if not the ultimate consumers? Annie Leonard's claim about the primacy of consumer identity is useful to revisit in this context: "We have become a nation of consumers. Our primary identity has become that of consumer, not mothers, teachers, farmers, but consumers. The primary way that our value is measured and demonstrated is by how much we . . . consume." Leonard is speaking specifically about the United States, but her claim could be extended to the whole of global consumer culture, whose borderlessness is mirrored by the postidentity nature of zombies, whose tattered garments and style frozen at the moment of death give hints of former social roles that have ceased to matter. The sole telos of zombies is to consume. As though interpreting to the letter of the law the corporate world's putative objective of turning everything under the sun into consumable material,[3] the zombie as a manifestation of this cultural logic subscribes to a mantra of privatization, commodification, and consumption that is so perfect as to turn it on humans themselves, darkly figuring the ultimate consequences of our faith in consumerism as our own subjugation—our own falling prey—to its law.

The AMC original cable series *The Walking Dead* (2010–present), which boasts a steadily increasing viewership in the millions, adds a further twist to this deadly immanence. The show takes place in the postapocalypse of a zombie outbreak that has devastated life as we know it, leaving the nearest city, Atlanta, and its surrounding area in ruins, with the occasional sign of survivors and more generally populated by zombies wandering, alone or in groups, always in search of live flesh. In the final episode of its first season, a lone scientist (Noah Emmerich), bunkered down in the massive complex of Atlanta's Center for Disease Control, reluctantly gives shelter to the small group of survivors whose story the series had thus far traced. The group relaxes into the miracle of refuge only to learn that the scientist has become so fatally disillusioned with the dismal prospects for humanity that he has irreversibly programmed the destruction of the CDC complex. In the final moments before its monumental explosion, the scientist whispers something into the hero's ear (Andrew Lincoln) that the audience does not hear, which we can only interpret as a kind of orally delivered suicide note. It is not until the final episode of the second season that the content of this message is revealed: all of humanity, the scientist has discovered, is infected with the zombie plague. In other words, regardless of how a living human dies—by zombie wound or no—an undead fate awaits. The immanence of zombie "life" is so complete as to reach into the erstwhile terrain of the metaphysical, categorically colonizing death itself, proscribing any and all classically transcendental aspect of the afterlife.

This grim formulation of a universal zombie fate recalls anew—in what has come to figure as a kind of warning bell leitmotiv of this entire study— Foucault's definition of biopower as control not simply over whether a subject is executed or spared, but over the quality of life in all its duration. Here that control is extended to death itself. Our cultural law of consumption, if we accede to reading zombies as its representation, is therein imagined as exerting a sway of immanence of such far-reaching proportions as to dictate the terms of life *and* death.

A mesmerizing scene from the penultimate first-season episode of *The Walking Dead*, in which the CDC scientist plays back the fMRI imaging of his own wife's process of zombification, shows a complete blackout of brain activity during death followed by the illumination of the most primitive areas of the brain stem that govern—what? The survival instinct? Basic sensory perception? The impulse and desire to consume? Are the undead truly dead, or are they in fact alive, in a new definition of "life" governed purely and exclusively by appetite? Read in this way, *The Walking Dead* shows how the feeling soma will be its own ruin. Paring down the figure of nonrational self-governance that epistemologically underwrites capitalist democracy to its barest bones—literally—this representation posits the feeling soma as occasioning the demise of its own organic systemicity. While the size of the feeling soma as zombie postnation waxes infinite, its morality and self-determination wane to the point of disappearance; the feeling soma is stripped of all powers of cognition except the recognition of its own appetite for destruction, a turn of phrase that recalls the eponymous landmark Guns N' Roses album that set to music what a contemporaneous rock documentary called the "decline of Western civilization."[4] As represented in the *Walking Dead*, the cultural motif of the zombie apocalypse suggests that there is no escape from the power of consumerism as a decline of civilization: the threat that holds us so captive, perhaps, as an audience, is this commentary on our own propensity toward consumption, on the ways in which we have been "hooked" and "hijacked"—as Moss and Kessler have argued, respectively, in the case of processed food—into physiological addiction to our patterns of consumption and emotionally wedded to our identity as consumers. As a cultural figure, the zombie touches precisely that nerve, provocatively asking if consumption can, in fact, consume us to the point of consuming ourselves, in pursuit of our primordial satisfaction, for all eternity.

On Wanting: Toward Epistemic Anagnorisis

I am hoping that my reader will appreciate the zombie apocalypse as the obverse of happiness in a bottle—as two sides of the proverbial single coin. And I wish to reiterate that it is not the objective of this study to take sides, but rather, and simply, to show them both, together, as functions of the same epistemic discourse of affect, as representations of the feeling soma.

Whenever notions of the organic, of the nonrational, of the emotional, of the fluidly self-governing are deployed in cultural production, where they are naturalized as part of the human condition, it is my hope and objective to have presented herein a model of analytic denaturalization such that these concepts may be weighed and considered as constructs participating in a larger epistemological discourse that is interpellating us—greeting us and ushering us into—a terrain already marked by the conceptual preeminence of the feeling soma in the service of capitalist democracy. That is, simply put, that we will learn to read and interpret the discursive supports of capitalist democracy and to disinter them from the foundations of our cultural psyche in order to interrogate the role they are playing in both our affirmations and our critiques of our cultural present, in our denunciations of injustice and formulations of a better future.

This vision of an epistemological common—of epistemic affect, at our current historical juncture, as I have been arguing in this study—could help us to see the commonalities between otherwise unthinkably diverse cultural interventions. Take, for example, Wendy Brown's suggestion that we reinvent ourselves as a political collective—a "we" instead of an "I"—and that we take as our telos the negotiation of pain, which she argues is foundationally constitutive of our contemporary political subjectivity (in other words, what I have been calling a denunciation of ill-being), and invest that subject with a "language of reflexive 'wanting'" in order to achieve a "partial dissolution of sovereignty into desire," understanding the subject, now, as "an effect of an (ongoing) genealogy of desire" that works toward a kind of subjectivity—and, therefore, power—that is neither "sovereign nor conclusive" ("Wounded Attachments" 407).

Can we see in Brown's politically positive—in the sense of being emancipatory and constructive—project of "wanting" the echoes of a whole corpus of theoretical thought that has privileged the open-ended and nonconclusive, the flowing and the feeling, as somehow more powerful than the fixed, the reified, the insensible? The individual and the vertical (for Brown, encapsulated in the Nietzschean "I," her de facto analogue for the Cartesian subject) decried in favor of the collective and the horizontal? (I recall a like-minded presentation at the 2011 MLA Presidential Forum by Judith/Jack Halberstam in which s/he visually cited the Muppets—with a photo of the whole crew—as having taught the current generation the power of the collective, the revolutionary power of togetherness to "learn to unlearn.")

I see in Brown's hopeful formulation of "wanting" as much of an echo of the feeling soma as I do in Josep Mascaró's upbeat affirmation that we were born to drink Coke, or, in the negative image of the same conceptual photograph, in zombies' implacable appetite for destruction, where homeostatic well-being has gone horribly and terminally wrong. In saying this, I do not stand in judgment; I simply seek to point out that a singular epistemic figure of nonrational homeostatic well-being is informing this broad range of cultural production—from scholarly political critique to profit-boosting advertising spots to popular television shows. Understanding it as the epistemic counterpart of *homo œconomicus*, the feeling soma is intrinsically neither good nor bad. That is, epistemic affect does not have a positive or negative ontology. Its moral coding as such comes from its analysis as an instrument of power; a favorable analysis will deem it positive, whereas an unfavorable analysis will deem it negative. As always, the political position from which we perform the analysis of affective discourse will determine the moral code to which we cleave therein. If we accept McDonald's smiles, we are "lovin' it"; if we reject those smiles as what Hardt and Negri call "affective labor" or a false mask obscuring other forms of exploitative behavior, then we are "not lovin' it"—a contestatory slogan that peppers the Internet.

The central conceit of the present study is to hold up a mirror: is there a self-discovery to be had by looking therein? Is there a passage of awareness to be traversed from epistemological blindness to insight? If so, will that cultural insight work to reveal the structure, sign, and play of our economic and political game? The communication—production and reception—of affective information travels as a type of cognition that is somatic rather than rational, tending toward the preclusion of critical thought. Are we losing our minds in coming to our senses? Or may we yet find "reason" and its power of self-expression and agency in the epistemological territory of affect?

Toward the Superstructure of Capitalist (In)Equality

In the course of this project, I have often been asked about exceptions to affective epistemicity. What lies outside this logic? I would answer that vertical rationality continues to lie outside, but its public face is much diminished. Growth, profit, and privilege are the powerful conceptual and practical vestiges of imperialism that have survived the shift of paradigm and episteme in the transition to free-market democracy. They are the principles of conquest, royal wealth, and divine right recast in democratic free-market clothes. The logic of verticality makes appearances where we expect them and even where we don't. In the former category, the steady eclipse of national economies by corporations, continual allegation of human rights violations and environmental devastation by corporations, the increasing collusion between, and even de facto fusion of, governments and corporations, annual profit earnings in the billions by the most powerful corporations are all naturalized aspects of persistent verticality legitimized by a logic of a rationalized right to amass capital ad infinitum and wield the power it affords. Consider the so-called American Dream, a national myth that promises an equal chance for everyone in the United States has an equal opportunity to become successful, rich, and happy without limits. The rhetorical sleight of hand of equal opportunity is that democracy and fair distribution of resources exists only in the hypothetical; in reality, only a lucky few achieve this prosperity. Pablo Larraín's 2010 film *No* places a cynical parroting of the American Dream in the mouth of a Pinochet campaign manager in the lead-up to the 1989 plebiscite: the correct strategy for capturing the country's vote, he argues, is to hold out the promise that under Pinochet anyone can achieve wealth—"ojo," he says, "cualquiera; no todos" ("mind you," . . . "anyone; not everyone"). Scriptwriter Pedro Peirano brilliantly and succinctly represents the hidden verticality within the concept of equal opportunity, which, thus laid bare, helps to explain why the U.S.-led neoliberal world would be willing to tolerate the worst kind of socioeconomic asymmetries on the gamble that they can catapult themselves into the superrich 1 percent, as the Occupy movements have dubbed the cadre of billionaires and corporations who, respectively, control nearly half of U.S. private wealth and constitute half the world's largest economies.

Theorists and activists like David Harvey (2005) and Naomi Klein (2007) have endeavored to show how material inequalities within capitalism are structural rather than aberrant—no small task, given that capitalism views itself as inherently democratic.[5] French economist Thomas Piketty's *Capital in the Twenty-First Century* (2014 [2013]) has, in effect, lent the power of quantitative analysis to their position with its simple formula $r > g$ (return on capital is greater than growth) that both explains and calculates this structural inequality of wealth within capitalism. Economist and public intellectual Paul Krugman cogently summarizes Piketty's formulation as a "break[ing of] ranks" with the predominant tendency to analyze economic inequality as a function of unequal income and, in its place, a "startling" return to an older, even Marxist, tradition of analyzing economic inequality as a function of unequal possession of capital ("Why We're in a New Gilded Age").

Krugman avers that Piketty "throws down the intellectual gauntlet . . . with his book's very title" and "its obvious allusion to Marx," marveling, "Are economists still allowed to talk like that?" I ask the same question, replacing "economists" with "humanists," cognizant that the scope of the present study effectively throws down the same intellectual gauntlet, including—by uncanny coincidence?—an unapologetic return to Marx that has tacitly informed my thinking throughout, and that I will here explicitly acknowledge:

In *The German Ideology* (circa 1845–1846), Karl Marx and Friedrich Engels propose that it is by means of ideology that the dominant class achieves the perpetuation of economic inequality: ideology—the aggregate of "ruling ideas" (64)—creates a false consciousness throughout the social order that works to attenuate and override the cognitive dissonance of this circumstance of material economic inequality. The shape of this relationship of false consciousness is one of inversion—"in all ideology men and their circumstances appear upside-down as in a *camera obscura*" (47)—that is, ideology obscures material inequalities by fabricating an opposite truth.[6]

Piketty's *Capital in the Twenty-First Century* provides a mathematical formula for capitalist inequality, and warns that, absent governmental intervention to limit the return on capital (which regulatory intervention headless capitalism will always resist as a tyrannical deprivation of freedom), the inequalities generated by capitalism will ultimately undermine democracy itself.[7] Where *Capital in the Twenty-First Century* defines material economic conditions of capitalism as we know and live it, *Coming to Our Senses* seeks to define its ideology. I have endeavored herein to lay bare the epistemological paradigm of the feeling soma—the infinitely capacious brotherly-sisterly "we" that positively emotes its way to an egalitarian good life of comforts and fairness (life, liberty, and the pursuit of happiness)—which works to naturalize a system that structurally produces a contrary reality of staggering inequality by neutralizing, at the deepest cognitive level, any resistance. My proposition may feel supremely uncomfortable when taken to its ultimate implications: we are epistemologically grounded by the feeling soma as much in our moments of most fervent dissidence as in our moments of most fervent acquiescence, for the feeling soma has foundationally informed our very structures of knowledge and models of political action. It is in this sense that Foucault's notion of epistemicity insists on the diffuse character of power, expanding the one-to-one relationship of causal responsibility between "ruling ideas" and "ruling class" (Marx and Engels 64) to society at large. Affective epistemicity is our diffuse ideology; biopower a name for the control it exerts over us. Consider the willingness of the American public to accept staggering neoimperialist inequalities only in the discursive packaging of egalitarian inclusivity and positive sentiment and the backlash against anything that runs counter to it. Republican U.S. presidential candidate Mitt Romney may have lost the 2012 election well in advance when he was captured on secret video tracing a patent hierarchy between the haves and the have-nots and openly disparaging the latter; it was, in contrast, the campaign predicated on positive and universal affect by incumbent Barack Obama, no less supportive of the free-market economy, that carried the day. The public expects a face of loving global oneness, even when this "face" is patently little more than a mask. When massive negative press greeted news of Facebook's covert manipulation of users' news feeds to study the phenomenon of emotional contagion, an experiment conducted in collaboration with Cornell researchers—and, for a brief moment, it was suggested, before being just as quickly retracted, the Pentagon—[8] savvy CEO Sheryl Sandberg apologized in the language of emotion: "We never meant to upset you" (Krishna).

Free-market capitalism is not just about economics and moneymaking; it engenders a way of thinking—a way of "thinking" as a way of feeling—a way of organizing what Jacques Rancière calls the "distribution of the sensible" in the world. But where Rancière sees politics, the call by the "we" to be afforded more power and resources by the police order of the aesthetic regime, in short, the call for greater democracy, as a dissident call from below, I would argue that what the present thesis of epistemic affectivity suggests is that the democracy-seeking "we" is itself coeval with the very police order of the aesthetic regime and that, as a project, the "distribution of the sensible" is a captured category. This is because Rancière's democracy-seeking political "we" is, itself, indistinct from the police order that controls the aesthetic regime. There is no outside to the "we" and therefore no possibility of dissidence that cannot be reabsorbed within, or, conversely, that can stand apart from, the signifying machine of free-market democracy.

In other words, if capitalism were only the vector-oriented and rationalizing profit machine as it is often cast in Manichaean terms (like *Avatar*'s

RDA and its CEO Parker Selfridge), then it might possibly be stoppable, as was formal empire before it. But capitalism also, and even more primordially, styles itself as revolution, not the status quo. And that revolutionary force is one that works on a model of happy democratic all-inclusiveness—hence capitalism's oft-cited ability to absorb, encompass, assimilate everything, even its harshest criticism or resistance. As an affective model, it expands toward plenitude, well-being, immanence; there is nothing that lies without. It is this epistemological structure that keeps capitalism on the cutting—revolutionary—edge of itself because, from this epistemological vantage point, it is never static or repressive, but rather always dynamic and embracing: a body moving ever toward optimal health.

And yet the denunciation of ill-being—as a failure of the democratic-capitalist project, as a betrayal of its promise of health, prosperity, and happiness—in voices that claim pain, suffering, and rage, are growing just as loud. Although I have used a vocabulary of emotion and health to describe these poles, the reality of ill-being is, ultimately, one heavily marked by violence. "Silent spring": the ecological violence denounced by Rachel Carson (1962) as the death of nature by human chemicals; as she warned the U.S. Senate in 1963, "Our heedless and destructive acts enter into the vast cycles of the earth and in time return to bring hazard to ourselves" (Griswold). "Slow violence": Rob Nixon's (2011) like-minded vision of planetary devastation as time-elapsed on a massive scale across regions and populations: "a violence that occurs gradually and out of sight, an attritional violence that is typically not viewed as violence at all [because it] is neither spectacular nor instantaneous, but rather incremental and accretive, its calamitous repercussions playing out across a range of temporal scales" (2), and its primary victimization of the "unseen" poor, "those people lacking resources who are the principal casualties of slow violence" (3). "Disposable people": the some twenty-seven million people, by Kevin Bales's 1999 count (8), who are effectively enslaved in the modern world wherein "slaveholders, businesspeople, even governments hide slavery behind smoke screens of words and definitions," in a phenomenon that is "not a 'third world' issue but a global reality" (260). "Horrorism": Adriana Cavarero's 2007 term for the contemporary violence that has "sprea[d] and assume[d] unheard-of forms," a violence for which the concepts of "'terrorism' and 'war'" are no longer sufficiently denotative (2); in its emotional dimension, horror precludes escape; in its political dimension, horror destroys subjectivities as well as bodies. And, finally, simply, "violence": namely, that of capitalism, which, from a philosophical angle, Slavoj Žižek considers a "systemic" violence that goes unperceived because, "something like the notorious 'dark matter' of physics," it is "inherent to th[e] normal state of things" (2008: 2). Žižek concludes his meditations by urging "abstention" from the "very frame of decision" that structures capitalist-democratic power in order to reveal the "vacuity of today's democracies"; he recommends withdrawal from participation, from critique, from dialogue, from protest. "Sometimes doing nothing is the most violent thing to do," Žižek avers (*Violence* 217), glossing this notion by citing Alain Badiou's view that "it is better to do nothing than to contribute to the formal ways of rendering visible that which Empire already recognizes as existent" (216).[9]

In the same breath with which Žižek advocates abstention from the democratic-capitalist project—going off the grid—he also makes an assertion that he acknowledges may strike his reader as "crazy and tasteless," namely, that the violent regimes in our modern history have not been "violent enough." That is, no form of protest, intervention, dissent, or aggression has managed to achieve liberation from imperialist structures past or present (217). The desire for a utopian escape from a cultural system that captures and engulfs, rendering epistemologically self-same, every form of "doing something," and the twin desire for an instrument of violence capable of bursting asunder the dark matter of capitalist-democratic empire to accomplish that impossible getaway both attest to Žižek's discomfort within the strictures of full enclosure on the totalizing plane of capitalist-democratic immanence. But his desires for transcendence and revolutionary violence for the sake of human progress beyond the logic of empire belong, epistemologically, to reason, with its verticalities, its thinking heads—whether imperial or insurgent—its teleologies. Capitalist democracy admits none of these conceptual precepts; they are epistemologically anathema to its fundamentally horizontal universality in which the happy flow of life is the only "telos." In this regard, Žižek effectively proposes little more than a nostalgic swap of the epistemological master present for the epistemological master immediately past, in the latter of which violence was justified and even celebrated as a means to an end and reason upheld as the basis for mounting a political action believed capable of achieving political transcendence. But affective epistemicity can no longer tolerate deliberate violence, no matter how lofty of cause; hence Žižek's intuition that his yearning for as much may strike his reader—epistemologically immersed, after all, within affectivity—as "crazy and tasteless."

If Žižek yearns for violence, for its power of change, at least, if not for its blood, then it bears reflection that violence is always vertical, always underwritten by hierarchy, whether established or aspiring. That is, whether the perpetrators of violence are powerless underdogs acting from below or powerful elites from on high, both seek to intervene within and influence the distribution of power and resultant access to resources along a vertical axis. Violence is conceptually anathema to the affective principle of free-market democracy with its tenets of brotherhood and equal opportunity, which explains why democratic governments cannot openly engage in it without the cloak of rhetoric (i.e., fighting for freedom and democracy) or, more powerfully, of business, outsourcing their most objectionable vertical violence as "security contracting." Journalist Jeremy Scahill, author of *Blackwater* (2007), calls the eponymous company a "neoconservative Praetorian Guard for a borderless war launched in the immediate aftermath of 9/11" ("Blackwater Founder"). Indeed, the commercial paramilitary services of the former private security agency Blackwater were instrumental in the Iraq War and were retained during the politically conservative and liberal presidencies, respectively, of George W. Bush and Barack Obama alike, despite criticism levied by Blackwater founder Erik Prince against the latter: "It's a shame the [Obama] administration crushed my old business, because as a private organization, we could've solved the boots-on-the-ground issue, we could have had contracts from people that want to go [to the Middle East] as contractors; you don't have the argument of U.S. active duty going back in there [to combat the Islamic State]. . . . [Blackwater could have] gone in there and done it, and be done, and not have a long, protracted political mess that I predict will ensue" (Suebsaeng). Prince's statement acknowledges the unacceptability of governmentally sponsored violence and the comparative efficiency and impunity of a company. Indeed, the 2014 trial of four Blackwater operatives for the Iraqi civilian massacre known as "Baghdad's Bloody Sunday" lasted a matter of weeks and convicted only a handful of operatives, leaving the company's founder untouched (Scahill, "Blackwater Founder"), whereas the investigation of what the *New York Times* calls a "decade-long debate over torture," which produced the 2104 U.S. Senate Torture Report, took five years, compiled over six thousand pages (only some six hundred of which comprise the declassified public version), and implicates an unquantifiable number of responsible parties and governmental institutions, though in and of itself it is not constitutive of any formal indictment.

Whether yearned for as a romanticized part of anticolonial revolutionary times past (which participated epistemologically in the paradigm of colonialist rationality), wielded with relative impunity by capitalist corporations, covertly exercised with the consequence of a "long, protracted political mess" by putative democracies, or, perhaps even more interestingly—and frighteningly—woven into our capitalist-democratic cultural fabric in the form of bullying,[10] violence is nevertheless squarely anathema to and prohibited within capitalist-democratic affectivity. From within the epistemological framework of affectivity, the contradiction of violence is treated as an autonomic failure—the source of illness, disease, unhappiness—the irruption of verticality within the conceptually dominant plane of horizontality that is decried and denounced as something gone wrong that requires remediation. Despite the fact that violence inherently violates the epistemological framework of affectivity, its popular critique—in terms of critiques with "trending" power to go viral—is enunciated from within an affective framework.

In his defense of "violent" inactivity, Žižek's warns that "doing something" ultimately remits to and reifies dominant structures of power (*Violence* 217). If protestors invoke the epistemological supports of affectivity to communicate their critiques of violence, whether a violence sponsored by states, institutions, or culture at large, is this protest always already a captured category, tantamount to a subsuming of culture—and would-be counterculture, by capitalist-democratic immanence? Must it be understood as the affirmation and reification of dominant structures of power? But shouldn't it be understood as the form of protest that is considered most culturally powerful and intelligible? Or is it necessarily both dissidence and reification all at once? Did not Žižek "do something" by speaking to the then budding Occupy Wall Street movement, his voice projected in waves by the human microphone?

Just what are our available avenues for and lexicons of civic political participation? Is the hashtag #todossomosayotzinapa (We Are All Ayotzinapa) a gesture of solidarity with the forty-three rural Mexican students, brutally murdered for unknown reasons by *narcotraficantes* in collusion with the police and local politicians, tantamount to a "doing something" that only demonstrates the vacuity of the capitalist-democratic matrix? What about members of the U.S. National Basketball Association team Miami Heat who posed dressed in hoodies with their heads bowed to reference the attire and death of Trayvon Martin, the young and unarmed black man killed in 2012 by a white man exonerated at trial, a photo that LeBron James posted with the hashtag #WeAreTrayvonMartin? The five St. Louis Rams National Football League players who, in a nationally televised game, raised their arms together in the "hands up, don't shoot" gesture in solidarity with Michael Brown, another unarmed black man slain, this time by a white police officer in Ferguson, Missouri, in 2014? The 131 Mexican students who made a YouTube video displaying their university identification cards one by one to defend their legitimate right to civic protest against then presidential candidate Enrique Peña Nieto, sparking the "Yo Soy 132" ("I Am [Number] 132") movement that propagated the students' dissident stance on a national level, which generated enough public pressure to hold unprecedented nationally televised presidential candidate debates? Or the so-called die-ins of 2007 and 2014 in which protestors lay down silently as though dead, their bodies strewn over large swaths of ground, the former in protest of the Iraq War on the Capitol lawn, the latter in protest of the deaths of Michael Brown and Eric Garner, the black man suffocated to death in a choke hold by a white police officer on Staten Island? The December 2014 wave of die-ins that swept the United States in concert with the movement #blacklivesmatter brought the civil rights "sit-in" of the 1960s to a level of affective biopolitics. Are these not examples of what Žižek, in his Occupy Wall Street speech, calls the "free egalitarian community of believers united by love" ("Slavoj Žižek")?

But Žižek also warns the OWS protestors against "false friends" ("Slavoj Žižek"). Would this latter category include Facebook, whose monotonous daily thoughtwork consists of teaching a billion users that their only practically and epistemologically available action verb is "to like"? What about Coca-Cola Light (aka Diet Coke), which opportunistically riffs on this limited vocabulary by exhorting the world to "choose love over like," positing an illusory opposition that masquerades as a discerning and even morally inflected expansion of our action verbs, when, in fact, there is no real choice at all, but rather only an exacerbating concatenation of the two terms that further wends around us the chains of our epistemologically affective captivity? Or the online bank PayPal, self-defined as the "world's most-loved way to pay and be paid" ("What Is PayPal?")? PayPal's first global campaign "Powering the People Economy" strives to "give a contemporary, human and populist voice to a brand that does amazing things for everyday people," namely, "help[ing] people take control of their money and use it in any way they want, through seamless and delightful experiences" and "making life better in tangible, practical and magical ways that . . . pu[t] people, not institutions, first" ("PayPal Brand Campaign"), thus unabashedly appro-priating the language of political self-determination and blending it with positive affect and even fantasy. In September 2014 PayPal ran a full-page ad in the *New York Times* with the tagline "People Rule" (Johnson), a terse summary of the sentiment expressed in a one-minute companion YouTube video spot entitled "PayPal Voices":

> We Are the People, who have built a whole new way to live, dream, and be. We employ ourselves, and vote with our money. Our phone is our wallet. . . . We can buy and sell and rent and send . . . lend a twenty to a friend from the coffee bar and share-car. We are unstoppa-ble, with our thumbs. Just One Touch to buy just about anything. . . . We live on all devices, and are as mobile as nature intended. . . . We have magical money, not bound by bank or bill. . . . Consider yourself invited to "The People Economy."

The visual accompaniment of this narrative presented in caption form is a fast-paced montage of diverse human faces of every shape, color, and style; the audio accompaniment is a composite voice, which suggests itself as that of this multitude enunciating, in perfect synchronicity, the written words the opening and closing quotation marks denote as the directly cited speech of this "we." A we that is the embodiment of foundational democracy, a we that is boundlessly mobile, autonomous, part of a fluid set of equivalencies in which communication, technology, nature, life, relationships, and money all morph conceptually into one another in analogy to the swiftly changing faces. The final "invitation" to join this immanent we is rhetorically struc-tured as the revelation of an a priori envelopment and belonging.

Does not this same "we" undergird the long list of aforementioned contestations and promotions alike? If we consider PayPal alongside the infamous decade-old hacker group Anonymous, which has, in fact, staged a "digital protest" again PayPal for its perceived unfreedoms, then we can appreciate how similarly these two sometime antagonists frame themselves. The hybrid audio track of "PayPal Voices" is evocative of Anonymous's signature use of a voice changer that reproduces a single voice in several octaves at once, blending them all together in simultaneity to create an audio disguise that assumes the form of multiplicity. Like PayPal, Anony-mous also speaks in the first-person plural; Anonymous's tagline "We are legion" conceptually resonates with "People Rule," both asserting power in the fact of extrainstitutional plurality, where an implicit immanent common of the "we" becomes the only cultural institution of which to speak. This we is "more powerful than ever," claims PayPal in the closing frame of its "Voices" video; "You should have expected us," echoes Anonymous, albeit in a more menacing tone, in an expression of omnipresent omnipotence in which the antagonistic "you" is subsumed, like the "you" "invited" to join PayPal, within a borderless immanence. Where PayPal represents its plurality with a fast-moving stream of diverse faces, we might conceive of Anonymous's plurality as fast-moving stream of diverse online posts and activity. But Anonymous also has a visual representation overwhelmingly associated with the iconic Guy Fawkes mask popularized by the 2005 film *V for Vendetta*, in which the futuristic freedom fighter V combats a fascist state regime that derives its power from media control, using a Guy Fawkes mask to liken his own subversion to the historical example of the failed Gunpowder Plot of 1605 in which Fawkes had planned to incite revolution by blowing up the English Parliament building. The poster for the 2012 documentary film about Anonymous, *We Are Legion*, depicts several rows of headless male torsos clad in identical black and white business attire superimposed on a Guy Fawkes mask. Street footage within the film includes interviews of three different unnamed protestors, each also wearing Guy Fawkes masks, whose content reiterates the themes that should by now seem predictable: "We stand for freedom, the power of the people," says one; "We have members throughout society, in all stratas [sic] of it worldwide. Yet we have no leadership," says the second. "It's one voice, it's not individual voices, that's why we don't show our faces, that's why we don't give our names, we're speaking as one collective," says the last, as, in the background, a line of riot-masked police officers rushes by on foot, batons in hand. A single protestor wearing a Guy Fawkes mask also graces the poster for the 2012 documentary film *Occupy Love*, which attests to the consistent presence of both Guy Fawkes masks and Anonymous in the global "Occupy" protests of the early 2010s. At his feet lies a hand-letter sign that reads: "Always know you are loved—the Universe." The Anonymous Facebook page "Re-LOVE-ution," which, as its banner image announces, focuses on what it calls "Operation Green Rights," echoes the discursive movements that should also by now be so familiar, namely, making love and nature the twin ideals and propellers alike of social change.

The objective of this long list of examples, and, indeed, of this entire study, has been to show that the capitalist-democratic power of immanence, of horizontal all-beingness, along with the very real violence that its discourse is so frequently made to cloak, is not without rhyme or reason, but rather turns on the logic of the feeling soma. Perhaps if we begin to "do something" in the epistemological dimension, that is, by interrogating the deployment of emotion in all contexts—happiness, love, pride, health, sorrow, hate, indignation, disease—we may yet begin to loosen the capitalist-democratic ties that bind at their source so that we may imagine and carry out political activity that accomplishes something other than "mask the nothingness of what goes on" (Žižek, *Violence* 217).

Regardless of the direction in which our political inclinations lead us to position ourselves with respect to affective discourse—its production as much as its reception—it is of the essence to note its power, a power to engender a mirror response of analogous emotional bent and therefore to perpetuate its own discursive life and a power to shape the ways in which we conceive of the very shape, possibilities, and limits of knowledge. Emotional discourse is no longer to be scorned or dismissed, but to be taken seriously as a cultural force central to the definition of life in the global West. The language of this global community, knit together by the apparatus of a new media technology that both facilitates and drives the discursive rendition of the world as an affective "we," is not the language of reason but the language of emotion and feeling. Where there is unfreedom, it will rely on affective discourse to accomplish its repression. Where there is contestation, it will also rely on affective discourse to accomplish its subversion. In order to comprehend discourses of power and its contestation alike in a world defined by capitalist democracy, we—the "we" of the title of this book, the we who inhabit that world—must come to our senses: we need to comprehend, in rational terms, emotional language and its epistemic rendition in the figure of the feeling soma.

Notes

Preface: Tracking the Feeling Soma

1. See both the Saatchi and Saatchi Lovemarks portal, which collects and displays users' narratives of love for favorite products, and Saatchi and Saatchi CEO Kevin Roberts's *Lovemarks: The Future Beyond Brands*.

2. Any mention of "hegemony" in Hispanist circles will immediately evoke Jon Beasley-Murray's claim that "there is no hegemony and never has been" (ix) with which he begins his 2010 *Posthegemony*, a text that has become a disciplinary standard. Beasley-Murray uses the term *posthegemony* to denote a postideological cultural landscape in which the withering of social teleologies only reveals a status that is, essentially, the opposite of Althusser's "always already"—for Beasley-Murray, the appropriate descriptor would be, perhaps, "never actually." "Nobody is very much persuaded by ideologies that once seemed fundamental to securing social order. . . . Social order was never in fact secured through ideology" (ix); "the myth of the social contract is over" (284).

My persistent use of the term *hegemony*, however, does not run as counter to Beasley-Murray's position as might appear. Beasley-Murray defines *posthegemony* as a function of "affect, habit, and an immanent multitude," averring that "politics is biopolitics"; "at stake is life itself" (284). I coincide thoroughly with Beasley-Murray in this definition; I view ours as largely a terminological difference. Where Beasley-Murray delineates the end of one epoch and the beginning of another as the transit from hegemony to posthegemony, I trace that same transit as the end of rational colonial politics and the beginning of affective free-market politics in which free-market democracy, as a model, is the new cultural hegemon on a global scale.

It is worth noting that in analogy to the way I salvage the term *hegemony* for application to what Beasley-Murray characterizes as a "posthegemonic" world, in *Marx and Freud in Latin America* (2012), Bruno Bosteels shows how the supposedly obsolete discourses of Marxism and psychoanalysis persist in cultural and political narrative in contemporary Latin America, particularly informing their critiques of a status quo of terror and violence.

3. I would like to note an affinity of what we might call intertemporal structure and intertextual play between my study and Graff Zivin's *Figurative Inquisitions* (2014). Graff Zivin traces what she terms "Inquisitional logic" (xii) from its origins in imperial Spain to its appearance in "practices of interrogation, torture, and confession" (xi) in the post-9/11 cultural world. Thus making a sweeping historical arc connecting the fifteenth century to the twenty-first, Graff Zivin also considers the place of Inquisitional logic on a cross-sectional plane of contemporary global culture, moving easily in and out of regions and across genres, from the U.S. to Latin America and the Iberian Peninsula, from journalism and cultural theory to film and literature. In this regard, I appreciate Graff Zivin's book as an important precursor to my own, establishing, as she does, new terms of regional, temporal, and textual engagement for the field of Hispanist cultural criticism.

I would be remiss if I did not also recognize the extent to which the late María Rosa Menocal's *Shards of Love* (1994) serves as a precursor to us both, insofar as it posits a fundamental historical affinity between the turbulent multiculturalism of 1492 and Menocal's present, the postmodern globalization of the early 1990s, within which the analysis moves between regions, time periods, and genres, from the mozarabic *jarcha* to Dante and Petrarch to Eric Clapton. *Shards of Love* remains a model of scholarly creativity and even audacity in privileging a free play of concept over the conventional disciplinary constraints of regional and temporal specialization.

4. My endeavor to trace the evolution of affect in the conceptual dimension through time and place, essentially a archaeological diagnostics, or the historiography of an episteme, coincides with Joshua Lund's efforts in compiling a cultural history of the concept of hybridity, which he describes as a "metacritical study," an exercise in "tracking the ways in which the idea of hybridity has been thought, specifically in Latin American writing" (ix), with the ultimate stakes of thereby creating a tool for analyzing and assessing "how the coloniality of power continues to operate on the site of the nation, which of its operations is transgressed, which maintained,

which reinforced, and which might be stopped" (188). My own attempts to trace the epistemological dimension of affect in contemporary cultural discourse has the analogous objective of offering itself up as a tool for the measuring and comprehension of contemporary biopolitics that turn on affective interventions and manipulations. The conceptual fabric of my politics may not be readily intelligible or legible within a field traditionally concerned with Marxism and its legacy, deconstruction, subalternity, and politics of cultural difference—I think here, for example, of Román de la Campa's *Latin Americanism* (1999) and Alberto Moreiras's *The Exhaustion of Difference: The Politics of Latin American Cultural Difference* (2001)—but my study of affect approaches these same questions of ethics, sovereignty, and power from an angle that might at first glance seem oblique, but simply approaches them through the filter of the epistemological. In this sense, I feel a solidarity of intention—if not entirely of method—with the group of Latin Americanists described by John Beverley in *Latin Americanism After 9/11* as generating a critical production on the strength of deconstruction that is "both a *critique* but also a new *form* of Latin Americanism" (43). I also feel an intellectual solidarity with Abraham Acosta insofar as he attempts to challenge, loosen, unravel the knots of reified disciplinary assumptions about resistance in *Thresholds of Illiteracy* (2014). Acosta's thematics of analysis revolve around a more traditional Latin American subalternity than mine do—*indigenista* narrative, *testimonio*, the EZLN, and border politics—but I nevertheless consider myself to be making an analogous push for the reconsideration and expansion of the standing theoretical limits of Latin Americanist thought.

5. I see a strong resonance with this mode of conceptualizing the relationship between Latin America and the United States in the relationship envisioned by Mariano Siskind in *Cosmopolitan Desires* between the Latin America desirous of joining the "global order of modernism" and the metropolis thus envisioned as world literature: "My point throughout the book," explains Siskind, "is that marginal literatures (however we define the subaltern materiality of their marginalities) expose the hegemonic making of modernist global mappings" (18). The Latin American *deseo de mundo* ("desire for the world," 3) thus reveals the mechanisms of the world it seeks to join, participating in the same currents of knowledge, imagination, and representation from a marginal position, however defined. Siskind's tracing of the Latin American *deseo de mundo* in many ways echoes Carlos J. Alonso's mapping of the quest for modernity in *The Burden of Modernity: The Rhetoric of Cultural Discourse in Spanish America* (1998), where Alonso's vision of the relationship between literary center and periphery is analogous to Siskind's. My perspective on the relationship between Latin America and the United States is in many ways a fusion between Siskind's *deseo de mundo* and Alonso's burden of modernity, on the one hand, and, on the other, Ericka Beckman's notion of capital fictions in which a desire for capital—the "promise of bananas" (191)—becomes a "foundational myth of Latin American societies" (197). Beckman helps us to consider the extent to which capital

relations between Latin America and the economic metropolis—neocolonialism, in a word—are textually inscribed in Latin American cultural production. I depart from precisely this same premise in my analyses of the perspectival differential between Latin American and U.S. cultural production, understanding Latin American cultural production to be self-conscious of its literary and economic marginalization vis-à-vis the developed world, especially the United States, while simultaneously participating in the literary and economic paradigmatic network that embraces both regions—and extends to global proportions.

Prelude: Affective Contours of Knowledge

1. In this same vein, within the field of Hispanism, Aníbal González argues in *Love and Politics in the Contemporary Spanish American Novel* that a "new sentimental novel" (144) has arisen in Latin American letters during roughly the same time period, which González dates from 1969 to the present (as listed in his appendix of relevant titles, 147–48). González suggests that this "new sentimental modality" (viii) is a reaction to the end of revolutionary politics and their commercially successful literary counterpart, the so-called Boom of Latin American literature in the 1960s, although he ultimately leaves the question of how this new modality originates open-ended (ix). This periodization is entirely consonant with my contention that affect begins to be visible in the wake of the cold war and the "universal triumph" of liberal democracy.

2. Another deeply personal study in cultural theory whose format and epistemological construction might be productively analyzed alongside Stewart's *Ordinary Affects* is Beatriz Preciado's *Testo Junkie* (2013), in which the consideration of the history of pharmaceuticals and pornography since the mid twentieth century, and the impact of this history on sexual identity and erotic desire, is intertwined with autobiographical meditations on the effects of testosterone on the author's body and psyche.

3. Stewart's waxing lyrical as denotative of the discursive terrain of affect calls to mind a contribution to Patricia Ticineto Clough's and Jean Halley's *The Affective Turn* in which author Hosu Kim analyzes the experience of a young Korean immigrant's learning of English as a second language. Kim's hybrid poem-essay is among the most explicitly poetic of recent contributions to affective scholarship, but it serves to underscore a tendency toward the poetic that is recurrent in the scholarly treatment of affect, as though evincing a tacit consensus that poetry were the expressive vehicle most closely related to affective communication—that poetry constitutes the linguistic form best suited to the expression of affective content. Collectively, scholars of affect seem to be giving themselves certain poetic license in the use of poetry in order to access—in a mimetic way—the experiential and conceptual field that they are seeking to describe in scholarly terms.

4. It is worth noting that, as historical contemporaries, Deleuze and Guattari and Williams both stage a struggle of sorts between affect and reason. In Williams this relationship is dialectical; in Deleuze and Guattari it is adversarial. But in both there is a question of whether affect will submit to the dominion of reason. Since Williams posits a dialectic in which affect precedes reason as an inevitable eventuality: affective preinstitutionality will, sooner or later, give way to rational institutionalization. In this regard, in Williams, reason is posed as dominant in an eternally repressive sort of way of affect, which is styled, in contrast, as unruly, spontaneous, and effervescent. These characterological traits—which also heavily populate the mid-century discourse of revolution—are indeed accorded dissident status in Deleuze and Guattari, where the body without organs that manifests them in its antiteleological and free-spirited self-pleasuring is capable of countering the capitalist machine associated with rationalized productivity tantamount to organic colonization.

Along with Williams and Deleuze and Guattari, Roland Barthes's *Le Plaisir du texte* (*The Pleasure of the Text*, 1973) comes readily to mind, for example, as vertebrally positing an opposition of reason and affect in two different models of reading: the first, a placid and unremarkable pleasure associated with the cultural bourgeoisie and its forms of rational order; the second, a jouissance riding the border between pleasure and pain cast as a desirable epistemological mechanism for the interruption of organized convention. (Barthes's opposition between two different models of reading is also suggestive as a precursor and analog for Stewart's two different models of writing.)

The recurrent motif of a structural and systemic contest between reason and affect in poststructuralist discourse (Williams, Deleuze and Guattari, Barthes) could be connected to psychoanalytic discourse, which sets up the same contest but with the reverse outcome. For Freud, the pleasure principle is an unbridled libidinous stage in early development that must be overcome by the rational overlay of heterocentric logic. The early "polymorphous perversion"—whose negative connotations could not be more pronounced—is inferior, base, undisciplined, and dangerous if unchecked. Heterocentric redirection and mastery of the libido, in contrast, represents the proper functioning of the ego and constitutes a functional passage toward rational order that underwrites the phenomenon of civilization itself.

It is not only mid-century poststructuralist thought that restages this contest between reason and affect, but inverting its outcome so that a triumphal affect destabilizes the rational social order, now associated with civilization in Freud, now associated with capitalism (as a synecdoche for Western civilization) in Deleuze and Guattari. The artistic vanguards of the early twentieth century write this opposition into their discursive program for cultural freedom embodied in such operations as surrealist automatic thought, which privileged the expression of the nonrational unconscious—a highly affective unconscious, to be sure—as a way of countering reified patterns of thought associated with rational cultural convention.

In this regard we might position poststructuralist thought, and its championing of affect as nonrational and contestatory, as the cultural inheritance of the political aesthetics of the vanguard and an evolving critique of the psychoanalytic dominion of reason over pleasure.

I submit this lengthy note to my reader not only as a deeper reflexion on the relationship between affect, poststructuralist discourse, and psychoanalysis, but also—and perhaps more importantly—as a skeletal example of the kinds of genealogies that the consideration of affect as episteme could open up in a diachronic analysis of cultural production and discourse from the Age of Revolution through to the global moment that this study takes as its central focus.

5. Stewart's politicized treatment of affect resonates with that of two anthologies, *The Affective Turn* (2007) and *The Affect Theory Reader* (2010), in which respective editors Patricia Ticineto Clough and Jean Halley (2007) and Melissa Gregg and Gregory J. Seigworth (2010) present collections of essays that work loosely—and intentionally so—toward the theoretical definition of affect in cultural discourse. These interventions construct a politics of affect that effectively posits itself with a certain ideological charge as against a sometime, and negatively connoted, politics of rational discourse. These two anthologies frame affect in a way that connotes an a priori resistance to conservative politics and discourse. Indeed, in both texts' introductions, which serve as a definitional aegis for the otherwise heterogeneous set of essays that follow, there is a marked and insistent ascription to affect of such qualities as rupture, multiplicity, fluidity, and resistance to definitive conclusions and analysis, with the result of inscribing affect studies and affect theory within a philosophical tradition of anticapitalism and antirationalism most heavily associated with Deleuzean thought (e.g., the bodies without organs of the *Anti-Oedipus*, the rhizome of *A Thousand Plateaus*, the notion of intensity in the cinematic theory of Deleuze focused on sensory perception and affective engagement between film and spectator). Affect can "do things" (to quote the speech-act phrasing of Peninsular Hispanist Jo Labanyi's 2010 "Doing Things: Emotion, Affect, and Materiality" on the interpretive use-value of affect), and it can do them without engaging the traditionally Cartesian apparatus—e.g., exclusively mental thought, critical evaluation, rigorous synthesis.

Introduction: Headless Capitalism

1. The conventional manner of conceiving of homeostasis is simply as a set of autonomic functions (e.g., the circulation of blood and respiration). Damasio refines this definition significantly by expanding the definition of the nonrational and automatic functions of the body to include a sequential chain of affective processes that is ascending in its complexity. First the senses apprehend external (or remembered) stimuli, which provokes a corresponding emotional state (understanding emotion

as a generalized but preconscious somatic circumstance). This in turn produces a consciousness of emotion in the brain that Damasio calls feeling (understanding this feeling-as-consciousness as a product of the brain, yet prerational in that it has been produced without the engagement of the rational cognitive apparatus whose engagement Damasio characterizes as a second-order operation that happens once feeling has been established).

2. In addition to Damasio's evocation of Spinoza (in opposition to Descartes) in exploring the "feeling brain," Hardt and Negri look to Spinoza for their definition of affect (108, 374n9). Spinoza is also to be found in the concept of immanence by way of Deleuze, who develops the term while championing Spinoza. The journal *Polygraph* dedicated its 2004 issue, for example, to the question of immanence versus transcendence, in which a cadre of prominent philosophers (Jean-Luc Nancy, Alain Badiou, Žižek) and Hispanists (Alberto Moreiras, Bruno Bosteels), among others, engage in what we might consider a Spinoza-Descartes debate routed through Deleuze's intellectual debt to Spinoza (Salván and Rodríguez).

3. Obama's "hope" campaign also recalls Bill Clinton's signature use of the 1977 Fleetwood Mac song "Don't Stop (thinking about tomorrow)" in his 1992 presidential campaign.

4. Clough and Halley's *The Affective Turn* joins a growing list of titles in a de facto affect series published during the last fifteen years by Duke University Press that have become landmarks in the emergent field of affect studies within the humanities and the social sciences, including, among others: Eve Kosofsky Sedgwick's *Touching Feeling: Affect, Pedagogy, Performativity* (as well as her seminal anthology coedited with Adam Frank, *Shame and Its Sisters*), Kathleen Stewart's *Ordinary Affects*, Sara Ahmed's *The Promise of Happiness*, Jane Bennett's *Vibrant Matter: A Political Ecology of Things*, and Melissa Gregg and Gregory J. Seigworth's *The Affect Theory Reader*. In the natural sciences, Oxford University Press has twenty-nine titles to date in its Series in Affective Science, also established in the mid-1990s, with the bulk of its titles published in the 2000s (see Oxford University Press's online catalog, "Series in Affective Science").

5. The late Teresa Brennan works toward an ontological definition of affect in an even broader context than media culture, aiming to "stan[d] neo-Darwinism on its head" with the contention that "what is at stake with the notion of the transmission of affect is precisely the opposite of the sociobiological claim that the biological determines the social. What is at stake is rather the means by which social interaction shapes biology" (74).

6. Foucault's definition of the episteme in this 1977 interview is "retrospective" because it glosses his original use of the term in *The Order of Things* (published in the original French in 1966). This retrospective gloss circles back to recuperate the term after his own rejection of it in favor of "discursive formation" in the subsequent *Archaeology of Knowledge* (1969). This latter terminological substitution (of "discursive

formation" for "episteme") was intended to lay charges of structuralism to rest, since the intervening events of May 1968 (the failed student protests and worker strikes that announced the demise of modernist leftism) had ushered in poststructuralism as a new theoretical position critical of a structuralist school now perceived as part and parcel of the repressive state. Foucault responded to these ideologically unflattering charges by underscoring, through the terminological shift to "discursive formation," that, as an intellectual category, the episteme was to be understood as a product of social-scientific discourse contingent upon its material historical circumstance, not as a product of some abstract ordering principle of knowledge. But I submit that this definitional precision should not—as the fact of his "retrospective" definition demonstrates—be interpreted to mean that Foucault abandoned the central idea of the episteme as an ordering principle of social thought operative on an epochal scale and extending from the scientific to the cultural.

7. The full title of Fox's treatise is *The line of righteousness and justice stretched forth over all merchants, &c. and an exhortation unto all friends and people whatsoever, who are merchants, tradesmen, husbandmen, or sea-men, who deal in merchandize, trade in buying and selling by sea or land, or deal in husbandry, that ye all do that which is just, equal and righteous in the sight of God and man one to another, and to all men; And that ye use just weights and just measures, and speak and do that which is true, just and right in all things.*

8. Peter Brooks's *The Melodramatic Imagination* might be productively considered as an important counterpart to Eustace's study of the role of emotion in underwriting the American Revolution, insofar as Brooks argues that melodrama—a social narrative of emotionality—emerges to codify bourgeois society in the era of the French Revolution. Likewise, Matthew Bush's *Pragmatic Passions: Melodrama and Latin American Social Narrative*, citing Brooks as a key influence, contends that melodrama is,. likewise, a central narrative modality in Latin American letters from the early nineteenth-century independence era forward. "For this reason," Bush boldly asserts, it is necessary to begin to consider melodrama not as the exception, but as the rule of Latin American literature. . . . [and] the dominant narrative made when Latin American literature speaks about politics and social development (22).

9. In the documentary film *The Corporation*, Charles Kernaghan, executive director for the Institute for Global Labour and Human Rights, gives anecdotal insight into corporate production practices: "One day [in the Dominican Republic] we found a big pile of Nike's internal pricing documents. Nike assigns a timeframe to each operation. They don't talk about minutes. They break the timeframe into ten thousandths of a second. You get to the bottom of all twenty-two operations: they give the workers 6.6 minutes to make the shirt. It's $0.70 an hour in the Dominican Republic. That's 6.6 minutes; equals $0.08. These are Nike's documents. That means the wages come to three tenths of one percent of the retail price. This is the reality. It's the science of exploitation."

10. A brief consideration of the history of the World Wide Web reveals, in its most skeletal version, a strong correlation with post–World War II U.S.-led global capitalist hegemony. The earliest conceptual blueprints and avatars of the Internet emerged in the late 1950s in connection with the communicative needs of the emergent U.S. military-industrial complex. The Advanced Research Projects Agency (ARPA, which would later become DARPA, the Defense Advanced Research Projects Agency), created in 1957 to lead space exploration, would over the next fifteen years turn its attention to computing and develop ARPANET as the practical realization of ARPA director Joseph C. R. Licklider's humoristically coined 1963 vision of an "intergalactic computer network." This first network linking the computer mainframes of large corporations, government agencies, and universities went public in 1972, spawning other such corporate-government-academic networks across the United States and Europe. In 1982, when Reagan-Thatcher neoliberalism was firmly taking root, ARPANET adopted the transmission control protocol/internet protocol (TCP/IP) that would allow these networks to communicate with one another: the Internet was born. Meanwhile, the concept of personal computing was in development; Macintosh released its first personal computer in 1984. Finally, in 1989, World Wide Web was developed as a global hypertext system connecting a network of sites, thus creating a virtual topography for the Internet, by Tim Berners-Lee at CERN (the Geneva-based European Organization for Nuclear Research) and released to the fledgling computing public in 1991, just as the fall of the Soviet Union was giving way to Fukuyama's "end of history": the global triumph of capitalist liberal democracy. For a history of the Web, see—among other myriad sources—Richard T. Griffiths's online "History of the Internet," Robert H. Zakon's "Hobbes' Internet Timeline 10.1," and Noah Wardrip-Fruin and Nick Montfort's *New Media Reader*, especially the final part, "Revolution, Resistance, and the Launch of the Web" (587–798), which concludes with an essay coauthored by World Wide Web architect Tim Berners-Lee (791–98).

11. A growing body of scholarship also attests to what we might label the "neocolonial" power of new media, in keeping with growth- and profit-oriented capitalist practice and discourse. Edward S. Herman and Robert Waterman McChesney's *The Global Media: The Missionaries of Corporate Capitalism* emphasizes the concentration of the global media in "three or four dozen large transnational corporations" and warns that "such a concentration of media power in organizations dependent on advertiser support and responsible primarily to shareholders is a clear and present danger to citizens' participation in public affairs, understanding of public issues, and thus to the effective working of democracy" (1). Robin Mansell and Michele Javary develop a similar line of argumentation in "New Media and the Forces of Capitalism."

12. In an analysis of the political iconography of democracy, Susan Buck-Morss meditates on the persistence of sovereign exception as an epistemological contradiction with respect to democracy's foundational revolutionary spirit:

The question we need to ask is why Thomas Jefferson's call for permanent revolution is not predictive of the history of democracies in modern times—why it is so difficult to cut off the head of the king so that it stays off, why popular sovereignty consistently resurrects an aura of quasi-mystical power around the sovereign figure—which since Hobbes's *Leviathan* has been recognized as a human artifact, a merely mortal god. . . . In a democracy where only the citizens have the legitimate right to declare a state of exception to the law, the real scandal occurs when an executive branch usurps that power and is allowed to get away with it.

(172)

While this question about sovereign democratic exception may still obtain, I would argue that its most relevant iteration for global neoliberalism would be in regard to sovereign *free-market* exception.

13. Both the United Nations Declaration of Human Rights (1948) and the Declaration of Alma-Ata (1978) calling for the worldwide protection and promotion of health resonate with the notion of a feeling soma and the primordial claim that its structure supposes to the homeostatic patrimony of well-being. Both declarations invoke all of humanity as their purview and explicitly politicize well-being, in political and physiological terms, as the "right" of every human being in the global body politic.

14. In regard to the epistemological potential of affect, Ruth Leys takes a certain cluster of "new affect theorists" (Damasio, Massumi, and others) to task for what she views as overdetermining the separation between reason and affect with a resultant exclusion of intentionality and cognition from affective processes. I do not pretend to assess the merits of how affect and reason are characterized in the empirical and ontological dimensions; I can only read Leys's intervention as indicative that a debate is underway in order to identify with greater precision the physiological distinctions—or hybridities—between rational and affective processes, and that this debate ultimately reflects the perception of an epistemological contest between their respective possibilities (or limits) of signification. But insofar as I infer Leys's central concern to be that affect's possibilities of signification not be atrophied by a scientific approach of definition that shortchanges and structurally stunts its epistemological power, I consider her argument to be analogous to mine—hers in a scientific context, mine in the context of cultural representation. That is, where Leys seeks to prevent affect from being dismissed as an epistemological force on physiological grounds of justification, I seek to foreground the epistemological power of affect as a cultural construct and to enable cultural critics to identify and interpret its markers with an awareness of their potency of signification.

15. Frederick Luis Aldama makes an equally damning assessment of *Babel*, calling it a "failure" on the grounds that director Alejandro González Iñárritu "ignored con-

nections between neurological emotion and reason systems" (139), a charge that goes unexplained, yet whose terms of analysis echo those of A. O. Scott's negative evaluation. Aldama also argues that the "interrelations among [*Babel*'s] stories are artificial and do not depict or illuminate in any way the forces that unify our planet, namely, the capitalist system, which dominates through oppression and exploitation" (105).

I would argue that González Iñárritu's representation of emotion is itself constitutive of his geopolitical analysis of the capitalist system. *Babel* has three story lines that involve four countries: the United States, Morocco, Mexico, and Japan. As the film progresses, a Global North-South pattern becomes clear: as regions, the United States and Japan are characterized by death (suicide, infant mortality) and persistent depression (emotional isolation, marital estrangement) and are also the source of guns. When those guns travel south—and this is a key connector of the story lines—they bring death and pain along with them to regions that are otherwise characterized by unconditional family love and togetherness. The arrival of the guns in the Global South sets in motion events of misguided aggression (a shooting contest between brothers, a drunken flouting of customs and border officials) that, like a boomerang of intensification, only bring that aggression back to roost on the Global South (ominous disappearance, definitive deportation, death in a shoot-out with police). The emotional patterns of the film reflect the patterns of power, money, and authority on a global level: the Global South is thoroughly abused, wounded, and left to deal with its humiliation, grief, and pain of loss by the Global North; the Global North, as a function of this painful resolution of events, experiences a certain catharsis toward the recuperation of positive affect, particularly in the area of family togetherness. The film concludes with the rekindling of the U.S. couple's marital love and the reaffirmation of the Japanese father's emotional availability for his daughter. In this sense the film stages a classic tale of North-South economic dependency theory in emotional terms. But viewers must be willing to accept emotional patterns as intellectual currency in order to appreciate the critique they mount.

16. In a relevant study, Laura Podalsky's *The Politics of Affect and Emotion in Contemporary Latin American Cinema* (2011) surveys the extent to which emotion pervades contemporary cinematic representation in Latin America.

17. "15-M" refers to May 15, 2011 (in Spanish, "15 de mayo"—hence the sequence of the acronym), the date of the opening protest in Madrid's Puerta del Sol.

1. The Feeling Soma

1. The title of the *autobloggreen* blog post making the 2011 announcement "Whole Lotta Prius Love" (Loveday) also reiterates the association between love and consumption that has become both standard practice in the advertising industry and a recurrent motif of sustainability discourse.

2. Antonin Artaud, the French writer best known for his theorization of a "theater of cruelty," lived with the Tarahumara in the mid 1930s. Like McDougall, Artaud also had a revelatory experience in their company, but for him it centered on peyote rituals rather than running, which he chronicled in *D'un Voyage au pays des Tarahumaras* (*Voyage to the Land of the Tarahumara*; *The Peyote Dance*), published a decade later in 1945. Also, like McDougall, Artaud saw in the Tarahumara a naturalistic antidote for what he considered the decadence of Western civilization.

3. Although a cottage industry has sprung up around the denunciation of the ills of U.S. industrialized food—and its permeation of the rest of the globe—two authors have particularly focused on the sugar-salt-fat triumvirate and its role in the success of processed food. David A. Kessler, former head of the U.S. Food and Drug Administration, has written precisely such an exposé explaining how the sugar-fat-salt combination physiologically overrides the homeostatic capacity to moderate food intake by activating the reward system: *The End of Overeating: Taking Charge of the Insatiable American Appetite* (2009; adapted as a "teen" book: *Your Food Is Fooling You: How Your Brain Is Hijacked by Sugar, Fat, and Salt* [2012]). Pulitzer Prize winning *New York Times* journalist Michael Moss echoes Kessler in *Salt, Sugar, Fat: How the Food Giants Hooked Us* (2013), in which he recapitulates Kessler's information about the brain's reward system and its endlessly deferred "bliss point" and gives a history of the development of the processed food industry in the United States that ultimately turns on the questions of profit and competition. I will discuss the sugar-fat-salt triumvirate further in chapter 3.

4. Interestingly, anthropologist Dean Snow suggests that European cave handprints may be preponderantly female (Messer). While this research does not come explicitly to bear on the question of other representational images such as hunting or running, it does throw into relief the masculinist bent of McDougall's imaginative fabrication of the "Running Man" as humanity's first cultural protagonist. Further, that this archetypal narrative of humanity's first cultural protagonist—founder of the "first fine art" of running, object, as such, of the first artistic representation—should also include a heterocentric boy-meets-girl coupling completes a portrait of the social in which cultural and sexual reproduction are, once again, conceptually intertwined.

5. A filmic adaptation of the eponymous 1992 P. D. James novel.

6. Cuarón is a vanguard director of what has been hailed as a renovation of the national Mexican cinema that has languished since its "Golden Age" of the 1940s and 1950s (when it was the "Hollywood of the South"). But, as is evidenced by his list of Oscar nominations that have broken out of the "foreign film" category, as well as his U.S. directorial credits (chief among them the third Harry Potter film in 2003), and the cosmopolitan scope of his filmic narratives, Cuarón's filmmaking does not cleave to the mold of the national Mexican cinema of old. Like fellow directorial compatriots Guillermo del Toro and Alejandro González Iñárritu—who, along with Cuarón, have been dubbed the "Three Amigos" in Hollywood circles—Cuarón has

become a global figure in film direction and production. On the subject of Mexicanness and its borders, González Iñarritu concisely articulates the shared ethos of the Three Amigos: "Cinema is universal, beyond flags and borders and passports" (Rohter). In this regard, Cuarón forms part of a broader tendency toward the redefinition of the Latin American cultural agent in universal terms.

Deborah Shaw's *The Three Amigos* foregrounds this postnational character of their films in the book's subtitle, *The Transnational Filmmaking of Guillermo del Toro, Alejandro González Iñárritu, and Alfonso Cuarón*; Celestino Deleyto and María del Mar Azcona also consider these three filmmakers to have an appeal that is both local and international, thus redefining *mexicanidad* (6).

7. Sayantani DasGupta proposes a race-based interpretation of the film in which Kee is the "subaltern surrogate" (198) to the "white heterosexual family unit" (197), "carr[ying] her pregnancy *for* the First World protagonists" in a "motherhood not born of autonomy but of a personal and ideological colonization" (198). This hermeneutic model reads Kee alongside the other "dumb beasts" "tame[d]" by Theo—dogs who don't bark, a kitten climbing his leg, his lone sighting of a deer—and views her as being discursively likened to the cows that surround her as she reveals her pregnancy to him: "Kee is all fertility, 'savage' simplicity, bestiality, and childlike trust" (188). While this interpretation certainly has merit, my analysis reads the representation of posthumanist animality as part of the conceptual paradigm that holds the morality of the natural world in higher regard than that of a humanity mired in materialistic (read: capitalist) resource hoarding and infighting. As DasGupta's terminology suggests, the film adopts a scale of social critique for this infighting that is geocultural, evocative of the emerging geopolitical division of the world into a Global North and South: the first world of old and the third world, respectively, with the old second world having tellingly disappeared in this new bipartite nomenclature predicated, above all, on respective generalized levels of economic development. It may well be true that this representation of a higher morality coded in positive affective terms begs interpretation for its racialization—the browner Global South, in this vision morally superior for its nobility of character in the face of its adversity through chronic victimization, saves humanity through its intimacy with nature, whereas the whiter Global North, morally inferior for the violence of its hierarchical power and resource-mongering, rots in the decadence of abundant yet sterile capital—yet, if that is so, then I would argue that such a reading works to affirm, rather than undermine, the film's message of geocultural critique.

2. We Are the World

1. Eltit has posited a continuity between the economic and cultural politics of military dictatorship and democracy—whether left-leaning or conservative—in *Emergencias*

(2000), an anthology of journalistic pieces most centrally reflecting on the dictatorship and its aftermath. This postulate was also vertebral for the theoretical orientation of the *Revista de Crítica Cultural* (Journal of Cultural Criticism) directed from 1990–2008 by compatriot Nelly Richard—founded, precisely, in the juncture of the transition to democracy following the 1989 plebiscite that put an end to the Pinochet regime—in which Eltit was also involved as a key contributor to the journal's pages and conceptual architecture.

2. *Crude* has a near mirror-image antecedent in *Trinkets and Beads*, a 1996 documentary film celebrated on the independent film circuit and in the academic sector with an award from the Latin American Studies Association for its chronicling of the David-and-Goliath struggle of the Ecuadoran indigenous Huaorani people against exploitation for oil and the Christian missionaries who have historically facilitated the penetration of Huaorani territory by a succession of international oil companies. The title refers to a quip made by an American present at a ceremony in which the daughter of the Ecuadoran president gives her gold earrings in exchange for tribal consent to drill on Huaorani land; when the president's daughter, acting as a de facto proxy for the Dallas-based oil company Maxus (acquired in 1995 by Argentina's Yacimientos Petrolíferos Fiscales), remarks that she got the better end of the deal, the American jokes that Manhattan was obtained in much the same way, "with trinkets and beads."

3. Shortly after the October 2014 Brazilian presidential elections, an already months-old investigation into Petrobras corruption by the Brazilian Federal Police exploded into public view. "Operação Lava Jato" (Operation Car Wash), as it has been dubbed, denominates an allegedly "vast kickback scheme," as the *Economist* has described it ("Scandal in Brazil"), in which the *Wall Street Journal* reports over ten billion reales are involved in "atypical financial operations" (Connors, Trevisani, and Kiernan). Dozens of executives at Petrobras and related companies have been arrested; scores of politicians have also been implicated, including, possibly, the newly reelected president Dilma Roussef (along with former president Luiz Inácio Lula da Silva, who had faced an analogous scandal involving Petrobras corruption in 2005); a protest on the scale of some ten thousand people on November 15, 2014, called for Roussef's impeachment (Phillips). Meanwhile, Roussef herself claims that this investigation "may change the country forever . . . by ending impunity" ("Petrobras Scandal").

As I read the *Washington Post*'s online coverage of the Petrobras scandal, I cannot help but notice the irony of the overhead banner advertisement for Chevron's Human Energy project, featuring the face of a middle-aged smiling woman of indiscernible ethnicity under the transparent dome of a greenhouse, surrounded by green plant tops, a visual accompanied by the following caption: "We treat the land like we live here. Because we do." This juxtaposition of, on the one hand, a report of corporate malfeasance, which invites interpretation as a lack of responsibility and care, with, on the other hand, a slogan of corporate responsibility, care, and even co-citizenship, paints a Janus-faced portrait of big oil, one of the world's most powerful industries. Chevron asserts its social and environmental stewardship in a display of the "double" bottom line phenomenon that I am trying to underscore; in the Petrobras story the *Washington Post* tracks down the missing component of the economic in the form of many billions of missing dollars that may never be recovered, much less enjoyed by society or environment.

4. In citing dependency theory as an amalgam, I am thinking in the aggregate of several interventions in the domain of economic theory from the 1950s to the 1970s that were particularly central to Latin American economic discourse: Raúl Prebisch's *The Economic Development of Latin America and Its Principal Problems* (1950) advanced the argument that exporters of commodities (underdeveloped countries) would face deteriorating terms of trade over time in the same measure that exporters of manufactured goods (industrialized countries) would accrue more favorable terms of trade (known as the "Prebisch-Singer thesis" because of Hans Singer's publication in the same year of an independent study drawing similar conclusions). André Gunder Frank's *Capitalism and Underdevelopment in Latin America: Historical Studies of Chile and Brazil* (1967) developed the idea that Latin America had been part of a capitalist center-periphery relationship since the sixteenth century and that, after independence, this same relationship continued with Britain, which appropriated Latin America's economic surplus and thereby stymied continental economic sovereignty. Fernando Henrique Cardoso and Enzo Faletto's *Dependencia y desarrollo en América Latina* (1969) argued, in a far more positive light, that the center-periphery relationship did not foreclose the possibility of "dependent development," since a hybrid economic state would result in the periphery by virtue of investment by the center. Eduardo Galeano's *Las venas abiertas de América Latina* (1971) recapitulated the thesis of a five-century extractive oppression of the continent, now identifying the United States as Latin America's newest economic exploiter. Here I am not concerned with a comparative parsing of the particular angles of each dependency theorist's argument, but rather with their conceptual distillation: what they share is a vision of global power as asymmetrical, unevenly distributed between center and periphery, and fundamentally economic in nature.

3. *"Becoming well beings"*

1. Along with Octavio Getino, codirector of their cinematic call to guerrilla arms *La hora de los hornos* (1968), Solanas authored "Hacia un Tercer Cine: apuntes y experiencias para el desarrollo de un cine de liberación en el Tercer Mundo" ("Toward a Third Cinema: Notes and Experiences for the Development of a Cinema of Liberation in the Third World") in 1969, one of the most enduringly influen-

tial manifestos from the markedly leftist Nuevo Cine Latinoamericano (New Latin American Cinema) of the 1960s. In it Solanas and Getino analyze the politicized Latin American film production of the era as a "Third Cinema" in contrast to the "First" and "Second" cinemas, respectively, of Hollywood and the auteur cinema best exemplified in the French New Wave. Third Cinema, in contrast to the other cinemas, rejects the capitalist logic of story, structure, and production technology, instead placing all these in the service of a revolutionary agenda.

2. Goodlad, Kaganovsky, and Rushing cite Egner's "Seeing History in 'Mad Men.'"

3. The anthology Mad Men, *Women, and Children* is, to my mind, particularly emblematic of this scholarly approach to the show, exploring, among other themes, the working/career girl of the 1960s, the archetypal opposition between Jackie Kennedy and Marilyn Monroe, the traditional American family, African American domestic help and marginalization, civil rights, motherhood and domesticity, and children's perspectives on the Baby Boomer years.

4. In this sense, it is no small irony—yet telling of the consumer culture it diagnoses—that *Mad Men* has inspired feverish retro consumerism, from period business attire to midcentury modern furniture and decor to collectible Barbie dolls of four *Mad Men* characters (see Stoddart's detailed inventory of *Mad Men* franchising and consumer inspiration, 4–8).

Mad Men has also inspired a bevy of critical scholarship, largely in the form of edited volumes. One of the most interesting in regard to *Mad Men*'s consumer appeal is *Mad Men and Philosophy* (ed. Carveth and South), in which the list of contributors, subtitled "Some Real Mad Men and Women" (247–51), substitutes biographical quips on the theme of love for *Mad Men* in place of traditional scholarly credentials, e.g., "An avid music lover, [George A. Dunn] hopes to be reincarnated as Joan Holloway's accordion" (248); "Landon W. Schurtz . . . does occasionally enjoy vodka martinis" and is "[a] lifelong lover of bowling, cars with fins, and Formica-and-chrome furniture" (250); "If the academic job market does not improve in the near future, Tyler [Whitney] would consider working with Harry Crane in the television department at Sterling Cooper Draper Pryce" (251). Another contributor, George Teschner, jokes that "he had the choice of advertising and teaching philosophy and has come to believe there is little difference between the two" (251); this comment sums up the spirit of the volume, and, more broadly, of the intellectual commodification that *Mad Men* has unleashed, somewhere between pleasurably guilty and unapologetic.

5. Lair and Strasser also cite this opening sequence as a key component of what they call *Mad Men*'s "masculinity-in-crisis narrative" (179), alongside Don Draper's pitch of the Kodak slide projector wheel as a nostalgia device, which Lair and Strasser view as definitional of that crisis as an emotional wound bound up with a yearning for love (178). Where, on the strength of this foundational interpretation, Lair and Strasser move forward to analyze *Mad Men*'s crisis of masculinity as the product of

the feminist and civil rights movements on the social horizon, I argue that this crisis is more deeply embedded within the fabric of midcentury postwar U.S. consumerist cultural hegemony itself. To my mind, *Mad Men*'s genius lies in creating a cultural mise-en-scène whose subterranean wounds give the lie to its opulent aesthetic, showing how social destabilization in the form of countercultural movements could be understood as having arisen from that very contradiction. Edgerton concurs, considering one of *Mad Men*'s most "distinguishing and innovative aspects" to be the dedication of its first three seasons to the "seemingly calm cultural period before the storm" of the early 1960s pre-Kennedy assassination years, a time that Edgerton views as one in which the "seismic developments" of the countercultural Sixties "simmered . . . beneath the placid exterior of post-war America before finally boiling over with a pent-up fury that took many people in the country by surprise" (xxviii).

6. Hernandez and Holmberg view Draper's character as a composite between "Adam in his new Eden" and a U.S. "frontier hero," both of which ultimately remit to the overarching notion of a "regeneration narrative" (16) that "call[s] into question . . . America's amnesiac romance with itself" (17). In this same vein, I thank Priscilla Wald for bringing to my attention the extent to which Draper is the mid-century analogue of F. Scott Fitzgerald's WWI veteran and self-made bootlegging millionaire Jay Gatsby, whose true name is Jimmy Gatz, hailing from rural farming country (*The Great Gatsby*, 1925). Michael Bérubé also makes this comparison in passing (353). Draper and Gatsby both seek to commit to oblivion their original names and agrarian pasts, redefining themselves in postwar prosperity and thus serving as synecdoches for the respective refashionings of twentieth-century America as a function of world war and shifting geopolitics that increasingly favor the United States as an emergent superpower. While Edenic and frontier narratives may have their place in the analysis of Don Draper's character, I believe that *Mad Men* reads most compellingly as an archaeology of contemporary consumerism and the global cultural might of the U.S. derived from that market power.

7. The foundational role of the Lucky Strike account and the surrounding context of the anxiety stemming from the Surgeon General's report, in turn spurring the use of publicity to influence public opinion, establish a historical arc between *Mad Men* and a seminal campaign credited as giving birth to the field of public relations itself. This one-time event with international media dissemination was the 1929 "Torch of Liberty" campaign staged by Edward Bernays—nephew of Sigmund Freud—in which female models marched with lit cigarettes in the New York City Easter parade, wearing banners that proclaimed the cigarettes—which, furthering the *Mad Men* connection, were Lucky Strikes—"torches of liberty." See Ewen's *PR!* (1996) and Tye's *The Father of Spin* (1998), the latter of which features an early twentieth-century inset photo of a woman raising a lit cigarette to her lips. Investigative reporters Sheldon Rampton and John Stauber (2000) cite Bernays's "Torch of Liberty" campaign as a seminal moment in the development of public

relations as an industry that would cultivate the manipulative distortion of evidence in order to override health concerns in the promotion of toxic products. In this sense, Brandt's *The Cigarette Century* (2007) offers up an academic version of the proposition set forth by *Mad Men*, namely, that cigarettes are at the center of the publicity-driven consumerism—of unhealthy consumption—that defined the United States of the twentieth century.

8. Best known for his film *Cidade de Deus* (*City of God*, 2002), a narrative film chronicling the rise of organized crime in the eponymous slum of Rio de Janeiro between the 1960s and the 1980s, Fernando Meirelles has received some dozen nominations for Academy Awards, Golden Globes, and prizes at Cannes.

9. In this way, *Blindness* makes use of a central metaphorical contrast between blindness and sight as a sensorial disposition toward capitalism or its antithesis, respectively, that is analogous to the opposition between superficial sight (the English "I see you") and true vision (the N'avi "I see all of you") in *Avatar* as explicated in an impromptu language lesson. As in *Blindness*, these two contrasting terms in *Avatar* encapsulate the cultural politics of each race—the exploitative neocolonial capitalism of humans versus the harmonious equitable sharing of the N'avi. In each case, the sense of sight—and therefore the sensing, perceiving body—is used as a vehicle to represent possibilities on the scale of the social. Indeed, extensive attention could be devoted exclusively to the study of the use of the senses to represent sociopolitical schema.

10. Likewise, in *Children of Men* (2006), what appears to be a morning glass of water contains the self-euthanizing product "Quietus"; in both *La Ciénaga* (The Swamp, 2001) and *Y tu mamá también* (2001), water associated with the normative bourgeois culture of capitalist exploitation is dirty, contaminated, and unpotable.

11. Venegas offers an analysis of how *The Motorcycle Diaries*, in the context of Gael García Bernal's playing the role of the young Ernesto Guevara, constitutes a "process of re-articulation through iconicity combined with stardom" (141); this fusion of the "*guerrillero* and the star," Venegas argues, "brings together insurrection and historical reconstruction as a weak form of politics in global film culture" (145) that "re-purpose[s] cultural and political memory into a politically correct, capitalist enterprise . . . reinforces the notion of memory and place as repositories of sentiment, and redefines revolution as pleasurable within the arena of consumption" (161). Implicit in this characterization of market politics as "weak" is the estimation of comparatively strong Cuban revolutionary politics. It is true that revolutionary Cuba eschewed market forces in its early years—it could certainly be argued that this revolution, which, in its origins, was neither socialist nor Soviet, was essentially a struggle against U.S.-led free-market capitalism and its politico-military complex. This is less true in the post-Soviet "Período Especial en Tiempo de Paz" (Special Period in Times of Peace), a time when dire economic crisis and extreme austerity led the regime to act as a "gatekeeper" for a controlled capitalist economy in Cuba (see Corrales).

But I would like to nuance the opposition between revolutionary politics and market politics by adding an epistemological filter to our comparative lens before judging the relative strength and weakness of the politics on each side. In what might be a contentious estimation, I would nevertheless assert that revolutionary politics participate in the imperialist logic of rational epistemicity, with its framework of teleological drive and conquest, albeit through the via negativa of anti-imperialist struggle. Consider, for example, Santiago Colás's masterful 1995 analysis of Cuban revolutionary discourse as desirous of colonial structures past or Antonio José Ponte's short story collection *Cuentos de todas partes del Imperio* (2000), whose imperialist referent is clarified in its English translation as *Tales from the Cuban Empire* (2002). The market politics characterized by Venegas as turning on "sentiment" and "pleasurable . . . consumption" may well undercut the power of revolutionary politics proper, but I would argue that they are no less powerful; they are simply germane to a different epistemological paradigm. It is precisely the participation of *The Motorcycle Diaries* in affective epistemicity on a narrative level that I wish to explore in my reading of the film. *The Motorcycle Diaries* certainly commodifies insurrection and historical reconstruction in a package of sentiment and pleasure; included within that package, as we will see, however, is also a critique of injustice as pain and disease. I caution against the wholesale glorification of imperialist politics of rationality past and the condemnation of free-market politics of affectivity present and instead urge the sober contemplation of both periods as two very different, yet both powerful, politico-economic paradigms functioning in obeisance to broader self-legitimizing epistemological currents. This is the way to begin thinking through what Venegas references in her title, but leaves entirely unarticulated in the body of her essay, as a "New Revolutionary Imagination" of capitalist market forces.

12. In his study of the intersection between theology and Third Cinema, which includes a reading of *The Motorcycle Diaries*, Antonio D. Sison echoes this interpretation, characterizing these indigenous tableaux vivants as embodiments of a "praxical imperative that haunts the memory of Ernesto . . . and representations of the call for social change" (80).

13. Ching, Buckley, and Lozano-Alonso also view Ernesto's crossing of the river as significant in the filmic representation of his revolutionary future: "The analogy to Che's eventual life as a revolutionary leader in this scene is obvious. He throws aside concern for his own well-being out of an inherent embrace of the masses and their suffering. They, in turn, are drawn to him and become the malleable force that he will lead to a better future through revolution and mass activism" (249). Ching, Buckley, and Lozano-Alonso's interpretation of Ernesto as "ignor[ing] his asthma" (248) and "throwing aside concern for his own well-being" construes his character as adopting a mind-over-matter posture; this classically hierarchical mind-body dualism finds analogy in the relationship that Ching, Buckley, and Lozano-Alonso envision between Ernesto as a Pygmalion-like leader and the "malleable" masses that will

follow him, in an interpretation that collapses the filmic Ernesto and the historical Che, whose writings did in fact evince the belief that a revolutionary vanguard elite was necessary to guide the masses toward their own liberation and betterment. Guevara's canonical 1965 letter known as "El socialismo y el hombre en Cuba" (Socialism and the New Man in Cuba), for example, asserts that a revolutionary *vanguardia* in the form of a leadership of guerrilla fighters is required to awaken the *pueblo* that he describes as a *masa todavía dormida*—an "as yet sleeping multitude," though *masa* also means "dough" in Spanish, a polysemanticity that resonates with the adjectival description by Ching, Buckley, and Lozano-Alonso of the "malleable" character of the masses that the filmic Ernesto will mobilize as he becomes el Che.

Yet I would argue that *The Motorcycle Diaries* does not in fact participate in this epistemically rational verticality of mind-body dualism and thinking-head leaders vis-à-vis subordinate masses. On the contrary, in the first regard, it stages Ernesto's potentially fatal river swim more as a leap of faith toward well-being than as an act of stoic negation thereof. It also insists on Ernesto's systematic efforts at achieving indistinction from the lepers-as-masses. The filmic Ernesto rejects every form of hierarchy, from symbolic white gloves in treating lepers to birthday celebrations that exclude them; if he "leads" the lepers—or the doctors and nuns, for that matter—it is through horizontal inspiration and affect-driven example rather than by vertical imposition. Both the river crossing scene and the film as a whole register a shift away from the vertical dynamics of top-down vanguard militancy to which the real-life Guevara subscribed. This twenty-first-century filmic reconstruction of revolutionary politics on an epistemological axis of free-market affectivity is what is of central interest for the present study.

14. Although I have structured this analytic cluster to show how a hemispheric cultural pattern emerges in the form of a divide between U.S. film as diagnosing capitalist ill-being and Latin American film as proposing an alternative well-being, there are certainly exceptions to this pattern. David Fincher's *Fight Club* (1999) which stages a national guerrilla revolution against U.S. capitalist consumerism that culminates in the destruction of the edifice of credit debt, as the central romantic protagonists look on holding hands in a tender high-school-sweethearts kind of embrace (although they may or may not be dead—but that would be the subject of a longer analysis), is but one example of U.S. cultural production that takes its narrative beyond denunciation and into corrective contestatory action to restore the well-being perceived to have been lost to a stranglehold of consumerist ill-being.

4. Legs, Love, and Life

1. Over the past twenty years, there has been a groundswell of scholarship in business studies on emotional advertising. A small sampling of the now established

subfield includes the following titles: Agres, Edell, and Dubitsky, *Emotion in Advertising* (1990); Feig, *Marketing Straight to the Heart* (1997); Robinette et al., *Emotion Marketing* (2000); Travis, *Emotional Branding* (2000); Gobé and Zyman, *Emotional Branding* (2001); O'Shaughnessy and O'Shaughnessy, *The Marketing Power of Emotion* (2002); Feig, *Hot Button Marketing* (2006); Hansen, Christensen, and Lundsteen, *Emotion, Advertising, and Consumer Choice* (2007); Du Plessis, *The Advertised Mind* (2008); Hill and Simon, *Emotionomics* (2009); Hill, *About Face* (2010).

This marketing interest in emotion should properly be understood as an interdisciplinary field in the sense that its lessons are drawn from the explosion in neuroscientific research on emotion during the same post-Soviet time period. *Neuromarketing* and *emotionomics* are thus roughly commensurate business neologisms, with the following titles attesting specifically to the central role of neuroscience in maximizing the emotional exploitation of advertising: Zurawicki, *Neuromarketing* (2010); Du Plessis, *The Branded Mind* (2011); Dooley, *Brainfluence* (2011).

2. The use of the term *posthuman* is generalized to several different fields and phenomena: some use it to denote a roboticized cybernetic body "evolved" through artificial intelligence, e.g., Fukuyama's *Our Posthuman Future* (2000); others use it to denote a vision of monstruous human alterity, such as zombies as a representation of afterlife, e.g., Christie and Lauro's edited volume *Better Off Dead* (2011), and others use it to denote a vision of the planetary animal kingdom in which humanity's place and role are redefined as being alongside those of other species and/or as imbricated within the natural ecosystem, e.g., Wolfe's *What Is Posthumanism?* (2009). The discussion in this chapter will explore that last meaning ascribed to posthumanism, but it bears noting that emotion plays a role as a pivotal analytic in each of these cases: the robotics of emotion are considered the final frontier of artificial intelligence; the question of empathy is key in the analysis of radical human alterity; and, as I will consider at some length here, emotion is what links humanity to animals and planet—in a word, to other life—in the understanding of the posthuman as what I will call a democratization of the animal kingdom and, indeed, all of sentient life. I would therefore hazard the hypothesis that what links the multiple definitions of the posthuman is an interest in the status of humanity itself and that an interrogation of emotion as a connective (i.e., relationship-, group-, and community-building) agent—whether to animals, cyberhumans, or radical Others (the undead, aliens, etc)—is what links these otherwise heterogeneous optics on humanity.

3. Dawkins's *The Selfish Gene* (2006 [1976]) revolutionized the field of evolutionary biology with the argument that the gene is "selfish" in that it is always seeking to maximize its chances of survival; even selflessness in the form of altruism is, in this light, essentially selfish. Yet Dawkins devotes the entire introduction of his thirtieth-anniversary edition to an apology for its title and asks his readers to "mentally delete" the "rogue sentence" where he had earlier urged, "Let us try to

teach generosity and altruism because we are born selfish" (ix). Without disavowing any of its original content, Dawkins nevertheless tries to frame his book differently, asserting that, "if anything, [it] devotes more attention to altruism" (viii) and might just as well have been called "*The Cooperative Gene*" (ix). The updated discursive through line of Dawkins's book makes it fully concordant with de Waal's efforts at "putting the altruism back into altruism" (*The Age of Empathy*) and affirms the hypothesis that the cultural exigencies of discourse have shifted away from selfishness and toward selflessness.

4. A full study of the shifting relationship between reason and affect would provide a diachronic account of their discursive relationship. Although it is spare and perhaps reductively skeletal, I have signaled at least some key topoi in what would be the early twentieth-century installment of this discursive historiography in my abbreviated discussion of the relationship between psychoanalysis and poststructuralism (see "Prelude," note 4).

5. See the "Avatar" entry in Box Office Mojo for detailed statistics on the film's lifetime gross and rank.

6. Of all political figureheads of the Latin American leftism unexpectedly renewed during the first decade of the twenty-first century, Hugo Chávez (1999–) has been the most radical, with his populist politics and the nationalization of petroleum, and the most openly antagonistic toward the United States government and economic system, particularly during the presidency of George W. Bush (2000–2008). Although at no time has the U.S. government issued any formal threat of military intervention, a video game released by Pandemic Studios in 2008, *Mercenaries 2: World in Flames*, does simulate—in mercenary form—the U.S. invasion of Venezuela. The video game begins with a coup d'état, followed by the game's central and sustained objective of battling China to gain control over the country's oil supply. The Chávez government interpreted this game as "preparation work for a real invasion" ("Venezuelan Anger at Computer Game"), especially in light of the fact that in 2003 Pandemic Studios had created the army training simulation *Full Spectrum Warrior* as a CIA contractor. In 2009 Venezuela enacted legislation banning violent video games with a fine and multiyear prison sentence for violators.

7. In a review of *Avatar*, Sara Palmer argues that disability studies theorist Robert McRuer's concept of "compulsory able-bodiedness" is "central to the narrative logic of Jake Sully's character"—that is, a compulsion to prefer able-bodiedness over disability as the result of a normative social desire. See McRuer's "Compulsory Able-Bodiedness and Queer/Disabled Existence."

8. In addition to emphasizing the motif of legs, we might also track the motif of obesity, comparing *WALL-E* on this basis, for example, to Pablo Trapero's *Mundo grúa* (Crane World, 1999), in which "Rulo" ("Curly," Luis Margani), a middle-aged blue-collar worker, is denied employment operating a construction crane in Buenos Aires because of a medical report defining him as obese and therefore a hazard the

insurance company will not permit. At stake in this film is the question of Rulo's free will, posited in analogy—albeit with greater subtlety—to the central thematics of *WALL-E*: is Rulo's obesity in fact a syndrome of the lifestyle imposed by capitalist culture—in other words, an expression of capitalist ill-being? The film presents Rulo as being boxed into his way of life: he works—or looks for work—during the day, comes home to a loveless existence in which the television is his only company, eats in large quantities while watching mindless programs, and falls asleep on the sofa. The physician who diagnoses him with "Pickwick" syndrome, a cardiopulmonary complication of obesity that manifests itself as sleep apnea, guesses that this is Rulo's routine, making its predictability suggestive of a larger cultural pattern in which Rulo is not the exception but the norm. The backdrop that defines this ill-being is what the film's title announces: a capitalist machine of progress—a culture of "more"—symbolized by the crane, which towers over a panoramic view of the city in an opening shot, as though it were king of the urban expanse. Rulo accepts this symbolism and speaks to his son of his aspiration to work the crane as the ultimate expression of personal freedom ("Voy a estar solo, voy a poder leer, escuchar la radio, si quiero tirar un pedo me tiro un pedo" ["I'll be alone, I can read, listen to the radio, if I want to fart, I fart"]), yet the film shows that it is precisely the logic of the "crane world" that dicatates Rulo's subservience to a lifestyle that systematically submerges him into increasing depths of unfreedom, progressively depriving him of his health, his livelihood, his love interest and friends, even his most meager income, and, finally, of his most cherished memory and greatest source of solace, when, in the closing moments of the film, he confesses to having lost the pleasure of recounting his brief glory as a member of a two-hit-wonder rock band. Rulo's band, Séptimo Regimiento (Seventh Regiment), is modeled on the real-life Séptima Brigada (Seventh Brigade); the latter's two successes, "Paco Camorra" (1969) and "Juan Camelo" (1970) are fictionally credited to Rulo in the film. This historical detail forms part of a larger neorealist aesthetic: the almost exclusive use of nonprofessional actors, their use of their given names (Rulo's full diegetical name is Luis Margani, the real-life name of the actor who plays him), the gritty and slow-paced hand-held camerawork shot in black and white. Just as Italian neorealism sought to denounce the social ills of postwar fascism, so does *Mundo grúa* seek to denounce a contemporary set of social ills: those arising from the capitalist model of progress that not only fails to provide well-being but generates its opposite in the form of systemic and ineluctable ill-being for the masses.

9. Rescue consumption becomes the mantra of the multibillion international online auction company eBay in its "ReLove" Earth Day 2013 campaign that seeks to rebrand "used" items as "pre-loved" items whose purchase is tantamount to "giving pre-loved items new life," which, eBay argues, is "good for the planet, too" through a "virtuous cycle [of] using our shared resources wisely." "Here's to falling in Re-Love, again and again," eBay concludes, urging an affect-driven "green" consumption that demonstrates the increasing cultural hegemony of the notion of love as

consumption. That is, the idea of a loving rescue consumption is no longer simply the purview of a contestatory discourse but characteristic of the rhetoric of corporate consumerism itself.

10. Brown's "Wounded Attachments," originally published in 1993 as journal article in *Political Theory*, also appears as a chapter in her subsequent 1995 Princeton University Press book *States of Injury*.

11. The commercial was still viewable on the Nike website some three years after the 2008 Olympics for which it was made. I would speculate that its subsequent removal had as much to do with obsolescence as with the public scandals that erupted around at least two of the athletes featured therein: Lance Armstrong was convicted in 2012 of doping for sports performance enhancement, stripped of all his Tour de France racing titles, and banned from competitive cycling; in 2013 Oscar Pistorius shot and killed his girlfriend, South African model Reeva Steenkamp, and in 2014 was sentenced to five years in prison for homicide. Nike had intended for these athletes to symbolize courage and love; their scandals certainly undercut these associations.

12. As a cultural text, this film is by far the least mainstream of any I analyze in this study. Yet it has made its way onscreen at a significant list of film festivals: Fifth-Seventh Berlin International Film Festival ("Berlinale," 2007); Festival de Cine Centroamericano Ícaro (winner, Best Production 2007); NewFilmmakers Film Festival (New York City, 2007); Pioneer Theater's "SAVNY Lovely Surveillance—Students from the Savannah College of Art and Design" (New York City, 2007); Del Corazón (HeART) Film Festival (El Paso, Texas) (2007); Twenty-Second Latin American Film Festival (North Carolina, 2008), including a visit to Duke University; Iberoamerikanische Filmtage, IV Festival de Cine Iberoamericano (Künstlerhaus k/haus Kino, Vienna, 2008); Third Latin American Film Festival (Oaxaca, 2009); Vancouver Latin American Film Festival (2009); and Jaman online archive of international cinema (ongoing).

13. Escobar Galindo offers a retrospective account of the relationship between his and Dalton's poems in the context of the Salvadoran violence of the 1970s in "El duelo por el 'Duelo . . . '" ("The Mourning of 'Mourning . . . ,'" 2006). In a case of tragic irony that remains judicially unresolved, Dalton is said to have been assassinated by members of his own political party (see Campos's "El asesinato de Roque Dalton" for a detailed discussion of the circumstances surrounding Dalton's death).

14. *Ever Amado*'s denouement of familial imagery in the sky is virtually identical to that of Sean Penn's *Into the Wild* (2007), a narrative film about the real-life story of Christopher McCandless, a young Emory graduate from a family of means who renounces Western materialism and what he considers its fundamental violences in order to live alone in the Alaskan wilderness. As part of his renunciation, McCandless leaves behind his given name (becoming "Alexander Supertramp") and his family as well as his money and material possessions. The film makes the question of

the family—as a synecdoche for loving relationships in general—the pivotal through line of McCandless's story. Penn interprets McCandless's philosophical journey as one that leads him back to the social sphere that he has squarely renounced, giving heavy emphasis to a marginalia notation in Leo Tolstoy's *Family Happiness* (1859) that seems to be one of the last that McCandless made before his death in isolation: "Happiness is not real unless shared." On the strength of this analysis, Penn casts McCandless's death as a return to his family: as he is in his final moments, gazing at the light from the sun, the sky seems to open up, and in that space a smiling Chris rushes into his parents' waiting arms in a final embrace. Whereas Penn's film ends on this note of the de facto reintegration of the double bottom line of the environmental and the social, concluding with a series of images of the people whose lives McCandless touched engaging each other with feeling as the implicit legacy of his communication of well-being, *Ever Amado* has no such happy ending, coming to rest only on genocidal violence and the perversion of nature in an effective eulogy for the double bottom line.

15. Although Michael Hardt does not give love a leftist ontology—that is, claim it as an essentially leftist phenomenon—he does gesture toward the identification of a variant of love with use-value for the political left (2007, 2009).

16. Writing about Mexican and Spanish cinema at the end of the twentieth century, Claudia Schaefer argues that its "dissonance and indigestion" (172) have the salutary effect of unsettling the middle class from the boredom of the status quo and may even contain the "possibility of emancipation from our dream state" (172) "These films," Schaefer continues, "should haunt Western society for some time to come since they bring the unexpected into view without creating an aura of fascination and wonder to surround the brutality of the images" (172). Though she is writing about films that somewhat antecede Reygadas's production, and at a period in time when one might argue that the "unexpected" was just around the corner in the form of global economic crisis, these descriptors are nevertheless equally apt for Reygadas's filmography.

17. Excerpt from Bello's "Silva a la agricultura de la zona tórrida" ("Ode to the Agriculture of the Torrid Zone," 1826):

> Mas ¡oh! ¡si cual no cede
> el tuyo, fértil zona, a suelo alguno,
> y como de natura esmero ha sido,
> de tu indolente habitador lo fuera!
> ¡Oh! ¡si al falaz rüido,
> la dicha al fin supiese verdadera
> anteponer, que del umbral le llama
> del labrador sencillo,
> lejos del necio y vano

fasto, el mentido brillo,
el ocio pestilente ciudadano!
¿Por qué ilusión funesta
aquellos que fortuna hizo señores
de tan dichosa tierra y pingüe y varia,
el cuidado abandonan
y a la fe mercenaria
las patrias heredades,
y en el ciego tumulto se aprisionan
de míseras ciudades,
do la ambición proterva
sopla la llama de civiles bandos,
o al patriotismo la desidia enerva;
do el lujo las costumbres atosiga,
y combaten los vicios
la incauta edad en poderosa liga?
[But oh! If your land,
fertile zone, is surpassed by none,
this having been the work of nature,
if only it had been of your indolent inhabitant!
Oh! If he finally knew how to put
true fortune ahead of false noise,
fortune that calls to him from the threshold
of the simple laborer,
far from fatuous and idle
pomp, deceptive brilliance,
pestilent urban leisure!
For what ill-fated illusion
did they whom fortune made lords
of such blessed lands, profitable and diverse,
abandon their care,
and to a mercenary faith,
the hereditary homelands
and in the blind tumult
of miserable cities imprison themselves
where wicked ambition
fans the flames of civil strife,
or indolence enervates patriotism;
where luxury poisons customs,
and vices embattle
unsuspecting youth in a powerful bind?]

Conclusion: Affective Biopower

1. In the afterword of the Darwin edition ("Universality of Emotional Expression? A Personal History of the Dispute"), Paul Ekman argues that the categorical rejection of a universal character of culture in favor of its malleability was a "one-sided view [that] developed in part as a backlash against Social Darwinism, eugenics and the threat of Nazism" (368). Immensely influential anthropologists such as Margaret Mead and Gregory Bateson were steadfast in their resistance to the idea of what Mead called "inborn differences" because of the potential for political misuse and abuse of such ideas. Ekman explains how these political misgivings impeded the study of human universals, namely the emotions: "[Mead's] concern that racists would misuse evidence of biology based individual differences led her to attack any claim for the biological basis of social behavior, even when biology is responsible for what unites us as a species, as in the case of universal expressions of emotions" (369).

2. Research that has gathered momentum from the mid-1990s forward on mirror neurons—brain cells that fire both in the viewing of another's actions and in their subsequent enactment by the viewer—approaches this question of emotional mirroring from a neurophysiological point of view (see, e.g., Sandra Blakeslee's *New York Times* Science section summary of mirror neurons "Cells that Read Minds"). Some researchers also explore the extent to which mirror neurons are linked to empathy and behaviors of togetherness (e.g., neuroscientist Marco Iacoboni's *Mirroring People* [2008], which underwent a subtle but significant change of subtitle in its paperback release indicative of its principal argumentation and presumed readerly interest alike: *The Science of Empathy and How We Connect with Others* [2009]).

3. The documentary film *The Corporation*, for example, explores this question of the privatization of the globe. Interviewee Maude Barlow, Canadian political and environmental activist, says, "There are those who intend that one day everything will be owned by somebody, and we're not just talking goods here. We're talking human rights, human services, essential services for life. Education, public health, social assistance, pensions, housing. We're also talking about the survival of the planet. The[re are] areas that we believe must be maintained in the commons or under common control or we will collectively die. Water and air." In an interview that follows Barlow's commentary, the interviewer then explicitly follows up on this point with free-market advocate Michael Walker, asking, "It sounds like you're advocating private ownership of every square inch of the planet. Every cubic foot of air, water." "Absolutely," Walker responds.

4. Guns N' Roses' 1987 *Appetite for Destruction* is ranked number 4 on *Rolling Stone's* top one hundred debut albums of all time. It came out too late to be included in *The Decline of Western Civilization Part II: The Metal Years* (1988), but this second volume of the three-part documentary that chronicles the punk-rock music

282 CONCLUSION: AFFECTIVE BIOPOWER

scene in the context of cultural decay resonates heavily with the content of the Guns N' Roses album, which characterizes daily life as a "jungle" where one "bleeds" and submits to self-destructive or decadent vice—drugs and sex, at turns—hoping all the while for a providential "paradise city" to counter this sadomasochistic jungle.

5. In *A Brief History of Neoliberalism*, David Harvey asks whether asymmetrical inequalities presumed to be outliers of a system presumed to be fair and egalitarian are not in truth better understood as structural; in *The Shock Doctrine*, Naomi Klein argues that capitalism has achieved its global spread on the strength of a vulture-like preying upon crises that are either natural or engineered. In this same vein, Jean Franco's *Cruel Modernity* (2013) attests to the extent to which Latin American modernity has been constructed on a foundation of torture and violence, whether in dictatorships or the drug war. Though Franco's analysis is more trained on culture than economics, the idea of "modernity" in Latin American scholarship is inextricably linked to the question of the continent's relationship to global capital. Though the relationship between Latin American dictatorships and the development of neoliberal economies has been long established—the Milton Friedman–trained "Chicago Boys" who became Augusto Pinochet's advisers in Chile being the most infamous referent of this phenomenon—Franco's omission of any regional identifier in her title allows her to "gradually buil[d] a theory of the cruelty of modernity as such" (Bosteels, Review of *Cruel Modernity*, 221).

6. For Marx and Engels, ideology is a phenomenon of consciousness produced by lived material existence: "Men are the producers of their conceptions, ideas, etc.—real, active men, as they are conditioned by a definite development of their productive forces and of the intercourse corresponding to these, up to its furthest forms. Consciousness can never be anything else than conscious existence, and the existence of men is their actual life-process" (47).

7. A 2014 test of theories of American politics may indicate that Piketty's future is here, as John Cassidy quipped when he described the study's provenance as the "Dept. of Academics Confirming Something You Already Suspected." Political scientists Martin Gilens and Benjamin I. Page summarized their findings as "provid[ing] substantial support for theories of Economic-Elite-Domination and for theories of Biased Pluralism, but not for theories of Majoritarian Electoral Democracy or Majoritarian Pluralism" (564), which the BBC interpreted in lay terms thus: "US Is an Oligarchy, Not a Democracy."

8. For the publication of the Facebook experiment, see Kramer, Guillory, and Hancock, "Experimental Evidence of Massive-Scale Emotional Contagion." For the retraction of the relationship between the U.S. Army and the Cornell researchers, see the note of correction at the foot of the Cornell news story on the experiment: Segelken and Shackford, "News Feed."

9. Žižek's citation is the last of Badiou's "Fifteen Theses on Contemporary Art" published by *Lacanian Ink* in 2003.

10. Bullying has become a national topic of discussion and concern in the United States. The 2011 documentary film *Bully* forms part of a larger "Bully Project" whose website announces the goal of screening the film and bringing the awareness issue to ten million children. The 2012 Mexican narrative film *Después de Lucía* (*After Lucía*) also unflinchingly takes on the subject matter of school bullying in a devastating portrait of a young girl mercilessly harassed and dehumanized by her peers after a video of her sexual activity goes viral in their affluent school community.

Works Cited

Abreu, Carlos. "Sustentabilidade? O que é Sustentabilidade?" *Atitudes Sustentáveis,* 16 October 2008. http://www.atitudessustentaveis.com.br/sustentabilidade/sustentabilidade/ (15 September 2011).

Acedo, Alfredo. "Monsanto y el petate del muerto." *Americas Program,* 24 March 2011. http://www.cipamericas.org/es/archives/4200 (15 September 2011).

Acosta, Abraham. *Thresholds of Illiteracy: Theory, Latin America, and the Crisis of Resistance.* New York: Fordham University Press, 2014.

Agamben, Giorgio. *Homo Sacer: Sovereign Power and Bare Life.* Trans. Daniel Heller-Roazen. Stanford: Stanford University Press, 1998. (*Homo sacer: Il potere sovrano e la nuda vita.* Torino: Einaudi, 1995.)

Agres, Stuart J., Julia A. Edell, and Tony M. Dubitsky. *Emotion in Advertising: Theoretical and Practical Explorations.* New York: Quorum, 1990.

Ahmed, Sara. *The Promise of Happiness.* Durham, NC: Duke University Press, 2010.

Aldama, Frederick Luis. *Mex-Ciné: Mexican Filmmaking, Production, and Consumption in the Twenty-first Century.* Ann Arbor: University of Michigan Press, 2013.

Alonso, Carlos J. *The Burden of Modernity: The Rhetoric of Cultural Discourse in Spanish America.* Oxford: Oxford University Press, 1998.

Althusser, Louis. "Ideology and Ideological State Apparatuses (Notes Towards an Investigation)." In *Lenin and Philosophy and Other Essays*, 121–76. Trans. Andy Blunden. New York: Monthly Review Press, 1971. ("Idéologie et appareils idéologiques d'État." *La Pensée* 151 [June 1970]: 3–38.) Louis Althusser Archive, Marxists Internet Archive Library. http://www.marxists.org/reference/archive/althusser/1970/ideology.htm (15 September 2011).

Amato, Mike. "The Coca-Cola Hilltop Ad: 40 Years of Apple Tress and Phosphoric Acid." *Huffington Post*, 13 April 2011 (updated 13 June 2011). http://www.huffingtonpost.com/mike-amato/coca-cola-hilltop-ad_b_847672.html (28 April 2015).

Amores perros. Dir. Alejandro González Iñárritu. Writer Guillermo Arriaga. Perf. Emilio Echevarría, Gael García Bernal, Goya Toledo. Altavista, Zeta, 2000.

Andrei Rublev. Dir. Andrei Tarkovsky. Perf. Anatoli Solonitsyn, Ivan Lapikov, Nikolai Grinko. Mosfilm, 1966.

"Anuncio Coca-Cola—destapa la felicidad (Josep Mascaró)." *Mr-Ad*, n.d. http://www.mr-ad.es/anuncio-coca-cola-destapa-la-felicidad-josep-mascaro.html (15 September 2011).

"'Argentina es un país ocupado y colonizado' (por la Barrick Gold)." *Urgente24.com*, 11 March 2011. http://www.urgente24.com/noticias/val/5293–150/argentina-es-un-pais-ocupado-y-colonizado-%28por-la-barrick-gold%29.html (15 September 2011).

Arlidge, John. "I'm Doing God's Work: Meet Mr Goldman Sachs." *Sunday Times*, 8 November 2009. http://www.timesonline.co.uk/tol/news/world/us_and_americas/article6907681.ece (15 September 2011).

Armstrong, Nancy. *How Novels Think: The Limits of British Individualism from 1719–1900*. New York: Columbia University Press, 2006.

Artaud, Antonin. *D'un Voyage au pays des Tarahumaras*. Paris: Fontaine, 1945. (*Les Tarahumaras*. Paris: L'Arbalète, 1955; "Concerning a Journey to the Land of the Tarahumaras." Trans. David Rattray. *City Lights Journal* 2 [1964]; *The Peyote Dance*. Trans. Helen Weaver. New York: Farrar, Straus and Giroux, 1976.)

@freedomrebel. "Nike . . . The King of Social Injustice . . . Sweatshops." *Zoo*, 24 March 2009. http://tpzoo.wordpress.com/2009/03/24/nikethe-king-of-social-injusticesweatshops/ (15 September 2011).

@mazsa. "The Single Greatest Deficiency." *United Persons*, 17 February 2010. http://theunitedpersons.org/blog/avatar-the-single-greatest-deficiency (15 September 2011).

@ToKatz. "Trudy Chacón: The Most Heroic of All." *Avatar Forums*, 4 February 2010. http://www.avatar-forums.com/characters/5475-trudy-chacon-most-heroic-all/ (15 September 2011).

Avatar. Dir. James Cameron. Perf. Sam Worthington, Zoë Saldana, Sigourney Weaver. Twentieth Century Fox, Dune, Ingenious Film Partners, Lightstorm, 2009.

"Avatar." Box Office Mojo. http://www.boxofficemojo.com/movies/?id=avatar.
htm (28 November 2014).

Babel. Dir. Alejandro González Iñárritu. Writer Guillermo Arriaga. Perf. Brad Pitt,
Cate Blanchett, Gael García Bernal. Anonymous Content, Babel Productions
(II), Central Films, Dune Films, Media Rights Capital, Zeta Film, 2006.

Badiou, Alain. "Fifteen Theses on Contemporary Art." Trans. Peter Hallward. *Lacanian Ink* 22 (Drawing Center, 4 December 2003). http://www.lacan.com/
issue22.php (18 April 2015).

Bales, Kevin. *Disposable People: New Slavery in the Global Economy.* Berkeley: University of California Press, 1999.

Barrett, Paul M. "Amazon Crusader. Chevron Pest. Fraud?" *Bloomberg Newsweek,*
9 March 2009, 1–9. http://www.businessweek.com/magazine/content/11_12/
b4220056636512.htm (15 September 2011).

Barsalou, Lawrence W. "Grounded Cognition." *Annual Review of Psychology* 59
(2008): 617–45.

Barthes, Roland. *Camera Lucida.* Trans. Richard Howard. New York: Hill and
Wang, 1981. (*La Chambre claire.* Paris: Gallimard, 1980.)

———. *The Pleasure of the Text.* Trans. Richard Miller. New York: Hill and Wang,
1975. (*Le Plaisir du texte.* Paris: Seuil, 1973.)

Batman Begins. Dir. Christopher Nolan. Perf. Christian Bale, Michael Caine, Ken
Watanabe. Warner Bros., Syncopy, DC Comics, Legendary, Patalex, 2005.

BBC. "Study: US Is an Oligarchy, not a Democracy." *Echo Chambers,* 17 April 2014.
http://www.bbc.com/news/blogs-echochambers-27074746 (19 April 2015).

Beasley-Murray, Jon. *Posthegemony: Political Theory and Latin America.* Minneapolis: University of Minnesota Press, 2010.

Beavan, Colin. "Today Is Answer the Critics Day." *No Impact Man,* 26 March 2007.
http://noimpactman.typepad.com/blog (15 September 2011).

———. "How Is the Idea of Progress Part of Your Practice?" *Guggenheim Forum.*
http://www.guggenheim.org/new-york/interact/online-forum/declarations/
invited-contributions?tmpl=component (15 September 2011).

Beck, Ulrich. *Risk Society: Towards a New Modernity.* Trans. Mark Ritter. London:
Sage, 1992. (*Risikogesellschaft. Auf dem Weg in eine andere Moderne.* Frankfurt:
Suhrkamp, 1986.)

———. *World at Risk.* Cambridge: Polity 2008.

———. *World Risk Society.* Cambridge: Polity, 1999.

Beckman, Ericka. *Capital Fictions: The Literature of Latin America's Export Age.*
Minneapolis; London: University of Minnesota Press, 2013.

Bellamy Brothers. "Let Your Love Flow." *Let Your Love Flow.* Warner Bros., 1976.

Bello, Andrés. "Silva a la agricultura de la zona tórrida." *Obras completas (Vol I):
Poesías,* 65–75. Caracas: Ediciones del Ministerio de Educación, 1952 [1826]. Biblioteca Virtual Miguel D. Cervantes. http://bib.cervantesvirtual.com/servlet/

SirveObras/01327220800793166644802/p0000004.htm#I_35_ (15 September 2011).

Bennett, Jane. *Vibrant Matter: A Political Ecology of Things.* Durham, NC: Duke University Press, 2009.

Bentham, Jeremy. *The Principles of Morals and Legislation.* Amherst, NY: Prometheus, 1988. (London: E. Wilson and W. Pickering, 1823 [1789]).

Berlant, Lauren. *Cruel Optimism.* Durham, NC: Duke University Press, 2011.

Bersuit Vergarabat. "Madre hay una sola." YouTube (BersuitVEVO), 30 November 2009. http://www.youtube.com/watch?v=NpZUlfWpUP8. 15 September 2011.

———. "Madre hay una sola." *Testosterona.* Universal Music Argentina, 2005.

———. "El tiempo no para." *Y punto.* Belgrano Norte S.R.L., 1992.

Bérubé, Michael. "A Change Is Gonna Come, Same as It Ever Was." In *Mad Men, Mad World: Sex, Politics, Style, and the 1960s,* 345–59. Ed. Lauren M. E. Goodlad, Lilya Kaganovsky, and Robert A. Rushing. Durham, NC: Duke University Press, 2013.

Beverley, John. *Latin Americanism After 9/11.* Durham, NC: Duke University Press, 2011.

Bewitched. Creator Sol Saks. Perf. Elizabeth Montgomery, Dick York, Dick Sargent, Agnes Moorehead. ABC, 1964–1972.

Black, Donald W. "A Review of Compulsive Buying Disorder," *World Psychiatry* 6.1 (February 2007): 14–18. http://www.pubmedcentral.nih.gov/articlerender.fcgi?tool=pubmed&pubmedid=17342214 (15 September 2007).

Blakeslee, Sandra. "Cells That Read Minds." *New York Times,* 10 January 2006. www.nytimes.com/2006/01/10/science/10mirr.html (19 April 2015).

Blindness. Dir. Fernando Meirelles. Perf. Julianne Moore, Mark Ruffalo, Gael García Bernal. Miramax, 2008.

Boltanski, Luc and Ève Chiapello. *The New Spirit of Capitalism.* Trans. Gregory Elliott. London; New York: Verso, 2005. (*Le nouvel esprit du capitalisme.* Paris: Gallimard, 1999.)

Bosteels, Bruno. *Marx and Freud in Latin America: Politics, Psychoanalysis, and Religion in Times of Terror.* New York: Verso, 2012.

———. "Review of *Cruel Modernity*, by Jean Franco." *Revista Hispánica Moderna* 68.2 (2015): 221–26.

Bourdieu, Pierre and Jean-Claude Passeron. *Reproduction in Education, Society, and Culture.* Trans. Richard Nice. London: Sage, 1977. (*La Reproduction: Élements pour une théorie du système d'enseignement.* Paris: Minuit, 1970.)

Brandt, Allan M. *The Cigarette Century: The Rise, Fall, and Deadly Persistence of the Product That Defined America.* New York: Basic Books, 2007.

Brennan, Teresa. *The Transmission of Affect.* Ithaca, NY: Cornell University Press, 2004.

"Britain's Brown Urges Moral Values at G-20." *CNN Politics,* 31 March 2009. http://articles.cnn.com/2009-03-31/politics/britain.g20_1_global-values-financial-crisis-moral?_s=PM:POLITICS (15 September 2011).

Brooks, Max. *The Zombie Survival Guide: Complete Protection from the Living Dead.* New York: Three Rivers, 2003.

Brooks, Peter. *The Melodramatic Imagination: Balzac, Henry James, Melodrama, and the Mode of Excess.* New Haven: Yale University Press, 1976.

Brown, Wendy. *States of Injury: Power and Freedom in Late Modernity.* Princeton: Princeton University Press, 1995.

——. "Wounded Attachments." *Political Theory* 21.3 (August 1993): 390–410.

Buck-Morss, Susan. "Visual Empire." *Diacritics* 37.2–3: 171–98.

Bully. Dir. Lee Hirsch. Perf. Ja'Meya Jackson, Kelby Johnson, Lona Johnson. The Bully Project, Where We Live Films, 2011.

The Bully Project. http://www.thebullyproject.com/ (12 December 2014).

"Bush: Kyoto Treaty Would Have Hurt Economy." MSNBC.com Politics, 30 June 2005. http://www.msnbc.msn.com/id/8422343/ns/politics/t/bush-kyoto-treaty-would-have-hurt-economy/ (15 September 2011).

Bush, Matthew. *Pragmatic Passions: Melodrama and Latin American Social Narrative.* Madrid, Frankfurt: Iberoamericana, Vervuert, 2014.

Calderón Hinojosa, Felipe. "XI. Mensaje del Presidente Calderón en el marco de su Segundo Informe de Gobierno." *Lupa Ciudadana*, 4 September 2008. http://www.lupaciudadana.com.mx/SACSCMS/XStatic/lupa/template/declaracion_detalle.aspx?n=36956 (15 September 2011).

——. "Eje 4. Sustentabilidad Ambiental." Plan Nacional de Desarrollo. *Presidencia de la República, México*, 2007. http://pnd.calderon.presidencia.gob.mx/sustentabilidad-ambiental.html (15 September 2011).

Campos, Marco Antonio. "El asesinato de Roque Dalton." *La Jornada Semanal* 977 (24 November 2013). http://www.jornada.unam.mx/2013/11/24/sem-marco.html (18 April 2015).

Caparrós, Martín. *Contra el cambio: Un hiperviaje al apocalipsis climático.* Barcelona: Anagrama, 2010.

Cardoso, Fernando Henrique, and Enzo Faletto. *Dependencia y desarrollo en América Latina.* Mexico City: Siglo XXI, 1969.

Carson, Rachel. *Silent Spring.* New York: Houghton Mifflin, 1962.

Carveth, Rod, and James B. South. Mad Men *and Philosophy: Nothing Is as It Seems.* Hoboken, NJ: Wiley, 2010.

Cassidy, John. "Is America an Oligarchy?" *New Yorker,* 18 April 2014. http://www.newyorker.com/news/john-cassidy/is-america-an-oligarchy (19 April 2015).

Castells, Manuel. *The Rise of the Network Society.* Malden, MA: Wiley-Blackwell, 2010.

Castillo, José. "Carlos Reygadas" (interview). Trans. Camilo Detorrela. *BOMB* 111: Film (Spring 2010). http://bombsite.com/issues/111/articles/3452 (15 September 2011).

Cavarero, Adriana. *Horrorism: Naming Contemporary Violence.* Trans. William McCuaig. New York: Columbia University Press, 2009. (*Orrorismo: Overro della violenza sull'inerme.* Milan: Giangiacomo Feltrinelli, 2007.)

Cazuza. "O tempo não pára." *O tempo não pára*. Polygram, 1988.

Che: Part One. Dir. Steven Soderbergh. Perf. Benicio del Toro, Oscar Isaac, Demián Bichir, Julia Ormond. Wild Bunch, Telecinco, Laura Bickford, Morena, Ministerio de Cultura, Picaso, Guerrilla, Section Eight, 2008.

Che: Part Two. Dir. Steven Soderbergh. Perf. Benicio del Toro, Demián Bichir, Franka Potente. Wild Bunch, Telecinco, Laura Bickford, Morena, Ministerio de Cultura, Guerrilla, Londra, 2008.

Chevron. "Conservation—Chevron Corporate Advertisement." YouTube (Chevron), 2 August 2010. http://www.youtube.com/user/Chevron?gclid= CJOH4tCHvKQCFc9L5QodVVo71A#p/c/F23280D7E4254DAC/7/ YEmoN9CdqOE (15 September 2011).

———. "Tomorrow—Chevron Corporate Advertisement." YouTube (Chevron), 4 August 2010. http://www.youtube.com/user/Chevron?gclid=CJOH4tCH-vKQCFc9L5QodVVo71A#p/c/F23280D7E4254DAC/14/1jnFNRdfvyc (15 September 2011).

———. "We Are Chevron Latin America—Chevron Corporate Advertisement." You-Tube (Chevron), 2 August 2010. http://www.youtube.com/user/Chevron? gclid=CJOH4tCHvKQCFc9L5QodVVo71A#p/c/F23280D7E4254DAC/10/ _DcIc3bc5fQ (15 September 2011).

———. "We treat the land like we live here. Because we do." Chevron Human Energy. Banner ad in the *Washington Post*. n.d. http://www.washingtonpost. com/blogs/worldviews/wp/2014/11/17/operation-carwash-in-brazil-causes-normally-staid-business-meeting-to-go-off-script/ (30 November 2014).

Un chien andalou. Dir. Luis Buñuel and Salvador Dalí. Perf. Pierre Batcheff, Simone Mareuil. Luis Buñuel, 1929.

Children of Men. Dir. Alfonso Cuarón. Perf. Julianne Moore, Clive Owen, Chiwetel Ejiofor, Clare-Hope Ashitey, Michael Caine. Universal, Strike, Hit & Run, 2006.

Ching, Erik, Christina Buckley, and Angélica Lozano-Alonso. *Reframing Latin America: A Cultural Theory Reading of the Nineteenth and Twentieth Centuries*. Austin: University of Texas Press, 2007.

Christie, Deborah, and Sarah Juliet Lauro, eds. *Better Off Dead: The Evolution of the Zombie as Post-Human*. New York: Fordham University Press, 2011.

La Ciénaga. Dir. Lucrecia Martel. Perf. Mercedes Morán, Gabriela Borges, Martín Adjemián. 4k, Wanda Visión, Code Red, Cuatro Cabezas, TS Productions, 2001.

A Civil Action. Dir. Steven Zaillian. Perf. John Travolta, Robert Duvall, Kathleen Quinlan. Touchstone, Paramount, Wildwood, Scott Rudin, 1998.

Clough, Patricia Ticineto, and Jean Halley, eds. *The Affective Turn: Theorizing the Social*. Durham, NC: Duke University Press, 2007.

Coca-Cola. "Candles." (McCann Erickson, New York) 1977.

———. "Encuentro." Dir. Andy Fogwill (McCann Erickson, Madrid). 2009. You-Tube (cocacola), 30 June 2010. http://www.youtube.com/watch?v=Vi5qqvuex-GU (15 September 2011).

———. "Hilltop." Dir. Roberto Malenotti (McCann Erickson, New York). 1971. In Ted Ryan, "The Making of 'I'd Like to Buy the World a Coke.' *Coca-Cola Journey*, 1 January 2012. http://www.coca-colacompany.com/stories/coke-lo-re-hilltop-story (28 April 2015).

———. "The Library." Dir. Jorge Calleja (Weiden+Kennedy, Amsterdam). 2009. You-Tube (cocacola), 4 August 2009. http://www.youtube.com/watch?v=rKVokR6I-hos (15 September 2011.).

———. "Smile-izer." mycoke.com, 2010. http://www.mycoke.com/htmls/smileizer/Smileizer (15 September 2011).

"Coca-Cola: Encounter." *Shape+Colour*, 13 March 2009. http://shapeandcolour.wordpress.com/2009/03/13/coca-cola-encounter/ (15 September 2011).

Colás, Santiago. "Of Creole Symptoms, Cuban Fantasies, and Other Postcolonial Ideologies." *Publication of the Modern Language Association* 110.3 (May 1995): 382–96.

"Collective Wisdom: 'We Are Smarter Than Me.'" National Public Radio, 1 November 2007. http://www.npr.org/templates/story/story.php?storyId=15817758 (15 September 2011).

The Colony. Perf. Michael Raines, John Valencia, Becka Adams. Discovery Channel, 2009–2010.

Connors, Will, Paulo Trevisani, and Paul Kiernan. "Petrobras Scandal Widens, Earnings Delayed: Former Engineering Director at Brazil's Oil Firm Arrested Along with 17 Others; Shares Plunge." *Wall Street Journal*, 14 November 2014. http://online.wsj.com/articles/petrobras-former-director-arrested-in-corruption-investigation-1415968811 (30 November 2014).

Coronil, Fernando. "The Future in Question: History and Utopia in Latin America (1989–2010)." In Craig Calhoun and Georgi Derluguian, eds., *Business as Usual: The Roots of the Global Financial Meltdown*, 231–92. New York: New York University Press, 2011.

The Corporation. Dir. Mark Achbar and Jennifer Abbott. Perf. Mikela J. Mikael, Rob Beckwermert, Christopher Gora. Big Picture Media Corporation, 2003.

Corrales, Javier. "The Gatekeeper State: Limited Economic Reforms and Regime Survival in Cuba, 1989–2002." *Latin American Research Review* 39.2 (2004): 35–65.

Crude. Dir. Joe Berlinger. Perf. Pablo Fajardo, Steven Donziger, Trudi Styles. Entendre, Radical Media, Red Envelope, Third Eye, 2009.

Dalton, Roque. *Poemas clandestinos.* San Salvador: Universitaria, 1982 [1974].

Damasio, Antonio. *Descartes' Error: Emotion, Reason, and the Human Brain.* New York: Harper Perennial, 1995.

———. *Feeling of What Happens: Body and Emotion in the Making of Consciousness.* New York: Houghton Mifflin Harcourt, 1999.

———. *Looking for Spinoza: Joy, Sorrow, and the Feeling Brain*. Orlando, FL: Harcourt, 2003.

Dargis, Manohla. "Action!" (review of *The Hurt Locker*). *New York Times*, 21 June 2009. http://www.nytimes.com/2009/06/21/movies/21darg.html (15 September 2011).

Darwin, Charles. *The Expression of the Emotions in Man and Animals*. Ed. Paul Ekman. Oxford: Oxford University Press, 1998 [1872].

DasGupta, Sayantani. "(Re)Conceiving the Surrogate: Maternity, Race, and Reproductive Technologies in Alfonso Cuarón's *Children of Men*." In Marcelline Block and Angela Laflen, eds., *Gender Scripts in Medicine and Narrative*, 178–211. Newcastle upon Tyne: Cambridge Scholars, 2010.

Dawidoff, Nicholas. "The Civil Heretic." *New York Times Magazine*, 25 March 2009, 1–8. http://www.nytimes.com/2009/03/29/magazine/29Dyson-t.html (15 September 2011).

Dawkins, Richard. *The Selfish Gene*. Oxford: Oxford University Press, 2006 [1976].

Dawn of the Dead. Dir. George A. Romero. Perf. David Emge, Ken Foree, Scott H. Reiniger. Laurel Group, 1978.

The Decline of Western Civilization Part II: The Metal Years. Dir. Penelope Spheeris. Perf. Steven Tyler, Joe Perry, Alice Cooper. New Line Cinema, 1988.

de la Campa, Román. *Latin Americanism*. Minneapolis: University of Minnesota Press, 1999.

Deleuze, Gilles and Félix Guattari. *A Thousand Plateaus: Capitalism and Schizophrenia*. Trans. Brian Massumi. Minneapolis: University of Minnesota Press, 1987. (*Mille plateaux: capitalisme et schizophrénie*. Paris: Minuit, 1980.)

———. *Anti-Oedipus: Capitalism and Schizophrenia*. Trans. Robert Hurley, Mark Seem, and Helen R. Lane. Minneapolis: University of Minnesota Press, 1977. (*L'Anti-Oedipe: capitalisme et schizophrénie*. Paris: Minuit, 1972.)

Deleyto, Celestino, and María del Mar Azcona. *Alejandro González Iñárritu*. Urbana: University of Illinois Press, 2010.

Dependencia sexual. Dir. Rodrigo Bellott. Perf. Alexandra Aponte, Roberto Urbina, Jorge Antonio Saavedra, Ronica V. Reddick, Matthew Guida. BoSD, Bods, 2003.

Derrida, Jacques. "The Animal that Therefore I Am (More to Follow)." Trans. David Wills. *Critical Inquiry* 28.2 (Winter 2002): 369–418. ("L'animal que donc je suis [à suivre]." In *L'Animal autobiographique: Autour de Jacques Derrida*, 251–301. Ed. Marie-Louise Mallet. Paris: Galilée, 1999.)

———. "Structure, Sign and Play in the Discourse of the Human Sciences" ("La structure, le signe et le jeu dans le discours des sciences humaines," 1966). Trans. Alan Bass. In *Writing and Difference*, 278–95. Chicago: University of Chicago Press, 1967.

Después de Lucía. Dir. Michel Franco. Perf. Tessa Ia, Hernán Mendoza, Gonzalo Vega, Jr. Pop Films, Filmadora Nacional, Lemon Films, 2012.

de Waal, Frans. *The Age of Empathy: Nature's Lessons for a Kinder Society*. New York: Harmony, 2009.

———. *The Bonobo and the Atheist: In Search of Humanism Among the Primates*. New York: Norton, 2013.

———. *Primates and Philosophers: How Morality Evolved*. Ed. Stephen Macedo and Josiah Ober. Princeton: Princeton University Press, 2006.

———. "Putting the Altruism Back into Altruism: The Evolution of Empathy." *Annual Review of Psychology* 59 (January 2008): 279–300.

Diarios de motocicleta. Dir. Walter Salles. Perf. Gael García Bernal, Rodrigo de la Serna, Mercedes Morán. Focus Features, 2004.

La dignidad de los nadies. Dir. and perf. Fernando "Pino" Solanas. Cinesur, 2005.

Dooley, Roger. *Brainfluence: 100 Ways to Persuade and Convince Consumers with Neuromarketing*. Hoboken, NJ: Wiley, 2011.

Draper, Robert. "Obama's BFF." *New York Times Magazine*, 26 July 2009. http://query.nytimes.com/gst/fullpage.html?res=9903E3DA143AF935A15754C0A96F-9C8B63 (15 September 2011).

Du Plessis, Erik. *The Advertised Mind: Groundbreaking Insights Into How Our Brains Respond to Advertising*. London: Kogan Page, 2008.

———. *The Branded Mind: What Neuroscience Really Tells Us About the Puzzle of the Brain and the Brand*. London: Kogan Page, 2011.

Dupré, Louis. *The Enlightenment and the Intellectual Foundations of Modern Culture*. New Haven: Yale University Press, 2004.

Dyce, Andrew. "3 'Avatar' Sequels to Be Released in 2016, 2017 & 2018." Screen Rant, n.d. http://screenrant.com/avatar-2-3-4-sequels-2016-2017-2018/ (18 April 2015).

Dyer-Witheford, Nick. *Cyber-Marx: Cycles and Circuits of Struggle in High-Technology Capitalism*. Urbana: University of Illinois Press, 1999.

Eagleton, Terry. *The Meaning of Life*. New York: Oxford University Press, 2007.

Eakin, Emily. "I Feel, Therefore I Am." *New York Times*, 19 April 2003. http://www.nytimes.com/2003/04/19/books/i-feel-therefore-i-am.html (23 October 2011).

eBay. "What is ReLove?" Blog post by jillprimost. 1 April 2013. http://green.ebay.com/greenteam/blog/Introducing-Relove/11702 (14 April 2013).

Edgerton, Gary R., ed. Mad Men: *Dream Come True TV*. New York: I. B. Taurus, 2011.

Egner, Jeremy. "Seeing History in 'Mad Men.'" *New York Times*, 16 July 2010. www.nytimes.com/interactive/2010/07/16/arts/television/20100718-mad-men-timeline.html (25 November 2014).

Ekman, Paul. *The Face of Man: Expressions of Universal Emotions in a New Guinea Village*. New York: Garland, 1980.

Elkington, John. *Cannibals with Forks: The Triple Bottom Line of Twenty-First Century Business*. Bloomington, MN: Capstone, 1997.

Eltit, Diamela. *Emergencias: escritos sobre literatura, arte y política.* Ed. Leonidas Morales. Santiago: Ariel, Grupo Planeta, 2000.

———. *Mano de obra.* Santiago: Seix Barral, 2002.

Enemies of War. PBS, n.d. http://www.pbs.org/itvs/enemiesofwar (15 September 2011).

"Enough About You." *Utne Reader,* May–June 2011. http://www.utne.com/arts/enough-about-you-christopher-lasch-culture-of-narcissism.aspx (15 September 2015)

"Entrevista con Carlos Reygadas." *Primordiales,* n.d. http://www.primordiales.com.ar/entrevistas/entrevista_con_carlos_reygadas.htm (15 September 2011).

Equilibrium. Dir. Kurt Wimmer. Perf. Christian Bale, Sean Bean, Emily Watson. Dimension, Blue Tulip, 2002.

ER. Creator Michael Crichton. Perf. Anthony Edwards, George Clooney, Julianna Margulies. NBC, 1994–2009.

Erin Brockovich. Dir. Steven Soderbergh. Perf. Julia Roberts, Albert Finney, David Brisbin. Jersey, 2000.

Escobar Galindo, David. *Duelo ceremonial por la violencia.* San Salvador: Universitaria, 1971.

———. "El duelo por el 'Duelo . . . '" laprensagráfica.com, 20 May 2006. http://archive.laprensa.com.sv/20060520/opinion/483679.asp (15 September 2011).

Eustace, Nicole. *Passion Is the Gale: Emotion, Power, and the Coming of the American Revolution.* Chapel Hill: University of North Carolina Press, 2008.

Ever Amado. Dir. Víctor Ruano. Perf. Ernesto Hernández, Juliana Works. Santasombra, 2007. http://www.santasombra.com/html/ever_amado.html (15 September 2011).

Ewen, Stuart. *PR! A Social History of Spin.* 1996. New York: Basic Books, 1996.

Fanon, Frantz. *The Wretched of the Earth.* Trans. Constance Farrington. New York: Grove, 1963. (*Les Damnés de la terre.* Paris: Maspero, 1961.)

Farah H., Ivonne, and Luciano Vasapollo, eds. *Vivir bien: ¿paradigma no capitalista?* La Paz: CIDES-UMSA, Sapienza Università di Roma, Oxfam, 2011. http://www.slideshare.net/ecuadordemocratico/libro-vivir-bien-paradigma-no-capitalista (15 September 2011).

Feig, Barry. *Hot Button Marketing: Push the Emotional Buttons that Get People to Buy.* Cincinnati: Adams Media, 2006.

———. *Marketing Straight to the Heart: From New Product Development to Advertising—How Smart Companies Use the Power of Emotion to Win Loyal Customers.* New York: AMACOM, 1997.

FernGully: The Last Rainforest. Dir. Bill Kroyer. Perf. Samantha Mathis, Christian Slater, Robin Williams. FAI, Youngheart, 1992.

Festa, Lynn M. *Sentimental Figures of Empire in Eighteenth-Century Britain and France.* Baltimore: Johns Hopkins University Press, 2006.

Fields, R. Douglas. *From Dementia to Schizophrenia: How New Discoveries About the Brain Are Revolutionizing Medicine and Science.* New York: Simon and Schuster, 2009.

Fight Club. Dir. David Fincher. Perf. Brad Pitt, Edward Norton, Helena Bonham Carter. Fox 2000, Regency, Linson, Atman, Knickerbocker, Taurus, 1999.

Fineman, Martha Albertson. "The Vulnerable Subject and the Responsive State." *Emory Law Journal* 60.2 (2010): 251–75.

Finfrock, Jesse. "Q&A: John Elkington." *Mother Jones,* November/December 2008. http://motherjones.com/environment/2008/10/qa-john-elkington (15 September 2011).

Fisher, Eran. *Media and New Capitalism in the Digital Age: The Spirit of Networks.* New York: Palgrave Macmillan, 2010.

Fitzgerald, F. Scott. *The Great Gatsby.* New York: Scribner's, 1925.

"*Forbes* Global 2000 Leading Companies." May 2014. http://www.forbes.com/global2000/list/ (30 November 2014).

Foucault, Michel. *The Archaeology of Knowledge.* Trans. A. M. Sheridan Smith. New York: Vintage, 2010. (*L'Archéologie du savoir.* Paris: Gallimard, 1969.)

———. *The Birth of Biopolitics: Lectures at the Collège de France, 1978–1979.* Ed. Michel Senellart, François Ewald, and Alessandro Fontana. Trans. Graham Burchell. New York: Palgrave Macmillan, 2008. (*Naissance de la biopolitique: Cours au Collège de France, 1978–1979.* Ed. Michel Senellart. Paris: Gallimard, Seuil, 2004.)

———. "The Confession of the Flesh" ("Le jeu de Michel Foucault"). Trans. Colin Gordon. *Power/Knowledge: Selected Interviews and Other Writings, 1972–1977,* 194–228. Ed. Colin Gordon. New York: Pantheon, 1980.

———. *The History of Sexuality:* vol. 1: *An Introduction.* Trans. Robert Hurley. New York: Vintage, 1990. (*La Volonté de savoir.* Paris: Gallimard, 1976.)

———. *The Order of Things: An Archaeology of the Human Sciences.* Trans. Alan Sheridan. New York: Vintage, 1994. (*Les Mots et les choses: Une archéologie des sciences humaines.* Paris: Gallimard, 1966.)

Fox, George. *The line of righteousness and justice stretched forth over all merchants, &c. Selections from the Epistles of George Fox,* 73–79. Ed. Samuel Tuke. London: Edward Marsh, 1848 [1661]. https://play.google.com/store/books/details/Samuel_Tuke_Selections_from_the_Epistles_of_George?id=AXRCAAAAcAAJ (18 April 2015).

Franco, Jean. *Cruel Modernity.* Durham, NC: Duke University Press, 2013.

Frank, André Gunder. *Capitalism and Underdevelopment in Latin America: Historical Studies of Chile and Brazil.* New York: Monthly Review Press, 1967.

Frazer, Michael L. *The Enlightenment of Sympathy: Justice and the Moral Sentiments in the Eighteenth Century and Today.* New York: Oxford University Press, 2010.

Friedman, Thomas L. "Something's Happening Here." *New York Times,* 11 October 2011. http://www.nytimes.com/2011/10/12/opinion/theres-something-happening-here.html (23 October 2011).

Fukuyama, Francis. *Our Posthuman Future: Consequences of the Biotechnology Revolution*. New York: Farrar, Straus and Giroux, 2000.

——. *The End of History and the Last Man*. New York: Free Press, 1992.

——. "The End of History?" *National Interest* 16 (Summer 1989): 3–35.

Galeano, Eduardo. *Las venas abiertas de América Latina*. Mexico City: Siglo XXI, 1971.

Galindo, Mario and Inés Muñoz. "Entrevista al subcomandante Marcos." *Archivo Maru*. 1 January 1994. http://www.bibliotecas.tv/chiapas/ene94/01ene94a .html (15 September 2011).

Gallagher, John, and Ronald Robinson. "The Imperialism of Free Trade." *Economic History Review*, n.s. 6.1 (1953): 1–15.

Galloway, Alexander R., and Eugene Thacker. *The Exploit: A Theory of Networks*. Minneapolis: University of Minnesota Press, 2007.

García Espinosa, Julio. "Por un cine imperfecto." (1969.) In Fundación Mexicana de Cineastas, ed., *Hojas de cine: Testimonios y documentos del Nuevo Cine Latinoamericano*, 3:63–77. Mexico City: Secretaría de Educación Pública, Universidad Autónoma Metropolitana, Fundación Mexicana de Cineastas, 1988. Biblioteca Digital Centro de Información e Investigaciones, Fundación del Nuevo Cine Latinoamericano, 2011. http://www.cinelatinoamericano.org/biblioteca/fondo. aspx?cod=2333 (15 September 2011).

García Lorca, Federico. "New York: Oficina y denuncia" (*Poeta en Nueva York*, 1929). In *Antología comentada*, vol. 1: *Poesía*, 240–42. Ed. Eutimio Martín. Madrid: la Torre, 1988.

The Garden. Dir. Scott Hamilton Kennedy. Perf. Danny Glover, Daryl Hannah, Antonio Villaraigosa. Black Valley, 2008.

GasLand. Dir. and perf. Josh Fox. HBO, International WOW, 2010.

Gibbs, Nancy. "Emotional Intelligence: The EQ Factor." *Time*, 2 October 1995. http://www.time.com/time/magazine/article/0,9171,983503,00.html (15 September 2011).

Gilens, Martin, and Benjamin I. Page. "Testing Theories of American Politics: Elites, Interest Groups, and Average Citizens." *Perspectives on Politics* 12.3 (September 2014): 564–81.

Gjelten, Tom. "Cyberwarrior Shortage Threatens National Security." National Public Radio, 16 April 2010. http://www.npr.org/templates/story/story.php?story-Id=128574055 (15 September 2011).

Gobé, Marc and Sergio Zyman. *Emotional Branding: The New Paradigm for Connecting Brands to People*. New York: Allworth, 2001.

Goldstein, Jacob. "The SEC's Case Against Goldman Sachs." National Public Radio, 16 April 2010. http://www.npr.org/templates/story/story.php?story-Id=126046693&sc=nl&cc=nh-20100417 (15 September 2011).

Goleman, Daniel. *Emotional Intelligence: Why It Can Matter More Than IQ*. New York: Bantam, 1995.

González, Aníbal. *Love and Politics in the Contemporary Spanish American Novel.* Austin: University of Texas Press, 2010.

Goodlad, Lauren M. E., Lilya Kaganovsky, and Robert A. Rushing. "Introduction." In Lauren M. E. Goodlad, Lilya Kaganovsky, and Robert A. Rushing, eds., *Mad Men, Mad World: Sex, Politics, Style, and the 1960s,* 1–31. Durham, NC: Duke University Press, 2013.

Goodyear, Dana. "Man of Extremes: The Return of James Cameron." *New Yorker,* 26 October 2009. http://www.newyorker.com/reporting/2009/10/26/091026fa_fact_goodyear (15 September 2011).

Google. *Project Re: Brief.* "Advertising Reimagined: Coca-Cola 'Hilltop.'" n.d. http://www.projectrebrief.com/coke/ (28 April 2015).

Gore, Al. *The Assault on Reason.* New York: Penguin, 2007.

Graff Zivin, Erin. *Figurative Inquisitions: Conversion, Torture, and Truth in the Luso-Hispanic Atlantic.* Evanston, IL: Northwestern University Press, 2014.

——, ed. *The Ethics of Latin American Literary Criticism: Reading Otherwise.* New York: Palgrave Macmillan, 2007.

Grandin, Greg. *Empire's Workshop: Latin America, the United States, and the Rise of the New Imperialism.* New York: Metropolitan, 2006.

Greenade. http://www.greenade.cl/ (15 September 2011).

Gregg, Melissa, and Gregory J. Seigworth, eds. *The Affect Theory Reader.* Durham, NC: Duke University Press, 2010.

Griffiths, Richard T. "History of the Internet, Internet for Historians (and Just About Everyone Else)." *Universiteit Leiden.* http://www.let.leidenuniv.nl/history/ivh/frame_theorie.html (15 September 2011).

Griswold, Eliza. "How 'Silent Spring' Ignited the Environmental Movement." *New York Times.* 21 September 2012. www.nytimes.com/2012/09/23/magazine/how-silent-spring-ignited-the-environmental-movement.html (30 November 2014).

Guevara, Ernesto "Che." "Mensaje a los pueblos del mundo a través de la Tricontinental." *Tricontinental* special supplement, 1967. Cátedra Ernesto Che Guevara. *Rebelión,* 28 July 2002. http://www.rebelion.org/hemeroteca/argentina/tricontinental280702.htm (15 September 2011).

——. "El socialismo y el hombre en Cuba." 1965. Archivo Che Guevara, Marxists Internet Archive—Sección en español. n.d. https://www.marxists.org/espanol/guevara/65-socyh.htm (25 November 2014).

Guns N' Roses. *Appetite for Destruction.* Geffen, 1987.

Gunther, Marc. "Stonyfield Stirs Up the Yogurt Market." CNN Money, 4 January 2008. http://money.cnn.com/2008/01/03/news/companies/gunther_yogurt.fortune/index.htm (15 September 2011).

Haden, Petra. "Let Your Love Flow." Toyota, 2009. http://www.toyota.com/prius-hybrid/commercial.html (15 September 2011).

Halberstam, Judith (Jack). "Learning to Unlearn." MLA Presidential Forum: "Language, Literature, Learning." Chicago, 2011.

Hamilton, Jon. "Einstein's Brain Unlocks Some Mysteries of the Mind." National Public Radio, 2 June 2010. http://www.npr.org/templates/story/story.php?storyId=126229305 (15 September 2011).

Handel. "Alexander's Feast" (1736). Perf. Harry Christophers, the Sixteen & the Symphony of Harmony and Invention. In *Children of Men (Music from the Motion Picture)*. Varèse Sarabande, 2006.

Hansen, Flemming, Sverre Riis Christensen, and Steen Lundsteen. *Emotion, Advertising, and Consumer Choice*. Copenhagen: Copenhagen Business School Press, 2007.

Happy Feet. Dir. George Miller, Warren Coleman, and Judy Morris. Perf. Elijah Wood, Brittany Murphy, Hugh Jackman. Warner Bros., Village Roadshow, Kennedy Miller, Animal Logic, Kingdom Feature, 2006.

Hardt, Michael. "About Love" (six parts). European Graduate School, 2007. YouTube (egsvideo), 24 June 2007. http://www.youtube.com/watch?v=ioopkoppabI (15 September 2011).

———. Transcription of intervention in "Otro mundo, otra política." Primer Festival Mundial de la Digna Rabia, San Cristóbal de las Casas, Chiapas, Mexico. 4 January 2009. Centro de Documentación sobre Zapatismo, n.d. http://www.cedoz.org/site/content.php?doc=955&cat=124 (15 September 2011).

Hardt, Michael, and Antonio Negri. *Commonwealth*. Cambridge: Harvard University Press. 2009.

———. *Empire*. Cambridge: Harvard University Press, 2000.

———. *Multitude*. Cambridge: Harvard University Press, 2004.

Harvey, David. *A Brief History of Neoliberalism*. Oxford: Oxford University Press, 2005.

Healthiest Nation—Move. U.S. Healthiest. YouTube (HealthiestNation), 25 September 2008. http://www.youtube.com/watch?v=rIZ56OrLQ5k (15 September 2011).

Hedges, Chris. *War Is a Force That Gives Us Meaning*. New York: PublicAffairs, 2002.

Hein, Kenneth. "Nike Just Does It Anyway." *Adweek*, 17 July 2008. http://www.adweek.com/news/advertising-branding/nike-just-does-it-anyway-104309 (15 September 2011).

Heller-Roazen, Daniel. *The Inner Touch: Archaeology of a Sensation*. New York: Zone, 2007.

Hello, Dolly! Dir. Gene Kelly. Perf. Barbra Streisand, Walter Matthau, Michael Crawford. Chenault, Twentieth Century Fox, 1969.

Herman, Edward S., and Robert Waterman McChesney. *The Global Media: The Missionaries of Corporate Capitalism*. London: Cassell, 1998.

Hernandez, Melanie, and David Thomas Holmberg. "'We'll start over like Adam and Eve': The Subversion of Classic American Mythology." In *Analyzing* Mad Men: *Critical Essays on the Television Series,* 15–44. Ed. Scott F. Stoddart. Jefferson, NC: McFarland, 2011.

Herrera Vegas, Rodrigo. "Qué es la sustentabilidad." *lanacion.com,* 16 October 2009. http://www.lanacion.com.ar/1186719-que-es-la-sustentabilidad (15 September 2011).

Hill, Dan. *About Face: The Secrets of Emotionally Effective Advertising.* London: Kogan Page, 2010.

Hill, Dan, and Sam Simon. *Emotionomics: Leveraging Emotions for Business Success.* London: Kogan Page, 2009.

The Hillside Singers. "I'd Like to Teach the World to Sing (In Perfect Harmony)." *I'd Like to Teach the World to Sing.* Metromedia. 1971.

La hora de los hornos: Notas y testimonios sobre el neocolonialismo, la violencia y la liberación. Dir. Fernando "Pino" Solanas and Octavio Getino. Grupo Cine Liberación, 1968.

Hume, David. *A Treatise of Human Nature.* Ed. David Fate Norton and Mary J. Norton. Oxford: Oxford University Press, 2000 [1739]. Project Gutenberg eBook, 13 February 2010. http://www.gutenberg.org/files/4705/4705-h/4705-h.htm (15 September 2011).

The Hurt Locker. Dir. Kathryn Bigelow. Perf. Jeremy Renner, Anthony Mackie, Brian Geraghty. Voltage, Grosvenor Park, Film Capital Europe Funds, First Light, Kingsgate, Summit, 2008.

Iacoboni, Marco. *Mirroring People: The Science of Empathy and How We Connect with Others.* New York: Picador, 2009. (*Mirroring People: The New Science of How We Connect with Others.* New York: Farrar, Straus and Giroux, 2008.)

Illouz, Eva. *Cold Intimacies: The Making of Emotional Capitalism.* Cambridge, UK: Polity, 2007.

An Inconvenient Truth. Dir. Davis Guggenheim. Perf. Al Gore, Billy West. Lawrence Bender; Participant, 2006.

"Informe de Sostenibilidad 2008 de Endesa Chile." United Nations Global Compact. http://www.unglobalcompact.org/COPs/notable/1952 (15 September 2011).

InfoSur: Sitio oficial del partido Proyecto Sur. "Solanas visitó Villa del Parque." 13 May 2011. http://infosur.info/?p=7394 (15 September 2011).

Into the Wild. Dir. Sean Penn. Perf. Emile Hirsch, Vince Vaugh, Catherine Keener. Paramount Vantage, Art Linson, Into the Wild, River Road, 2007.

Jally, Sut. "Advertising at the Edge of Apocalypse." In *Critical Studies in Media Commercialism,* 27–39. Ed. Robin Andersen and Lance Strate. New York: Oxford University Press, 2000.

James, P. D. *The Children of Men.* New York: Knopf, 1992.

Japón. Dir. Carlos Reygadas. Perf. Alejandro Ferretis, Magdalena Flores, Yolanda Villa. No Dream, Mantarraya, Hubert Bals Fund, Solaris, Instituto Mexicano de Cinematografía, 2002.

Johnson, Lauren. "PayPal Strikes Blow Against Apple in New Ad Campaign." *Adweek,* 16 September 2014. http://www.adweek.com/news/advertising-branding/paypal-strikes-blow-against-apple-new-ad-campaign-160163 (18 April 2015).

Joyce, Christopher. "Worries Over Water as Natural Gas Fracking Expands." National Public Radio, 2 August 2011. http://www.npr.org/2011/08/02/138820966/worries-over-water-as-natural-gas-fracking-expands&sc=nl&cc=nh-20110802 (15 September 2011).

Juan de los muertos. Dir. Alejandro Brugués. Perf. Alexis Díaz de Villegas, Jorge Molina, Andros Perrugoría. La Zanfoña Producciones, Producciones de la 5ta Avenida, 2011.

Kessler, David. *The End of Overeating: Taking Control of the Insatiable American Appetite.* Emmaus, PA: Rodale, 2009.

——. *Your Food Is Fooling You: How Your Brain Is Hijacked by Sugar, Fat, and Salt.* New York: Roaring Brook, 2012.

The Killers. "All These Things that I've Done." *Hot Fuss.* Island Def Jam Music, 2004.

The Kills. "Wait." *Keep on Your Mean Side.* Domino, 2003.

Klein, Naomi. *The Shock Doctrine: The Rise of Disaster Capitalism.* New York: Metropolitan, 2007.

Koop. "Strange Love." *Koop Islands.* Diesel Music, 2003.

Kramer, Adam D. I., Jamie E. Guillory, and Jeffrey T. Hancock. "Experimental Evidence of Massive-Scale Emotional Contagion Through Social Networks." *Proceedings of the National Academy of Sciences* 111.24 (June 17, 2014): 8788–90. http://www.pnas.org/content/111/24/8788.full (18 April 2015).

Krishna, R. Jai. "Sandberg: Facebook Study Was 'Poorly Communicated.'" *Wall Street Journal Digits,* 2 July 2014. http://blogs.wsj.com/digits/2014/07/02/facebooks-sandberg-apologizes-for-news-feed-experiment/ (2 November 2014).

Krugman, Paul. "Why We're in a New Gilded Age." Review of *Capital in the Twenty-First Century,* Thomas Piketty. *New York Review of Books,* 8 May 2014. http://www.nybooks.com/articles/archives/2014/may/08/thomas-piketty-new-gilded-age/ (19 April 2015).

Krugman, Paul and Robin Wells. "The Busts Keep Getting Bigger: Why?" *New York Review of Books,* 14 July 2011, 1–2. http://www.nybooks.com/articles/archives/2011/jul/14/busts-keep-getting-bigger-why/ (15 September 2011).

Labanyi, Jo. "Doing Things: Emotion, Affect, and Materiality." *Journal of Spanish Cultural Studies* 11.3–4 (2010): 223–33.

Lair, Daniel J. and Daniel S. Strasser. "*Mad Men*'s Mad Men: Multiple Masculinities and the 'Masculinity-in-Crisis' Narrative." In Danielle M. Stern, Jimmie Manning, and Jennifer C. Dunn, eds., with assistance from Igor Ristic. *Lucky Strikes and a Three Martini Lunch: Thinking About Television's* Mad Men, 177–89. Newcastle upon Tyne: Cambridge Scholars, 2012.

Lane, Anthony. "Edge of Dark: 'Blindness' and 'Rachel Getting Married.'" *New Yorker,* 6 October 2008. http://www.newyorker.com/arts/critics/cinema/2008/10/06/081006crci_cinema_lane (15 September 2011).

Lasch, Christopher. *The Culture of Narcissism: American Life in an Age of Diminishing Expectations.* New York: Norton, 1991 [1979].

Latouche, Serge. "Serge Latouche: Gran ideólogo del decrecimiento" (two parts). YouTube (SubtUtiles), 19 May 2008. http://www.youtube.com/watch?v=fvBsi-P3hAmA (15 September 2011).

——. "Et la décroissance sauvera le Sud . . . " *Le Monde diplomatique,* November 2004. http://www.monde-diplomatique.fr/2004/11/LATOUCHE/11652 (15 September 2011).

Latour, Bruno. *Reassembling the Social: An Introduction to Actor-Network-Theory.* New York: Oxford University Press, 2005.

Leonard, Annie. *The Story of Stuff: How Our Obsession with Stuff Is Trashing the Planet, Our Communities, and Our Health—and a Vision for Change.* New York: Free Press, 2010.

——. "The Story of Stuff." *The Story of Stuff Project,* 2007. www.thestoryofstuff.com (15 September 2011).

Leys, Ruth. "The Turn to Affect: A Critique." *Critical Inquiry* 37 (Spring 2011): 434–72.

Libert, Barry and Jon Spector. *We Are Smarter than Me: How to Unleash the Power of Crowds in Your Business.* Upper Saddle River, NJ: Pearson Prentice Hall, 2007.

Licklider, Joseph C. R. "Memorandum for Members and Affiliates of the Intergalactic Computer Network." 23 April 1963. Essays. Kurzweil: Accelerating Intelligence, 11 December 2001. http://www.kurzweilai.net/memorandum-for-members-and-affiliates-of-the-intergalactic-computer-network (15 September 2011).

Lie to Me. Created by Samuel Baum. Perf. Tim Roth, Kelli Williams, Brendan Hines. Twentieth-Century Fox Television, 2009–11.

Loveday, Eric. "Whole Lotta Prius Love: Toyota's Hybrid Sales Top 3 Million Worldwide." *autobloggreen* 9 March 2011. http://green.autoblog.com/2011/03/09/prius-toyota-hybrid-sales-3-million/ (31 March 2013).

Ludmer, Josefina. "Literaturas postautónomas." *Ciberletras* 17 (July 2007). http://www.lehman.cuny.edu/ciberletras/v17/ludmer.htm (23 October 2011).

Macan-Markar, Marwaan. "En el fondo, el Banco Mundial no es verde." *Otramérica,* 11 April 2011. http://otramerica.com/radar/en-el-fondo-el-banco-mundial-no-es-verde/101 (15 September 2011).

Macarthur, Kate. "Coke Unveils New Ad Theme: 'Happiness in a Bottle.'" *Advertising Age,* 30 March 2006. http://adage.com/article/news/coke-unveils-ad-theme-happiness-a-bottle/108091/ (15 September 2011).

MacKenzie, Ian. "The Revolution Is Love." fiercelightfilms, 18 November 2011. http://www.youtube.com/watch?v=BRtc-k6dhgs (21 March 2013).

Mad Men. Created by Matthew Weiner. Perf. Jon Hamm, January Jones, John Slattery, Elisabeth Moss, Vincent Kartheiser, Christina Hendricks. American Movie Classics (AMC), 2007–15.

Madrick, Jeffrey G. Age of Greed: The Triumph of Finance and the Decline of America, 1970 to the Present. New York: Knopf, 2011.

———. "How Can the Economy Recover?" New York Review of Books, 23 December 2010, 1–3. http://www.nybooks.com/articles/archives/2010/dec/23/how-can-economy-recover/ (18 April 2015).

Madison, Lucy. "House Republicans Reject Climate Change Science." CBS News, 16 March 2011. http://www.cbsnews.com/8301-503544_162-20043909-503544.html (15 September 2011).

Manovich, Lev. "New Media from Borges to HTML." In Noah Wardrip-Fruin and Nick Montfort, eds., The New Media Reader, 13–25. Cambridge: MIT Press, 2003.

Mansell, Robin and Michele Javary. "New Media and the Forces of Capitalism." In Andrew Calabrese and Colin Sparks, eds., Toward a Political Economy of Culture: Capitalism and Communication in the Twenty-First Century, 228–43. Lanham, MD: Rowman and Littlefield, 2003.

Marcovitch, Heather, and Nancy E. Batty, eds. Mad Men, Women, and Children: Essays on Gender and Generation. Lanham, MD: Lexington, 2012.

Mariátegui, José Carlos. Siete ensayos de interpretación de la realidad peruana. Lima: Amauta, 1928.

Marks, Laura U. The Skin of the Film: Intercultural Cinema, Embodiment, and the Senses. Durham, NC: Duke University Press, 2000.

Marx, Karl, and Friedrich Engels. The German Ideology. Ed. C. J. Arthur. New York: International, 1970 [1845–46].

Massumi, Brian. Parables for the Virtual: Movement, Affect, Sensation. Durham, NC: Duke University Press, 2002.

McCready, Louise. "Dr. David Kessler, Author of The End of Overeating, on Why We Can't Stop Eating." Huffington Post, 6 May 2009. http://www.huffingtonpost.com/louise-mccready/d-kessler-author-of-emthe_b_195676.html (15 September 2011).

"McDonald's® Unveils 'i'm lovin' it™' Worldwide Brand Campaign; Superstar Justin Timberlake Featured in English Language Vocals." Highbeam Research, 2 September 2003. http://www.highbeam.com/doc/1G1-131665979.html (15 September 2011).

McDougall, Christopher. Born to Run: A Hidden Tribe, Superathletes, and the Greatest Race the World Has Never Seen. New York: Knopf Doubleday, 2009.

McRuer, Robert. "Compulsory Able-Bodiedness and Queer/Disabled Existence." In Lennard J. Davis, ed., *The Disability Studies Reader*, 383–92. 3d ed. New York: Routledge, 2010.

"Mediapost.com Names Subaru of America Automotive Marketer of the Year." *Subaru Global*. 17 Dec. 2008. http://www.subaru-global.com/news2008n000876.html (15 September 2011).

Memoria del saqueo. Dir. and perf. Fernando "Pino" Solanas. ADR, Centre National de la Cinématographie, Cinesur, 2004.

Mendelsohn, Daniel. "The Wizard" (review of *Avatar*). *New York Review of Books*, 25 March 2010, 1–3. http://www.nybooks.com/articles/archives/2010/mar/25/the-wizard/ (15 September 2011).

Menocal, María Rosa. *Shards of Love: Exile and the Origins of the Lyric*. Durham, NC: Duke University Press, 1994.

Messer, A'ndrea Elyse. "Women Leave Their Handprints on the Cave Wall." *Penn State News*, 15 October 2013. http://news.psu.edu/story/291423/2013/10/15/research/women-leave-their-handprints-cave-wall (18 April 2015).

Morales Aima, Evo. General Debate Statement for the Constitutional Republic of Bolivia. *United Nations General Assembly 61st Session*. 19 September 2006. http://www.un.org/webcast/ga/61/gastatement19.shtml (15 September 2011).

Moraña, Mabel, and Ignacio M. Sánchez Prado, eds. *El lenguaje de las emociones: Afecto y cultura en América Latina*. Madrid: Iberoamericana Verveurt, 2012.

Moreiras, Alberto. *The Exhaustion of Difference: The Politics of Latin American Cultural Studies*. Durham, NC: Duke University Press, 2001.

Moss, Michael. *Salt Sugar Fat: How the Food Giants Hooked Us*. New York: Random House, 2013.

Mundo grúa. Dir. Pablo Trapero. Perf. Luis Margani, Adriana Aizemberg, Daniel Valenzuela. Instituto Nacional de Cine y Artes Audiovisuales, Lita Stantic, Matanza, 1999.

"My Water's on Fire Tonight (The Fracking Song)." YouTube (davidmholmes), 10 May 2011. http://www.youtube.com/watch?v=timfvNgr_Q4 (15 September 2011).

Nancy, Jean-Luc. *Being Singular Plural*. Trans. Robert D. Richardson and Anne E. O'Byrne. Stanford: Stanford University Press, 2000. (*Être singulier pluriel*. Paris: Galilée, 1996.)

The New Seekers. "I'd Like to Teach the World to Sing (In Perfect Harmony)." *We'd Like to Teach the World to Sing*. Philips, 1971.

Newitz, Annalee. "When Will White People Stop Making Movies Like 'Avatar'?" *io9*. 18 December 2009. http://io9.com/5422666/when-will-white-people-stop-making-movies-like-avatar (15 September 2011).

Night of the Living Dead. Dir. George A. Romero. Perf. Duane Jones, Judith O'Dea, Karl Hardman. Image Ten, Laurel Group, Market Square Productions, Off Color Films, 1968.

Nike. "Courage." nike.com, 2008. http://www.nike.com/nikeos/p/nike/en_US/courage?p=courage (15 September 2011).

Nike+ Human Race. nike.com, 21 October 2009. http://nikerunning.nike.com/nikeos/p/nikeplus/en_US/humanrace/?id=race_day (31 July 2010).

Nissan. "Innovation for the Planet." nissanusa.com. http://www.nissanusa.com/leaf-electric-car/video/view/innovation_for_the_planet#/leaf-electric-car/video/view/innovation_for_the_planet (15 September 2011).

"Ni un metro más de soja: Pino lanza su corriente rural." Noticias Congreso Nacional, 21 February 2011. http://www.ncn.com.ar/08/noticiad.php?n=9862&sec=2&ssec=&s=noticiad (15 September 2011).

Nixon, Rob. *Slow Violence and the Environmentalism of the Poor.* Cambridge: Harvard University Press, 2011.

No. Dir. Pablo Larraín. Perf. Gael García Bernal, Alfredo Castro, Antonia Zegers. Fabula, Participant Media, Funny Balloons, Canana Films, 2010.

No Country for Old Men. Dir. Ethan Coen and Joel Coen. Perf. Tommy Lee Jones, Javier Bardem, Josh Brolin. Paramount Vantage, Miramax, Scott Rudin, Mike Zoss, 2007.

No Impact Man: The Documentary. Dir. Laura Gabbert and Justin Schein. Perf. Colin Beavan, Michelle Conlin. Eden Wurmfeld, Shadowbox, 2009.

Occupy Love. Dir. Velcro Ripper. Perf. Amr Adel, Angaangaq Angakkorsuaq, Colin Beavan. Fierce Love Films, 2012.

"Occupy Love." Facebook. https://www.facebook.com/occupylovefilm?ref=ts&-fref=ts (21 March 2013).

Occupy Wall Street. http://occupywallst.org/ (18 October 2011).

"Occupy Wall Street." Facebook. https://www.facebook.com/Gilded.Age?fref=ts (15 May 2013).

"Old Washington Consensus Is Over: Gordon Brown." *Pressrun.net,* 3 April 2009. http://www.pressrun.net/weblog/2009/04/old-washington-consensus-is-over-gordon-brown.html (15 September 2011).

Organizing for America. Project of the National Democratic Committee. N.d. http://my.barackobama.com/page/content/ofasplashpresident/ (27 November 2009).

Orr, Christopher. "The Mini-review: *The Hurt Locker.*" *New Republic,* 24 July 2009. http://www.tnr.com/blog/the-plank/the-mini-review-the-hurt-locker (15 September 2011).

O'Shaughnessy, John, and Nicholas Jackson O'Shaughnessy. *The Marketing Power of Emotion.* New York: Oxford University Press, 2002.

Oxford University Press. "Series in Affective Science." http://www.oup.com/us/ catalog/general/series/SeriesinAffectiveScience/ (23 October 2011).

Palmer, Sara. "Old, New, Borrowed and Blue: Compulsory Able-Bodiedness and Whiteness in *Avatar*." *Disability Studies Quarterly* 31.1 (2011). http://www.dsq-sds.org/article/view/1353/1473 (15 September 2011).

Pandemic Studios. *Full Spectrum Warrior*. 2003.

———. *Mercenaries 2: World in Flames*. 2008.

The Passion of the Christ. Dir. Mel Gibson. Perf. James Caviezel, Monica Bellucci, Maia Morgenstern. Newmarket, 2004.

Patnaik, Dev. *Wired to Care: How Companies Prosper When They Create Widespread Empathy*. Upper Saddle River, NJ: Financial Times, 2009.

PayPal. "PayPal Brand Campaign Puts People Back in Charge of Their Money: First Global Campaign in PayPal's History." Press Releases. 30 April 2014. https://www .paypal-media.com/press-releases/paypal-brand-campaign-puts-people-back-in.

———. "PayPal Voices." YouTube, 8 September 2014. http://www.adweek.com/ news/advertising-branding/paypal-strikes-blow-against-apple-new-ad-cam-paign-160163.

———. "What Is PayPal?" n.d. https://personal.paypal.com/il/cgi-bin/?cmd=_ render-content&content_ID=marketing_il/How_does_PayPal_work (11 December 2014).

Péguy, Charles. *L'Argent*. Paris: Gallimard, 1932 [1912].

Perez, Rosangel. "Occupy Wall Street with Love." 7 October 2011. http://spiritual-networks.com/Soulfuldance/photo/occupy-wall-street-one-love/occupy-wall-street-with-love/.

Pert, Candace. *Molecules of Emotion: The Science Behind Mind-Body Medicine*. New York: Scribner, 1997.

Petrobras. "Comercial Era de Sustentabilidade." YouTube (PetrobrasNoCabore), 6 November 2008. http://www.youtube.com/watch?v=jGEMJ1UHqxo&playnex-t=1&list=PLB619EBFC8D001C66 (15 September 2011).

———. "Environment and Society." petrobras.com.br, 2009. http://www.petro-bras.com.br/en/environment-and-society/ (15 September 2011).

———. Investor Relations. Dow Jones Sustainability Index. petrobras.com.br. 2013. http://www.investidorpetrobras.com.br/en/dow-jones-sustainability-index-djsi. htm (30 November 2014).

———. "We Lead Sustainability Ranking." petrobras.com.br, 16 May 2011. http:// www.petrobras.com.br/en/news/we-lead-sustainability-ranking/ (15 September 2011).

"Petrobras Scandal May Change Brazil Forever, Roussef Says." *Reuters*, 16 No-vember 2014. http://www.reuters.com/article/2014/11/16/us-brazil-petro-bras-corruption-idUSKCN0IZ0PY20141116 (30 November 2014).

Phillips, Dom. "'Operation Carwash' in Brazil Causes Normally Staid Business Meeting to Go Off Script." *Washington Post,* 17 November 2014. http://www .washingtonpost.com/blogs/worldviews/wp/2014/11/17/operation-carwash-in-brazil-causes-normally-staid-business-meeting-to-go-off-script/ (30 November 2014).

Piketty, Thomas. *Capital in the Twenty-First Century.* Trans. Arthur Goldhammer. Cambridge: Belknap, 2014. (*Le Capital au XXIe siècle.* Paris: Seuil, 2013.)

Pocahontas. Dir. Mike Gabriel and Eric Goldberg. Perf. Irene Bedard, Judy Kuhn, Mel Gibson, Linda Hunt, Christian Bale. Walt Disney, 1995.

Podalsky, Laura. *The Politics of Affect and Emotion in Contemporary Latin American Cinema: Argentina, Brazil, Cuba, and Mexico.* New York: Palgrave Macmillan, 2011.

Polygraph 15/16 (2004). *Immanence, Transcendence, and Utopia.* Ed. Marta Hernández Salván and Juan Carlos Rodríguez.

Ponte, Antonio José. *Cuentos de todas partes del Imperio.* Angers: Deleatur, 2000. (*Tales from the Cuban Empire.* Trans. Cola Franzen. San Francisco: City Lights, 2002.)

Pratt, Mary Louise. *Imperial Eyes: Travel Writing and Transculturation.* 1992. New York: Routledge, 2007.

Prebisch, Raúl. *The Economic Development of Latin America and Its Principal Problems.* New York: United Nations, 1950.

Preciado, Beatriz (Paul B.). *Testo Junkie: Sex, Drugs, and Biopolitics in the Pharmacopornographic Era.* Trans. Bruce Benderson. New York: Feminist Press at City University of New York, 2013.

Project Muse. "The Global South." http://muse.jhu.edu/journals/the_global_ south/ (15 September 2011).

Protevi, Jon. *Political Affect: Connecting the Social and the Somatic.* Minneapolis: Minnesota University Press, 2009.

Rama, Ángel. *The Lettered City.* Trans. John Charles Chasteen. Durham, NC: Duke University Press, 1996. (*La ciudad letrada.* Hanover, NH: Ediciones del Norte, 1984.)

Rampton, Sheldon, and John Stauber. *Trust Us, We're Experts: How Industry Manipulates Science and Gambles with Your Future.* Los Angeles: Tarcher, 2000.

Rancière, Jacques. *The Politics of Aesthetics: The Distribution of the Sensible.* Trans. Gabriel Rockhill. New York: Continuum, 2004. (*Le Partage du sensible: Esthétique et politique.* Paris: La Fabrique, 2000.)

"Report of the World Commission on Environment and Development." United Nations General Assembly, 11 December 1987. 15 September 2011. http://www. un.org/documents/ga/res/42/ares42–187.htm.

Ridley, Matt. "Humans: Why They Triumphed." *Wall Street Journal,* 22 May 2010. http://online.wsj.com/article/SB10001424052748703691804575254533386933138.html (15 September 2011).

Rifkin, Jeremy. *The Empathic Civilization: The Race to Global Consciousness in a World in Crisis.* New York: Penguin, 2009.

Roberts, Kevin. *Lovemarks: The Future Beyond Brands.* New York: powerHouse, 2005.

Robinette, Scott, Claire Brand, Vicki Lenz, and Don Hall, Jr. *Emotion Marketing: The Hallmark Way of Winning Customers for Life.* New York: McGraw-Hill, 2000.

Rohter, Larry. "The Three Amigos of Cha Cha Cha." *New York Times,* 23 April 2009. http://www.nytimes.com/2009/04/26/movies/26roht.html (21 February 2013).

Rolling Stone. "The Best 100 Debut Albums of All Time." 15 May 2013. http://www.rollingstone.com/music/lists/the-100-greatest-debut-albums-of-all-time-20130322 (18 April 2015).

Rushkoff, Douglas. "Think Occupy Wall St. Is a Phase? You Don't Get It." *CNN,* 5 October 2011. http://www.cnn.com/2011/10/05/opinion/rushkoff-occupy-wall-street/index.html (18 April 2015).

Ryan, Ted. "The Making of 'I'd Like to Buy the World a Coke.'" *Coca-Cola Journey,* 1 January 2012. http://www.coca-colacompany.com/stories/coke-lore-hilltop-story (28 April 2015).

Saatchi and Saatchi. Lovemarks. n.d. http://www.lovemarks.com/ (28 April 2015).

Salván, Marta Hernández, and Juan Carlos Rodríguez, eds. *Immanence, Transcendence, and Utopia.* Special issue of *Polygraph* 15–16 (2004).

Sánchez Prado, Ignacio M. *Screening Neoliberalism: Transforming Mexican Cinema, 1988–2012.* Nashville: Vanderbilt University Press, 2014.

Santasombra. "*Ever Amado*: Synopsis." 2009. http://www.santasombra.com/html/ever_amado.html (15 September 2011).

Saramago, José. *Ensaio sobre o cegueira.* Lisbon: Caminho, 1995.

Schaefer, Claudia. *Bored to Distraction: Cinema of Excess in End-of-the-Century Mexico and Spain.* Albany: State University of New York Press, 2003.

Scahill, Jeremy. "Blackwater Founder Remains Free and Rich While His Former Employees Go Down on Murder Charges." *Intercept,* 22 October 2014. https://firstlook.org/theintercept/2014/10/22/blackwater-guilty-verdicts/.

———. *Blackwater: The Rise of the World's Most Powerful Mercenary Army.* New York: Nation, 2007.

"Scandal in Brazil: The Petrobras Affair." *Economist,* 8 September 2014. http://www.economist.com/blogs/americasview/2014/09/scandal-brazil (30 November 2014).

Schlussel, Debbie. "About 'The Hurt Locker': Yes, It's a True Story; No, It's Not 'Left-Wing.'" *Debbie Schlussel,* 3 March 2010. http://www.debbieschlussel.com/18418/about-the-hurt-locker-yes-its-a-true-story-no-its-not-left-wing/ (15 September 2011).

Scott, A. O. "Emotion Needs No Translation." Movie Review: *Babel* (2006). *New York Times*, 27 October 2006. Web. http://movies.nytimes.com/2006/10/27/movies/27babe.html (15 September 2011).

Sedgwick, Eve Kosofsky. *Touching Feeling: Affect, Pedagogy, Performativity*. Durham, NC: Duke University Press, 2002.

Sedgwick, Eve Kosofsky, and Adam Frank, eds. *Shame and Its Sisters: A Silvan Tomkins Reader*. Durham, NC: Duke University Press, 1995.

Segelken, H. Roger, and Stacey Shackford. "News Feed: 'Emotional Contagion' Sweeps Facebook." *Cornell Chronicle*. 10 June 2014. http://www.news.cornell.edu/stories/2014/06/news-feed-emotional-contagion-sweeps-facebook (15 September 2011).

Séptima Brigada. "Juan Camelo." Disk Jockey, 1970.

———. "Paco Camorra." Disc Jockey, 1969.

Shaun of the Dead. Dir. Edgar Wright. Perf. Simon Pegg, Nick Frost, Kate Ashfield. Universal Pictures, StudioCanal, Working Title Films, 2004.

Shaw, Deborah. *The Three Amigos: The Transnational Filmmaking of Guillermo del Toro, Alejandro González Iñárritu, and Alfonso Cuarón*. Manchester: Manchester University Press, 2013.

Sicko. Dir. and perf. Michael Moore. Dog Eat Dog, Weinstein, 2007.

Siskind, Mariano. *Cosmopolitan Desires: Global Modernity and World Literature in Latin America*. Evanston, IL: Northwestern University Press, 2014.

Sison, Antonio D. *Screening Schillebeeckx: Theology and Third World Cinema in Dialogue*. New York: Palgrave Macmillan, 2006.

Smith, Adam. *Theory of Moral Sentiments*. Ed. Ryan Patrick Hanley. Intro. Amartya Sen. New York: Penguin, 2010 [1759].

———. *The Wealth of Nations*. Library of Economics and Liberty. London: W. Strahan and T. Cadell, 1776. http://www.econlib.org/library/Smith/smWN.html (15 September 2011).

Smith, Paul Julian. *Mexican Screen Fiction: Between Cinema and Television*. Malden, MA: Polity, 2014.

Sobchack, Vivian. *Carnal Thoughts: Embodiment and Moving Image Culture*. Berkeley: University of California Press, 2004.

Solanas, Fernando "Pino," and Octavio Getino. "Hacia un Tercer Cine: Apuntes y experiencias para el desarrollo de un cine de liberación en el Tercer Mundo." In Octavio Getino, ed., *A diez años de "Hacia un Tercer Cine,"* 37–56. Mexico City: Filmoteca UNAM, 1982 [1969].

———. *La hora de los hornos: Notas y testimonios sobre el neocolonialismo, la violencia y la liberación*. Grupo Cine Liberación, 1968.

Sontag, Susan. *Against Interpretation*. New York: Farrar, Straus and Giroux, 1966.

Stewart, Kathleen. *Ordinary Affects.* Durham, NC: Duke University Press, 2007.

Stoddart, Scott F., ed. "Introduction." In *Analyzing* Mad Men*: Critical Essays on the Television Series,* 1–11. Jefferson, NC: McFarland, 2011.

Suebsaeng, Asawin. "Blackwater Founder Wants to Fight Ebola, ISIS, and for the GOP to 'Get Off Their Ass.'" *Daily Beast,* 19 September 2014. http://www.thedailybeast.com/articles/2014/09/19/blackwater-founder-wants-to-fight-ebola-isis-and-for-the-gop-to-get-off-their-ass.html (18 April 2015).

Super Size Me. Dir. and perf. Morgan Spurlock. Kathbur, The Con, Studio on Hudson, 2004.

Taibbi, Matt. "The Great American Bubble Machine." *Rolling Stone,* 5 April 2010, 1–8. http://www.rollingstone.com/politics/news/;kw=[3351,11459 (15 September 2011).

The Take. Dir. Avi Lewis and Naomi Klein. Perf. Freddy Espinoza, Naomi Klein, Avi Lewis. Barna-Alper, Canadian Broadcasting Corporation, Klein Lewis, National Film Board of Canada, 2004.

Terada, Rei. *Feeling in Theory: Emotion After the "Death of the Subject."* Cambridge: Harvard University Press, 2003.

Tobias, Scott. "Japón (review)." *A.V. Club.* 19 March 2003. http://www.avclub.com/articles/japon,5722/ (15 September 2011).

Tolstoy, Lev Nikolayevich (Leo). *Family Happiness.* Trans. Louise and Aylmer Maude. (1859.) Tolstoy Library Online. n.d. http://magister.msk.ru/library/tolstoy/english/tolsl19e.htm (15 September 2011).

Toyota. "The Making of 'Harmony.'" Toyota, 2008–11.

———. Prius "Harmony." 2011 Toyota Prius TV Commercials. toyota.com, 2008–11. http://www.toyota.com/prius-hybrid/commercial.html (15 September 2011).

———. Prius "MPG." Toyota, 2008–11.

———. Prius "Solar." Toyota, 2008–11.

Travis, Daryl. *Emotional Branding: How Successful Brands Gain the Irrational Edge.* New York: Crown Business, 2000.

Trinkets and Beads. Dir. Christopher Walker. 1996.

Tye, Larry. *The Father of Spin: Edward L. Bernays and the Birth of Public Relations.* New York: Crown, 1998.

U2. "One." *Achtung Baby.* Island. 1991.

U.S. Healthiest. http://www.ushealthiest.org (15 September 2011).

United Nations. Dialogue with the Global South. 2005. http://www.un.org/globalsouth/ (15 September 2011).

V for Vendetta. Dir. James McTeigue. Perf. Hugo Weaving, Natalie Portman, Rupert Graves. Warner Bros., 2005.

Varoufakis, Yanis. "Beyond the Crisis: Markets, Planning, and a Utopian Vision (Inspired by the American National Football League)." *Thoughts for the Post-2008*

World, 15 June 2011. http://yanisvaroufakis.eu/2011/06/15/beyond-the-crisis-markets-planning-and-a-utopian-vision-inspired-by-the-american-national-football-league/ (15 September 2011).

Venegas, Cristina. "The Man, the Corpse, and the Icon in *Motorcycle Diaries*: Utopia, Please, and a New Revolutionary Imagination." In A. Aneesh, Lane Hall, and Patrice Petro, eds., *Beyond Globalization: Making New Worlds in Media, Art, and Social Practices,* 138–61. New Brunswick, NJ: Rutgers University Press, 2012.

"Venezuelan Anger at Computer Game." BBC News, 25 May 2006. http://news.bbc.co.uk/2/hi/5016514.stm (15 September 2011).

Verdú, Vicente. "El 15-M es emocional, le falta pensamiento." *El País,* 17 October 2011. http://politica.elpais.com/politica/2011/10/17/actualidad/1318808156_278372.html (23 October 2011).

Vidal, John. "Bolivia Enshrines Natural World's Rights with Equal Status for Mother Earth." *Guardian,* 10 April 2011. http://www.guardian.co.uk/environment/2011/apr/10/bolivia-enshrines-natural-worlds-rights (15 September 2011).

Vijay, Amar. "James Cameron Talks Avatar Sequels." *Empire,* 26 November 2014. http://www.empireonline.com/news/story.asp?NID=42852 (29 November 2014).

Virilio, Paul. *The Information Bomb.* New York: Verso, 2000. (*La Bombe informatique.* Paris: Gal-Lée, 1998.)

The Walking Dead. Created by Frank Darabont. Perf. Andrew Lincoln, Steven Yeun, Sarah Wayne Callies. American Movie Classics (AMC), 2010– .

WALL·E. Dir. Andrew Stanton. Perf. Ben Burtt, Elissa Knight, Jeff Garlin. Pixar Animation, 2008.

Wardrip-Fruin, Noah, and Nick Montfort, eds. *The New Media Reader.* Cambridge: MIT Press, 2003.

Wasserman, Todd. "Coke Ad from Spain Has Grown Men Falling to Their Knees Crying." Brandfreak.com. 12 March 2009. http://www.brandfreak.com/2009/03/coke-ad-from-spain-has-grown-men-falling-to-their-knees-crying.html (15 September 2011).

Waste Land. Dir. Lucy Walker, Karen Harley, and João Jardim. Perf. Vik Muniz. Almega Projects, O2 Filmes, 2010.

We Are Legion: The Story of the Hacktivists. Dir. Brian Knappenberger. Perf. Anon2World, Anonyops, Julian Assange. Luminant Media, 2012.

"*We Are Smarter Than Me*: About the Book." *We Are Smarter Than Me,* 2008. http://www.wearesmarter.org/book.asp (15 September 2011).

We Are the 99%. 20 October 2011. http://wearethe99percent.tumblr.com/ (18 April 2015).

Weber, Max. *The Protestant Ethic and the Spirit of Capitalism.* Ed. Richard Swedberg. Trans. Talcott Parsons. New York: Norton, 2009. (*Die protestantische Ethik und der Geist des Kapitalismus* [1919].)

Weisman, Jonathan and Alistair MacDonald. "Obama, Brown Strike Similar Notes on Economy." *Wall Street Journal,* 3 April 2009. http://online.wsj.com/article/SB123871661163384723.html (15 September 2011).

"Welcome to 'The Coke Side of Life.'" Coca-Cola Press Release. Corporate News, Articles and Press Releases. Corporate Archive. 30 March 2006. http://icaa.eu/company/Coca-Cola/article/8546.html (15 September 2011).

Westen, Drew. *The Political Brain: The Role of Emotion in Deciding the Fate of the Nation.* New York: PublicAffairs, 2007.

"Why Do Voles Fall in Love?" *Emory Magazine* 72.1 (Spring 1999). http://www.emory.edu/EMORY_MAGAZINE/spring99/features_pgs/voles.html (15 September 2011).

"Why Natural Gas?" America's Natural Gas Alliance, 2011. http://www.anga.us/why-natural-gas (15 September 2011).

Williams, Linda. *Hard Core: Power, Pleasure and the "Frenzy of the Visible."* Berkeley: University of California Press, 1989.

Williams, Raymond. "Structures of Feeling." In *Marxism and Literature,* 128–35. Oxford: Oxford University Press, 1978 [1977].

Wolfe, Cary. *What Is Posthumanism?* Minneapolis: University of Minnesota Press, 2009.

———. *Animal Rites: American Culture, the Discourse of Species, and Posthumanist Theory.* Chicago: University of Chicago Press, 2003.

———. *Zoontologies: The Question of the Animal.* Minneapolis: University of Minnesota Press, 2003.

Wright, Robert. "Building One Big Brain." *New York Times,* 6 July 2010. http://opinionator.blogs.nytimes.com/2010/07/06/the-web-we-weave/ (15 September 2011).

Young, Jeffrey R. "Crowd Science Reaches New Heights." *Chronicle of Higher Education,* 28 May 2010. http://chronicle.com/article/The-Rise-of-Crowd-Science/65707/.

Zakon, Robert H. "Hobbes' Internet Timeline 10.1." Zakon.org, 15 December 2010. http://www.zakon.org/robert/internet/timeline/ (15 September 2011).

Žižek, Slavoj. "Slavoj Žižek at Occupy Wall Street: We Are Not Dreamers, We Are the Awakening from a Dream Which Is Turning Into a Nightmare." Posted by Sarah Shin. *Verso Books.* 10 October 2011. http://www.versobooks.com/blogs/736-slavoj-zizek-at-occupy-wall-street-we-are-not-dreamers-we-are-the-awakening-from-a-dream-which-is-turning-into-a-nightmare (18 April 2015).

———. *The Ticklish Subject: The Absent Centre of Political Ontology.* London: Verso, 1999.

———. *Violence: Six Sideways Reflections.* New York: Picador, 2008.

————. "Welcome to the Desert of the Real (Reflections on WTC)." 7 October 2001. European Graduate School. http://www.egs.edu/faculty/slavoj-zizek/ articles/welcome-to-the-desert-of-the-real/ (15 September 2011).

Zurawicki, Leon. *Neuromarketing: Exploring the Brain of the Consumer.* New York: Springer, 2010.

Index

Able-bodied: in *Avatar*, 276*n*7; ecolove only for, 225, 226; love and well-being linked to, 185–86, 193; *see also* Legs and leglessness

Academy Awards, 154, 190, 272*n*8

Acosta, Abraham, 256*n*4

Adaptive evolution, 52, 55–60, 64, 67–69, 266*n*4

Addiction: to consumption, 66, 80, 136, 139–40, 143–45, 154, 196; in *Mad Men*, 136, 139–40, 143–45; to sugar-fat-salt triumvirate, 37, 66, 144–45, 241, 266*n*3; in U.S., 169–70; to war, 80, 190–91; well-being and, 38

Advertising: emotional, neuroscience of, 19, 274–75*n*1; legs and leglessness in, 186; love in, xiv, 174, 177, 225, 256*n*;

pro-profit sustainability narratives in, 186; *see also Mad Men*; *specific companies and commercials*

Aesthetics, in cultural studies, xix

Affect: antiprofit, sustainability discourse and, 108–15; in cinema, 19–20, 43–44; defined, 17–18, 22, 261*n*5; diversity of, 22; Hardt and Negri on, 243, 261*n*2; as horizontal, 22–23, 253–54; as immanent, 22–23; as imperative of both sides, 205–7; psychoanalytic discourse on, 259*n*4; psychological research on, 233; reason dependent on, 18; sources for contemporary, xxii; in sustainability discourse, 122; U.S. and Latin America's shared, xviii–xix, xxii–xxv; well-being as imperative